THE
LIBRARY
OF
QUMRAN

On the Essenes, Qumran, John the Baptist, and Jesus

Hartmut Stegemann

WILLIAM B. EERDMANS PUBLISHING COMPANY
GRAND RAPIDS, MICHIGAN / CAMBRIDGE, U.K.

BRILL ACADEMIC PUBLISHERS
LEIDEN / NEW YORK / KÖLN

The Publication of this work was aided
by a grant from Inter Nationes, Bonn

Originally published as
Die Essener, Qumran, Johannes der Täufer und Jesus
© 1993 Verlag Herder, Freiburg im Breisgau, Germany

English translation © 1998 Wm. B. Eerdmans Publishing Co.

Published jointly 1998 by
Wm. B. Eerdmans Publishing Co.
255 Jefferson Ave. S.E., Grand Rapids, Michigan 49503 /
P.O. Box 163, Cambridge CB3 9PU U.K.
and by
Brill Academic Publishers
P.O. Box 9000, 2300 PA Leiden, the Netherlands

Printed in the United States of America

03 02 01 00 99 98   7 6 5 4 3 2 1

Library of Congress Cataloging-in-Publication Data

Stegemann, Hartmut.
[Essener, Qumran, Johannes der Täufer und Jesus. English]
The library of Qumran, on the Essenes, Qumran, John the Baptist,
and Jesus / Hartmut Stegemann.
p.   cm.
Includes index.
ISBN 0-8028-6167-9 (pbk : alk. paper)
1. Dead Sea scrolls — Criticism, interpretation, etc.   2. Qumran community.
3. Dead Sea scrolls — Relation to the New Testament.   4. Essenes.   I. Title.
BM487.S78813   1998
296.1'55 — dc21   97-38525
CIP

Brill ISBN 90 04 11 2103

Contents

CHAPTER ONE

Discoveries

At the northwest end of the Dead Sea, 12 kilometers south of Jericho and 32 kilometers north of the En Gedi oasis, lies a solitary set of ruins. Larger heaps of rubble, such as might represent an entire ancient city, are called *tells* by the Arabs, while smaller heaps, the ruins of only a few buildings, are called *khirbeh*.

From antiquity, the Bedouin have called this place in the vicinity of the Dead Sea *Khirbet Qumran*. The name Qumran may mean "moon hill," since the bright hilltop against the brownish-red countryside, as viewed from the Dead Sea, may once have reminded folk of the pale disk of the moon sinking behind the horizon. It may, however, simply mean "humpback hill," which would likewise appropriately designate the particular form of this pile of ruins. The pronunciation of the place name is *koom-RAHN*.

The area of the landscape on which Khirbet Qumran lies consists of one of the steep rock precipices of a low range of mountains forming a terrace on the threshold of the Judean Desert. It is a thick layer of marl that once arose from the deposits at the bottom of the Dead Sea. For scores of millennia, however, the surface of the Dead Sea has lain some 50 meters below this terrace and today is more than 400 meters below sea level. Flowing down from the western slopes, brooks, which appear in the rainy season, have eaten their way through the marl and thereby created the rugged Wadi Qumran. Ages ago the brooks had already cut through the terrace and gnawed their way into the side of the channel thus created. Like a giant's fingers, the brooks running from the terrace in the north reach down into the valley below. The Arabs call streams like these, which in the rainy season can transport roaring torrents of water into the valley but otherwise are dry, by the name of *wadi*. Israelis call the same natural phenomenon a *naḥal*.

Perched atop the last ledge of the old marl terrace before it becomes a

1

precipice plunging down to the Dead Sea, more than a kilometer from today's west bank of the Sea and high over the floor of Wadi Qumran, stands Khirbet Qumran. Nowadays Qumran is a tourist attraction, with an air-conditioned restaurant, a parking lot for buses, and even a few palm trees. Half a century ago — and for thousands of years before that — the most that would be seen here were Bedouin with their tents and their herds of goats and sheep, when winter rain had greened the desert and provided pastureland for a few weeks. The Bedouin tribe of the Ta'amireh has regarded this area as its property in every age, regardless of how political boundaries might run or what state has sovereignty here at a given moment.

Since 1850 researchers have also shown an interest in the area around Qumran from time to time. The graves there are striking, in that they are placed so that the dead lie facing north and are separated from the earth around them by clean-cut slabs of stone. Thus the departed neatly awaited their resurrection to an everlasting life in the north — the direction to which they lay turned — where the Garden of Eden was thought to have been. Such a funerary custom is not known to have been practiced elsewhere in the Holy Land of ancient times. Meanwhile, of course, such graves have been discovered near En Ghweir, some fifteen kilometers to the south of Qumran. In the arid desert by the Dead Sea, by way of exception, a number of things have remained recognizable that in the rest of the country have long since rotted away or fallen victim to the conditions of time. This special funerary practice alone, however, at first induced no one to investigate the hill of ruins of Qumran and its broader vicinity.

Everything changed after seven writing scrolls turned up in Jerusalem in the late autumn of 1947 and the beginning of 1948, discovered by Bedouin the winter before in a rock cave near the northwest end of the Dead Sea. In 1949, this cave — 1.3 kilometers north of Qumran — was investigated by researchers. There they found remnants, pieces broken off, from four of these scrolls, a few other manuscript fragments, potsherds from numerous clay jugs, and rotted linen covers, which had once served to enwrap the scrolls.

The Bedouin recounted how one of their shepherd boys, Muhammad ed-Dhib, "the Wolf," had discovered the cave by accident when he had climbed up into the rocks after a runaway goat. What else happened just then can no longer be sorted out very well. Some still usable clay jugs found in the cave had been taken by the Bedouin as containers. They are said to have used a few of the scrolls for their campfires, the area being so sparsely wooded, but these probably gave off more bad smell than real heat in the cold nights. What were they to do with these rare finds?

Several months after their unexpected lucky find, the Bedouin went to Bethlehem, their market town, and called on a Christian cobbler named Khalil Iskander Shahin, known in the area as "Kando." Doubtless they hoped the shoemaker could make them cheap sandals or some other useful item out of the old leather of the scrolls. Instead, Kando bought the leather scrolls for a few coins. Later, probably at the end of July 1947, he took four of these scrolls to his spiritual superior, Syrian Metropolitan Athanasius Yeshua Samuel, in Jerusalem, who paid him the equivalent of $97.20 for them.

Three other scrolls were acquired in a similar fashion at the end of 1947 by an archaeologist of Hebrew University in Jerusalem, Professor Eliezer Lipa Sukenik. He was the father of then Israeli secret police officer Yigael Yadin, who was chief of staff of the Israeli army during the war of independence in 1948-49 and later became Professor of Archaeology and then, for a time, a cabinet minister and Vice Premier of the State of Israel. On June 28, 1984, Yadin died at the age of 67. When the State of Israel became politically independent in 1948, these three scrolls, which his father had bought, were already the property of Hebrew University. Since then they have formed the basic stock of Israeli property from the Qumran finds.

These are the most important of the facts about which there is any clear understanding today. A discussion of what else may have played out in the years 1947-51 — what other persons were involved in these events in various ways, the story of individual scrolls until they came into scholars' hands — would take up several volumes of reports and surmises. (One clear exception is the fate of certain items that were cautiously buried in a moist garden to keep them from the eyes of officialdom — private possession of such archaeological finds being unlawful — and left there for a long time, so that they suffered further irreparable damage.) John C. Trever, in his book *The Untold Story of Qumran* (see p. 270, below), has said all that is to be said on the subject. The following paragraphs will provide an adequate condensation of what out of all of this is really relevant for an understanding of the manuscript finds.

At the end of 1951, researchers began to investigate the broader area of these scroll caves. They also took a number of random samples from the hill of ruins at Qumran that proved unproductive. It was thought that, above and beyond the isolated manuscript deposits in the caves, there would scarcely be anything else interesting to discover in such a remote area.

But in February 1952 Bedouin found near the first cave and in the same cliff another cave that contained extensively decomposed remnants of a number of manuscripts. That got the searches going again. Now investigators systematically searched 270 caves and crags along the mountain cliff, but despite all efforts they discovered only one more scroll cave, about one kilometer north of the first one discovered. In the interior of this cave, searchers found very small fragments of a few scrolls, along with a huge number of shards of broken clay jars.

At the entrance of this third manuscript cave, hidden under some stones, lay two scrolls of copper sheeting so thoroughly oxidized that at first they could not be unrolled. When they finally were unrolled in 1956, it became evident that the two copper scrolls belonged together. A long sheet of copper had only been rolled up into two separate parts. The text of the *Copper Scroll* is impressed into the sheeting. It is a catalogue of sixty-four localities where enormous treasures had been hidden — mostly bars of silver and gold — with precise information as to the location and content of each cache.

As early as 1953, Heidelberg Professor Karl Georg Kuhn had surmised this to be the content, when both parts of the *Copper Scroll* had lain in a showcase in the Rockefeller Museum in Jerusalem. He had deciphered pieces of the text, which were recognizable from without in mirror fashion. Since the letters had been engraved into the thin sheeting, they showed up embossed, in reverse, on the outside of the scroll. At first, his contention that the writing on the scrolls was a treasure catalogue was regarded as rather absurd in the scholarly world. With the opening of the scrolls, it was splendidly confirmed.

Archaeological interest in the Qumran settlement reached its climax, however, only after the withdrawal once more of researchers in March 1952. Now the Bedouin began to do some searching on their own, and in August of the same year they discovered a fourth cave that contained remnants of nearly 600 scrolls. This cave, however, was not way off somewhere on the rocky landscape, as the others had been, but in a spur of the marl terrace, quite close to the ruins of Qumran.

Naturally the investigators carried out searches in this cave as well. There, amidst rubble and cracks in the floor of the cave, they found some more manuscript fragments, which supplemented the material that would later be purchased from the intermediaries of the Bedouin. But above all, it was now crystal clear that the ruins of Qumran, only a few meters from this cave and never investigated very carefully, must hold very great promise.

This latest discovery also occasioned the numbering, in the order of their discovery, of the caves that had already come to light, pairing each numeral with a *Q,* for Qumran, in order to distinguish these manuscript caches from those that had been discovered elsewhere, for example in Wadi Murabbaʿat. Following these designations in the Qumran literature is always an indication of the content of the manuscript, usually in conventional scholarly abbreviations. The abbreviation 1QIsa, then, designates a scroll discovered in the first cave of the Qumran complex containing the text of the biblical book of Isaiah. If several manuscripts of a given work come from the same cave, they are distinguished by way of small superscript letters. For example, the two Isaiah scrolls from the first cave are called 1QIsa[a] and 1QIsa[b]. Further, the manuscripts of the respective caves received serial numbers. When the fragments are too small to determine the contents, these numbers are simply listed, for example, 4Q521.

In the excavation campaigns of the years 1952 to 1958, the archaeologists, namely, French Dominican Roland de Vaux and his assistants, discovered that a settlement had existed on the site of today's Qumran. The settlement dated as far back as the time of the Israelite kings, from about the middle of the ninth century B.C. De Vaux and his team were able to identify the remains of a deep cistern, a high defense tower, and some buildings. With the fall of the southern Kingdom of Judah in 587 or 586 B.C. this settlement was destroyed by the Babylonians. Not until around 100 B.C. were the remains of this old settlement cleared of their rubble, restored, and developed into a place of activity for a larger number of people.

For all historical inferences, it is especially important that two kilns for the production of clay jars were found that dated from the beginning of this newly erected settlement. The manufacture of these jars establishes the continuous operation of this new settlement until its destruction in A.D. 68.

Nowhere but in Qumran was this special pottery produced. Individual pieces of this kind discovered elsewhere in Palestine can have come only from Qumran. After all, the settlers surely sold a part of their production to others, for example to inhabitants of Jericho, in order to purchase wares that they were unable to produce themselves. At all events, the same pottery has been found not only in the ruins of the settlement itself, but also in the ruins of certain maintenance buildings in the vicinity, in the manuscript caves, and in other caves of the cliff near Qumran. Accordingly, there can be no doubt whatever that all of these finds are most intimately connected with the Qumran settlement that dated from about 100 B.C. to A.D. 68.

In the course of their excavations at Khirbet Qumran, archaeologists discovered several more caves in the marl terrace. In 1952 they discovered Cave 5. In 1955, they discovered Caves 7, 8, and 9, which contained the remains of some scrolls, as well as Cave 10, which contained remnants of the possessions of its one-time inhabitants, among them a shard from a clay jar with the first two letters of a name, but no scrolls.

The Bedouin found two more caves in the rock cliff of the Judean Desert. In September 1952 they found Cave 6 some 300 meters west of Qumran, right by the path leading up from the rock cliff into the mountains. This cave contained the remains of some thirty-five scrolls. And finally, in 1956, they found Cave 11 some 250 meters south of Cave 3, nearly 2 kilometers from Qumran. In this cave were more than twenty scrolls, some of which were still well preserved, although most had extensively rotted away.

That is all to date. A stroke of luck could bring to light more Qumran caves containing scrolls. But we should not expect a great deal any more. This becomes clear when the various sorts of finds from the individual caves are investigated more closely and brought into relationship with one another. The puzzle produces an overall picture that is quite complete (see below, Chapter 5, pp. 58-79).

CHAPTER TWO

Starting Points

In all of the Qumran caves together, nearly 900 different scrolls and other manuscript documents, or their remnants, have been found. That is a very large number and calls for comment.

Originally, some 1,000 documents were deposited in the ten manuscript caves. A part of these were discovered and removed very early, in antiquity and in the Middle Ages. Over the course of the millennia, other scrolls have crumbled to dust or have clumped together, due to moisture, into hard wads that can no longer be separated. Furthermore, in the vast majority of cases only a few fragments of the once extensive scrolls are available, often no more than a single fragment. Often these fragments are so minuscule that even today no one has managed even to identify the literary works from which they come. The language of the text — Hebrew, Aramaic, or Greek — the formation of the individual letters, the thickness and color of the manuscript material — leather or papyrus — variations in line spacing, or origin in a particular cave are often the only starting points just to determine which of these fragments may have once belonged together. Peculiarities of style, or the use of characteristic words, help determine the kind of content that these almost completely destroyed scrolls might once have had. In many cases, however, the remnants of once extensive scrolls are so small that it is impossible even to establish whether their text was composed in Hebrew or Aramaic.

In the Qumran finds, actual scrolls of which at least half of the original text has been preserved intact number only nine, plus a single sheet of leather. From Cave 1 we have (1) a magnificently preserved scroll of the entire text of the biblical book of Isaiah; (2) a rather fragmentary scroll of the same book, (3) an embellished retelling in Aramaic of parts of the book of Genesis; (4) a commentary on the book of Habakkuk; (5) an extensively preserved master

6

manuscript with an agenda for the celebration of the annual covenant festival, a treatise on the doctrine of the two spirits, a disciplinary rule, a community rule, and a list of blessing formulas; (6) a depiction of the coming decisive battle between the powers of light and darkness; and (7) an extensive collection of hymns. From Cave 4 we have (8) an isolated sheet of leather containing four scriptural citations without commentary. From Cave 11 we have (9) an extensively preserved scroll containing parts of the Psalter. Probably likewise from Cave 11 we have (10) the celebrated *Temple Scroll,* which was confiscated from Kando in Bethlehem during the Six Day War of 1967. (The State of Israel nevertheless indemnified him in the amount of $105,000 for his misfortune.)

This *Temple Scroll* is still extensively preserved in its original overall length of some nine meters, although the first one-fourth has completely crumbled away and the other earlier portions are preserved only fragmentarily. But about half of the original text is still intact. Best preserved is the 7.34-meter-long scroll from Cave 1, which offers the text of the book of Isaiah almost without lacunae.

The 2.42-meter-long *Copper Scroll* found at the entrance to Cave 3 is also completely preserved. However, it cannot be listed as one of the actual Qumran manuscripts.

The Status of Publication

All extensively preserved manuscripts were published in their entirety as early as 1950-56, except (9) the manuscript of Psalms, which was not published until 1965, since it could not be purchased until 1961, and (10) the *Temple Scroll* confiscated in 1967, which was not published until 1977. All remaining manuscripts from Cave 1 — all of them fragmentary — were published in 1955. Everything found in Caves 2, 3, and 5-10 appeared as early as 1962 in the official Oxford series, Discoveries in the Judaean Desert (of Jordan). Between 1965 and 1985 almost all of the texts from Cave 11 were also published, though, with the exception of the Psalms manuscript, entirely outside the official series. Material still unpublished from Caves 1-3 and 5-11 comprises only a few small fragments from Cave 11 that are particularly difficult to decipher.

The criticism of delay in the publishing process, which has flared up in recent decades, therefore applies exclusively to the text finds from Cave 4. The same is true of the supposition of a willful concealment and of the accusation that certain individual scholars are unwilling to allow other researchers to collaborate in the various editions.

According to present count — which could still come in for slight adjustment in the course of further research — altogether some 566 manuscripts come from Cave 4. In at least 40 cases, however, their remains are so fragmentary that nothing can be done with them any longer. What we have from 140 other manuscripts is available in its entirety in official volumes or independent monographs. Of 150 further manuscripts, the best preserved pieces, in some cases everything available, have appeared in contributions to journals, in commemorative collections, in published dissertations, and in congress volumes. Among the entirely unpublished remainder are 40 biblical manuscripts, which are of interest from the standpoint of textual history but which scarcely offer anything new in terms of content. At all events, that is a total of 370 of the 566 manuscript fragments from Cave 4.

Nothing else is available from Cave 4 except fragments of a scant 200 nonbiblical manuscripts, whose content is still potentially recognizable, but which have not yet been officially published. Most of these are texts parallel to already known works, and of course they occasionally complete the received state of the text considerably. But little is completely new. The texts comprise sapiential collections, liturgical material, hymns, prayers, community regulations, calendar tables, and sundry scribal works, at most 60 distinct works all told, of which several copies are sometimes fragmentarily preserved. Little, however, remains of once intact works whose content is new. Among these are a few writing exercises, calculations, or the documentation of business transactions and the like. That is everything from Cave 4 — and thereby from all of the Qumran finds as a whole — whose official publication is still outstanding.

Quite obviously, all of these data are valid only for the official corpus of publications. This means that the manuscripts in question have been published by the researchers officially entrusted with their deciphering and their treatment in a scientifically responsible fashion — therefore with pictures of the manuscripts, transcription of the text in its original language, translation into a modern language, and clarification of more difficult textual readings and matters of content. Producing this kind of scholarly edition of a text is very laborious. It takes a great deal of time and requires various expenditures, such as for trips to the original manuscripts in Jerusalem, for the creation of expensive infrared photos of the fragments, or for efforts to clarify difficulties of content.

At the moment, sixty-four scholars are working to make the not yet officially published remaining manuscripts from Cave 4 available to the public at least by the end of this century. The publishing house in England that issues the official series, Discoveries in the Judaean Desert (of Jordan), has, however, always required several years to publish the typescripts submitted. But there are grounds for hope that things will go more quickly in the future.

Further, since June 1993 there has been an official microfiche edition, published by E. J. Brill of Leiden in the Netherlands, with photographs of all of the Qumran fragments, including all not yet definitively published material. So nothing whatever is "secret" any longer.

The Age of the Manuscripts

The great number of Qumran manuscripts that we have — manuscripts a good three centuries in the making — has, for more than three decades now, enabled scholars to pursue the development of the manuscript tradition during this time span phase by phase, and thereby to establish precisely the moment of the production of each individual manuscript. In particular, during the years 1952-61 the Jewish paleographer Solomon A. Birnbaum and Frank M. Cross, later a Harvard professor, established reliable criteria and methods for dating the manuscripts of the Qumran Scrolls.

The margin of error in the dating established by these scholars is usually twenty-five years in each direction. In other words, a date of highest probability set at 100 B.C. has a tolerance span ranging from 125 to 75 B.C. In such a case, it is certain that the manuscript dated "circa 100 B.C." was produced neither before the year 125 nor after the year 75. In many cases the margin of error for the dating is even narrower.

Other scholars, however, basically doubt that an ancient manuscript can ever be dated so precisely, or else they register dissenting opinions as to the composition of certain manuscripts in the era in question. And so they date many of the Qumran manuscripts only in the Christian era and boldly derive from them "the information they contain on Christianity" — despite the fact that manuscript experts have long since established that these scrolls are 100 to 150 years older, so that they come down to us from a time when there were no Christians at all. But such polemicizing in the face of "established" science is regarded as a vain attempt to escape conclusions that have already solidified and is instantly and unreservedly greeted by the scholarly community most closely connected with the Scrolls as stabs in the dark and wishful thinking. How is the question to be decided in unprejudiced fashion? Who is right?

In such a case, sound demonstrations can be provided only by natural science. As early as 1950, one of the linen covers in which scrolls from Cave 1 were wound were tested by the carbon-14 method, and it was established that this linen was from A.D. 33, with a 200-year margin of error either way, thus from the period 167 B.C. to A.D. 233. There was no way to be more precise at that time, and considerable amounts of material were needed for each separate test. And larger parts of the scrolls should not be sacrificed. Meanwhile, however, measurement procedures have become substantially more precise and can be carried out on minuscule quantities of material, so that the precious manuscripts suffer scarcely any harm when a sample is taken from them.

In 1990, ten manuscripts from Qumran and Masada, as well as four dated business documents from around their time, were tested by an institute of physics in Zurich according to the newest methods. In all cases, test results coincided with the dates of the business documents and with the earlier determinations of the manuscript experts. The margin of error of the dates established in this fashion was now only twenty years each way, and only in difficult cases — for example, when the manuscript leather had been chemically treated in the museum — up to forty-five years in either direction.

In these cases, the writing material originally used in a given manuscript — which is, after all, the only material that can be investigated in such a test — has proved to be at most slightly older than its writing. That ought to come as no special surprise, however, since at that time no one would have used freshly tanned leather for the preparation of a scroll or a document. Usable material was the end product of a lengthy production process and also had to be well aged, as we know to be the case today with good wine, smoked meat, or lumber. Manuscript leather that was too fresh could warp, become brittle, or be torn. But that would have irreparably ruined a scroll that had been painstakingly prepared from it. Thus, adequately aged material was used for the preparation of the scrolls whenever possible. Finally, the animals whose hide was worked into manuscript leather had already lived a certain number of years before they were slaughtered as sources of sufficiently solid pelts. From what phase in their life a sample taken from the manuscript leather comes, however, will not be taken into specific consideration at all, since maximal differences here will amount only to about a mere decade.

Only in a single case did the writing material used in this manuscript test turn out to be some 200 years older than its writing. Here, by way of exception, someone either reused an uninscribed part of an old manuscript, or else drew his writing material from a long-forgotten store of the same. The decisive thing is that in no single case did this test show any writing material to be younger than the dating of its writing by manuscript experts decades before.

These experts' critics, who held many of these manuscripts to be 100-150 years younger, have thereby been clearly and definitively shown to be in the wrong. Sensational literature, television programs, and countless stories in the press, of course, continue to delude the public even today with alleged facts presented as certified findings, shoving aside everything that natural science and paleography have long since worked out as basic, inescapable fact.

Indeed, among the nearly 900 scrolls and other manuscript documents from the Qumran finds, there is no single work whose oldest copy in our possession was not prepared until Christian times, and so only after Jesus' appearance on the scene around A.D. 30. Only further copies of older works were produced as late as the time between A.D. 30 and the destruction of the Qumran settlement in A.D. 68. Any opinion to the contrary is without any scientific foundation.

CHAPTER THREE

The Scrolls and the Modern Public

Already in the years 1950-55, when the best preserved — and thus, then as now, the most important — Qumran finds were published, high excitement reigned, filling columns of newsprint and generating numerous books. Even in those days the questions asked were the same as today: Was the figure of Jesus, as the New Testament presents it, original and unparalleled, or was it only a pale copy of an earlier "Teacher of Righteousness," to whom such great importance is attributed in the new texts? Did the Essenes already regard their Messiah as a "Son of God" to whom God himself had "borne witness," so that Christian interpretations of Jesus' divine sonship and virgin birth would be nothing more than an old cliché adopted out of transparent interests? Were Baptism and Holy Communion already practiced at Qumran long before there were Christians? Were the Essenes who once lived at Qumran "Christians before Jesus," so to speak?

Within a decade, however, all of the excitement died down. Almost all of the texts in the Qumran finds that might have given answers to such questions had already been published by that time, along with a good many other fragments from the various Qumran caves, especially those that could help clarify the disputed questions of that time. From the outset, all serious examination of the available materials led to the unambiguous conclusion that Jesus and early Christianity were considerably different from the figures and forms of ancient Judaism that could be extracted from the newfound texts.

The lasting impression left after the early phase of Qumran research, though, was not one of healthy disillusionment with over-eager expectations. Instead, the Qumran finds were now regarded as a rather boring affair. A glance at the scholarly literature on the subject over the last three decades proves this. References to the sources of ancient Judaism consisted, then as before, essentially of citations of later Rabbinic works. At most, a few scattered data from the Qumran texts turned up among the sources listed in the vast majority of scholarly studies of the Old and New Testament. One almost has the impression that the wealth of manuscript finds from the Dead Sea did not even exist. Their composure regained, scholars around the world left the investigation of these finds to a few specialists whose further editions of the texts, however, slumbered in the scholarly libraries like Sleeping Beauty. Like the broader public, the scholarly world was no longer interested.

The Dead Sea Scrolls Deception

This situation abruptly changed in the summer of 1991. In that year a team of authors, Michael Baigent and Richard Leigh, published a book entitled *The Dead Sea Scrolls Deception.* The book appeared on the German market under the title *Verschlusssache Jesus: Die Qumranrollen und die Wahrheit über das frühe Christentum (Jesus under Lock and Key: The Qumran Scrolls and the Truth about Early Christianity).* For more than two years, *Der Spiegel* carried it on its weekly list of best-selling nonfiction, and it topped that list for almost a year. Well over 300,000 copies were sold during those two years. The media jumped in for all they were worth. Conferences and talks were everywhere crowded to overflowing, their audiences seeking to know what to make of the assertions of this best-seller.

The original English title of this book reads simply, *The Dead Sea Scrolls Deception.* The book captured only rather moderate attention abroad. Its sensational success in Germany is to be explained not least of all by the fact that "Deception" was transformed into "Lock and Key," and "the Dead Sea Scrolls" — which scarcely interested anyone any more — was replaced with the name of "Jesus," which is such a powerful draw in Germany, even though the content of the book has next to nothing to do with Jesus. The original title in English was far more appropriate.

The astounding effect of the German edition of *The Dead Sea Scrolls Deception* was due to three propositions. All three are false, to be sure, but together they explain a success on the book market that outstrips even the promise of the seductive German title.

First, it is declared that "less than twenty-five percent of the material" of the Qumran finds had by then been published (p. 38 of the original English edition). A good four decades after the discovery of these manuscripts, that would of course have been most remarkable and would have urgently demanded an explanation.

Second, the two authors claim to have discovered that this astonishing delay in the publication process was ultimately due to machinations of the

Vatican, which is supposed to have tried its best from the outset to prevent these texts from ever coming to light, since they were dangerous for Church teaching. Whoever attacks the Vatican in such a manner can always count on awakening a great deal of interest.

Third, the authors claim actually to have managed to ferret out why the still secret Qumran texts constituted such an explosive threat. In 1983, American scholar Robert Eisenman had already proclaimed that the Qumran finds showed that the early Christians of Palestine — especially the original community in Jerusalem — together with other Jewish groups of their times, had waged an armed underground struggle against the Roman forces of occupation. Jesus himself, Eisenman had explained, was scarcely the peace-loving savior that the New Testament presents, but a combative rebel in the political conflicts of his time.

This, according to the presentation in *The Dead Sea Scrolls Deception*, was now — thanks to Robert Eisenman — all the more clear from the Qumran material. Here was why the Vatican was keeping as much of it as possible under lock and key, with the result that only a small portion of the texts had thus far been published — obviously, only relatively innocuous material. Any additional fragment that might one day emerge would surely be a spark in the tinderbox of Church doctrine. So ran the fantasies of the book.

A best-selling team of authors, Baigent and Leigh had pulled off their first major coup in 1982, with a book entitled *Holy Blood, Holy Grail.* The book appeared in Germany in 1984 under the title, *Der Heilige Gral und seine Erben: Ursprung und Gegenwart eines geheimen Ordens: Sein Wissen und seine Macht (The Holy Grail and Its Legacy: A Secret Order Yesterday and Today — Its Knowledge and Power).* The principal secrets revealed in this book were that Jesus was married to Mary Magdalene; the marriage had produced a daughter; Jesus had survived his crucifixion and recovered from his wounds, but the traumatic experience had motivated him to show the better part of valor and move with his little family to security in southern France. Hence King Arthur's Round Table and the gleam of the Grail.

You can make what you want of a hack job like this. In any case, it sold well. The third edition appeared in Germany in 1990. The market even managed to cope with a sequel, which appeared in 1986 under the title, *The Messianic Legacy.* In 1987 it was published in German as *Das Vermächtnis des Messias: Auftrag und geheimes Wirken der Bruderschaft vom Heiligen Gral (Legacy of the Messiah: Mission and Secret Activity of the Brotherhood of the Holy Grail).* Here the consequences of Jesus' marriage with Mary Magdalene are extended to the resistance of the Kreisauer circle in the Third Reich, the Mafia and the Vatican in Italy, and the orders of nobility and the activity of Charles de Gaulle in France.

After this fine success, Baigent and Leigh sought a new subject in the now tested and obviously lucrative area of books about Jesus. And they came upon a treatise, published in 1983, *Maccabees, Zadokites, Christians and Qumran: A New Hypothesis of Qumran Origins,* by Robert Eisenman, a professor of Middle East studies teaching in Long Beach, California. Here the Qumran settlement is presented as a kind of monastic community consisting of members of the Jerusalem priesthood at the time of Jesus. The most important installation of this settlement was an imposing library.

The discovery of Eisenman's book served Baigent and Leigh as a launching pad for their new book project. After all, the most celebrated best-seller of the day was Umberto Eco's *The Name of the Rose* (1980). Everyone knows what its author managed to make out of the motif of a medieval monastic library reeking with mysteries. Baigent and Leigh evidently thought it would be worthwhile to emulate this example in hopes of a similar success. The pair of authors claim to have researched their subject for years. Their only misfortune is that they are dealing with a real library, so that all of the errors they commit are detectable, while Umberto Eco's monastic library — despite all of the realistic elements of the overall picture — ultimately remains a fictional creation that the author was able to shape as romantically as he pleased.

How powerfully the basic concept of *The Dead Sea Scrolls Deception* is stamped by Umberto Eco's example is shown by the two references to the best-seller contained in *The Dead Sea Scrolls Deception.* In the view of the latter's authors, the monastery and library depicted in Eco's book "reflect the medieval Church's monopoly of learning, constituting a kind of 'closed shop', an exclusive 'country club' of knowledge from which all but a select few are banned — a select few prepared to toe the 'party line' " (p. xviii). Transferred to Qumran contexts, this medieval Church enclave of monks becomes an exclusive team of twentieth-century editors working in Jerusalem's Dominican convent with its École Biblique and refusing outsiders any glance into the secrets of the closely guarded scrolls.

Functioning as a subsidiary of such devious monastic secrecy in *The Dead Sea Scrolls Deception* is the Rockefeller Museum in Jerusalem, where the countless fragments from the Qumran caves were once assembled and prepared for publication. "The 'Scrollery' in which they conducted their research has a quasi-monastic atmosphere about it. One is reminded again of the sequestration of learning in *The Name of the Rose.* And the 'experts' granted access to the 'Scrollery' arrogated such power and prestige to themselves that outsiders were easily convinced of the justness of their attitude" (p. 32).

What is meant by this "attitude" is illustrated by a quote from a conversation with a researcher who is not a member of this circle of Qumran "specialists": "Manuscript discoveries bring out the worst instincts in otherwise normal scholars" (p. 32). Such "worst instincts" of monks are, as we know, a leading motif in Umberto Eco's book as well. Transferred to relations in the old Scrollery of the Rockefeller Museum (photographs 18-26 in *The Dead Sea Scrolls Deception*), their effect is of course worse than painful, and they say more about the mentality of the two authors than about the relations described by them.

It is worth noting how *The Dead Sea Scrolls Deception* carries Umberto Eco's library motif further. Analogous relations are suggested for the old Qumran settlement, with its central library; for the Dominican convent in Jerusalem, with its wealth of materials; and for the Rockefeller Museum in Jerusalem, whose Scrollery performs a quasi-library function. The same religiously conditioned, devious secrecy reigns everywhere. The overall conditions of the three "monastic libraries" are regarded as comparable and are interpreted interchangeably, as it were. What might happen in one case is mirrored in the other two.

There is a similarity here with Stefan Heym's *Ahasver*, with its equivalent of three time levels. In *The Dead Sea Scrolls Deception*, Robert Eisenman perceives the role of the diabolically helpful Bringer of Light, Lucifer, as standard for all three places. A novel might express many a profound undertone with such an approach. A nonfictional work fails to do even partial justice to any of the three different places of activity, but blocks off its own and its readers' view of the differences. Aficionados of *The Name of the Rose*, however, are bound to be fascinated by the coincidences and regard anything that echoes the mood of Eco's book as plausible. Anything presented is taken at face value.

Finally, it is interesting to observe how the central theme of *The Dead Sea Scrolls Deception* progressively developed over the course of the book's preparation. In the earliest stages the two authors had simply not arrived at the motif, so characteristic of Eco's *The Name of the Rose*, of an exclusive circle of strict secrecy as a possible analogy to the team of Qumran scholars in Jerusalem. Even in Eisenman's 1983 book, his later experience of vain attempts to gain access to the originals of the Qumran manuscripts is still missing. Consequently, the motif of an exclusive circle was at first not invoked by Baigent and Leigh. Only when a press campaign launched in the United States — whose principal intent was to gain access to the Qumran manuscripts allegedly kept under lock and key — reached the pair of authors did they hit on their main theme (pp. xvii-xviii; cf. pp. 99-103, 118-26). In the final version of the book, the idea of a circle of conspirators sworn to secrecy — with Cardinal Ratzinger at the center of the spider web — became the leading motif, along with Ariadne's thread in the labyrinth of the Qumran finds and their consequences.

The new book of the learned best-selling authors Baigent and Leigh is expertly fashioned. It is written entirely in the style of a serious nonfictional report, richly adorned with documents, evidence, photographs, and tables.

This inspires confidence, although very few readers are in a position to verify what might be correct here and what not, especially when it is simply insinuated or even cloaked in silence.

When the media get hold of such a book, what really counts is the jacket copy. The dust jacket of the English edition provocatively states, "Why a handful of religious scholars conspired to suppress the revolutionary contents of the Dead Sea Scrolls." And the inner fold promises that *The Dead Sea Scrolls Deception* finally reveals how "the content of a large part of the eight hundred ancient Hebrew and Aramaic manuscripts remains concealed from the general public." The basis of these formulations is the authors' assertion that four decades after the beginning of the publication process "less than twenty-five per cent" of the Qumran material has appeared (p. 38).

Even at that time (1991), the truth was that things stood just the other way around. Of all the material from the finds, at least eighty percent was available in official publications. How did the two authors arrive at their sensationalistic false information, which they used as the basis of all of their suspicions against the Roman Catholic Church? They tell us themselves on pages 37-38 and guarantee it in note 17 on pages 238-39 (page 189 of the German edition). They claim to have learned from their research that a twenty-four volume series, Discoveries in the Judaean Desert (DJD), was the intended framework for the publication of all of the Qumran texts. Only eight volumes of this series had appeared by then, and of these, two were devoted to the manuscripts found at Wadi Murabbaʿat and Naḥal Ḥever. Thus, only six of the twenty-four actual Qumran volumes had appeared. That would in any case have been one-fourth. But one of these six volumes — DJD 4, which contains the manuscript of the Psalms found in Cave 11 — presents only a single scroll. So all calculations yielded the perception that, until now, "less than twenty-five percent of the material" had come to light, or — as the book jacket of the German edition puts it — "seventy-five percent of the some eight hundred manuscripts composed in ancient Hebrew and in Aramaic are withheld from the public."

It simply escaped the authors and their strange calculations that nearly the whole body of more extensively preserved Qumran manuscripts had already appeared *outside* the DJD series. The scrolls in Israeli possession, long since published, had never been intended for publication in the DJD series — only the "Jordan" fragments available in the Rockefeller Museum. And many of these also had long since appeared *outside* this series, in a number of special oversized volumes, in contributions to scholarly journals, in congress volumes, in commemorative collections, or in exhibit catalogues. Indeed, all this comes to at least eighty percent of the material of the Qumran finds. None of these special editions, which together contained several times more material than had by this time appeared in the DJD series, is in any way included in the calculations of the authors of *The Dead Sea Scrolls Deception* — even though a number of these "forgotten" scrolls are explicitly listed on pages 179-91 of the German edition of their book. Not one of the extensive manuscripts listed there is included in their calculation of the "total material" already published!

How can research be so shoddy, when the matter at hand is something as important as establishing the current publication status of the Qumran manuscripts? Any specialist could easily have supplied the correct information. But the authors seem to have asked no one. Of course, *The Dead Sea Scrolls Deception* would have come to nothing if its authors had known the actual state of affairs. Their big gun would have exploded like an overblown balloon. But the reading public is helplessly delivered over to such dilettantes. How would anyone know that the truth is just the opposite of what is asserted here? Presumably the authors themselves did not know this and had no intention of deceiving anyone, but they had become victims of their own incompetence — which of course is no excuse at all. Objectively, at any rate, their contrivance is a heavy-handed deception.

But what have the Roman Catholic Church, the Vatican in general, and Cardinal Ratzinger in particular to do with all of this? One of the main things that the two authors had discovered in their years of research and now were backing up with extensive documentation of various kinds is a particular hypothesis, presented with impressive persuasiveness. According to this hypothesis, the publication of the whole body of Qumran material had been entrusted from the beginning to a Church-controlled team of seven Roman Catholic scholars, who by the time the book was written had published only such texts as could do no harm to Catholic doctrine. This cartel of conspirators against the truth manages to prevent anyone else from looking into the still unpublished material of the finds. Team members who have died are replaced by others who likewise refrain from breaching the wall of secrecy. Had there been no doughty warriors like Robert Eisenman, who made this scandal public, Rome's machinations would probably never have come to light. So we read in *The Dead Sea Scrolls Deception*.

Actually, the original team of seven scholars was responsible only for those Qumran manuscripts that had come to the Rockefeller Museum, on Jerusalem's east side — in particular, the huge quantity of fragments from all of the Qumran caves. Nearly all of the extensively preserved scrolls have never been in the Rockefeller Museum. They are in the possession of the State of Israel, are kept in the Shrine of the Book in the Israel Museum on the west side of Jerusalem, and have long since been published, some by Israelis and others by American scholars. Quantitatively, these Israeli scrolls alone make up nearly half of the material from the Qumran finds. None of it has been "kept secret." Everything has always been published as promptly as possible.

Nor has the Qumran material kept in the Rockefeller Museum — all of it fragmentary — ever been sorted in terms of which texts to publish and which to withhold from publication. The most important ordering principle has always been exclusively from which caves the material has come, which is the only way to sort the fragments properly.

As early as 1962, the members of the team of editors had already published, regardless of content, everything that had been found in Caves 1-3 and 5-10. The same procedure had been carried out by the Dutch Academy of Sciences and certain American institutions with the materials from Cave 11 that they had taken over in 1960. These manuscripts are likewise in the Rockefeller Museum, but have been published not by the team of "seven chosen ones," but by other scholars, Dutch and American.

Had Church interests played any role, one would expect that some part of the finds from *all* of the Qumran caves would have been withheld. But that has never occurred.

In order to bestow plausibility on its hypothesis, *The Dead Sea Scrolls Deception* resorts to a bag of tricks. It asserts, first, that all of the members of the editorial team "were, in fact, Roman Catholic priests, attached to, and residing at, the École Biblique" (p. 100). In this religious house — just as at their workplace, the Scrollery of the Rockefeller Museum — these priests are said to have been under the constant observation of the Director of the École Biblique, Père Roland de Vaux, as the local guardian of Rome's interests. The only member of the team to have rebelled against this clerical supervision is said to have been John Marc Allegro, who was English. But he, we are told, was promptly silenced by the Vatican.

Actually, only three of the original team members named in *The Dead Sea Scrolls Deception* were Roman Catholic: Polish Abbé Józef T. Milik, French Abbé Jean Starcky, and American Monsignor Patrick W. Skehan. And only the former two lived, when they were in Jerusalem, at the Dominican convent of the École Biblique. Monsignor Skehan lived somewhat farther away, in East Jerusalem, at the Albright Institute, which he directed. There too all non-Catholic members of the team lived: Frank M. Cross, a Presbyterian, later a Harvard Professor; John Strugnell, an Anglican at that time; Lutheran Claus-Hunno Hunzinger, who since has become Professor Emeritus of New Testament in Hamburg; and self-styled agnostic John Marc Allegro, whose father was Jewish and mother Anglican. Those living at the Albright Institute had no connection with the École Biblique, and Dominican Father Roland de Vaux was there only as an occasional guest.

Altogether overlooked in the heat of the fray by the authors of *The Dead Sea Scrolls Deception* was Dominican Father Dominique Barthélemy, from Fribourg in Switzerland, who of course lived in the Dominican convent and who in the first volume of the DJD series had published the biblical texts found in Cave 1. With him, indeed, *half* of the original team of eight were Catholic priests.

The common workplace of all of these scholars — ordinarily their sole common meeting place — was the Scrollery of the Rockefeller Museum. True, that room had been created and arranged with a careful eye to its purpose, but it did not operate after the fashion of a religious house. I can testify to that, since from 1964 on I worked there several times, until it was eventually dismantled and the Qumran fragments were moved to the basement of the Museum, where they still are today.

Furthermore, the portrait in *The Dead Sea Scrolls Deception* of Père Roland de Vaux, who died in 1971, as a narrow-minded watchdog of the faith in the service of Rome showers on his head all of the scorn with which the book consistently characterizes him and the whole École Biblique. Those who would like to know what Père de Vaux thought and what was of interest to him will easily find this in his scholarly magnum opus, *Ancient Israel: Its Life and Institutions*. It is a standard work of historical criticism, free of any dogmatism or cheap "Vatican toadying." The manner in which *The Dead Sea Scrolls Deception* seeks to establish its contrary suspicions concerning Père de Vaux's role in connection with the publication of the Qumran finds is fabricated and fraudulent. How Baigent and Leigh accomplish this fabrication may at least be illustrated by one characteristic example; numerous similar examples could be given.

Ever since it was founded in 1892, the École Biblique, whose director from 1945 to 1965 was Père de Vaux, has published the scholarly journal, *Revue Biblique*. *The Dead Sea Scrolls Deception* regards it as an organ steered by Rome from the outset, which only shows that the book's authors have never seen the journal's actual content. In the course of fifty years, the two authors maintain, the flood of contributions concerning the Qumran finds became visibly greater, to the point that Rome could no longer adequately control them just through *Revue Biblique*. What was to be done?

> In 1958, the École launched a second journal, *Revue de Qumran*, devoted exclusively to the Dead Sea Scrolls and related matters. Thus the École officially controlled the two most prominent and prestigious forums for discussion of Qumran material. The École's editors could accept or reject articles as they saw fit, and were thereby enabled to exert a decisive influence on the entire course of Qumran scholarship. (pp. 100-101)

Actually, *Revue de Qumran* has no connection whatever with the École Biblique. It was founded in 1958 by Abbé Jean Carmignac in Paris and until his death in 1986 was published by him alone. How *The Dead Sea Scrolls Deception* comes to the conclusion that he belonged to "Father de Vaux's team" and was "one of de Vaux's associates" (p. 69) remains completely undiscoverable. Abbé Carmignac never lived anywhere but in Paris, in very modest circumstances. As a scholar he had received no manner of promotion at the hands of his Church, nor would he have allowed himself to be influenced by the prospect of such a promotion. (See his own words in *Revue de Qumran* 1 [1958-59]: 3-6.) At any rate, he was in no close contact whatever with *Revue Biblique* and its publishers.

After Carmignac's death in 1986, French Qumran scholar Émile Puech became editor of *Revue de Qumran*. For several years now he has maintained quarters at the École Biblique. Michael Baigent, on his visit to Jerusalem in November 1989, met him there (pp. 65-66), and got the false impression, doubtless under the influence of local circumstances, that *Revue Biblique* and *Revue de Qumran* were nothing more nor less than twin undertakings and of course, given Baigent's presupposition, both under the patronage of Rome. The wire-puller behind the scenes is not Cardinal Ratzinger but, quite obviously, one of the two authors of *The Dead Sea Scrolls Deception*, who has used a specious finding of his shoddy research to make insinuations utterly devoid of any truth content.

The only concrete connection between the Qumran finds and the Vatican that there has ever been, and that *The Dead Sea Scrolls Deception* accordingly plays for all it is worth, is the fact that in the autumn of 1955 "£3,000 worth of Cave 4 material had just been purchased (with Vatican funds)" (p. 39; cf. p. 119). The two authors stumbled upon this sensational (for them) information "in the private correspondence file of John Allegro's papers " (n. 26 to p. 239). Everyone knows that the true interests of an enterprise — be it an industrial firm or the Vatican — are revealed best of all by the financial means it employs in order to gain influence. Has the Vatican here been caught using an underhanded means of acquiring influence?

Viewed impartially, this financial involvement on the part of the Vatican is entirely appropriate and is certainly generally known. But it does call for an explanation to nonspecialists. In the following paragraphs, this matter will afford us an opportunity to describe in greater detail the problems involved in the purchase of Qumran manuscripts. We will see how the purchase of manuscripts has entailed obligations in terms of property rights that have had repercussions even today for delays in the publication process. It will also be worthwhile simply to know what went on at that time.

Manuscript Purchases and International Law

From Cave 4 alone come some two-thirds — by number, not bulk — of all Qumran manuscripts. This cave was discovered in August 1952 by Bedouin and was extensively plundered. Searchers could salvage only scraps of the original cache. But the Bedouin and their intermediaries were at first unwilling to hand over their precious booty. There were good grounds for their hesitancy.

In 1949, the Syrian Orthodox Metropolitan in Jerusalem at that time, Mar Athanasius Samuel, had obtained from Kando four Dead Sea Scrolls, for an amount corresponding to $97.20 (see above, p. 3). At that time no one yet knew the real value of these finds. Scientific examination gave an estimate only in the summer of 1952. But the Bedouin and their intermediaries at first had no actual experience conducting business deals that could guide them in making further offers. They could not adequately test the market themselves, since the possession of the manuscripts was unlawful in the eyes of the state. The sale of further scattered items from Cave 1 and the discovery of Cave 2 in February 1952 had produced no satisfactory basis for calculation. So most of the material from further finds was cautiously withheld.

On February 13, 1955, Israeli Prime Minister David Ben-Gurion announced at a press conference in Jerusalem that in July 1954 the four scrolls in the possession of Mar Athanasius Samuel had finally been acquired in the United States for a total price of $250,000 for the Hebrew University in Jerusalem. These were proceeds on which the seller would be able to live in considerable comfort for the rest of his life — not to mention his truly remarkable margin of profit. Legally, it is true, the proceeds belonged to his Church. But a successor was chosen for his post in Jerusalem, which implies that Mar Athanasius would now be living in the United States as a wealthy private individual.

As early as 1950 and 1951, three of the Metropolitan's scrolls were published in their entirety and with an indication of their exact measurements. Among these was a manuscript of Isaiah, 734 cm. long and 26.2 cm. wide. Everyone knew these data, thanks to their publication. If you divided the total official purchase price of his manuscripts by four, the result was exactly $62,500 per scroll, and thus $3.25 for each of the Isaiah manuscript's 19,230 sq. cm. — at the rate of exchange at that time, about £1 or DM 14 per square centimeter.

The Israeli Prime Minister's announcement officially supplied the Bedouin and their intermediaries with what they needed to know — the real market value of the Dead Sea Scrolls or their fragments. Their stock-in-trade could at last be offered for sale, of course only in small quantities, due to the risk of its confiscation as unlawful property. For larger, intact pieces a surcharge was paid, since it was assumed that manuscripts would be torn up for the sake of a surcharge on individual fragments.

Several of the intermediaries involved at that time told me in 1964, independently of one another, that it was indeed this procedure that had been followed, and in particular that the *Isaiah Scroll* had been the basis of their price calculations. They showed me the edition of this scroll lying before us and regarded it as extremely honorable that they had chosen precisely the largest of the three already published scrolls as the basis of their calculations, since, had their criterion been any of the smaller scrolls, the price per square centimeter would have been considerably higher. That texts unknown until now could have been sold at even higher prices, owing to their special content, did not enter their heads at that time; they knew no Hebrew or Aramaic, and so were unable to assign a differentiated value to each of the manuscripts and fragments in their possession. A "Qumran square centimeter" therefore cost the official purchasers of all of the manuscripts and fragments still in Bedouin possession its basic price — aside from relatively small surcharges for pieces particularly well preserved. At times the sellers even stuck fragments together with adhesive tape, in order to obtain the coveted surcharge for larger, intact pieces.

In September 1952, the Bedouin had already emptied Cave 6 as well, with its fragments of further scrolls. Finally, in February 1956, they discovered the last cave to date, Cave 11, with its several still extensively preserved scrolls, which may be partially withheld by their possessors even today.

But most of those sharing in the possession of Qumran finds between 1955 and 1958 wanted to get rich quick. Accordingly, after February 13, 1955, intensive buying and selling of these valuable goods got under way in Jerusalem and continued for some three years. Many fine individual pieces were also sold to tourists, who rarely knew the official market price and so paid more than professional buyers were paying. Only a few of these privately obtained fragments have become accessible to scholarship today. Many others are noted to be still missing when one seeks to ascertain, from the remnants of a decomposed manuscript, its materially reconstitutable content. In any case, most new material from the Qumran finds was purchased at that time, with financial resources from all over the world, for scientific analysis in the Rockefeller Museum, where it conveniently complemented the stock of basic pieces already available from the various caves.

Most of the funds for these quantities of fragments came from the United States, England, France, and the Netherlands. The German state of Baden-Württemberg also took part in 1955 with DM 50,000. With these funds, fragments of manuscript material from Cave 4 were obtained to the extent of some 3,570 sq. cm., including the approximately 500-sq.-cm. remains of a commentary on the book of Nahum. For purposes of comparison: an ordinary 8½" × 11" sheet of copying paper measures some 603 sq. cm. "Vatican finances" sufficed for the purchase of just 3,000 sq. cm. — a relatively small proportion of all of the material when one realizes that, just by itself, the *Isaiah Scroll* measures 19,230 sq. cm. Another larger purchase of fragments from Cave 4, some 40,000 sq. cm. of material, required at that time an outlay of around $130,000.

These specifics and comparative values are needed if we are to understand that the money from the Vatican was indeed more than just a drop in
the bucket. In relation to overall expenditures, however, it was so small that
an effective influence over the *whole* project of editing all the Qumran texts
amassed in the Rockefeller Museum could not have been achieved, even if
that had actually been the contributor's goal. But this was certainly never the
case. The Vatican made its contribution just as other institutions did; only, the
others usually contributed substantially higher sums.

Even more important for an understanding of these matters is another
factor, one which is generally ignored. Anyone sharing in the purchase of
manuscript materials discovered by the Bedouin acquired, in return for his or
her financial outlay, only *half* of the *ownership* rights thereto, while all *publication* rights rested with those researchers who had been sent to Jerusalem
by the contributing countries. This was the legal status of the Rockefeller
Museum and the École Biblique, which obtained many of the Qumran fragments with financial means of their own.

The Rockefeller Museum itself was opened to the public as a private
foundation in 1938 with the official designation "The Palestine Archaeological
Museum." Until November 1966 it was administered by the Jordanian Min-
istry of Antiquities in Amman. All manuscripts found in the Qumran caves
qualified as "antiquities" and so were automatically the property of the Jordanian state. Thus, they actually ought to have all belonged in the state
museum of the capital city, Amman, even if the Bedouin from the Ta'amireh
tribe were accustomed to regard such property rights traditionally and, therefore, altogether differently. However, Jordan had always participated in the
endowment and maintenance of the private Rockefeller museum as well and
had transferred to it storage rights over the Jordanian manuscripts until their
publication. And so the official series of publications containing the Qumran
fragments to be found in the Rockefeller Museum was entitled, until 1968,
Discoveries in the Judaean Desert *of Jordan*. Beginning with volume 6, which
appeared in 1977, the words "of Jordan" were dropped.

These affairs were complicated by the fact that the Bedouin, who had
arbitrarily appropriated this state property, were willing to give it up only for
considerable sums of money. At that time, the State of Jordan was unwilling
to pay the required sums that could be regarded in international law as a kind
of finder's fee. Accordingly, the private Rockefeller Museum and the École
Biblique helped with their own finances. But mainly foreign contributors were
involved. In accordance with worldwide convention, the investment of foreign
money corresponds to a division, under contract, of the antiquities thus obtained, in equal portions to the country of origin and to the country contributing
the money. Thus, with the investment of DM 50,000 from Germany, it was
strictly agreed which of the materials thereby obtained would now belong to

Jordan and would be delivered to Amman, and which were to be accounted as belonging to the half that would one day reach Baden-Württemberg — the contractually specified legal owner being the University Library of Heidelberg.

How this system once functioned is easy to verify by considering the disposition of the texts from Cave 1. After all 72 fragmentary texts from this cave were published in 1955, 23 of the manuscripts remained in the Rockefeller Museum, 10 were taken to the Museum in Amman, where they are still to be found, and the remaining 39, which were first purchased by the École Biblique but then acquired by the Bibliothèque Nationale in Paris, were finally given a place at the latter (see DJD 1 [1955], p. xi). The fragments of all 130 manuscripts found in Caves 2, 3, and 5-10 were divided in the same fashion, after they had been published in 1962. Thus, for example, the two parts of the *Copper Scroll* from Cave 3 have since been on display in the Museum at Amman.

In the assignment of property rights of this kind, it is of course desirable to avoid letting each foreign contributor simply go off with its newly acquired half of the property. What had been gathered together over the course of the years in the Rockefeller Museum were several thousand larger and smaller fragments, with the individual parts of a manuscript frequently the legal property of entirely different contributors. For these countless fragments to be worked on in anything like a reliable manner by researchers, they all had to be kept together, at first, at the Rockefeller Museum.

The unavoidable problems were solved as long ago as the 1950s in terms of a gentlemen's agreement that all *publication rights* — even for the Jordanian manuscripts — were obligatorily assigned to the members of the international team of scholars that was obliged to perform the concrete work. Only when individual larger manuscripts, or groups of fragments filling a further volume of the official edition, had been published, could the *owners* have disposition of them. For example, in 1968 the Germans were permitted to carry off "their" manuscript of the *Commentary on Nahum* to Heidelberg, since it had just been published by J. M. Allegro. If, in the course of work on a manuscript, it appeared that several proprietors shared in its ownership, the manuscript was to belong to the party that already possessed the most; that party then had to compensate the other part-owners proportionately by trading to them other fragments from its earlier manuscript acquisitions. The difficult tasks of coordination were contractually entrusted, for the scholarly aspect of the matter, to Père Roland de Vaux, and for proprietary concerns, to the competent authority in Amman.

Only with knowledge of this background can one understand that when it came to scholarly work on the Qumran manuscripts in the Rockefeller Museum, the criteria applied from the outset were not arbitrary personal interests but very complicated legal agreements. Further adjustments had to be made in all precision when Père de Vaux died in 1971 and Père Pierre Benoit took his place, and again when the latter died in 1987 and Professor John Strugnell, then of Harvard University, replaced him. Since Strugnell's untimely departure in 1990 for reasons of health, legal relationships have become rather confused. The legal rights once represented by Père Roland de Vaux have thus far not been applied to other authorities with all precision. They are laid claim to and held in trust — in continuous contact with Amman — by the Israel Antiquities Authority. However, this claim is not generally acknowledged on the international level.

In the same way, the publication rights for respectively designated, precisely fixed groups of manuscripts — for example, all of the texts from a particular cave or, specifically, all the biblical manuscripts from another — were contractually distributed to the individual scholars of the editorial team, independently of respective proprietary titles. Thus, the British scholar John Marc Allegro eventually received exclusive personal publication rights for all biblical commentaries from Cave 4, including the *Commentary on Nahum,* which in terms of proprietary rights was a "German" manuscript. There was no other way to organize an orderly publication process and to exclude fundamentally every kind of arbitrary act. Each researcher would have preferred to publish only the most interesting findings out of all of these texts, instead of laboriously working up difficult and less rich material as well. Or foreign investors may have wanted to bring out early on, in their own countries, manuscripts not yet officially published, in order to make the investment of the large sums of money required to obtain them understandable to the public. But this would have resulted in texts being "published" in wholly inadequate fashion.

Of course, the downside of these protective agreements for the benefit of solid scholarly work was that any change in the composition of the editorial team, or in the responsibility for the publication of particular manuscripts, required corresponding changes in agreement among all legal partners. No member of the team could independently transfer publication rights to others; no additional expert could simply be added to the team. If a team member died or resigned, a successor had to be appointed in all due form. In each such case the competent authority in Amman had to cooperate, as did all the other proprietors of the manuscripts, if they were legally involved. This explains the relative rigidity of the system. Only when it became apparent that no member of the original team would likely be able to publish in his lifetime all of the texts entrusted to him did the Israelis begin to distribute the remaining workload on a larger scale. They attempted to do so in agreement with the responsible publishers and other authorities. But this continues to cause many kinds of difficulties even today, not least those of a legal sort.

In May 1961, Jordan nationalized all of the Qumran manuscripts in the Rockefeller Museum. In other words, it factually withdrew them from the ownership of their proprietors, but at the same time it offered them reasonable compensation. Some of these proprietors, for instance institutions in the United States, accepted the offer at that time, while others did not. In 1966, Jordan nationalized the Museum as well. And nothing in this legal situation changed when Israel occupied East Jerusalem in June 1967 and assumed the adminis-tration of the Rockefeller Museum. The buildings and the antiquities they house, including the Qumran manuscripts, are still the property of the Jor-danian state in international law. As for the very special legal position of East Jerusalem, which Israel regards as not belonging to the "occupied territories" but as an integral part of its own capital city, redoubled caution is exercised not to interfere with the continuing Jordanian rights.

The possibility that the State of Israel might confiscate the Qumran manuscripts in the Rockefeller Museum has not become a reality. To a large extent, this is probably because the Israelis cannot be sure that the previous proprietors of a part of these manuscripts — such as the United States, En-gland, France, the Netherlands, Germany, or the Vatican — would not reclaim their old rights. If this were to happen, a considerable number of the manu-scripts might end up wandering throughout the world instead of continuing to be properly cared for in Jerusalem. In case of doubt, a de facto right of possession will probably take complete precedence over a disputable right of proprietorship. This, at any rate, seems to be the opinion of the competent Israeli authorities at present.

Hopefully this explanation has clarified many elements in the compli-cated legal situation that otherwise would have escaped the reader's under-standing. The authors of *The Dead Sea Scrolls Deception* have evidently taken no particular care to become acquainted with these legalities. When they came upon something they failed to understand, they followed their suspicions rather than the facts — which, after all, they hoped to penetrate in detective fashion.

In 1955, the Vatican had acquired, by way of its financial commitment, property rights over at most 1,500 square centimeters of fragmentary material from the Qumran finds, which could perhaps eventually be exhibited in Rome's Bibliotheca Vaticana, an institution already richly blessed with ancient manuscripts, if the Vatican has not long since accepted Jordan's offer of compensation made in 1961. What these fragments offer in terms of content was never of any special interest to the Vatican. Since the purchased material could at that time be identified "in one afternoon" (*The Dead Sea Scrolls Deception,* p. 39), it was probably mostly a matter of remnants of biblical manuscripts, which are always easy to identify.

Père Roland de Vaux never laid claim to rights of publication of Qumran manuscripts on his own behalf. He was responsible only for archaeology and for the coordination of the editorial tasks. Up to half of these tasks were in the hands of non-Catholics from the start. Père de Vaux was in no way to blame for the temporary delay in the publication of Qumran texts. On the contrary, he did everything he possibly could to push the publication process forward expeditiously. Nevertheless, a volume of the official series in which he communicated archaeological findings, a volume he had himself prepared in 1960 together with Józef T. Milik and others (DJD 6), did not appear until 1977, six years after de Vaux's death. The reason for this delay can be read in the foreword of this volume (pp. v-vi). In any case, it has absolutely nothing to do with machinations on the part of the Vatican, as *The Dead Sea Scrolls Deception* is so fond of presuming.

Furthermore, the editors of the original team progressively sought to include other experts in their enterprise, as they were now awash in the difficulties of solid work on their manuscript material. The team member most strongly denounced in *The Dead Sea Scrolls Deception,* John Strugnell, had, by the time of the onset of his burdensome health problems at the end of 1990, already transferred most of his texts to others, especially to Israelis and Americans. Much of this material has already appeared in excellent editions. Frank M. Cross has kept back precisely eight of his original 127 Qumran biblical manuscripts as his particular contribution to the final edition, while he has long since transferred everything else — including the manuscripts he has himself worked on — to others. Much of this has also already appeared.

Hopefully these comments and clarifications will suffice to put unsuspecting readers in touch with the reality of the situation. Works of mystification in the style of *The Dead Sea Scrolls Deception* lead their own life, anyway. Because they have so little contact with reality, they can only be subjected to so much criticism. What makes them so effective is sometimes curious. For example, there is a rumor abroad that the State of Israel, which does of course control all of the still unpublished Qumran texts, has guaranteed the Vatican that it will continue to keep all of this manuscript material under lock and key, in order to obtain the Vatican diplomatic recognition that Israel has never had since 1948. This is the kind of blossom that springs from *The Dead Sea Scrolls Deception.*

The Best-seller, *Jesus and the Riddle of the Dead Sea Scrolls*

Australian Qumran researcher Barbara Thiering has taken advantage of the sensational success enjoyed by Baigent and Leigh on the book market. She had already written three books (1979, 1981, and 1983), in which she attempted to prove that the "Teacher of Righteousness" so often cited in the

Qumran texts was John the Baptist and that one of his historical adversaries, "the Liar," was none other than Jesus himself. The main authority for *The Dead Sea Scrolls Deception,* Robert Eisenman, identifies these two figures with, respectively, James the Just, one of the brothers of Jesus and leader of the early community in Jerusalem after Jesus' crucifixion, and his opponent, Paul, whom he holds to have been a converted secret agent of the Roman forces of occupation in Palestine.

All of these identifications become possible — and even then remain absurd — only if one dates the Qumran manuscripts that mention the "Teacher of Righteousness" and "the Liar" 100-150 years later than paleography and carbon-14 tests reveal them to be. But Barbara Thiering is no more interested in this evidence than Robert Eisenman is.

After her first three Qumran books failed to sell very well, Thiering finally found the right trick for joining the ranks of best-selling authors. Her most recent book, *Jesus and the Riddle of the Dead Sea Scrolls: Unlocking the Secrets of His Life Story,* appeared in 1992. It reached the German market just in time for Christmas 1993 under the alluring title, *Jesus von Qumran: Sein Leben — neu geschrieben (Jesus of Qumran: His Life — Written Anew).* Here Jesus is once more married to Mary Magdalene, as Messrs. Baigent and Leigh had already proposed in their first best-seller, *Holy Blood, Holy Grail.* Just as it did there, so also here the marriage produces a daughter, and Jesus once more survives his crucifixion. But then the two best-sellers follow different paths. After surviving the crucifixion, Jesus does not transport his wife and child to southern France but, according to Thiering, remains with them in Palestine, where Mary Magdalene gives him two sons. Finally, however, she leaves Jesus, who now marries Lydia, the dealer in purple from Thyatira in Asia Minor known from the Acts of the Apostles (Acts 16:14-15 and 16:40). After his crucifixion, Jesus continues his activity for at least thirty years, until he dies a natural death in Rome.

Ms. Thiering is also of the opinion that Jesus never designated himself "Son of God," that his virgin birth is only a myth, and that he was born in a place named Bethlehem that has nothing to do with David's birthplace of the same name a few kilometers south of Jerusalem. A photograph documents the place on the marl terrace, a few meters south of the Qumran assembly hall, where Jesus is supposed to have been crucified. Nearby Cave 7 is presented as the hiding place where he recovered from this mistreatment.

All of this is supposed to be demonstrable from combinations of New Testament findings, discoveries in the Qumran texts, and archaeological data. There is no connection, however, between any of this and even halfway-serious research, as Otto Betz and Rainer Riesner have already shown quite clearly in pp. 99-113 of their *Jesus, Qumran and the Vatican* (1993).

The Best-seller, *The Dead Sea Scrolls Uncovered*

A little more serious than Barbara Thiering's treasury of inventions is a book first published in 1992, *The Dead Sea Scrolls Uncovered,* coauthored by Robert Eisenman and Michael Wise. This book became a best-seller in Germany when it was published there in 1993. The title of the German translation runs, *Jesus und die Urchristen: Die Qumran-Rollen Entschlüsselt (Jesus and the First Christians: The Dead Sea Scrolls Uncovered),* the English title becoming the subtitle here. This explains a substantial part of the German edition's sales success. In terms of content, "Jesus" and "the First Christians" appear only marginally in the book. The transcription of fifty Hebrew and Aramaic texts — all of them very fragmentary — from Qumran Cave 4, with their translations, was prepared by Michael Wise. For twenty-two of these texts, reduced photographs of the corresponding manuscript fragments are supplied. The texts are divided into eight chapters.

Each chapter and each individual text is provided with an introduction written by Robert Eisenman. There he presents the same positions that had already found expression in *The Dead Sea Scrolls Deception,* except that this time they are extended by association with further data from the texts presented here.

This book claims that the most important of the still unpublished texts from Cave 4 — which Messrs. Baigent and Leigh identify in a remark on the back of the dust jacket as those texts that were "long suppressed" — are here for the first time being made available to the public. Granted, the latter is true in eighteen (at most) of the fifty cases. At the end of each chapter, "notes" are to be found with references to "earlier discussions" of these texts. At issue here is actually their earlier publication, the oldest of which date from the year 1956!

In certain cases, it is true, more of the text of a manuscript is offered than was reproduced in its earlier, partial publication. On the other hand, presentations of a text are sometimes used that the actual editors once distributed at conferences; but this use of other scholars' work is never acknowledged. Also, the use of other, previous publications of texts — a practice noticeable in several places — is generally not acknowledged. Instead, the book declares that it contains only "new" texts, altogether independently deciphered from photos — which is demonstrably false, again from multiple indications. Besides, the eighteen texts that are really being offered to a broader public for the first time here, texts that of course had likewise been long since known to the experts, are the smallest and most unimportant pieces in the entire volume.

Granted, Michael Wise and his assistants have expended a great deal of effort throughout, often improving the old textual readings on the basis of photos of manuscript fragments. But they have also occasionally worsened them. Unfortunately, the original manuscripts in Jerusalem were never looked at. The translations on whose basis alone the public can gain a working knowledge of the texts are sometimes catastrophic in the original English edition, often precisely in places where the content is decisive. The German-language edition is merely a faithful mirror of these blunders. One can therefore use the presentation of the texts offered in this book only with serious reservations. In fully half of the cases, experts themselves do not have a photo on whose basis to verify the textual readings and the suggested restorations for words partially destroyed in the original, entirely apart from the miserable quality of the reduced photos of the manuscripts.

The justness of this critique may be documented by a few characteristic examples. Texts 35 and 36, "The First" and "The Second Letter on Works Reckoned as Righteous" (English ed., pp. 180-200) — in actuality both texts are from the same "letter" — are almost word for word a transcription of a text that Professor Elisha Qimron of Beersheba had earlier distributed to the participants of scholarly conferences. But only two joint publications of Elisha Qimron and John Strugnell are cited in the book (pp. 219-20). In one of these publications from 1985, Qimron and Strugnell had reported on a few sentences from this letter. But they had not published the transcription actually used by Michael Wise — that of the complete text, as laboriously worked out by Strugnell and Qimron.

Text 50, "Paean for King Jonathan," was published in the spring of 1992 by the Jerusalem research couple Esther and Hanan Eshel, together with Ada Yardeni, in the Israeli scholarly journal *Tarbiz*. This article is the basis of Michael Wise's transcription of the text. The article comes in for no mention whatsoever in the book (see p. 281).

Worst of all, however, are the transcriptions of the texts. For example, if we translate the beginning of the first manuscript fragment (p. 21) with philological precision, then it reads: "[Hea]ven and earth shall be obedient to His Anointed Ones, [and all th]at is within it must never wander from the commands of the Holy Ones: You [pl]. who strive after the Lord, place all [your] strength in service to him." In this context — as often in the Qumran texts (see below, p. 206) — God's "Anointed Ones" are the biblical prophets (Isaiah, Jeremiah, and so on), whose directives the addressees of the text are to follow. The "commands of the Holy Ones" are nothing other than the commands of the five books of Moses, the Torah, which God revealed to Moses "through [his holy] angel" (cf. *Jubilees* 1:27-29; 2:1; Gal. 3:19). In a double declaration — scholarly language calls this style of expression, so frequent in the Bible, a "synthetic parallelismus membrorum" — both parts of the then current biblical canon, the Torah and the Prophets, are named in this text as a basis of orientation for obedience to God. The faithful are to

serve with all their might the fulfillment of what is demanded in the Torah
and the Prophets. This corresponds to general maxims in Judaism highly prized
even today — maxims that indeed have been formulated in especially beautiful language in this Qumran text.

But how does the same text read in Michael Wise's transcription? "[. . .
The Hea]vens and the earth will obey His Messiah, [. . . and all th]at is in
them. He will not turn aside from the Commandments of the Holy Ones. Take
[pl.] strength in His service, (you) who seek the Lord" (p. 23). In philologi-
cally indefensible fashion, the parallelism of members is disregarded and
thereby "the Messiah" read into a text that in no way contains it. To the plural
"the Holy Ones" corresponds, in the first part of the statement, the *plural*
"His [God's] Anointed Ones," not "His [God's] Messiah" in the *singular.*
The mistaken adoption of a singular form leads to the curious textual statement
that heaven and earth — therefore the whole world, including sun, moon, and
stars, together with all the angels — shall "obey" this Messiah. These statements would be entirely foreign to the mind of ancient Judaism, whether as
expressed in the Qumran texts or in any other tradition. In particular, the
powers of heaven never "obey" the Messiah, but only God.

This distorted text is singled out for special attention, with the banner
heading "The Messiah of Heaven and Earth" over the entire presentation of
the text (p. 19). Nothing could be further from the truth. But how should
readers who know no Hebrew surmise that something has been conjured
before their eyes that is simply nonexistent in reality? After all, the translation
is accompanied by the Hebrew original, and even by a photo of the manuscript
fragment. How could the reader fail to be impressed?

Furthermore, this text is deliberately given prominence as being especially important beyond what the book otherwise offers. Here, therefore, the
special teaching on the Messiah from the Qumran texts is supposed to be
placed before our eyes for the first time. Only, that teaching never existed in
this form.

Another example of misleading transcription is Text 49 of this book (pp.
269-73). The only completely preserved sentence of this small fragment reads:
"And furthermore [a delinquent has been admonished] because he used to
drink his own urine." This practice was common in folk medicine and is still
to be found today, especially among Hindus in India. But the Essenes, famed
for their therapeutic skills, obviously rejected this kind of medicine.

This part of the text is rendered incomprehensibly with "Furthermore,
he loved his bodily emissions," and this one finding once more becomes the
basis of the banner headline for the entire text. The formulation readily
suggests a sexual perversion. And this is indeed the direction in which Robert
Eisenman leads the reader when he cites in his introduction "sexual matters"
as the occasion for the inclusion of this reprimand (p. 272). But with the

Essenes a sexual deviation would have entailed punishment and not — as in this text — a simple admonition without sanctions. How is the lay reader to cope with such a strange transcription?

Perhaps these examples will suffice to show the main deficiencies of *The Dead Sea Scrolls Uncovered,* a best-seller thrown all too hastily onto the book market. The list begins with the slipshod selection of often scarcely readable, reduced photographs corresponding to less than half of the fifty fragmentary texts allegedly used in the book. The level of deficiency increases with the transcription and with its translation. But most of all, adequate aids to interpretation are wanting. What Robert Eisenman has contributed in this respect is more of an exercise in association and guesswork — often a helpless exercise — than any solid practical information. That is a pity. After all, for many readers this book will be the only occasion they will have in their lives to go beyond a few superficial ideas about the content of the Qumran Scrolls and deal with actual reproductions of the texts. Such readers should not have been left in the lurch only for the sake of getting another sensational book onto the market as quickly as possible.

The haste with which this book appeared has its adequate explanation in the wish to be quick to share in the readership interest generated by *The Dead Sea Scrolls Deception.* The case is similar with other books, which by and large have already been dealt with by Otto Betz and Rainer Riesner in their *Jesus, Qumran and the Vatican* and therefore can be passed over here.

CHAPTER FOUR

The Excavations

Khirbet Qumran

No sooner had Père Roland de Vaux and his assistants finally begun intensive work in the excavations at Khirbet Qumran in 1952, than they came upon a deep layer of ashes. Buried within it were a large number of Roman arrow-heads. The last inhabitants of this settlement had therefore not fled as the Roman troops attacked but had entrenched themselves in the buildings of the settlement. They had no chance against the superior Roman force. Particularly fatal was that, in this area so lacking in building materials, the roofs of the buildings had been thatched with palm twigs and reeds. For the flaming arrows of the attackers, this was pure tinder.

Skeletons were not found in the ruins. Thus, with their settlement afire, the inhabitants fled into the open but were struck down there or taken prisoner. The once so orderly life conducted here ended in complete disaster.

Subsequently the Romans rebuilt some of the buildings that had been destroyed and stationed a military post here. The view from Qumran stretches far into the distance. The gateway to the Judean Desert, through the upper course of Wadi Qumran, can also be closely monitored. This was strategically relevant.

In the second Jewish revolt, A.D. 132-35, one of the detachments com-manded by the leader of the revolt, Bar Kochba, settled in here. Coin finds at Qumran give evidence of both the long-term stationing of the Roman military post and the later presence of the insurgents.

The Jews called this place *meṣad ḥaśîdîm,* meaning "Fortress of the Pious Ones," that is, "Fortress of the Essenes." A letter from the correspon-dence maintained among Bar Kochba's groups of fighters found at Wadi Murabbaʿat contains this latter old place name (DJD 2 [1961], pp. 163-64).

"Essene" is simply an anglicization of the old Greek transliteration of the Aramaic *essēn,* which — like its Hebrew counterpart, *ḥasîdîm* — means "the pious ones." This large Jewish religious party, called in its time the "Essenes," the "Pious Ones," had once been the proprietor of the Qumran settlement, and this circumstance was still familiar to the insurgents of the Bar Kochba episode.

The Romans and the insurgents under Bar Kochba reused only a few small buildings at the foot of the guard tower or built new ones for their purposes. Subsequently these edifices collapsed. No one ever lived there again. It all lay untouched until today, as did the larger parts of the settlement, which survived the millennia undisturbed, resting under the layer of ashes that dates from A.D. 68.

From 1952 onward researchers attempted to find out what lay hidden under these collapsed Roman buildings and the layer of ashes with its covering of bright drifts of sand. Excavations revealed basement walls and remains of buildings for a settlement that was admittedly small but respectable enough for its situation. Today the north entrance of this building complex is some 75 meters wide and stretches — narrowing slightly — some 50 meters in a southerly direction. There are also a number of extensions in the area of the entrance and a large cistern or water reservoir at the southeast end.

The entire settlement installation is divided into three main complexes. Seen from the north entrance, on the left is the actual dwelling area, once two stories high; on the right is a complex of domestic economy buildings; and straight ahead, blocking one's path, on the south end, is the only assembly hall of the settlement, which served at the same time as a dining hall.

Under the harsh conditions of antiquity, life and business in this place were only possible because of the double precautions taken and the arrangements made. Together they guaranteed a fairly self-contained existence in this remote place, which was almost unbearably hot throughout the greater part of the year.

For the settlement's water supply, the occupants installed a large dam and reservoir high in the mountains, in the upper course of Wadi Qumran. In the winter rainy season this system enabled the settlers to store considerable quantities of water. From this installation — beginning with rock tunnels that had been created here and there — a water canal, extensively preserved even today, leads down to the settlement. Once inside the settlement it divides. Here, once upon a time, it supplied a whole series of cisterns — water reservoirs for various produce-processing installations and ritual baths and for the kitchens.

Ain Feshkha

Other economic needs were served primarily by a large complex of buildings and agricultural areas two to three kilometers to the south. There the mountain range of the Judean Desert practically borders on the Dead Sea, leaving just enough room for a road. Where the mountains do not come quite so close to the shore, a freshwater pond, called Ain Feshkha, lies in the narrow coastal strip. *Ain* is the Hebrew-Arabic word for "spring," and *Feshkha* is the proper name of the place where the spring flows. The one-time settlers also brought water here by way of a number of conduits leading down from the mountain cliff.

With the help of this irrigation, in the broader area around Ain Feshkha to the north, reaching more than halfway to the Qumran settlement, date palms were cultivated along with vegetables and cabbages. Seeds from the yield of these date plantations have been found in massive quantities everywhere in the area of Ain Feshkha, in the Qumran settlement, and in the caves of the vicinity. The cultivation of produce and so many other fruits of the earth was of course impossible here, because the soil was too salty.

Of the reeds that thrive round Ain Feshkha so richly even today, mats were woven in those days, as floor coverings, and for roofs. Wicker baskets and bags for the transportation of goods were also made. From the palms and their roots, canes could be made, or spoons, or combs, or many other implements, of the sort found in Qumran and in the surrounding caves. But the palms were above all the source of firewood, for the kitchen and for industrial uses.

The area used for agriculture, stretching some 2 kilometers to Ain Feshkha, was protected from floods and landslides from the mountains by a stone wall one meter wide and one meter high. The northern half of this wall dates all the way back to the time of the Israelite kings, before the Exile, as does a small building on its northern end. The later Qumran settlers, the Essenes, repaired the old wall and extended it southward all the way to Ain Feshkha. At about the middle of the entire wall, they erected a large, new building measuring 12 square meters with three interior rooms, which probably served for the storage of farm implements and for the temporary storing of fruits from the harvest.

Some 100 meters north of the circular spring of Ain Feshkha lies a larger complex of structures and installations.

Farthest toward the Dead Sea, two large, walled basins stand side by side, one flanked by two side basins. A smaller basin, lying in front of the two main basins, supplied them both with water. The water was brought westward from higher land, past the cliff, by a particularly ample aqueduct. Baffles at the inlet of this aqueduct provided a protective wall, diverting excess water — as well as the overflow from the basins — into the Dead Sea.

This extensive installation served for the production of rawhide. The various basins were needed for different stages in the production process. The hides of animals, with intermediate layers of tanning materials, were piled up from the floor of the basin. Large stones were then placed atop the stack to weigh it down. Several of these stones were found here in the course of the excavations. The enormous use of water, which was supplied by the conduit from the mountains, was essential to the production of leather.

A few steps to the southwest of this tannery lay a building measuring 24 meters long and 18 meters wide that originally had two stories. The lower story was solidly built of stone, while the upper story was constructed of wooden beams and planks. An entryway on its eastern, narrow side was a passage — wide enough for beasts of burden — into the inner court, which was surrounded by storage rooms. Part of the space in these rooms was used to store the finished product of the tanning process; part of it was for the wicker mats, baskets, and hauling bags manufactured in the spacious outer court from the reeds growing around Ain Feshkha.

Another entryway — immediately to the left, next to the passage — led into an office. Behind this was a room in which coins were found in the course of the excavations. It served as a treasury and archives. To the left, in the inner court, is a stairway leading up to what was once the upper story, in which several living rooms were to be found. From one of these living rooms of the upper story comes a magnificent limestone vase 70 centimeters high and adorned with an inscription. During the fiery destruction of the building it fell through the burning planks of the second floor and shattered on the stone floor of the storeroom beneath.

Close to the southwest corner of this main building begins an outbuilding 34 meters long but only 5 meters wide. The back wall of this building — on its north side — is made of solid masonry. The front side originally had eleven large entrances. The inner sections of this building were stables for donkeys, which hauled materials and goods. Trade with outsiders was apparently intensive.

As far as can be determined, the buildings and the other installations in the vicinity of Ain Feshkha served exclusively for the production of rawhide and reed products. The coins, potsherds, and the stone vase found here are from the same era as the settlement of Qumran, from ca. 100 B.C. to its destruction in A.D. 68.

The coins and a weighing stone also found from that time show further that not only were goods produced here, but trade was carried on as well. It may be that the community sold its own goods here and purchased supplies for themselves. Finally, an important commodity was crumbled asphalt, which occasionally broke away from the bottom of the Dead Sea and washed up on the shore. This commodity was an expensive one in those days. Traces of supplies of this coveted material were found still preserved in the ruins of Qumran.

Buildings and Installations of the Qumran Settlement

The Main Building

At the heart of the Qumran settlement stood a two-story, square building, each wall measuring 15 meters on the outside. As in the case of the two-story building near Ain Feshkha, here too the lower story was made of stone, while the upper one was built of wooden beams and planks.

Those entering the settlement by the main entrance to the north, by which tourists are usually led in today, found this building on the left, immediately behind the old guard tower. Through the entrance at the northwest corner one entered upon a long hall. To the right of the hall a stairway led up to what was once the second story. From there, a bridge led to the upper story of the guard tower, which could be reached only by this means. The lower story of the guard tower was without any openings and contained particularly well-secured sleeping quarters and storerooms for emergencies, such as an assault by plunderers. There was also surely an arsenal of weapons here for defense against such assaults — for which one had always to be on the watch — as well as a permanent observation post.

Likewise on the upper floor of the two-story building, to the east, was a large, bright scriptorium approximately 14 meters long and 4.5 meters wide, where leather and papyrus scrolls could be inscribed. Clay benches, writing tables, and inkwells were found in the course of the excavations. They had tumbled into a stone-walled room below when the settlement was burned.

The other areas of the upper story probably served as living quarters. True, archaeologists can no longer determine their arrangement and precise functions, since everything was made of wood and burned up without a trace. As in the lower story, there was surely a wide hall here, leading from the stairway to the scriptorium. The remaining space measured altogether some 10.5 meters in length — seen from the hall — and 5.8 meters in breadth. That would have been insufficient for separate rooms grouped around an inner court. But one can imagine two sleeping rooms separated by a middle wall that were entered from the hall; in these rooms ten to twelve sleeping places with their heads to the walls could have been arranged to the right and left of a middle aisle. If "closets" for clothing and personal items were not in the hall area outside but were inside the sleeping rooms instead, then there were would have been somewhat fewer sleeping places; but some forty men could still have spent the night here.

In the lower story, the hall leads straight into a large room, set at an angle, whose original purpose remains in question. Here excavations uncovered the remains of the scriptorium above, which had plunged down to the first floor. Most likely this long, slanting room was a workshop. Here on wooden tables the leather sheets were cut to size, sewn together into long scrolls, and inscribed with writing lines and column demarcations. Leather buckles and laces were then mounted on the end of each scroll, and both edges of the scroll, which was often many meters in length, were trimmed so precisely that they formed a perfectly true line from beginning to end. Bookbinders do much the same thing today, when they press and trim a book so that the cover and the pages are of exactly the same size. At any rate, the length of the room, some 13 meters on the inside, would have been appropriate for the production of scrolls.

On the right of this hall on the ground floor stands the doorway to the library. Here there are three rooms, which are otherwise completely closed off from the outside. The first room, with low seats or benches built along the walls, was the reading room. No daylight entered here — an advantage for the extended use of the bright scrolls, which even today quickly darken when exposed to harsh light for lengthy periods. Persons read in the scrolls mainly by the light of oil lamps, which shone from stands or from wall fixtures. Members of this community were strictly obliged to spend one out of every three nights over the course of the year — or one-third of every night — "in the Book," that is, in the Torah, the five books of Moses. They were to "read in the Book and study the Law and praise God together" (1QS 6:7-8). To do this, of course, was possible only by lamplight.

In this reading room, at an angle to the right, opposite the entrance door, was the entrance to the library itself, where the some 1,000 manuscripts and documents later deposited in the caves were originally kept on shelves and in clay vessels. To the left lies the main room of the library, and to the right a smaller room holding scrolls that were seldom used or were damaged or discarded, together with archive material and whatever else might accumulate over the course of time in such a library.

In the literature of the Qumran finds, this reading room is generally regarded as the meeting room for the fifteen-member "community council." But if that is the case, it is difficult to explain the function of the two rooms behind it. There are two indicators ready to hand which suggest that this room actually functioned as a reading room. These indicators unfortunately were not mentioned in the excavation reports and therefore must be delineated more precisely.

First, to the left of the entryway to the reading room is a small opening in the wall no larger than a mouse hole. Anyone wishing to be admitted to the library rooms had to insert a fingertip-shaped stone through the hole with the applicant's name engraved on it. A stone like this bearing the name "Joseph" was found in the course of excavation. Inside the reading room, this stone fell into a bowl-shaped receptacle set in the wall. It was then up to the one in charge of the library to determine whether the applicant was to be admitted or not.

There was good reason for monitoring entry to the library. First, members of the community who had been temporarily excluded from all community affairs for some misbehavior were not allowed into the library. The same applied to any guests who had not yet received authorization to enter. Second, at that time almost no one was able to read without pronouncing the words aloud.

Accordingly, special library hours had to be maintained for the various grades of membership. Anyone who had decided to become an Essene was obligated from the outset to study the Torah and then works like the book of Isaiah and the Psalter. Other works — biblical books such as the prophet Ezekiel or Daniel or nonbiblical works such as community regulations or exegetical writings — were reserved for the proficient. Only full members of the community were permitted to read esoteric texts like the *Angelic Liturgy*. No one, therefore, could enter the reading room who was not authorized to hear what another was reading at the moment. Beginners were allowed little time in the reading room. They had to devote the rest of the day to committing what they had just read to memory and to proceed from there on their next visit to the reading room. The rigid control of the entryway served this orderly admittance system.

The technical apparatus for controlling the entryway could, of course, support the supposition that our "reading room" was really an assembly room reserved for the leading members of this community, so that anyone seeking to enter had to identify himself beforehand. While this hypothesis is somewhat problematic, we cannot entirely rule it out. And so the second indicator is especially important, since it makes sense only on the hypothesis that the rooms in question were library rooms.

Viewed from the entryway as one comes into the room, toward the left on the opposite wall, is a kind of window. It once served as a counter, across which items could be handed from one side of the wall to the other. Just within the window, a little lower than the sill, is a long stone platform, some one-half meter wide and nearly three meters long, with a poured plaster surface that is completely flat and that was once polished smooth by long use.

The only imaginable purpose of this striking installation would have been to meet the inevitable requirements of a scroll library. Whenever a reader wanted a particular work from the library stacks, the librarian would seek it out and hand it to him through this window to the reading room. Many of these scrolls were only 1.5 to 3 meters long, but many others extended to 10 meters, and a complete manuscript of the Torah — at least one fragmentary example was discovered in Cave 4 — would have been 25 meters long.

Scrolls were inscribed continuously from right to left. The applicant would receive a long scroll unopened only when he wanted to read it from the beginning. Otherwise, the librarian would unroll it for him on the platform to that part of the text where the applicant wanted to begin reading. As he unrolled the scroll to the left, the reader would simultaneously roll up the outside part of the scroll with his right hand. If he wished to study Isaiah 40, for example, he would receive the scroll of the book of Isaiah in two contiguous rolls connected by the sheet of leather on which Isaiah 40 was inscribed. Had the reader himself undertaken this rolling procedure on his lap while crouching in the reading room, the precious scroll would have been subject to damage all too easily.

The librarian also took care of rolling the manuscript back up on his special platform after it had been read. The long manuscripts had to be rolled up evenly and tightly if they were to stay durable. Rolling them up freehand or on the lap would have been technically unfeasible. In antiquity, scrolls did not yet have rods at the beginning and end with handles to facilitate rolling and unrolling, as is customary in synagogues today. Instead, the scrolls were hollow inside and had only protective sheets at the beginning and end, with no writing on them. This way the manuscript could be held tight by its two ends throughout the reading and then rolled up again without smudging the text.

After it had been studied and carefully rolled up again, the manuscript was returned to its place on the shelf. Some works had their titles inscribed on the outside of the manuscript. This procedure was helpful since it allowed one to determine the content of a manuscript without opening it. So far, though, the procedure has been verified only with three especially old writing scrolls. Otherwise, the scrolls had to be opened to the beginning of the text in order to know what was in them. But good librarians know, in most cases, what they have before them even without looking for a title or opening the text.

Other Structures of the Main Complex

Besides this two-story building housing the library, the workshop for scroll production, the scriptorium, and sleeping quarters, there were within the living complex, to the left, other structures necessary for the organization of life. Excavations here have brought to light a kitchen and a bakery with their associated pantries and storerooms, as well as several grain mills.

Near the east side of the two-story building stood a bathhouse for the washing away of perspiration and dirt. Immersion basins were reserved for ritual cleansing, which presupposed physical cleanliness. In the ritual basins the water had to flow in and out continuously, in order to express the symbolic force of the rite of immersion. "Flowing water" is "living water" in Hebrew, and at the same time means "water of life." This is how the symbolism of "everlasting life" comes into view, to which the ritual of immersion was originally related. For bodily cleansing, hot water was often used as well, but it was not allowed immediately to flow out unused when it had just been poured into the bathing basins. In these respects too, the cleansing bath and the bath of ritual immersion were completely different installations.

Toilets, on the other hand, generally did not exist in Qumran. For such needs one had to leave the settlement and walk a considerable distance over the countryside, dig a hole, squat without stripping, and finally fill up the hole again. One of the wooden hoes used for this was found in an excellent state of preservation in one of the Qumran caves.

Connected to the living complex on the south is the pottery workshop, with its two kilns. Here storage jugs for food and drink and clay vessels for the preservation of manuscript scrolls were produced, as well as jug covers, keys, bowls, jars, other containers, drinking bowls, oil lamps, and inkwells. The potter's wheel of the workshop was discovered near the kilns, and a few meters away the equipment for producing potter's clay from raw materials was found. The water to be added to the clay was drawn from the large cistern located there, which forms the termination of the entire aqueduct system.

The Economic Buildings

In the economic complex, there were spacious stables for a large number of donkeys, beasts of burden that had to transport rather large loads, such as rush mats, bundles of rawhide, harvest produce, or firewood from Ain Feshkha. But the donkeys were primarily needed for fetching supplies of commodities that could be produced neither in Qumran itself nor at Ain Feshkha. Here the principal items were grain, wine, and lamp oil, together with, as the need arose, linen for clothing, olives, melons, vegetables, fruits, smoked foods, or metal wares like knives and defensive weapons. All of this was usually purchased at the market in Jericho twelve kilometers away. It was paid for either in money or in kind, out of the wares of the Essenes' own production. The donkey stables were, so to speak, the garages of that time.

Outsiders also traded in Qumran. There was even a special installation for this, since obviously no stranger was allowed to enter the inner area of the settlement. But the inhabitants of Qumran desired trade contacts with outsiders, and this purpose was served by two small loophole-shaped openings built into the exterior wall of one of the buildings. The room to which these openings lead lies at a place on the west wall of the settlement that can still be reached on foot from outside, just before the west wall reaches the top edge of the marl terrace and progress outside the wall becomes impossible. Later this exterior entrance was walled up (cf. below, p. 56).

Three jars were found buried in the unpaved floor of the rear part of this double room. They contained a total of 561 coins. The floor served as a sort of treasury — just as people in modern times used to hide things under the floorboards of their homes. Trade with strangers proceeded in the following manner. Once the two sides had come to terms, the dealer on the outside handed his money or commodities into the one opening, while his counterpart on the other side of the exterior wall handed his item for exchange into the other opening. Thus, the money or commodities were exchanged by their owners simultaneously. Had a stranger simply handed his commodities through the opening, he would have been anxious about receiving nothing in exchange. Conversely, he would have been happy to take his merchandise back, had his counterpart paid him the money for it without being able to lay hold of it.

The same kind of double opening for trade in small articles is found from a later time in the outside walls of Christian monasteries in the Judean Desert. Evidently the monks did not like to admit strangers either. Oddly enough, these openings in the wall for external trade are never mentioned in the literature on the Qumran community. The stores of cash kept safely in the floor are usually judged to be forgotten hiding places for treasure, which is absurd.

The Fine-Leather Tannery

Within the economic area, there is another complex farther to the south of this double-room trading center with its adjoining storerooms. The purpose it served was at first a puzzle to the excavators of Qumran. Père de Vaux, in his preliminary report on the excavations — the final report still has not been completed — restricted himself to the observation that enormous quantities of water must have been used here. A huge fireplace was also found. But what purpose could fire and water together have once served here?

The puzzle's solution lies close at hand if one considers the special installations in the area. There are two large basins here. They both have solid walls and are coated with a waterproofing of clay. One basin is long and shallow, rests within the floor, and has a water intake. The other basin lies fully knee-high and is above the floor. It too is walled. In the case of this second basin, water must have been drawn with pails and poured into the basin.

It cannot have been a laundry. The installation is too extravagant for that. Further, the laundry of the Qumran settlement has been located with certainty in another complex of the economic area. But what is gathered together in this area are exactly those facilities that a tannery of fine, manuscript leather would need.

The shallow basin is perfectly suited for soaking the rawhide and for its further preparation with the required substances. Finally, the raised basin was needed in order to smooth the intended writing side of the leather with pumice, and to rub the other side until the leather was of the desired, often paper-thin, quality. For this, other aids were applied, which were not allowed to drain off unused, and so the basin had been walled until it had a sufficiently high rim. But above all, hot water, not just cold, was needed for the procedures that made the leather flexible. For this purpose, a large metal kettle was used, which once hung over the fireplace.

Unlike the production of rawhide, in which the hides of animals were piled up, then fulled and pressed, in the tanning of fine leather each individual animal skin had to be worked separately. Further, the scroll finds in the Qumran caves inform us that occasionally finishing touches were also given here to other kinds of leather, such as sheep and goat leather from the settlement's own flocks that had been partially prepared by the tannery at Ain Feshkha. Or, for example, antelope leather. Above all, though, this fine-leather tannery was the indispensable midway point between the shop producing rawhide and the scroll-production workshop on the ground floor of the two-story main building.

Other Economic Areas

It is difficult to tell what further installations the economic buildings once sheltered, because the corresponding tools disappeared without a recognizable trace when the Qumran settlement burned. There was probably a wool-weaving mill in which women especially were employed. In all likelihood there was also a turner's shop for producing handles for house utensils and lance shafts, arrow shafts and hoes, and all manner of wooden items: soup spoons and ladles, combs, writing instruments, clothes chests, and boxes for many different kinds of utensils — in a word, whatever was produced from wood in those days.

A cobbler shop would also have been indispensable. It would have produced such things as sandals and belts, thin leather straps and closures for manuscripts, or capsules for prayer straps (phylacteries) and doorpost texts (mezuzot).

Another area in the economic buildings looks as if a smith once worked here. There are stands for oil lamps and wall sockets, gridirons, pokers, and copper vessels, door hinges, bolts, locks and keys, arrowheads and knives, as well as other small essentials.

Everything constantly needed for daily life was, as far as possible, independently produced within the Qumran settlement, in order to reduce expenditures for purchase. But what the inhabitants themselves made, and what they purchased (above and beyond the raw materials), can scarcely be established more precisely.

The Assembly Hall

Next to the library, which was the central study hall, and the scriptorium, the most important installation for daily living in this settlement was the assembly hall, which encloses the entire group of buildings at its southern extent. Here all of the full members of the Essenes living in Qumran gathered thrice daily — for morning prayer, for the noon meal, and for supper.

One became a full member of the Essenes after a three-year probation at the earliest. After one year, the neophyte had to undergo an examination to establish whether he had acquired sufficient knowledge in the past year, and whether his concrete life praxis throughout that year had corresponded to an authentic Torah piety. Only those who passed this examination were promoted to the next stage of membership, and they became full members only after they passed the third yearly examination.

Those who had not yet reached full membership had to say their prayers alone and take their meals separately. Full members, by contrast, were under the formal obligation of praying and taking their meals only *together*.

The common meals in the assembly hall were always preceded by a prayer service. It is primarily for this reason that the entire course of the assembly was regarded as an act of worship requiring ritual purity. At the entryway to the assembly hall there is a large immersion basin into which everyone had to descend before entering the hall. A pipe from the aqueduct for this immersion basin leads along the westerly, front side of the assembly hall directly into the hall itself, which is considerably sloped at its other end. After mealtime, water from this pipe was used to clean the floor thoroughly of food scraps and any other rubbish.

Cleaning the floor was all the more necessary, since in Qumran one did not eat at tables but while sitting cross-legged on the floor. Eating and drinking bowls were placed right beside the diner. Nevertheless, assembling for a meal was called "gathering at table," and the work of preparing the hall for a meal was called "setting the table," since in the homes of Jerusalem and Judea it was customary to eat while reclining around low tables. So these customs marked linguistic usage. But the Essenes actually took their meals just as pilgrims in the outer court of the Jerusalem Temple would — on the bare floor. Had there been tables in this assembly building, it would have been quite impossible for the Essenes to practice their customary prayer ritual here.

The prayer service with which the common meals began was performed according to the same rite practiced in the Jerusalem Temple. In Jewish synagogues today, one prays standing. This was also the practice in the time of Jesus (cf., e.g., Matt. 6:5; Luke 18:11, 13). In the Temple, on the other hand, one first knelt to pray and then bowed down with arms stretched out straight ahead until the forehead touched the floor. We see this still today with Muslims in their mosques, although they do not stretch out their arms, but spread the palms of their hands next to their heads on the floor. In antiquity, this prayer posture was called "prostration," or *proskynēsis*. It was a special expression of reverence for God as the ruler over everything in the world. In the ancient orient, it was common to cast oneself down in this way before human rulers as well. The outstretched arms signaled that there was no lethal weapon being held in the hands. In the context of worship, this gesture signified complete surrender to God.

The inner room of the assembly hall in Qumran is 22 meters long and 4.5 meters wide, so that it is about 100 square meters in area. Two hundred men would surely have been able to pray here while standing. More than a hundred would have been able to take their meals at the same time while sitting. We must keep in mind, however, that in the Temple prayer ritual no more than six men were permitted to pray next to one another in each lateral row. Each row required a room depth of at least 1.75 meters, and at the front of the room there had to be enough free space for the prayer leader. As a result, this space was designed to accommodate the communal prayer and meals of at most six times ten, or sixty, men.

Sixty is therefore the maximum number of full members of the Essenes who can have lived at the same time in the Qumran settlement. Since a floor plan tends to reflect the upper limit that the architect has in view, we must estimate the number of those regularly present here as being even a little lower. We must therefore conclude that as a rule there were only about fifty Essenes in Qumran — surely not many more, but hardly any fewer either.

The Cemeteries

The same statistical result yielded by the floor space of the assembly hall is suggested by the number of graves in the cemeteries at Qumran. In antiquity the deceased were indeed transported to often distant burial places, if this corresponded to the wishes of the departed or their families. Jews preferred to have themselves buried in the holy city of Jerusalem, that is, in the cemeteries surrounding the city. As a rule, one moved to the desired burial place while still alive, since only in this way did one have any guarantee that one's last wish would be honored, and since climatic conditions were anything but favorable for transporting corpses. Even today in Jerusalem with its high elevation, burials take place on the day of death itself if at all possible — at least in summer. Given the climate at the Dead Sea, there is all the more reason to assume that everyone who died there was also buried there, and certainly no one was brought there from elsewhere to be buried — except folk from Ain Feshkha, three kilometers away, who were buried in wooden coffins that have occasionally turned up.

There is a main cemetery at Qumran with some 1,000 individual graves. This cemetery stretches from a point some fifty meters to the east of the settlement and covers the ground all the way to the edge of the marl terrace in the direction of the Dead Sea. A smaller burial ground lies somewhat deeper, on a ledge of the marl terrace, and a third is in the valley where Wadi Qumran passes from the area of the marl terrace onto the coastal strip. About 200 persons in all were laid to rest in these two smaller burial grounds.

In the course of the Qumran excavations, fifty-four of these graves have been opened over the course of time. In the main cemetery, these random samplings revealed only one grave in which a female had been buried; all of the other graves contained the remains of only men. In the smaller cemeteries were several graves of women and children, but also graves of men. Presumably only full members were buried in the main cemetery in Qumran, while the smaller cemeteries were reserved for those who had not yet attained full membership, as well as women, children, and strangers in the area who died unexpectedly.

From its foundation around 100 B.C. to its destruction in A.D. 68, the Qumran settlement stood some 170 years. If we assume that the number of graves in the main cemetery, approximately a thousand, roughly corresponds to the number of full members who died here during this time, then on average about six of them died each year. One could become a full member of the Essenes with the completion of one's twentieth year at the earliest. Many were probably older at the moment of their definitive acceptance. It would therefore be reasonable to assume that the average age at acceptance was twenty-two. On the other hand, examination of the skeletons has established that those buried in the cemetery were generally only twenty to thirty-five years of age, thirty on the average.

These observations and calculations result in an average stay of approximately eight years for a full Essene member in Qumran until his death. Statistically it makes no difference whether the number of inhabitants of the settlement varied during these 170 years, how many were here only a short time or spent the rest of a long life here, how many were overtaken by death suddenly and unexpectedly in Qumran, and how many returned to their homes hale and hearty. All of this is entirely inconsequential for the statistical average.

An average stay of eight years until one's demise and six deaths a year together mean that some forty-eight Essene full members usually lived in

Qumran — practically the same numerical value we have already reached in our consideration of the available capacity of the assembly hall.

Finally, we may assume that of the some 200 graves of the smaller cemeteries, approximately half contain the remains of men, and the other half those of women, children, and strangers. This means that on the average five candidates and four or five women lived in the Qumran settlement. Women who lived here must have been married; whether to full members or to candidates remains unknown. In any case, some ninety percent of the men here were without their wives. Since the men were usually between twenty-five and thirty-five years old, we can hardly assume that they had all divorced their wives or that their wives had already died. That would be true for only a part of the population of Qumran.

This finding, incidentally, shows that the Essenes living in Qumran were not hostile toward marriage. Yet it also shows that for most of them, their stay at Qumran entailed separation from their families, even if only for a time.

Living and Sleeping Quarters

Shortly after the discovery of Cave 2 at the beginning of 1952, Père de Vaux, his archaeological team, and Bedouin volunteers systematically searched a total of 270 caves. The caves were located in the western mountain cliff, from about four kilometers north to four kilometers south of Qumran. In 230 of these caves, no traces of human activity were found. Forty caves, on the other hand, had been used from time to time, between the fourth millennium B.C. and the present. Of course, few had been used as living quarters. As a rule these caves had served as weatherproof shelters, or for the storage of various things by persons who had temporarily stopped in the area, probably mostly shepherds in the winter rainy season. In twenty-six of the forty caves used over the course of millennia, various articles were found, including the remains of earthenware produced in Qumran. Theoretically, then, a portion of the Qumran settlers may have lived here. But would that have been practically possible?

The actual opportunities for comfort available to the Essenes living in Qumran were narrowly circumscribed. Even on the Sabbath they had to gather for morning prayer, midday dinner, and supper in the assembly hall of the settlement. But one of their Sabbath precepts, and one strictly to be observed, provides that no one may leave "his city" on the Sabbath to walk more than 1,000 cubits away — a scant 500 meters (CD 10:21). This figure surely refers to distance, not to the sum of all of the steps that a person would actually take. Applied to conditions in Qumran, "the town" of those living here was identical with the area of the buildings of the actual settlement, an area solidly bounded on its perimeter by masonry. Living quarters in its vicinity could not count as an integral component part of this "city." But that means that no member of the Essenes living in Qumran might live farther away from the settlement than a scant 500 meters. Otherwise he would necessarily have violated this Sabbath rule and thereby incurred a heavy penalty.

This eliminates the great majority of the twenty-six rock caves used by inhabitants of Qumran over the course of time and lying in the mountain cliff at least 200 meters from the settlement. Only some 300 meters from Wadi Qumran, in a northerly and in a southerly direction, Essenes could have lived in caves of the rock cliff. But Caves 1, 2, 3, and 11 are actually 1.2 to 2.3 kilometers from Qumran.

It has been demonstrated beyond doubt that caves lying beyond the 500-meter radius were used for the most varied purposes (apart from the scroll caches). This should probably be ascribed to occasional use by small cattle herders among the Essenes, who pastured their herds along the cliff as soon as it became green. This use was permitted on the Sabbath even twice as far, in an area up to almost 1,000 meters away from the "city" (CD 11:5-6).

In individual cases, those Essenes who had been excluded from the community for a limited time due to improper conduct may temporarily have lived in caves of the cliff more than 500 meters from Qumran. These caves were not members' regular living quarters, however. This has been established by renewed investigations. Not one of these twenty-six caves was arranged for regular dwelling purposes while Qumran was inhabited. All of them were left in their natural state and were used only occasionally.

So the only remaining possibility is that substantially more Essenes than is usually supposed actually lived within the Qumran settlement or in the immediately neighboring area of the marl terrace. It is all too easily assumed that there were 150-300 Essenes in Qumran, who mainly lived in rock caves along the mountain cliff or in huts among these caves, from Ain Feshkha in the south to Cave 3 in the north. But the reduction of this far too lofty number to an average of only about fifty-five full Essene members and candidates — through a demonstration of the actual capacity of the assembly hall and through a statistical consideration of the findings in the cemeteries — opens new perspectives on the question of living space as well.

It has already been suggested that, in the upper story of the two-story main building of the Qumran settlement, two sleeping rooms for about forty men were available. In the course of the excavations at Qumran, on the southern end of the ledge of the marl terrace on which the settlement lies, four additional living and work spaces reserved for scholars were discovered. These spaces could only be reached from the settlement, and they obviously belonged to the living area in the strictest possible sense. In one of these living and work spaces, that of Cave 8, one of the two prayer straps and the doorpost capsule of the last inhabitant were actually found, which proves that this "cave" was once a regular dwelling.

Outside of the settlement — within a relatively short radius — lie Caves 4 and 5, which originally were simply living caves. Cave 4 is particularly large and has a different interior arrangement. It actually has room for two to four persons, who could have lived here at the same time without disturbing one another. The smaller Cave 10, on the same ledge of the marl terrace, was simply a living space for one individual. There are several other such dwelling caves in the ledges of the terrace, which are not mentioned even once in the literature for the simple reason that neither scrolls nor articles used by the earlier inhabitants were found there.

Altogether at least fifteen men probably lived in caves of the marl terrace — including the four living and work spaces reserved for scholars — sometimes with their families. To reach this conclusion we need only take adequate account of the relative unpretentiousness of the time when it came to questions of housing and of the conditions in Qumran.

There were further living spaces in the upper story of the two-story building at Ain Feshkha. The administrator of this economic enterprise certainly lived there. If the need arose, his bookkeeper and the administrator of the agricultural areas to the north of Ain Feshkha would also have lived there, since the agricultural areas obviously had no actual living space. The remaining quarters in the upper story of the main building at Ain Feshkha were reserved for the tanners and the herders of small livestock.

The herders of the flocks of sheep and goats were usually on the move with their animals in any case. In summertime they could be high in the range of mountains, since at that time there was no longer enough decent grazing along the Dead Sea. They spent the night wherever there were suitable places and a fold for their herds was available. In the meantime their families could live in the main building at Ain Feshkha, as could the families of the tanners. The production of plaited mats, boxes, and carrying bags of rushes was women's work in any case, as was wool weaving. Family members were practically indispensable for the economic enterprise.

Furthermore, Ain Feshkha has no cemetery of its own. That means that whoever died there would have been buried in one of the Qumran cemeteries. Full members of the Essenes who died at Ain Feshkha would perhaps have been buried in the main cemetery near the Qumran settlement, and the other inhabitants of Ain Feshkha would doubtless have been buried mainly in the small cemetery at the point where one leaves Wadi Qumran for the coastal region of the Dead Sea. This would be a natural explanation for the relatively high proportion of women's graves here, some of them with children, since wives living in this region were probably employed in the production enterprises of Ain Feshkha and in agriculture.

Besides, excavations in the area around Ain Feshkha have unearthed no basin for ritual baths of immersion. That means that all full members of the Essenes in residence here were actually required to be present in the assembly hall of the Qumran settlement for morning prayer, dinner at noon, and supper. Perhaps they were granted temporary dispensations from these obligations, so that they had to go to Qumran only on the Sabbath, during the festival days, or on other occasions and then, if need be, spend the night in the Qumran settlement. Several smaller rooms in the entrance area of the Qumran settlement probably served to lodge these and other "guests" as the need arose.

There was enough room in the buildings of the Qumran settlement and in the residential caves of the surrounding marl terrace for all who dwelt here to live and to sleep. The assumption, customary but unsupported by any archaeological evidence, that the Qumran settlers generally lived in tents and huts in the wider vicinity, especially in the more proximate area of the scroll caves, is therefore completely superfluous and factually inaccurate.

Aerial photographs have recently shown that in ancient times there were no beaten paths from the manuscript caves in the mountain cliff to the Qumran settlement. This negative finding is thought to prove that there was no connection between the nearby residents of the cliff caves and Qumran — that the two regions must therefore be regarded as altogether independent of each other. The only true thing here is that the scroll caves in the cliff and nearby surroundings never served the Qumran dwellers as quarters. Those who were active in Qumran also lived and slept there. How the scrolls got into the rock caves is an altogether different question.

The Purpose of the Qumran Settlement and Ain Feshkha

The results of the excavations leave no doubt that the Qumran settlement and the economic buildings at Ain Feshkha were erected simultaneously about 100 B.C. and remained essentially unaltered until their destruction in A.D. 68. The evidence for this, other than the finds of coinage and ceramics in both places, is especially the architecture of the main building at each place, with its massively walled ground story and wooden upper story, as well as many sorts of further architectural details.

At the same time, the excavations have shown that the Qumran settlement must have been immediately preceded by another, relatively short-lived architectural phase. Therefore it is generally reckoned that the Qumran settlement was at first very modestly dimensioned but then expanded after some time.

Actually, the beginning phase of the Qumran settlement was nothing more than an enclosed construction yard. Here all of the materials were gathered of which there was need for the erection of the edifices. Beams and planks especially had to be fetched from far away. Building stones came from the nearer part of the mountain cliff. But the stonemasons, bricklayers, carpenters, and other construction workers had to live somewhere. First they got the old cistern from pre-exilic times working again and had it supplied by an aqueduct with only a gentle incline. At this cistern they also erected a few small living quarters; on the far side of the yard they built others for the two-story main building. Here the pottery ovens were also set up at this early stage and put into operation, since baked clay became necessary from the outset for many needs.

It is altogether conceivable that the large-scale construction work carried on mainly in Qumran but concurrently at Ain Feshkha lasted a number of years, until everything was ready to be used. The reservoir high in Wadi Qumran, with the aqueduct through the rock tunnel, was also installed during the construction phase, as were the aqueducts for the tannery at Ain Feshkha and for the agricultural areas to the north. The protective wall, one kilometer in length, and the buildings for agricultural use in the area of Ain Feshkha were probably completed at that time; date palms were planted; and step by step all installations were completed that would eventually be needed for the intended use of all the buildings, including even a well-stocked utensil room in the assembly building, as well as desks and benches in the scriptorium of the main building.

Evidently, neither the Qumran settlement nor the economic installations at Ain Feshkha developed slowly from small beginnings. Rather, there was a comprehensive construction plan for the entire project from the outset, and it was executed systematically before the future inhabitants moved in.

This construction plan reflects a clear center of interest: the *production of scrolls,* together with all preliminary stages of obtaining and working the leather from which the scrolls were made. Only secondarily was the study of these scrolls in view, within the framework of the religious life of those involved. But even study at Qumran served not least of all to acquaint the scroll copyists with the texts that they had to professionally transcribe.

Thus, the decisive point of departure for an understanding of the comprehensive planning and creation of the facilities at Qumran and Ain Feshkha can only be leather and scroll production. Comparable opportunities for study would have been much easier to obtain elsewhere in the towns and villages of Judea.

The production and working of leather was a difficult business in Palestine at that time. Tanning required, in the first place, tannin, which the barks of certain kinds of trees supplied. Also necessary were the feces of dogs or pigeons and other ingredients difficult to obtain. Because of their penetrating stench, tanneries generally had to be erected outside the inhabited areas of towns and villages.

Only in a few cases did the rabbis later concede to women the right to divorce their husbands on their own initiative. To these cases belonged that of the wife of a tanner, who could be granted a divorce even if she had expressly attested in the marriage contract that she was marrying her husband in full knowledge of his occupation (Mishnah *Ketuboth* 7:10). Even rabbis understood that, despite the best of intentions, one could hardly bear to be in the immediate vicinity of a tannery for a long period of time.

The Essenes, however, had evidently succeeded in replacing conventional methods of leather production with a technique that produced equal or better results through the application of minerals available from the Dead Sea — for example, potash. In any case, a chemical analysis of the sediment in the basins of the tannery at Ain Feshkha revealed no traces whatever of tannin, which was usually indispensable for the production of leather. Instead, what was found was essentially calcium carbonate. The tanning procedure in use at Ain Feshkha was evidently of a completely different kind from that in use elsewhere. Probably better qualities of manuscript leather were attainable in this way. And surely the new procedure did not cause the penetrating odor that surrounded other tanneries. Otherwise the two-story economic and residential buildings at Ain Feshkha would certainly not have been erected a mere ten meters from the basins of the tannery.

In order for this new procedure for leather production to be applied in volume, it obviously had to be practiced in a place and location close to the Dead Sea. In those days the large quantity of chemicals needed from the Dead Sea presumably could not be processed so as to make transporting them inland possible. This was probably the reason why the Essenes transferred their production and refinement of manuscript leather quite purposefully into the desert by the Dead Sea. The production of rawhide, which required a particularly large amount of water with raw materials from the Dead Sea but also a great deal of fresh water for rinsing, was established almost directly on what was then the bank of the Dead Sea at Ain Feshkha. The refinement of the leather, which demanded comparatively fewer raw materials but a higher number of personnel, was established instead at Qumran, which lay on the high marl terrace at some distance from the Dead Sea and which also had a much more favorable climate.

To obtain the leather used in the manufacture of manuscripts in Ain Feshkha and Qumran, the Essenes made use of extensive herds of sheep and goats. These animals yielded principally their hides for the tannery. Meat, wool, and milk were but happy by-products of this necessary animal husbandry.

In the Qumran settlement, no less than four different installations served the purposes of scroll preparation. There was the tannery for producing the delicate leather in the economic buildings; there was the scroll production room on the ground floor of the main building; there was the library, with its master manuscripts; and, finally, there was the large scriptorium in the upper story. Other than the kitchen, the assembly hall, also used as a dining hall, sleeping rooms, ritual and cleansing baths, storerooms, and stables, that was nearly everything to be found in this settlement.

Even the extensive aqueduct leading down from the mountain range was probably installed primarily for the operation of the fine-leather tannery. For drinking, cooking, washing, pottery manufacture, cleansing baths, and ritual baths alone, considerably less water would have sufficed and could have been fetched from the near vicinity without any problem, as the ancient Israelite settlers and the construction workers who were building Qumran did for some time. Only for the copious use of water by the tannery during all seasons of the year was the great reservoir in the mountains additionally necessary.

The great majority of scrolls from the Qumran finds were prepared from sheep or goat leather, and only a few from other kinds of leather or from papyrus. The enormous outlay necessary for the production of leather manuscripts would be altogether incomprehensible had it simply served the purpose of producing multiple copies of individual works, and replacements for worn-out scrolls, for the study needs of the Essenes living here. Such scrolls could have been obtained more easily elsewhere than by maintaining an operation of these proportions.

Archaeological findings in Qumran and Ain Feshkha thereby show that the extensive scroll manufacture installed here must have served local needs only in very small measure. The main intent, from the beginning, was obviously to provide the numerous local Essene communities throughout the land with the manuscripts they needed for study, religious practice, and pious edification.

With the proceeds from manufacturing scrolls, the Qumran settlers could obtain wares — especially grain, wine, lamp oil, and metals — that they were unable to obtain from their own production. Proceeds from the sale of other Qumran products — such as rawhide, wool, or pottery — could never have sufficed for living needs in the settlement. In the case of biblical manuscripts or edifying literature, their sale to other Jews would have posed absolutely no difficulties.

In the late version of the *Rule of the Community,* written around 100 B.C., there is a passage that research has always connected with the founding of the Qumran settlement. It consists in the instruction "to go out into the wilderness, so as to build his [God's] way, as it is written: 'Prepare in the wilderness the way of the Lord! Make straight in the desert a highway for our God!' (Isa. 40:3). This means the study of the Torah . . . and of what the Prophets have revealed through his Holy Spirit" (1QS 8:13-16).

What is to occur there in the wilderness is obviously the facilitation of the study of both parts of the Bible, the Torah and the writings of the Prophets, in a way that would not be possible elsewhere. This instruction has usually been understood to refer simply to the Qumran settlers' Bible study. Of course that leaves it unclear why this should take place precisely in the remote "wilderness" or "desert" *near the Dead Sea.* The Essenes could have regarded the immediate environs of the city of Jerusalem as "wilderness" (1QM 1:3).

The state of affairs would become more plausible, at any rate, were we to think concretely of the installations for the production of manuscripts — especially of the books of the Bible — as "making straight in the desert a highway." After all, it became technically possible to produce these manuscripts on a large scale only in the wilderness on the Dead Sea. Preparing the way for "the Lord, our God" would then have consisted especially in the extensive preparation of scrolls, and thus in the procurement of the indispensable prerequisites for the intensive study of the Holy Scriptures in the numerous Essene congregations all over the land.

Put in contemporary terms, the founding of the Qumran settlement, together with Ain Feshkha, was no different from the establishment of a publishing house, such as the Deutsche Bibelgesellschaft (German Bible Society), or the Katholische Bibelwerk (Catholic Biblical Project) in Stuttgart, with their own paper factory, printing shop, bindery, and mailing room. The task of founding this Essene "publishing house" had been imposed by God himself, through the prophet Isaiah. The Essenes complied about half a century after their foundation. Conventional methods of producing manuscript leather eventually were no longer equal to the great need for scrolls on the part of thousands of their members. And so new ways were necessary.

There is no reason why 1QS 8:13-16 should not be interpreted in this concrete fashion, even though this interpretation is not conclusive. At any rate, the results of archaeological investigation at Qumran and Ain Feshkha, as well as the date of this manuscript of the Essenes' *Rule of the Community,* fit this very concrete interpretation without forcing the text. The striking "there" in the introduction of the citation from Isaiah (1QS 8:13) has always occasioned the supposition that it refers to a very specific place, in which case it could most readily refer to the Qumran settlement. But it has usually been thought of as referring to the founding of the Essenes, rather than to an independent community in Qumran. The founding of the Essenes, however, took place a half century before the appearance of the Qumran settlement, and therefore was entirely independent of it. Accordingly, the striking "there" needs another referent. The founding of the "publishing house" is best suited for this referent.

The Fate of the Qumran Settlement

Contemplating the excavations of Qumran today, one could easily get the impression that everything that can be known about Qumran always went along in the same way, as indeed has been portrayed here, from the foundation of the settlement around 100 B.C. until its destruction in A.D. 68, and that the settlement was used in the same way during all of this time. This is essentially accurate, but calls for certain qualifications.

In the year 31 B.C., a powerful earthquake, the devastating effects of which the Jewish historian Flavius Josephus reports (*Jewish War* 1.370-79), also visited the region around the Dead Sea. It razed some of the buildings in existence at that time and caused the eastern part of the marl terrace to sink by two or three handbreadths. The fissure that then split the ground in the area of the complex is still quite visible today, as it traverses, lengthwise, one of the basins used for ritual immersion, so that it leaked and was unusable for the future. The earthquake also caused a fire in parts of the settlement, which brought customary operations to a halt.

Many buildings and installations were subsequently repaired or else rebuilt — in some instances with reinforced masonry — exactly as they were before. Other facilities — like the split basin or the collapsed tableware-pantry of the dining hall — were simply filled with rubble and closed. In a number of places, what had gone to ruin was simply rebuilt in the same place in a new form. In the library reading room, a former entrance to the archive was walled up and the sitting bench in that area lengthened. The external entrance to the openings in the wall of the trading room was closed. The principal installations, however, remained unchanged.

The damage done by the earthquake was so extensive that rawhide production in Ain Feshkha, and all of the undertakings having to do with scroll manufacture in Qumran, were interrupted for a rather long time. Neither in Qumran nor in Ain Feshkha have coins been found that clearly date from the later years of the reign of King Herod (to 4 B.C.), while from the early years of his reign (40-31 B.C.) a total of at least eleven coins have been found in the two places. Accordingly, it is generally assumed that the entire settlement complex lay fallow for the course of some three decades.

However, numerous scrolls from the Qumran caves clearly show that they were prepared precisely during the later years of King Herod's reign — surely nowhere else than in the Qumran settlement. The evidence of these manuscripts also indicates that the interim years were used as a creative pause to prepare new master manuscripts, replace worn-out copies with new ones, and complement the library holdings with other scrolls that until then had not belonged to its repertoire. The supplies of manuscript leather that had originally been intended for the continuation of voluminous production sufficed for these limited local requirements long after the earthquake.

So a smaller number of Essenes carried on with some of the usual activities in Qumran. The installations necessary for this were adequately repaired, but only little contact was maintained with the outside world. In particular, there was no longer any trade with outsiders at Qumran itself. This is why no coins have been found from these years. It is popular but hardly plausible to suppose that all of the Essenes left Qumran in 31 B.C. and took their extensive library with them elsewhere — Jerusalem is the destination most frequently supposed — and then returned to Qumran with their library several decades later (see below, pp. 161-62).

After a rather long period of time, however, the scrolls in daily use by Essenes in the cities and villages of Judea must have become rather worn. Not enough replacement copies could be produced elsewhere. After some time, then, it was decided to spare no difficulties and to rebuild everything in both Qumran and Ain Feshkha just as it once had been. Around the turn of the era at the latest, but perhaps as early as a few years after the devastating earthquake, to judge by archaeological findings, scroll production was probably once more in full swing, until the Romans annihilated the entire enterprise once and for all in 68 A.D.

The only things still standing or reactivated out of all these extensive facilities were some of the agricultural installations at Ain Feshkha. At least that is what must be concluded from the report of a later, Christian chronicler, whom Père de Vaux has cited in his *Archaeology and the Dead Sea Scrolls* (1973, p. 75). This report is so charming that here too it should not go without mention.

According to this later chronicler, centuries after the destruction of Qumran there was a group of Christian settlers who lived at Khirbet Mird and maintained gardens by the Dead Sea. They had them cultivated by an employee. When the settlers had need of vegetables, they sent their donkey to the garden all by himself, with an empty bag on his back. The animal would knock on the door of the gardener's dwelling with his head, allow himself to be laden with supplies, and return without fail to his owners.

Khirbet Mird lies high in the mountains, nine kilometers west of Ain Feshkha. An old footpath links the two places. There can be no doubt, then, that Qumran agriculture continued to afford good service, until no one bothered with it any more. Had the obedient beast not astonished and delighted the chronicler, we would have known nothing of the duration of the farming enterprises of the time. The report concerning this helpful donkey is the last connection between the past and present of Qumran.

CHAPTER FIVE

The Scroll Caves

With the eruption of Vesuvius in A.D. 79, a widely traveled man of many interests lost his life: Pliny the Elder. In the spring of A.D. 70, as a high-ranking officer in the detachment commanded by future emperor Titus, he had taken part in the siege of Jerusalem and had learned a great deal about the land and the people of Judea. Subsequently he recorded his findings in his magnum opus, *Natural History,* which he completed in A.D. 77.

In book 5, chapter 15, after describing the east shore of the Dead Sea, Pliny describes the west shore as well, moving progressively from north to south. Before mentioning the city of En Gedi, which was destroyed by Roman troops in the summer of A.D. 68, and Masada to its south, Pliny mentions the "Essenes." Having referred to them in chapter 4 as the only folk north of En Gedi, he describes the Essenes in this way:

> On the west side of the Dead Sea, but out of range of the noxious exhalations of the coast, is the solitary tribe of the Essenes, which is remarkable beyond all the other tribes in the world, as it has no women and has renounced all sexual desire, has no money, and has only palm-trees for company. Day by day the throng of refugees is recruited to an equal number of numerous accessions of persons tired of life and driven thither by the waves of fortune to adopt their manners. Thus through thousands of ages (incredible to relate) a race in which no one is born lives on forever; so prolific for their advantage is other men's weariness of life!

There is no other place that could be meant here but the Qumran settlement, which at that time lay about one kilometer from the shore of the Dead Sea. True, the excavations have shown that the men here by no means lived without women and without money, and the scrolls inform us that the

Essenes hoped indeed to live "thousands of centuries" into the future but did not believe that they were older than the world, which according to Jewish-biblical reckoning in A.D. 70 was only 3,830 years old. But that Pliny was referring to Qumran is beyond doubt. Pliny's presentation is of course full of fantasies, such as tourists might gather from the "locals," half understanding what they are told and then passing them on at home accompanied by all manner of florid embellishment, in order to astound their audiences and satisfy their eagerness to hear the curiosities of faraway lands. Had Pliny visited Qumran at the time, he would have observed that this settlement — like En Gedi — had been destroyed almost two years earlier, and that no Essenes lived there any longer. Still, Pliny's report constitutes an important contemporary testimony to the fact that the one-time inhabitants of Qumran were indeed Essenes.

The Date of Qumran's Destruction

The date of the destruction of Qumran can still be established rather precisely if we combine three different kinds of evidence — not only coins and historical tradition, as Père Roland de Vaux has done so convincingly (*Archaeology and the Dead Sea Scrolls* [1973], pp. 36-41), but also the condition of the scrolls in the various caves.

Coins

The revolt of the Jews against Roman rule in Palestine began in A.D. 66. From then on, the Jews annually minted new coins that bore the dates of the years of the revolt. Of the numerous coins found during the excavation of Qumran, eighty-three date from the second year of the revolt, but only five date from the third year — beginning in March or April of A.D. 68. After that we have no Jewish coins from Qumran at all from the revolt. Instead, we have Roman coins, and all of these are from the remains of the settlement above the layer of ashes that resulted from the destruction of Qumran. This find strikingly suggests that the Qumran settlement was destroyed rather soon after March/April A.D. 68, owing to the relatively few coins found from the third year of the revolt, at most two to three months after the beginning of spring.

Historical Tradition

The Jewish historian Flavius Josephus, who personally took part in the revolt as one of the military commanders in Galilee, has left us a very detailed and precise report of the Jewish war. Here we learn that on June 21, A.D. 68, the Roman Tenth Legion, the *Fretensis,* captured the city of Jericho and established a permanent camp there (*Jewish War* 4.450). There had previously been no Roman troops in the region. In the year 70 this legion — consisting of some 5,000 soldiers — marched off to storm Jerusalem. At the taking of Jericho, Vespasian, who became the Roman Emperor the following year, was present for a few days.

Josephus informs us that at one point Vespasian amused himself by having some Jews who were unable to swim fettered and thrown into the Dead Sea, in order to determine whether — without their being able to make any swimming movements — they would really float. It turned out that the water of the Dead Sea did indeed possess the buoyancy for which it was renowned. The persons thrown in headlong — from boats — would shoot back up straight as an arrow and peacefully drift about on the surface of the water (*Jewish War* 4.477).

According to Josephus, at the capture of Jericho the Romans had put to death the few inhabitants who had not fled in time (*Jewish War* 4.451-52). Where, then, did the nonvolunteer nonswimmers come from? When one reached the shore of the Dead Sea from Jericho, Qumran was only another five kilometers away. Would Vespasian have ridden to the Dead Sea only to hold a swim meet? A much more plausible hypothesis would be that shortly after taking Jericho with a troop of the Tenth Legion, Vespasian marched south in order to determine what enemy localities might be in that area. Thereby the military unit came upon the Qumran settlement, destroyed it in one fell stroke, and tested the buoyancy of the Dead Sea with a few Essene prisoners.

It cannot, of course, be established that everything happened in just this way and that it was precisely Qumran inhabitants who had to bear the brunt of the experiment. But it was standard procedure with the Romans to "restore peace" to the wider environs of a new base-camp — to cleanse it of potential pockets of resistance — before the surprised inhabitants could mobilize opposition. This sort of action served the strategic purpose of securing the new military base. By Roman standards, places like Qumran lay clearly within the narrower security zone around the new camp at Jericho. To the south, the mountain range at Ain Feshkha stretched to the Dead Sea like a roadblock. For the mounted Romans, the immediate vicinity of Jericho ended here.

The inhabitants of Qumran, with their constant trade contacts with Jericho, doubtless learned at once what had occurred there on June 21 and that the Romans had not marched on but had set up a fixed camp in the city.

That made the inevitable clear. The danger of Qumran being destroyed was probably not uppermost on their minds, but they had to reckon with it being plundered at any time. The most important thing the Qumran settlers possessed was their scrolls. They had to carry them to safety as quickly as possible. The cave finds still show clearly how hastily this was done and reflect in detail how the manuscripts were rescued.

The Condition of the Scrolls in the Caves

In the library, the first measure taken was to seek out the most important and best-preserved scrolls, especially those serving as exemplars for further copies. In case of doubt whether a manuscript actually was still fully in order, it was skimmed through from the beginning to the end. Scrolls that proved to be damaged were at first put to one side. In haste, though, the undamaged scrolls were not rolled up again into their original position. Other scrolls were known to be in order without anyone's looking at them. Both kinds of manuscripts — some rolled up backward, as it were, the others correctly — were covered with linen, packed in clay jars, and transported to that rock cave 1.3 kilometers away which in 1947 was the first to be discovered by the Bedouin and therefore named Cave 1. This careful a procedure was used with less than a hundred scrolls. Finally, the entrance to the cave was painstakingly walled up with stones so that it was unrecognizable from the outside, and it was still closed up when Muhammad ed-Dhib managed to get into the cave through a shaft in 1947 (see above, p. 2).

Second-choice manuscripts were not even examined for their state of preservation. They were simply stowed — without linen covers — in other clay jars and taken to Cave 3, which lay another kilometer farther to the north. In this procedure, some empty jars and bundles of manuscripts were transported separately, while other jars were first filled with scrolls and then moved to Cave 3. As far as it is still possible to ascertain, only rather well-preserved manuscripts were sent off to Cave 3 — no obviously damaged ones, none seen to be damaged on examination and put aside, and no archive materials.

Probably the plan at Qumran was to ship all still usable scrolls from the library to Cave 3 in quite a number of separate trips. True, this cave was a good two kilometers away as the crow flies, and every trip took nearly an hour. But it was also an especially secure hiding place. Cave 3 lies high in a steep cliff. If there was a load to carry, it could be reached only along a footpath leading along the cliff, and only some 250 meters to the south — near Cave 11 — does this path become more readily negotiable. The inhabitants of Qumran could be sure that the Romans would not discover this cache, if they advanced along the foot of the cliff — or even along the Dead Sea — to plunder Qumran.

From Cave 3, furthermore, one had an excellent overview of the entire area, all the way to Jericho. In those critical days, then, a permanent watch was certainly mounted by the Qumran settlers, with the duty to report at once if Roman troops were seen on their way to the south. Scarcely more than some thirty-five clay jars, and at best 140 manuscripts, had reached this hiding place when the alarm sounded.

As the Romans drew near from the direction of Jericho, the entrance to the cave was hastily and only haphazardly walled up with stones. The people working here could easily be seen from the level of the shore, especially in the clear air of the morning, when the Romans began their marches. This is why the utmost haste was in order.

Further loads of manuscripts came too late to be stashed in Cave 3. More than twenty scrolls, for which there were no more jars, or whose empty jars had made it in time to the now sealed Cave 3, were simply dumped on the floor of Cave 11, which was located at the beginning of the footpath. The entrance to Cave 11 was not visible from the direction of Jericho, and so there was time to block up at least this entrance so thoroughly that even investigators looking for caves did not discover it on their search in 1952 — only the sharp-eyed Bedouin did in 1956. Another load, with four jars full of scrolls, was stopped on the way and redirected to Cave 2. This cave was located 200 meters south of Cave 1 and had to be walled up in great haste; like Cave 3, it was all too easily observable from shore level.

In the Qumran settlement itself, the report of the approach of the Romans created a panic. Further loads were no longer taken to Cave 3. Instead, all other writings in the library were snatched up in great haste and without being examined were thrown together and taken by foot to Cave 4 only 250 meters away. Thus, among the scrolls reaching Cave 4 were those that had at first been laid aside when they were unrolled in the library and seen to be damaged. At any rate, only in Caves 1 and 4 have scrolls been found that, when opened, were seen to have the end of their text on the outside (e.g., 1Q22, 1Q27, 1QH, 1QM, 1QS, 4Q2, 4Q174, 4Q401) instead of on the inside, as would have been the case with a scroll rolled back up properly to be stacked in the library once more. Cave 4 was the largest living area in the nearest ledge of the marl terrace, to the west of the complex of the settlement's main buildings. It could be reached only from above, by way of steps hewn into the stone.

The last items of the library holdings had scarcely been brought down into the roomy Cave 4 along with the installations of the nearby residential Cave 5 when the Romans came in sight. The last thing the Essenes could still do was to close up the entrance of Cave 4 with brittle marl chunks and destroy and cover over the entry steps as best they could.

A load of scrolls that seems to have been on its way to Cave 3 but that had been brought back came too late. It was placed on the floor in a corner of the living area in Cave 5, which had been cleared of its ordinary contents and left uncovered, where excavators found it in 1952 in a state of decomposition but otherwise intact.

Another load of scrolls was temporarily deposited on the floor of Cave 6 at the ascent to the Judean Desert. An empty but well-preserved clay jar still stood alongside it when the Bedouin found this cave in 1952. These scrolls were surely placed near the path so that in case of a flight to the mountains they could be grabbed quickly and taken along. The person who stowed them here temporarily, however, did not flee but returned to the Qumran settlement like all the others, to defend it with all their might against the approaching Romans.

The short time available was also inadequate to carry to safety away from the settlement a considerable number of additional scrolls that were *outside* the library. On the southern end of the ledge of the marl terrace on which the Qumran settlement lies — accessible only through the settlement itself — were residential caves that also served as the workrooms of the scholars living in them. When Qumran excavators discovered these living quarters in 1955, one of them was so decomposed that only the rear wall of the room, chiseled into the soft marl stone, was still to be found. In the other three areas (Caves 7, 8, and 9), however, there were still shards of clay jars and remains of scrolls.

Conclusions

So the coin finds in Qumran, the report of Flavius Josephus, and the great haste with which the inhabitants of Qumran attempted to get all of the scrolls to safety in time show that Qumran must have been destroyed very shortly after June 21, A.D. 68. This surely occurred before the end of the month; otherwise, more work could have been done. Unfortunately, however, we do not know when the Qumran settlers decided to carry their scrolls to safety. The depositing of scrolls in Cave 1 and the sealing of that cave must have taken a whole day. The trips that the settlers managed to make to Cave 3 must have taken another. Everything else could have played out on the morning of the third day — that is, on June 24, A.D. 68 — at the earliest. However, if the decision to rescue the manuscripts was made only after a certain amount of hesitation, then the three days required for operations could have been a few days later.

This survey has shown how the various caves yielding manuscripts are connected in such different ways with the Qumran settlement and its fate in A.D. 68. The fact that the scroll caches were in all probability created in almost exactly the same order as they were later discovered — from Cave 1 in 1947 to Cave 11 in 1956 — is nothing more than a curious coincidence.

The inhabitants of the Qumran settlement fled the burning buildings after the attack by the Romans and were either slain in the open or taken prisoner. No one returned who would still have known of the scroll caches. Furthermore, the military base that the Romans built at Qumran may have contributed in its own way to the fact that subsequently no Essene put in an appearance in the area.

Other Viewpoints

Père Roland de Vaux himself, in his reports on the excavations of Khirbet Qumran and on the investigation of the individual scroll depository caves, held that everything found in these caves had come ultimately from a central library within the settlement. In none of the installations of this settlement, however, had any remains of scrolls been found at all. And so he left the question open, where this library could once have been accommodated. Nor did Père de Vaux entertain the thought that residential and workshop Caves 7, 8, and 9, at the southern end of the marl terrace, were integral parts of the whole installation in a stricter sense. To him they were simply a few more residential caves, as others in the nearer vicinity of the settlement surely were.

So it is no wonder that in the course of time other, completely different viewpoints have arisen. Let us enter more closely upon only three of them, since these three are totally contrary to what we have presented above, and because they currently play a role not only among specialists but also among the broader public.

Professor Norman Golb

One of these theories has been defended since 1980 by American Professor Norman Golb. Golb is of the opinion that Qumran was never inhabited by Essenes but instead was always a military base under the high command of Jewish authorities governing Jerusalem, until its destruction by the Romans. According to Golb, the scrolls have nothing whatever to do with this military base. They are from the Temple libraries and the libraries of wealthy private persons in Jerusalem and were carried to safety in the remote caves of the Judean Desert during the revolt against the Romans that began in A.D. 66.

Against a similar theory — advanced in 1960 by Münster Professor Karl Heinrich Rengstorf, who likewise held the Qumran scrolls to be parts of the Jerusalem Temple library — Père de Vaux had already objected that if this were so it would be impossible to explain why the scrolls in the caves had been found in the kind of clay jars produced at Qumran. Furthermore, in Professor Golb's theory it is difficult, to say the least, to explain why the scrolls were found not somewhere in caves of the Judean desert, but precisely in caves relatively close to the Qumran settlement, most of them only a few meters away. Nor does one understand why so much of the literature consists of works that are certainly of Essene origin and not, for example, of Pharisaic provenance. But above all, the finds in Caves 4, 5, 6, and 11, where the scrolls simply lay on the cave floor unpacked, show that they cannot have been transported here from far away. Without any protective packaging or carrying containers, they were set down in an entirely provisional fashion. Besides, Caves 5 and 6 were completely open, as were Caves 7, 8, and 9. Who would have subjected precious items laboriously transported from afar to such mishandling? On far too many points, the Golb theory is irreconcilable with established data.

The Worship-Cave Theory

Another opinion currently in favor actually goes back to the beginnings of Qumran research. As soon as it became known in 1948 that the scrolls that had turned up in Jerusalem were from a cave at the northwest end of the Dead Sea, Professor Eliezer Lipa Sukenik advanced the conjecture that they might have originated with the Essenes of whom Pliny the Elder had reported. No one at that time bothered with the ruins of Qumran. But the cave in question, Cave 1, had never served as living quarters.

This gave rise to the notion that the Essenes described by Pliny had lived in the immediate vicinity of Cave 1 in huts or tents, whose traces have meanwhile disappeared. When Caves 2 and 3 were discovered, further little groups of Essenes were hypothesized in connection with these caves, who were somehow in competition with the main group, the folk of Cave 1. When Cave 4 with its great mass of scrolls was discovered in 1952, the opinion arose that most of the Essenes had lived in the adjacent Qumran settlement, but that a series of splinter groups had settled in the wider vicinity, especially near Caves 1, 2, 3, and 11.

Since manuscripts were in these caves, along with clay jars, an occasional oil lamp, and even a tefilla or phylactery, the idea occurred to some that these caves might have been the centers of worship for such individual groups and that Cave 4 was therefore the chief place of worship for the inhabitants of the Qumran settlement. Because the various caves had each been stashed with a characteristic selection of texts, one could supposedly deduce which teachings the individual groups favored and how they thereby distinguished themselves from the others. The Essenes associated with Caves

1, 2, 3, and 11 were then to be regarded as dissident members of the Qumran community who had separated themselves from the main group.

Against this theory, one must first object that none of these caves shows unambiguous traces of a cultic purpose. Nowhere apart from the Qumran settlement — thus, nowhere in these caves — is there a single basin for ritual baths or a kitchen. This theory cannot explain why the devotees connected with Cave 11 never protected their precious scrolls with clay jars but simply set them down on the floor of the cave. Nor can it adequately explain why when opened so many of the well-preserved scrolls from Cave 1 did not show the beginning of the text, as other Cave 1 scrolls did, but the end.

But the main difficulty with this theory is both its inability to explain the curious finds in Caves 5 and 6 — why were there any scrolls there at all? — and its failure to consider that many manuscripts from completely different caves come from the hand of the same scribe. This fact indicates connections that should not be ignored. By contrast, Père de Vaux's old theory — that all of the scrolls discovered were once kept together in the settlement's central library — easily explains these facts. It is the only theory that has proven its worth over time and that also fits all the further evidence that has come to light since Père de Vaux's time.

The Donceels

At the time of his death in 1971, Père Roland de Vaux had not succeeded in completing a comprehensive final report on his Qumran and Ain Feshkha excavations. In numerous separate contributions, he gave preliminary reports of only the most important results of the individual excavation campaigns. Finally, in 1959 he offered the chief results in a series of public lectures under the auspices of the British Academy of Sciences. These lectures appeared in 1961 in French, and in 1973 in a revised English edition. For the time being, they remain the chief source of all relevant archaeological findings.

A few years ago, a young Belgian couple, researchers Pauline Donceel-Voutê and Robert Donceel, were entrusted by the École Biblique in Jerusalem with preparing a complete final report on the Qumran and Ain Feshkha excavations. Both of these archaeologists have since held the view that, until its destruction by the Romans, the Qumran settlement was neither a military base nor an Essene installation, but a private villa. For example, the large room in the upper story of the two-story main building, with its tables and benches, in no way served as a writing room for the preparation of scrolls, as others generally accept, but as the banquet hall of a villa. In the Donceels' theory, the manuscripts found in the caves have nothing to do with the villa but reached the vicinity of Qumran from somewhere else.

The overwhelming proportion of what excavations have by now re-vealed, however, is in no way reconcilable with the idea of a private villa. In particular, the central library rooms and the connection of the scroll finds with the Qumran settlement are completely ignored in the villa hypothesis, and the groundbreaking findings of Père de Vaux are prematurely rejected without better explanations being brought forward. Those who could afford villas in this part of Palestine built them in the oases of Jericho and En Gedi, not in the desert of Qumran, far removed from all culture. Or are the 1,200 graves perhaps evidence of a remote, lonely murder-villa?

Furthermore, objections to this theory also include practically everything that has already been cited against the Golb theory. Happily, Père Jean-Baptiste Humbert, archaeologist of the École Biblique, has recently taken the final report in hand himself. With this the villa phantom should come to its deserved end.

The Individual Caves 1 through 11

So far we have been considering the course of events whose end result was the various manuscript caves in the vicinity of Qumran and pointing up the weaknesses of other explanatory models. It will be worth our while, though, to take a closer look at the individual caves, for they contain some surprises.

Cave 1

When the Bedouin discovered Cave 1 at the beginning of 1947, they must have found everything there still quite undisturbed — exactly as the Qumran settlers had left it in A.D. 68. Only, more than half of the scrolls hidden there had extensively decomposed over the course of time. Through a shaft in the cave ceiling — by which Muhammad ed-Dhib had slipped into the cave — moisture had frequently entered and was thirstily soaked up by the clay jars. The jars always dried out, to be sure, but the manuscripts they contained more or less decayed. The jar containing the well-preserved manuscript of Isaiah must, by way of exception, have stood in an especially well-protected place. All of the destruction of these scrolls otherwise than through decay is of course to be laid to the account of their modern discoverers.

In Cave 1 there were at least 56, perhaps even more, well-preserved clay jars, in each of which one large, or two medium-sized, scrolls would fit. But substantially more than the approximately 80 scrolls or fragments thereof that can be shown to come from Cave 1 seem never to have been deposited here — 85 to 90 at the most. At the same time, these scrolls constituted the portion of the library holdings that the Qumran settlers saw as especially worthy of urgent rescue. This makes it all the more saddening that despite all of their care — only manuscripts of *this* cave were additionally wrapped in linen — so much of it has rotted away.

Cave 2

When the Bedouin found Cave 2 in 1952, it had already been opened. On the floor of the cave lay the shards of four clay jars and the remains of some 40 scrolls. At some point in an earlier time, someone discovered this cave, smashed the jars, opened some of the scrolls out of mild curiosity, and then tore them up. This long-ago discoverer had no use for them and so left everything scattered and unprotected on the floor.

This devastation cannot have occurred in recent times. The shreds of these scattered scrolls continued to rot away over the ensuing centuries, until the Bedouin finally took them for themselves in 1952. Originally at least 40 scrolls were deposited in this cave.

Cave 3

Cave 3 was once a gigantic dwelling cave, stretching deep within the mountain range. It was inhabited as early as the fourth millennium B.C., as well as during the age of the Israelite kings. Later, however, a powerful earthquake — probably the one that occurred in 31 B.C., which severely damaged the Qumran settlement as well — caused stones from the ceiling to come crashing down, to the extent that the deeper recesses of the cave were rendered entirely inaccessible. The same earthquake dotted the front areas with coarse gravel. The old entry vault now lies in smithereens on the floor of the cave. Conditions were probably the same when the scrolls were hidden here in A.D. 68.

When investigators discovered this cave in 1952, its entryway had long been open. Inside, they found shards of some 35 jars, but not a single intact jar. Of the some 70-140 smaller and medium-sized scrolls that one would have expected to find along with some 35 clay vessels of this kind, almost nothing remained. Of each of 24 scrolls, only one small fragment still exists; of 5 scrolls there are 2 fragments each; of 5 others we have 3-7 fragments each; of the rest, nothing whatever remains except an enormous number of uninscribed fragments of the original cover sheets. The fragments that have been preserved are frequently from the upper or lower edge of the scrolls, from their beginning, or from places with sewn edges. Pieces of this kind are characteristic of material that falls to the floor of a cave and lies unnoticed in the dark when old scrolls are opened. The faithful transcriptions of the inscribed remnants of 34 once extensive manuscripts barely fill two complete pages in the published volume (DJD 3 [1952], illus. xviii, xix).

What has happened here? Bedouin of the present day cannot have made off with the scrolls, since the rubble in which the small fragments were found had lain untouched for centuries. Nor, surely, had the scrolls rotted away beforehand, since even in those cases in which several fragments of the same manuscript are preserved, these are not from consecutive loci but from altogether different places in the original scrolls. The sole possible explanation for the strange discovery in Cave 3, then, is that hundreds of years ago someone was here who made off with the scrolls. On the other hand, the scrolls must have already lain in this relatively dry cave for centuries before that, until such time as the characteristic traces of decomposition that the discovered fragments manifest began to develop in the scrolls. Is there an explanation?

The Karaites

Sometime around A.D. 800, the Nestorian Patriarch Timotheus I of Seleucia, today's Baghdad, wrote his colleague Sergius, the Metropolitan of Elam. Timothy informed Sergius that he had received a report from reliable persons that some ten years before "books" had been found in a rock cave in the vicinity of Jericho. An Arab hunter's dog had disappeared into the cave, wrote the Patriarch, and since it did not emerge right away, the hunter had entered the cave and discovered the "books." The hunter had thereupon reported his find to the Jews in Jerusalem, who came in droves. They found books of the Old Testament there, the Patriarch went on, as well as others composed in Hebrew, and made off with them (in P. Kahle, *Die Kairoer Genisa* [1962], pp. 16-17).

The story fits the data of Cave 3 perfectly. The largest cave, Cave 11, was closed until 1956. The extensive manuscript holdings of Cave 4, likewise large and difficult to reach, lay there until the present day. But none of the other manuscript caves is large enough for a dog to have rummaged about inside for a lengthy period of time without his owner's being able to see it from the entrance of the cave or call it from fairly nearby, so that he had to go inside himself to find it. Finally, and tellingly, there are no other scroll caves "in the vicinity of Jericho" than those connected with the Qumran settlement. Everything comes together magnificently and takes on even more persuasive power when we ask what might have become of those "books" that Jews carried off in those days.

A scant half-century before the time of Patriarch Timotheus I, a descendant of David named Anan had founded in Mesopotamia a new movement in Judaism that still persists today. Its members were at first called Ananites, after their founder, but soon they began to be known as *Karaites,* since they rejected the Rabbinic tradition — the Mishnah and the Talmud — in its entirety and acknowledged only Old Testament writings as their binding authority. Jews refer to the study of the Old Testament as *kara.* These Karaites, then, constitute a Jewish reform movement similar to the Protestants of the sixteenth century in Christianity, who no longer accepted the validity of the teaching of the Fathers of the Church or scholasticism, but recognized "Scripture alone," in this case the Christian Bible, as the foundation of faith.

The Karaites quickly won many adherents in the Judaism of Mesopotamia, Palestine, and Egypt. Jerusalem and Cairo in particular immediately became centers of Karaite learning. The scrolls from the cave in the vicinity of Jericho have evidently had a strong influence on them. After all, these scrolls originated in their entirety in the *pre-Rabbinic* Judaism of Palestine, whose authority was still "Scripture alone," in the form of the Torah and the biblical books of the Prophets. Thus the Karaites regarded their basic anti-Rabbinic principle as confirmed by "cave folk" — as they called the old Qumran settlers — thanks to the circumstances of the discovery of their scrolls. Indeed, the Karaites may finally have taken their hard line only from these manuscripts: these old scrolls were especially harsh in their criticism of the Pharisees, the very group to which the Rabbinic tradition later appealed. That criticism corresponded to the Karaites' own tendencies. The Karaites eagerly studied the old scrolls — which are the direct source of many of their teachings, along with their calendar system — and even copied them anew, in order to have more copies or to replace scrolls that had become damaged.

One of the chief writings of the Jews who once resided in Qumran was a very extensive work composed around 100 B.C. It is usually referred to today as the *Damascus Document.* Fragments of ten copies were found in various Qumran caves. About one-half of the original text of this work has actually been known to modern scholarship since 1910, when Solomon Schechter published parts of old books that had been discovered in the discarded old stacks of a Karaite synagogue in Cairo at the close of the nineteenth century. The copies of the *Damascus Document* found there date from the tenth and twelfth centuries. Karaites had copied them from master manuscripts from the cave near Jericho — quite word for word, as the now-discovered parallel texts attest. The medieval copies are generally called the *Cairo Damascus Document,* owing to the place of their discovery.

Let us cite another example. The original Hebrew text of the *Wisdom of Jesus Son of Sirach,* which appeared around 190 B.C., had already been extensively known, since the beginning of our century, through medieval copies from the Karaite synagogue in Cairo. But these Karaite manuscripts contain various differences vis-à-vis the Septuagint and Vulgate text of these books, and one never knew whether to ascribe these differences to the freedom of the Greek translators — who always had a bit of the author in them — or to mistakes creeping in at the hands of a long chain of copyists. Some scholars even regarded the medieval manuscripts as later reverse translations of the text of Sirach from the Greek back into Hebrew.

In Cave 2, two small fragments of a scroll containing the Hebrew text of Sirach were found. Their textual arrangement corresponds exactly to the find in the Karaites' medieval copies. The Rabbis did not transmit the Hebrew text of Sirach. Accordingly, there is very good reason to assume that the Karaites at Cairo owed their text of Sirach directly to the "cave folk," just as they owed the *Damascus Document* to the finds in Cave 3. The great age of this version of the text is confirmed by a likewise fragmentary but more extensively preserved manuscript of Sirach from the mountain stronghold of Masada, which was destroyed in A.D. 74. Yigael Yadin edited this manuscript, which was copied in the period 100-50 B.C. Thus, the medieval copies of Sirach are practically direct Qumran finds — something that without the Qumran discoveries, of course, no one would ever have known.

It is not yet known what further "Dead Sea Scrolls" will still turn up in the enormous, only partially researched stacks of the old Karaite synagogue in Cairo, whether Karaite biblical manuscripts present versions of the text that are characteristic of the Qumran finds, and to what extent Karaite material may one day help us better understand difficult readings in the Qumran texts. The first and most important thing is that the medieval copies of the *Damascus Document* unambiguously trace their lineage to the manuscript discovery at the end of the eighth century in a cave near Jericho — in all probability, none other than today's Cave 3.

How many scrolls were found in Cave 3 by Karaites — and other Jews of Jerusalem — at the end of the eighth century is difficult to ascertain. There was probably no one in this cave before them: they found everything the way the Qumran settlers had left it. Inscribed remnants of 34 scrolls were found, but there had probably been considerably more. The shards of 35 clay jars correspond to a quantity on the order of some 70-140 scrolls. Of course, it is also possible that some of these jars were empty and were supposed to have been filled with the scrolls that were ultimately found in Caves 5 and 11 because they did not reach Cave 3 in time before it was sealed. On the other hand, one certainly cannot entirely rule out the possibility that many more manuscripts did reach this cave in time and were simply piled on the floor of the cave because no more jars were available or there was no time to take them to Cave 3. So there is a series of open questions here that will probably never be answered.

The *Copper Scroll*

Finally, however, there is another important find connected with Cave 3 — the *Copper Scroll* already mentioned in the first chapter of this book, with its catalogue of sixty-four treasure caches. It lay to the left at the entrance of the cave, covered with stones, and was discovered by investigators only in 1952 — not back in the Middle Ages. The sheer fact of the utterly different manner in which both finds were concealed — the scrolls inside the cave and the *Copper Scroll* at the entrance — suggests that they had different origins.

The textual content of the *Copper Scroll* makes these divergences evident. It shows that the scroll was produced only in A.D. 70 and hidden at the entrance of Cave 3. This entrance must have been so well sealed at that time that nobody could guess that a manuscript cave lay hidden behind the stone wall. Later, however, this relatively hastily erected sealing wall was broken up so extensively — by an earthquake or by the burrowing work of rats — that the Arab hunter's dog could get in. This hunter himself, or the Jews whom he led here, then thoroughly dismantled the remainder of the wall in order to be able to get into the cave. And so in 1952 the searchers found the entrance already open. When the *Copper Scroll* was deposited there, however, the cave was still shut up tight. Again its cover of stones protected it from discovery by those interested in the inside of the cave back in the Middle Ages. Despite their close proximity, the two caches have little to do with each other.

The *Copper Scroll* lists those sixty-four hiding places — mainly in Jerusalem, in the Judean Desert, and east of the Jordan — in which it had been possible to stash treasures of the Jerusalem Temple where they would be safe from insurgent Jews and enemy Romans during the political upheavals of A.D. 66 to 70. Manifold privileges had by then made the Jerusalem Temple the safest bank in all the Middle East. In the investment area it enjoyed a respect like that of Switzerland today. Many foreigners, merchants, and politicians held accounts there — a lucrative business for the Temple bank, due to the deposit taxes it levied. Apart from various objects of value described in the scroll, more than one hundred tons of gold and silver, in the form of coins and bars, had been brought to the sixty-four hiding places — a truly impressive store of deposits in the Temple bank at that time in addition to the actual Temple treasure.

The caches described in the *Copper Scroll* that we can still identify today are empty. The basis for the fact that they could be found even without using the *Copper Scroll* is stated in the text itself (DJD 3 [1962], pp. 212-15, 284-99), at its conclusion: "In the cliff north of Kochlit, where a cave with several burial places in the area of its entrance opens to the north, lies another copy of this catalogue, containing even more precise information concerning these hiding places, with all of the details of their precise location and of the valuables to be found therein" (pp. 215, 298). This much more precise main text of the treasure catalogue was probably known to the original possessors of all these valuables who had survived the war and the destruction of the Temple in A.D. 70, and it had probably been used for the rediscovery of the caches. The compendium of the catalogue hammered into durable copper and placed at the entrance of Cave 3, having been prepared only for safety's sake in case of emergency, was therefore not needed any more and was left to lie wherever it might be hidden.

As the Romans took Jerusalem in the summer of A.D. 70, they plundered — according to the report of Flavius Josephus — such rich hordes of treasure that the price of gold in Syria subsequently plummeted by half (*Jewish War* 6.317). Some of the treasure caches lying in the area of the Temple also fell into their hands. Josephus reports an instance in which they forced a priest responsible for the treasury administration, one Jesus ben Thebuti, to show them such a hiding place. It contained golden liturgical objects (6.387-89).

But we ought not to assume that the *Copper Scroll* is a catalogue of everything then belonging to the Temple treasury. It surely lists only those partial stocks that could be carried to safekeeping for the long term. Indeed, the comprehensive catalogue was probably composed only after the destruction of the Temple. After all, the booty from the Jerusalem Temple that was exhibited in the triumphal march held in Rome in A.D. 71 (*Jewish War* 7.148-50) — whose reproduction on the Arch of Titus can still astound us today and which partially came from treasure caches discovered in August of the previous year (6.387-91) — is *missing* in the inventory of the *Copper Scroll!*

Because the Temple had been destroyed, there had to be some way of knowing exactly where the rescued bank deposits and other valuables actually were. Since the Roman military controlled the entire country, it was impossible to gather these treasures together again somewhere. Thus, the *Copper Scroll* can be regarded as a register of only those holdings of the Temple bank that were still lying buried after the destruction of the Jerusalem Temple. Here the bank declares its deposits or "branches" in a way that tells the initiated everything and the layman nothing.

The basis of our certitude that the *Copper Scroll* catalogues only parts of the Temple treasure lies in the citation of certain names. The treasure list is composed in the Hebrew language. The sixty-four individual items listed are clearly separated from one another, so that each new item begins with a new line. At the end of seven such entries, the beginnings of proper names are found in Greek script. Each is the name of the one to whom the deposit in the Temple bank indicated in this entry belonged. It was precisely such personal deposits (*Jewish War* 6.282) that the treasury office had evidently carried to safety with all urgency, to protect itself from legal claims in case of accident.

The first two of these names — subjoined to items 1 and 4 — are particularly interesting. They are those of two members of the royal house of Adiabene — today, the Kurdish region between Kirkuk and Turkey in the Northeast of Iraq — named Kenedaios and Chageiras, who are also known from Josephus' reports. Sometime before, King Izates of Adiabene, his wife Helena, and his brother Monobazos had gone over to Judaism. Izates had seven of his sons reared in Jerusalem. The royal house of Adiabene kept three palaces there. Several members of the royal family took part in the insurrection against the Romans on the side of the Jews, but survived. Thanks to prudent precautions that included the preparation of the *Copper Scroll,* they — or their heirs — were able sometime after the political disaster to recover financial means adequate for their accustomed lifestyle.

The other five proper names in this register — with items 6, 7, 10, 14, and 17 — are just as interesting from the viewpoint of religious politics. The example cited, however, will probably be enough to establish the purposes actually served by the production of the *Copper Scroll.* At all events, it is clear that this scroll has no connection with the scrolls from the Qumran finds. Conjectures to the effect, for example, that what we have is a catalogue of the treasures of the Essenes, or that the Temple treasury office in Jerusalem had entrusted the Qumran settlers with this catalogue for safekeeping, are completely absurd. Cave 3, which is not at all visible from Qumran, just happened to attract two different circles of persons that otherwise have absolutely no connection with each other, as a particularly safe hiding place. When the *Copper Scroll* was deposited here, it had already been two years since any Essenes had been anywhere in the area at all.

Cave 4

In Cave 4 was hidden everything still left after the operation of hiding scrolls in caves of the mountain ledge had been broken off — above all, anything still in the Qumran library. Besides further scrolls, then, receipts, old writing exercises, and even uninscribed material found their way here. In today's reckoning the total comes to 566 manuscripts — or more precisely, items of various kinds.

In none of the other caves has such a broad array of library items been found (cf. p. 90, below), but only complete scrolls or their remnants. The number of manuscripts from Cave 4 shows that this must have been the greater part of the former library stacks — if only in quantity and not in contemporary significance. Scrolls of the first importance had already been carried to safety in Cave 1, and those of secondary consideration ultimately to Caves 2, 5, 6, or 11.

The shards of a few clay jars and the other things in Cave 4 have hardly anything to do with the manuscripts deposited here, but rather are part of the furnishings of the persons who used to occupy it, along with the transferred belongings of the persons who used to live in Cave 5 nearby. The manuscripts were essentially piled on the floor without protective packaging.

Although the openings of Cave 4 had been hastily sealed with pieces of marl, the cave did not remain undiscovered for long. The scrolls must first have lain here for centuries and have partly decomposed in their closed-off condition. But then — as in the case of Cave 2 — someone came and rummaged through everything, opened many of the manuscripts, shredded a considerable number of them, but finally left everything lying because he did not know what to do with them. Probably the soft marlstone, with which the entrance had been barricaded, had partially crumbled away in the course of the centuries, resulting in an opening that made somebody curious — someone who hoped to find treasures here, but who finally left disappointed. Whether this person took anything along as a souvenir can no longer be established.

The Bedouin who found Cave 4 in 1952 can at any rate not be its first discoverers. At that time, they already knew the value of these old writing scrolls, and indeed had ultimately dealt entirely differently with their rich finds from Cave 1 than had the first discoverers of Cave 4. They surely carried off everything from Cave 4 that they could lay their hands on there, before investigators caught them at it and secured the remaining material. The latter consisted of scraps of scrolls and potsherds that had already lain there for centuries just as investigators found them, partly covered with rubble or mischievously stuffed into chinks in the stone. Many of the fragments from Cave 4 show traces of long decomposition that can only have begun after the scrolls were opened and pieces of them were scattered on the floor of the cave. That had already happened many centuries before our time.

So of the numerous manuscripts of Cave 4, only a little material remained in comparison with what was originally deposited here — mostly very paltry pieces broken off from once impressive manuscripts. Only with relatively few manuscripts do we have anything like a larger portion of the original text.

Cave 5

In 1952 the excavators of the Qumran settlement found the remains of some thirty scrolls in dwelling Cave 5, which had otherwise already been completely cleared out in A.D. 68. The scrolls lay there completely unprotected amidst sand and dirt that had blown in over time. They were still quite untouched, but extensively decomposed. No jars were found in Cave 5.

Cave 6

Much the same thing happened with the thirty-five or so scrolls also deposited entirely unprotected in small Cave 6 and discovered by Bedouin in 1952. They were just as untouched, but just as extensively decomposed, as those in Cave 5. Beside them stood a well-preserved but unused clay jar.

Caves 7, 8, and 9

The dwelling and work spaces usually designated Caves 7, 8, and 9 were discovered by excavators of the Qumran settlement only in 1955. Here lay nothing but individual fragments such as fall scattered on the ground when old scrolls are opened.

In Cave 7, only one fragment each, or its imprint on a potsherd, was still found from seventeen manuscripts; from three other manuscripts, two fragments each; and none from any others. In the official edition, these pitiful remnants fill a single page of photographs (DJD 3 [1962], illus. xxx). Still less extensive are the three manuscripts from Cave 8, if we disregard the enlarged reproductions of the minuscule textual inscriptions of a tefilla and a mezuza (ibid., illus. xxxi-xxxv). In Cave 9, only a single fragment of a scroll was left — one too small even to determine whether it comes from a Hebrew or an Aramaic text (ibid., illus. xxxv).

Four clay jars whose shards lay in Caves 7 and 8 once had the function of containers into which the scrolls were placed after their reading. But these manuscripts had not previously decayed, as was the case with most of the other caves, but had long since been removed, leaving small remnants. The finds in all three caves correspond in principle to those that the searchers found in Cave 3 (see above, p. 68).

The scrolls cannot have been removed as early as A.D. 68 during the great rescue operation. At that time they were surely not yet so brittle that pieces of the sort found in Caves 7, 8, and 9 could have broken off. In some cases there are even imprints of manuscript text on clay shards. This means that clay jars and the scrolls inside them crumbled together, and the broken pieces of both pressed into one another over a rather long period of time. But how long did the manuscripts lie here, and why had they long since disappeared by 1955?

The Hexapla of Origen

Between A.D. 228 and 254, Origen created his celebrated Hexapla — a reproduction of the entire Old Testament in all of the six textual versions then known. In the case of the Greek Psalter, Origen had a further textual version at his disposal, "which was found in a clay jar near Jericho in the time of Antoninus, son of Severus" (Eusebius, *Ecclesiastical History* 6.16.3). Epiphanius of Salamis, in his *On Measures and Weights,* composed in A.D. 392, further reports: "In the seventh year of Antoninus, son of Severus, manuscripts of the Septuagint, together with other Hebrew and Greek writings, were found in clay jars near Jericho" (Migne, *Patrologia Graeca,* vol. 43 [1864], cols. 265-68). The "seventh year of Antoninus" can only be the last year of his actual reign, A.D. 211-17 — thus, a good decade before Origen began work on his Hexapla.

Clay jars with manuscripts in them have been found nowhere in Palestine except "near Jericho" — namely, in connection with the Qumran settlement. Greek scrolls or fragments of such are in evidence only in the case of two of the locations in which the Qumran manuscripts have been found.

Among the numerous manuscripts from Cave 4 are four copies of the Greek version of the books of the Pentateuch, together with fragments from four other Greek-language texts. But manuscripts were removed from Cave 4 by Bedouin only in 1952, never earlier. And so Origen's Psalter manuscript cannot have come from there.

On the other hand, searchers found in the living and work space that they had discovered and that we call Cave 7 the sparse remains of some twenty Greek-language scrolls that have otherwise disappeared. In neighboring living and work spaces, now known as Caves 8 and 9, scant remains were likewise found of Hebrew scrolls, whose main parts must also have been made off with at some earlier time. Finally, it is impressive that in the notices concerning manuscript finds in the time just before Origen, we hear only of clay jars, in which, among other things, the Psalter scroll was found and not — as in the medieval report of Timotheus I — of a cave in which manuscripts had been found. Actually Caves 7, 8, and 9 are rather open spaces without the proper character of "caves."

This depiction of the circumstances of the find exactly matches the findings in Caves 7, 8, and 9 of the Qumran settlement, with their Greek and Hebrew manuscripts; it does not fit any of the other locations where manuscripts were found. True, Greek biblical manuscripts from pre-Christian times have also been found in other caves of the Judean Desert, but not in clay jars. For example, a scroll of the Book of the Twelve Prophets (Hosea through Malachi) was found in a cave of the Nahal Hever (edited by Emanuel Tov, DJD 9 [1990]). It is practically certain, therefore, that the additional Psalter column in Origen's Hexapla reproduces the text of a scroll with which the former inhabitant of Cave 7 busied himself in A.D. 68 at the latest. What may have become of the other scrolls of Caves 7, 8, and 9 remains unknown.

Cave 10

In the present context, one could omit Cave 10, with its two letters of the alphabet on a clay shard. Not a single scroll fragment was found in this living area. Precisely for that reason, though, it is important to observe that Cave 10 is not one of those four living and work areas that, seen from the Dead Sea, lie in the *first* ledge of the marl terrace (Caves 7, 8, 9, and an area almost completely weathered away). It is often cited in connection with them and even indicated on maps. But Cave 10 lies instead on the west side of that *second* ledge of the marl terrace in which Caves 4 and 5 are also located. Cave 10, then, was simply a living area and did not function at the same time as a scholar's work area. The only way manuscripts would even have made it here would be if they had been part of the hiding operation. But that did not happen.

Cave 11

The last cave, Cave 11, was discovered by Bedouin in 1956 and was still tightly sealed at that time. Only bats, one tepid February evening, betrayed its existence. Twenty-three manuscripts — or fragments thereof — from this cave are known so far. Substantially more can scarcely have been deposited here originally. But it is not known how much manuscript material from this cave is still extant. One repeatedly hears of relatively well-preserved scrolls said to be still held in private possession. If there actually are such, they most likely must come from Cave 11, as is obvious in the case of the copy of the *Temple Scroll* that was confiscated from Kando in Bethlehem in 1967.

Some of the manuscripts from Cave 11 were of especially fine, thin leather, others of coarse leather. One clay jar was still here. What did not fit in the jar was set down on the bare floor of the cave, to be exposed from time to time to a great deal of moisture when strong downpours forced water in through chinks between the stones. A manuscript from Cave 11 containing the text of the biblical book of Ezekiel has dried and stuck together in such a way that it can no longer be opened at all. All of the other material from the cave of which we have knowledge up to the present time is at least severely damaged.

Conclusions

This survey of the manuscript holdings in the caves has shown that there must have been substantially more scrolls available in the Qumran library than have come down to us. Even Origen and his contemporaries profited from finds in the dwelling Caves 7, 8, and 9. The Karaites, founded in the eighth century A.D., received decisive impulse for their movement from the manuscripts of their "cave folk" that were discovered at that time in Cave 3. Only a few fragments of only *some* of these once numerous scrolls have remained up to the present in their original places of use or concealment.

Nevertheless, the great mass of all that was once available in the Qumran library has only become accessible to us today. The thorough search conducted by the Bedouin, especially, but also a bit of finder's luck on the part of investigators, ultimately have procured for us the overwhelming mass of what could still be available at all after the finds of the third and the eighth century, especially those of Cave 4. Severely damaged and extensively destroyed though it be, here we have the bulk of the material originally housed in the central library. The only material missing is what had already been transferred to other caves or left in the work areas of Caves 7, 8, and 9 (cf. p. 82, below). Of many manuscripts, very little or nothing remains; nevertheless, a satisfactory comprehensive picture can be drawn.

According to the usual reckoning, a total of approximately 800 scrolls and documents have come down to us wholly, partially, or in small fragments. In the editions of the manuscript materials from the individual caves, however, there are usually appendices that, under one or more serial numbers, list fragments of numerous other scrolls, whose content we are as yet unable to determine more precisely (e.g., 1Q69-70; 2Q33; 3Q14; 4Q517-520; 5Q25; 6Q31). Potentially, at least 70 additional scrolls are hidden here and in a stock of remnants consisting of fragments from Cave 4 whose content likewise is as yet unspecified.

Some 120 scrolls in all were probably removed in earlier times from Cave 3 and from the old living and work rooms that are Caves 7, 8, and 9 — as well as from the all but completely weathered away area on the southern end of the marl terrace — without leaving us a single, tangible fragment. Some material has surely decomposed completely, perished as building material for rats' nests, or fallen victim to some other annihilating fate.

If we take this all together, we arrive at a *grand total of some 1,000 scrolls and documents* that must have been available at the end of June, A.D. 68 in the central library of the Qumran settlement and in the living and work areas at the southern end of the marl terrace that were integrated into the settlement. Of nearly 900, at least fragments have been preserved. Thus far it has been possible to determine the content of some 660. Only in ten cases has more than one-half of the original text of these manuscripts been preserved (see above, pp. 6-7), and in only one case, an Isaiah scroll from Cave 1, is nearly all of the text preserved.

CHAPTER SIX

The Scroll Holdings of the Qumran Library

The scrolls held in the former Qumran library can be considered in various ways. Today we are primarily interested in what they can tell us that is new — things we have not known before. The apposite discoveries will be presented here in terms of that interest. Of course, those who once stocked the library, used it, and carried its contents to safety as best they could regarded their library in an entirely different manner. Only their interest can supply an explanation of all the material that was gathered together in this library over the course of some 170 years and that has in large measure become available to us today through the Qumran finds.

The Functions of the Qumran Library

If we combine the findings of the various manuscript caves — the variety of the materials found there and the manner in which they were concealed at the time — while keeping in mind the origin of these materials in the central library within the settlement, and while considering the comprehensive holdings of the library from the viewpoint of the interests of its users, we can divide all of the original material of this library into four different categories.

The first category in the library consisted of *master manuscripts,* which served principally as models for the preparation of further copies. Examples of this kind would be the completely intact *Isaiah Scroll* or the extensive scroll containing the community rules — both of which were prepared about 100 B.C. — as well as the scrolls with the great *Hodayot* hymn collection, or the presentation of the eschatological battle between light and darkness, which come from the last quarter of the first century B.C.

In A.D. 68, these and other scrolls found in Cave 1 were already 80-170 years old. Nevertheless, they show only relatively minor traces of use — for example, depressions on the outside from being held — although the works that they represent were among the Qumran settlers' most read books. This shows that the library had a relatively large number of copies of these scrolls. Master manuscripts such as these were evidently withdrawn for use in the scriptorium but were otherwise treated with the greatest possible care. Scrolls of this kind comprise a substantial part of the material found hidden in Cave 1, where they were carefully covered with linen wrapping and packed in clay jars. Severely damaged master manuscripts ended up exclusively in Cave 4 (cf. above, pp. 62-63).

A second category in the library consisted of scrolls for general use, especially for *study*. Notable among these are most of the following: the 33 copies of the Psalter, the 27 copies of Deuteronomy, the 20 copies of Isaiah, and the 16 copies of *Jubilees,* along with copies of other books of the Bible available in fairly large numbers, further traditional writings, and similar works of the Essenes themselves.

Several such copies were needed concurrently for the Essenes' prescribed communal study of the holy Scriptures and of the community's own statutes. The number of copies of a given work held in the Qumran library, then, may be an indication of the approximate number of participants involved in the common study of these writings — in the case of some works, a larger circle; in that of others, a smaller number of participants. Scrolls of this second category were found in all of the caves from Cave 1 through Cave 6, as well as in Cave 11 — thus, in all of the caves where scrolls were actually hidden.

A third category in the library consisted of works for *special studies* and *items of current interest.* For example, apart from the remaining library holdings that ultimately were hidden in Cave 4, Greek scrolls were in stock only in the living and work area known as Cave 7. There are only two copies of the *Temple Scroll,* both from Cave 11. One of these two copies was made only toward the end of the first century B.C., but then it was used so extensively that shortly thereafter it required major repairs. In this case there was a special interest for a time on the part of the library users. Several copies of Daniel were newly made toward the middle of the first century B.C., since this old prophetic book had aroused recent interest.

Thus, in many cases our findings are unambiguous. But with the majority of manuscripts from this third category that have been preserved, it is very difficult to exclude the possibility that they might instead belong to one of the other three library categories. There are actually very many works of which the Qumran library held only one, or at most two or three, copies. In many of these cases, we can regard it as probable that they served the interests of only a few persons. But there are many other conceivable reasons for works existing in such small numbers. For example, they may have been older works in which there was now only limited interest, or they may have been master exemplars of writings that were in more demand elsewhere than by the users of the Qumran library.

Most of the manuscripts of this kind are from Cave 4, with only a few coming from the other caves. Examples of texts in greater demand elsewhere could be such single copies as the splendid manuscript of the *Commentary on Habakkuk,* or the popular, freely developed presentation of parts of the book of Genesis in the Aramaic language, both from Cave 1. But fully 100 scrolls from the Qumran library are completely lost; of more than 200, the only remnants are so scanty that we have not yet succeeded in identifying their content. And that, after all, means that we do not know the content of some one-third of the original library holdings. This component may to a large extent have consisted of multiple copies of works that we do have — but of which ones?

The fourth category of the library consisted principally of *worn-out manuscripts.* Later on, it was customary in Judaism to store such worn-out copies in a side room of the synagogue — a place somewhat comparable to the sacristy in Christian churches. This happened, for example, in the case of the Karaite synagogue in Cairo from which we have the medieval copies of the *Damascus Document* and the book of Sirach (cf. above, pp. 69-71). It was also customary at times to place in the grave of a particularly pious person worn-out religious writings that had accumulated up to the time of his demise. In the random examination of certain graves in the Qumran cemeteries, however, no manuscripts whatever were found. Nor, surely, do the other graves contain manuscripts. In Qumran, no manuscript material that had become worn-out was removed from the buildings of the settlement for safekeeping but was kept instead in an adjoining room of the library.

Besides worn-out manuscripts, also belonging to the fourth category were the teffillin and mezuzot of the departed containing biblical texts; deeds; bookkeeping accounts; and parts of old manuscripts that could be re-used at one time or another for writing exercises or other purposes. One example may suffice here: a manuscript of the *Astronomical Book of Enoch (1 Enoch* 72–82), made around 200 B.C. and long since fallen into disrepair, was partially re-used for writing exercises.

Surely none of this discarded manuscript material would have survived the burning of the Qumran settlement in A.D. 68 had everything still in the library not been transported at the last moment totally unchecked — in bulk, as it were — to Cave 4. Only in this cave, at any rate, have such materials been found.

Even though not everything that ended up in Caves 1 to 11 has come down to us today, the picture presented here of the main classifications of the former central library may still be regarded as correct in its main features. What else can we establish?

Some of the manuscripts that come from the Qumran library are considerably older than the Qumran settlement itself, which was completed around 100 B.C. Thus they cannot have been prepared here but must have been brought here from elsewhere. Several master manuscripts were prepared precisely at the time when Qumran was settled. Whether these are from here or elsewhere cannot be established. After all, even when it can be demonstrated that a given scribe has continued to work in Qumran, he may have prepared his master manuscripts beforehand somewhere else and brought them here. Precisely as things got under way there was need for expert skills, until a rising generation trained in Qumran could step in.

At all events, some of the especially old master manuscripts show by their very existence that from the outset one of the prescribed purposes of the Qumran library was to serve the needs of the scriptorium, where work was done especially for others — the Essene communities in the cities and villages of Judea.

On the other hand, we must not forget the second and third categories of the library. The parts of the manuscript finds belonging to these categories show that the Qumran library served several kinds of study purposes at once.

There were men living in Qumran who had little or nothing to do with the actual production of manuscripts. During the day, they saw to the administrative, commercial, agricultural, and culinary needs of the settlement. At the same time they were — like all Essenes — obligated to participate, in the evening and on into the night, in the common study of the Torah, the Prophets, and the community rules. To this end, a corresponding number of copies of certain manuscripts had to be available in the library.

Furthermore, there were priests in Qumran who were responsible for the spiritual leadership of the community. They supervised the library and the production of manuscripts, led prayers at the daily prayer services, presided at community meals, and were jointly responsible for deciding legal questions of communal and private property. But these priests spent the bulk of their time working as scripture scholars, besides working on special studies for which appropriate library materials had to be available.

Probably it was leading priests like these who lived in the four living and work areas in the southern end of the marl terrace ledge on which the Qumran settlement lies. They may also have been the only ones authorized to withdraw scrolls from the library and study them privately. Those living in the caves of the marl terrace outside of the settlement had, like everyone else, to seek out the library reading room when they wanted to study or to examine scrolls.

In the eyes of the Qumran settlers, their library was, on the one hand, the main basis of their economic existence, and on the other, the principal locus of their educational opportunities and further studies. This view provides a sufficient explanation of why they sought to transport these library holdings to safety as best they could when the Roman threat became acute.

Other viewpoints than those just cited would be superfluous to give a plausible explanation of why certain kinds of these some 1,000 scrolls were gathered here over the course of approximately 170 years; why there were multiple copies of many works and only a few of others; and why this was a strictly Essene library, in which there were no works of Sadducees, Pharisees, or, of course, pagan authors such as Homer or the Greek philosophers.

Certainly only a limited part of the general holdings was in constant use, as is the case today with any library serving comparable purposes. Much material had long since worn out during the last decades of the library's existence, and much was only occasionally used. But all of the data together identify the interests that prevailed here over the course of time, interests now finally known to us thanks to the Qumran finds.

A particularly revealing discovery, finally, is that numerically the greatest part of all of the manuscripts of the Qumran finds whose contents are still available to us — fully 500 out of a total of some 660 — comes from Cave 4 alone. Here we are largely dealing with manuscripts of works of which not a single copy is known from the other caves. Obviously we must bear in mind that a great number of other copies from Caves 3, 7, 8, and 9 must have disappeared without a trace in earlier times. Further, in some 150 cases the remnants of scrolls coming from Caves 1 to 3 and 5 to 11 are so small that their content cannot even be precisely determined any longer. Surely, then, these other caves contained many sets of multiple copies of works whose availability in the Qumran library can be demonstrated at present only from the finds in Cave 4.

It is nevertheless striking which works have so far not been identified among the scrolls in the other caves but only in Cave 4, and even here for the time being in only one or two copies. Of the books of the Hebrew Bible, we find Joshua, Proverbs, Ecclesiastes, and 1 and 2 Chronicles, as well as Ezra/Nehemiah. Thus, we are dealing with a number of works probably composed in pre-Essene times — from the fifth to the middle of the second century B.C. — but also with many works from early Essene times, such as thematic midrashim (scholarly scripture studies), pesharim (commentaries on biblical Prophets), or liturgical material.

Cases like these suggest that in the last decades of the Qumran settlement's existence, there was no longer any great interest in these works. But a more precise verification of this judgment must be conducted for each separate case — for instance, by determining the date when the latest manuscript we have was produced or by appreciating peculiarities in content.

Generally, however, the following supposition is valid: works whose availability in the Qumran library is witnessed exclusively by finds from Cave 4 — and even here only by one or two manuscripts from a relatively early time — are in all probability of pre-Essene origin or, in cases of indubitable Essene composition, are relatively old and later came to be of only marginal interest in the community. Cave 4, after all, supplies us with the main holdings of the original library only *quantitatively* and is not representative from a *qualitative* standpoint. The best parts of those holdings are missing here, since they were carried to safety elsewhere (Caves 1, 2, 3, 5, 6, and 11).

The Contributions to Modern Scholarship

From the standpoint of scholarship, the Qumran finds of 1947-56 constitute a sensation. Previously, apart from legal documents and letters, we had no Aramaic manuscripts at all from pre-medieval Judaism, and only one Hebrew one, the Nash papyrus from Egypt. Here, on a little sheet from the second or first century B.C., was noted the wording of the Ten Commandments and of the "Shema Yisrael" (Deut. 6:4-9). Up until that time, nothing more was available. Now original manuscripts of Palestinian Judaism composed between the third century B.C. and A.D. 68 at the latest are available to scholarship in great abundance.

Even if the last fragments from these finds are published in the near future, it will still take decades of intensive research to process adequately the rich gains in insight that all of these texts have to offer in the study of Judaism, in the investigation of the Old and New Testaments, in the history of Hebrew and Aramaic, in broader Semitic studies, and in the study of religion. Still, the most important of the new insights can now be soundly won, now that four decades of Qumran research have passed and every last particle of all the material found until now is completely available to general scholarship,

It goes without saying that only some of the most important manuscripts from the Qumran finds can be dealt with in any detail in these pages. The "Suggestions for Further Reading" at the end of this volume (pp. 269-70) may be consulted for more detailed studies of the texts.

Biblical Manuscripts

All modern printed editions of the Hebrew Bible are based on Jewish manuscripts that were not produced until the Middle Ages. For this reason, we have never been certain just how reliable the traditional printed text of the Old Testament actually is. A transmission process spanning more than a thousand years might have entailed risks of many kinds: with every new copy, new mistakes could have crept in.

The oldest biblical manuscripts from the Qumran finds date from as early as the third century B.C. The almost completely preserved copy of the entire book of Isaiah is from around 100 B.C. Altogether the Qumran finds have given us nearly 200 biblical manuscripts, all of which must have been prepared before the summer of A.D. 68. Every one of them is more than 800 years older than the various medieval manuscripts that are the basis for the printed text of today's Biblia Hebraica. They now constitute a testimonial to a professionalism of the highest excellence on the part of the Jewish copyists of those 800 years: only in very few, relatively unimportant details do we observe inaccuracies or outright errors. The text of the Bible as we have it from the Middle Ages is virtually identical to the text a thousand years before.

The Qumran caves have yielded the remains of at least one copy of each of the books of the Hebrew Bible, with the sole exception of Esther. The exception is no coincidence. As corresponding finds from Cave 4 show, the Essenes held older, Aramaic versions of the Esther material in the highest regard. On the other hand, they rejected the Esther material in Hebrew developed by other Jews in the second century B.C. This is the material that the Biblia Hebraica presents and that has always served as the basis for the Festival of Purim still celebrated in Judaism today. A "foreign" work like that did not belong in the Qumran library, any more than the celebration of the Festival of Purim belonged in the Essene festal calendar. That was an affair of the Hasmonean rulers, who were regarded as rebellious, and of their sympathizers, the Pharisees. The tradition-conscious Essenes wanted nothing to do with this innovation.

At the same time, the exceptional case of the book of Esther indicates that all the other books of the Hebrew Old Testament, in those versions available in the Qumran library, were probably completed before the middle of the second century B.C. For the Essenes, these writings were received, accepted traditional-literature, no longer open to alteration in either scope or wording. Some of them — especially the Torah and the prophetic writings — enjoyed the highest authority. In any case, the Qumran library held not a single demonstrable copy of other books of the Old Testament that appeared only after the middle of the second century B.C. and that therefore reached our Bibles only by way of the Septuagint and the Vulgate, that is, through the Greek and Latin translations of the Old Testament: Judith, 1 and 2 Maccabees, and the Wisdom of Solomon.

The great significance of the Qumran finds for Old Testament scholarship can be illustrated by some further examples. Previously, certain works of the Hebrew Bible — namely, some of the books of the Prophets and especially the Psalter — were occasionally regarded as having been completed only in the second, or even the first, century B.C. Now, for the first time, we have manuscripts with the same text as the Biblia Hebraica that are clearly older than such late dates. In a manner that extends far beyond the examples cited, these manuscripts call for a rethinking in Old Testament Introduction, a scholarly discipline that deals with the process of how biblical writings were formed.

The Greek translation of the Hebrew Bible that appeared after the middle of the third century B.C., the Septuagint, contains deviations of many kinds in the understanding of the words and form of the text. Until now, these divergences have been readily ascribed to translators' whims or their subjective freedom in the shaping of their translation. Biblical manuscripts from the Qumran finds now show that, alongside the text of the Biblia Hebraica that we have received, other forms of the text of the Hebrew Bible also took shape in the pre-Rabbinic Judaism of Palestine, which the Septuagint has followed word for word. The deviations of the Septuagint from the text of the Biblia Hebraica go back essentially to intra-Palestinian divergences in the shaping of the text — and copyist errors in the Hebrew — that were simply unknown before the Qumran finds.

When it comes to the Torah — the five books of Moses — besides the Massoretic text of the Biblia Hebraica and the *Vorlage* of the Septuagint, there is a third form of the text. Until now it was known only through the textual tradition of the Samaritan Pentateuch, which arose between the fifth and second century B.C. The Samaritans still number three hundred today and even publish their own newspaper, but from the first century B.C. to the first century A.D. they controlled in much greater numbers the area around Shechem and their holy mountain Gerizim, midway between Judea in the south and Galilee in the north. The Samaritans have generally been blamed for any divergences from the traditional text of the Biblia Hebraica.

Thanks to the Qumran finds, we now know the "Samaritan" form of the text as a thoroughly familiar one in the Judaism of Palestine at that time and especially as one that was readily used by the Essenes. What has until now been regarded as a version of the Pentateuch newly created by the Samaritans turns out to be a form of the text that must have arisen before the "Samaritan Schism," probably as early as the fifth and fourth centuries B.C. There are only a few words in the Samaritan Pentateuch that we must continue to consider as deliberate alterations by the Samaritans, especially the occasional insertion of "Mount Gerizim" in places that traditionally mentioned only an unspecified "place of the sanctuary."

Finally, before the Qumran finds it was generally assumed that the translation of the text of the Hebrew Bible into the Aramaic vernacular, especially for purposes of the obligatory reading of Scripture in the synagogues, was exclusively an oral affair in pre-Rabbinic times. Now, thanks to the Qumran finds, we possess such Aramaic renderings of the text, called targums, for the books of Leviticus and Job in written form, the manuscript of the *Targum on Leviticus* having been completed in the second century B.C.

These targums show — as had always been supposed — that the population of Palestine during the time of the second Temple (from the sixth century B.C. to A.D. 70) was by and large ignorant of Hebrew. This is why we had been lacking Aramaic renderings of recognized forms of biblical texts. The fact that most of the Qumran manuscripts offer texts in the Hebrew language corresponds to the needs of a highly trained, tradition-oriented elite, which the Essenes represented almost uniquely. There was a corresponding phenomenon in the Christian Middle Ages, when the church elite spoke and wrote Latin. In ancient Judaism the written establishment of Aramaic renderings of books originally composed in Hebrew was a solution imposed by necessity. The Rabbis later suppressed them as far as possible. The Essenes still regarded them as reliable, even though they obviously used them only to a very limited extent.

The Qumran finds supply biblical scholars with a plethora of other very interesting material. Biblical manuscripts, commentaries, and textual citations unlock all manner of approaches to the history of the text. Free translations of biblical material, called paraphrases, repeatedly provide new ways of understanding the biblical transmission process, modes of transmission that occasionally are relevant even for Jesus and the New Testament. Elaborations of the prescriptions of the Pentateuch, as offered by the text of the *Temple Scroll* and a series of other pre-Essene works, provide an insight into the Jerusalem priesthood's treatment of the central materials of sacred tradition. All of the works of this sort that have become available for the first time through the Qumran finds actually made their appearance in Persian and early Hellenistic times, therefore between the sixth century and ca. 175 B.C.

Phylacteries

There are four places in the Pentateuch that especially emphasize that one should "take to heart" the directives of God and act accordingly. Two of the passages in question further require that these prescriptions be followed "while you are at home and while you are away." "Write them on the doorposts of your house and on your gates," the Israelites are told. "Bind them as a sign on your hand; fix them as an emblem on your forehead " (Deut. 6:7, 9, 8; 11:20; cf. Exod. 13:9, 16).

These ordinances have been followed by pious Jews to our very day, by way of writing these verses of the Torah on small pieces of leather or parchment and rolling up the pieces and inserting them into capsules. Since they are thereby "hidden," scholars call them "phylacteries," a word that comes from the Greek. The same word incidentally suggests that phylacteries once had an "apotropaic" significance: they were supposed to ward off "evil spirits." Nowadays, of course, this scarcely comes to mind.

Phylacteries are of two different kinds. One of their applications consists in inserting into a capsule — today generally of metal — a rolled-up piece of leather or parchment on which Deuteronomy 6:4-9 and 11:13-21 have been inscribed, and attaching this capsule to the right side of the doorway on the outside of a house or dwelling. On the exterior of this little roll is written the original name of God, *Shaddai,* whose initial letter is visible through a small opening in the capsule. Especially pious Jews touch these capsules, every time they pass them, with a finger, which they then kiss. The most pious kiss the capsule itself and sometimes attach it to their doorways almost as low as the floor, in order to demonstrate their humility before God by their especially deep bows. This kind of capsule is called a *mezuza* ("[belonging to the] doorpost").

The other kind of capsule intended for "taking to heart" the ordinances of God and "acting accordingly" are called *tefillin* ("prayer [accessories]"). They have always been of leather and are attached with straps to the forehead and the left hand (the left hand being the one nearer the heart) during ritual prayer. The hand tefilla encloses a piece of leather inscribed with Deuteronomy 6:4-9 and 11:13-21, as well as Exodus 13:1-10 and 13:11-16. Forehead tefellin contain the same biblical citations, but on four separate little leather rolls in separate compartments. The Bible itself regards "taking to heart" as a matter of the head, and the hand as the symbol of all "actions."

The oldest witnesses to these pious customs had until now been the *Letter of Aristeas* (A.D. 157-60) and Josephus (*Antiquities* 4.213). Now the Qumran finds demonstrate that the Essenes had already received them from tradition. To be sure, the two Deuteronomy passages in the mezuzot and tefillin of the Qumran finds are reproduced in more detail than later, namely, with the inclusion of the Ten Commandments and their context (Deut. 5:1–6:9) and the extended passage concerned with "circumcision of the heart" (Deut. 10:12–11:21) or renunciation of arbitrary behavior. But even the distinction between the single little inner box of the hand tefilla and the four divided compartments of the forehead tefilla was already customary among the Essenes.

In Cave 8 excavators found the mezuza and the hand tefilla of the last inhabitant, together with their textual content. Doubtless their small size caused both pieces to be missed by the scroll-discoverers of the third century

A.D. A forehead tefilla was found in Cave 5, a forehead or hand tefilla in Cave 1.

All other finds of this kind — 25 tefillin and 7 mezuzot — come from Cave 4. But that many people had never lived together here, and one mezuza would have sufficed for the entryway. This is the best proof of the fact that the Qumran library was both the collection and storage location of everything written that was regarded as "used." The hiding caves in the rocky landscape never had the function of storing "used" writings, but were deposits for the most important and best-preserved scrolls.

Apocrypha

The Apocrypha are those books of the Old Testament that are missing from the Biblia Hebraica and that have come into our Bibles only through the Septuagint and the Vulgate. Catholic Bibles still contain them today; Protestant Bibles usually do not, because Martin Luther called them "books not quite worthy of Scripture and yet useful and good to read" and banished them to a mere appendix to the Old Testament.

Only two of these Apocrypha — Sirach and Tobit — appeared before the middle of the second century B.C. Accordingly, only these two figure among the Qumran finds.

The Books of Tobit and Sirach

The oldest text of the book of Tobit up until now was its translation into Greek. Now there are four — unfortunately very fragmentary — manuscripts containing the original Aramaic text, along with another containing a secondary Hebrew translation. The original language shows that this work, so popular in New Testament times, must have appeared in the third century B.C. at the latest, and that the Greek translation is a largely literal rendering of the original text — something that, before the Qumran finds, was often doubted.

The other work is the sapiential book of Sirach, which was composed in Hebrew about 190 B.C. We have already dealt with this book in our presentation of the finds in Cave 3, since in the Middle Ages the Karaites had already found a copy hidden there and had copied it extensively (see above, pp. 70-71).

Pseudepigrapha

The Pseudepigrapha are those books of ancient Judaism that are not contained in the Biblia Hebraica, do not belong to the Old Testament Apocrypha, and have not come down to us in the Rabbinic tradition. They are all lumped together as "pseudepigrapha" — writings "falsely ascribed (to someone)" — since so many of these books appeared under the names of persons who from a historical viewpoint simply cannot have written them.

In ancient Judaism, sages of the past like Enoch, Noah, Job, and Daniel, or celebrated figures of tradition like Abraham, Moses, Joshua, David, Solomon, and Ezra, were regarded as experts in various professional fields. Such areas back then were astronomy, geography, the prediction of the future, legislation, poetry, and much besides. Authorship of new specialized books in these areas of science, the prediction of the future, or poetry was readily ascribed to recognized authorities of the past, their names being appealed to as a trademark.

Most of the ancient Jewish Pseudepigrapha were composed after the middle of the second century B.C. by non-Essenes and therefore never found their way into the Qumran library. Older "Pseudepigrapha" found there, like Job, Proverbs, Ecclesiastes, and the Song of Solomon, or the predictions of the future contained in the book of Daniel, were already regarded by the Essenes as fixed and integral parts of the Bible. Here, then, we are dealing only with such nonbiblical Pseudepigrapha as were already known before the Qumran finds, but were also found in the Qumran caves.

Thirty manuscripts of such Pseudepigrapha have so far been clearly identified among the Qumran finds: sixteen copies of the book of *Jubilees,* and fourteen manuscripts containing works of the Enoch literature. They have radically altered the approaches that had become customary in scholarship. Of epochal significance in particular has been their effects on research into apocalypticism. Until now the book of Daniel, composed in 164 B.C., had ordinarily been regarded as the oldest Jewish apocalypse and had been erected into the standard for all apocalypticism. The Qumran finds now force us to rethink the matter completely and to find totally new criteria for describing Jewish apocalypticism and its historical setting.

The Book of Jubilees

One such apocalypse is the book of *Jubilees.* It was among the favorite traditional writings of the Essenes from the beginning. The *Damascus Document* itself (ca. 100 B.C.) appeals to it for questions of the calendar (16:2-4). It is absolutely the only Jewish apocalypse written entirely in Hebrew —

consciously composed in the language of the Torah. It stands under the legislative authority of Moses. After preliminary revelations to Enoch, God has finally entrusted to Moses, through this book, everything concerning the true calendar. It consists principally of the 364-day solar calendar of ancient priestly tradition, which the Essenes — almost the only Jews of their time to do so — always faithfully followed.

Scrolls from the Qumran finds — all of them, unfortunately, very fragmentary — have preserved *Jubilees* in its original Hebrew. Before the Qumran finds, it was known almost exclusively from medieval manuscripts of the Ethiopian Church, which still today follows the calendar of *Jubilees*. Thanks to the Qumran finds, we now know that the Ethiopic version is true to the Hebrew original practically word for word, and we know this by way of manuscripts that antedate the later Ethiopic textual witnesses by a millennium and a half.

Ten of the sixteen scrolls of *Jubilees,* it is true, come from Cave 4. But over and above these are two each from Caves 1 and 2, as well as one each from Caves 3 and 11. This finding unambiguously shows that, to the very end, the Qumran settlers considered *Jubilees* one of the most important works of their traditional literature.

The date when *Jubilees* was composed remains in dispute. Most often the book is still regarded as coming from some time during the second third of the second century B.C. But this is surely much too late, if we keep in mind that *Jubilees* was a chief traditional authority for the Essenes from the beginning and that the Essenes were founded around 150 B.C. On the basis of the Qumran finds, we shall have to go back at least to the third century B.C. for the date of the composition of this work.

The Books of Enoch

Like *Jubilees,* the early Enoch literature had also been known until now almost exclusively through the biblical canon of the Ethiopian Church. This *Ethiopic Enoch* or *1 Enoch* is a composite work. It contains five books, each of which was originally independent, and all of which are apocalypses: (a) the Book of the Watchers (chaps. 1–36); (b) the Book of the Parables or Similitudes (chaps. 37–71); (c) the Astronomical Book (chaps. 72–82); (d) the Book of Dreams (chaps. 83–90); and (e) the Epistle of Enoch, with its many warnings, in which older Noah literature is also developed (chaps. 91–108).

In the Qumran finds we have (c) the Astronomical Book represented by four manuscripts that include none of the other Enoch books. These manuscripts show that *1 Enoch* contains only a secondary abridgment of this originally very extensive work. In the original version now available for the first time, it is established, for each individual day of a three-year cycle, through which of the six "gates of the East" the sun rises, and in which of the six "gates of the West" it sets on that day. Registered as well is on which day the full moon occurs, on which day the new moon occurs, and how much of the moon is visible on each day. Our own wall calendars today still indicate a part of these data, usually only full moon and new moon, but also occasionally the times of day for the rising and setting of sun and moon.

For the first time, the manuscripts from the Qumran finds make the original text of this apocalypse, which was composed in Aramaic, available to us. They show us that the Ethiopic version of the text reproduces the framing chapters of this work in extensive fidelity to the original but that it has replaced the detailed calendrical tables with abridgments.

The most important thing, however, is the following: the oldest scroll to contain the text of the Astronomical Book actually comes from around 200 B.C. It is therefore considerably older than the biblical book of Daniel, which was completed only in 164 B.C. However *Jubilees* is to be dated, the beginnings of Jewish apocalypticism, as revealed through the oldest manuscript of the *Astronomical Book of Enoch* from the Qumran finds, now have to be extended much farther back than the traditional date, namely, the completion of the book of Daniel.

There is also one manuscript of (a) the Book of the Watchers — out of a total of five — which was written already in the first half of the second century B.C. This work too, then, was certainly composed before the biblical apocalypse of Daniel. But if the beginnings of Jewish apocalypticism are characterized by calendrical tables in the style of the *Astronomical Book of Enoch,* and by reflections on the relationship between "fallen" angels and those still in God's good graces, along with all manner of cosmological excursions in the style of the Book of the Watchers, and if we also have a work like *Jubilees,* then the historical speculations of the biblical book of Daniel concerning the end times — what one usually calls eschatology — can no longer be the measure of all things when we attempt to specify what Jewish apocalypticism once was. Eschatology is almost entirely missing from what are now the oldest Jewish apocalypses. The Qumran finds have established a completely new standard here and provide scholarship with far broader horizons.

The original version of the *Astronomical Book of Enoch* is very extensive. Accordingly, a whole scroll was used for each new copy. The other Enoch books are joined together in the Qumran scrolls as a compilation. The order there is the same as in *1 Enoch.* The only one missing is (b) the Book of Parables or the Similitudes. There is no trace of it in all the Qumran finds. Therefore one may assume that it was composed only after the middle of the second century B.C. and that it comes from the hands of non-Essenes.

On these grounds, it is usually presupposed that the Similitudes appeared in the first century A.D., either in the pre-Christian decades or when there already were Christians. This is a hotly disputed problem, because the Similitudes contain the first evidence in ancient Judaism for the "Son of Man" as an individual figure having all of God's power and authority. Are Jesus' "Son of Man" sayings to be understood against this religio-historical background in pre-Christian Judaism, or were they originally Christian sayings that influenced the Similitudes of Enoch, which was composed later?

The opinions of scholars in this respect are still strongly divided. Only the Qumran finds have made us fully aware of the explosive potential of this matter.

The Book of the Giants

In at least one of the three Enoch compilations among the Qumran manuscripts, (a) the Book of the Watchers is followed by another Enoch apocalypse, the Book of the Giants. There are a total of six copies of this book. It has not yet been clarified, however, whether the other five copies likewise come from such compilations or whether — at least in part — they were independent scrolls. Of course, even without the clarification of this question it is certain that, from a literary viewpoint, the Book of the Giants is an independent work.

Before the Qumran finds, the Book of the Giants was mainly known from the fact that the religious founder Mani, whose teachings strongly influenced the Church Father Augustine in his youth, received it into his canon of sacred Scripture in the third century A.D. The Manichaeans spread it throughout the world as far as China, so that, for example, it is partially preserved even in Turkish languages such as Uighur. Until now the Book of the Giants was regarded as a composition of Mani himself, which explained the special interest it held for his followers. That it existed earlier is now witnessed by the Essenes.

The Book of the Giants deals with the "giants," who were born, according to Genesis 6:1-4, as a result of angels having intercourse with earthly women before the Flood. Accordingly, as humans these beings live not in heaven but on earth. But like their heavenly sires they are gigantic "as the cedars of Lebanon" (which grow to thirty meters); they have wings with which they can move from place to place quick as the wind; they are — like the angels — invisible and remain immortal until the end of creation, so that even the Flood was not able to do away with them.

These execrable giants are the mighty right arm of the demons, who ever lie in wait to tempt human beings to sin. Like their one-time sires, they are especially on the watch for women, who therefore must be very particularly protected from them. The Book of the Giants gives the names of their leaders, deals with their doings, and portrays their coming destruction at the Last Judgment, when the heat of the sun will burn their wings and they will be delivered in fetters to the blazing fires. Now, however, they continue to ply their mischief, and it is therefore important to have the most exact information possible about them.

Josephus has reported that it was part of the entry oath of the Essenes to promise to keep secret the names of the angels, good as well as evil (*Jewish War* 2.142). One who knew the angels' names had power over them. Several exorcism texts from the Qumran finds show how persons strove to conjure away the activity of the bad angels. The highly prized medical healing art of the Essenes consisted especially, as these exorcism texts show, in the conjuration of illness-causing demons. The latter stood under the lordship of the bad angels presented in the Book of the Giants. Exorcism compelled the bad angels to withdraw their dreadful assistants, so that the sick recovered.

As religio-historical background for understanding Jesus' expulsion of demons and the New Testament's negative evaluation of angels (e.g., 1 Cor. 6:3, 11:10), the Book of the Giants has special significance. Only the Qumran finds have shown us that it is a Jewish work and was already known in Palestinian Judaism before the time of Jesus.

New Pre-Essene Works

About 400 of the 660 manuscripts of the Qumran finds whose content can still be identified contain works that had previously been unknown and that therefore are completely new to us. We frequently have them in several copies, occasionally five to ten, at the most thirteen. All told, these 400 manuscripts represent no more than some 120 different works.

Only a portion of these works were composed by Essenes. Everything else is traditional literature whose cultivation was especially dear to the heart of the Essenes. All of the works received by the Essenes and handed down by them are from the time before the mid-second century B.C. How old each is individually, though, is still as disputed as the question of which writings from the Qumran finds come from an earlier time at all, and which were demonstrably composed by Essenes. In the following paragraphs, we will mention only a few of the most important works, ones that in all probability come from pre-Essene times, as well as certain literary forms whose works may in the main be pre-Essene.

The Temple Scroll

Probably the work most often designated as the *Temple Scroll* was written as early as about 400 B.C. For the Jerusalem Temple, which was central to Israel's intellectual world and practice of piety, it offers everything concerning the divine revelations available up to that time to David, Solomon, and the prophet Ezekiel, as a supplement to the older prescripts contained and required in the Torah (cols. 3–47). A new version of the law book of Deuteronomy 12–26 (cols. 51–66) likewise met the demands of that time. Presumably the *Temple Scroll* — or at least the presentation of the Temple contained therein — is that older work of tradition actually described in 1 Chronicles 28:11-19 as the blueprint for the Temple at Jerusalem composed by God and entrusted of old by David to Solomon.

The text of the *Temple Scroll* is conceived by its author as the sixth book of the Torah. The entire work is to be joined to the five books of Moses as of equal rank. In similar fashion, the foundation of the Torah, originally consisting only of the four books, Genesis through Numbers, had earlier been supplemented by Deuteronomy as a fifth book. In particular, the stylization of many directives as declarations of God in the first person singular is intended to document the fact that this book had the same authority as the other books of the Torah.

Since the five books of Moses had already been recognized around 400 B.C. by the Persian rulers as the exclusive civil law for Jews living in Jerusalem and Judea, it now proved to be impossible to introduce, after the fact, this further work composed shortly thereafter into the framework of what was generally accepted. Accordingly, the *Temple Scroll* never became an official part of the canon of biblical writings but was now handed down only by tradition-conscious priests such as those of the Essenes. From Cave 11 we have two copies of this work, one well-preserved and dating from the beginning of the first century A.D., the other from two to three centuries before and extensively decomposed.

Johann Maier's translation, with commentary, of the *Temple Scroll,* listed in the Suggestions for Further Reading at the end of this book (p. 269), is an excellent presentation of the content and significance of this ancient work.

Mosaic Works

We have several Mosaic works from the Qumran caves. Like the *Temple Scroll,* they take up prescripts of the Torah and subject them to further development.

One of them, in three fragmentary copies (1Q29, 4Q375, 376), deals among other things with the problem of how true and false prophets can be distinguished. In case of a concrete problem, the distinction is shown in the context of a rite of expiatory sacrifice performed by the high priest in the Temple. If, in the performance of this rite, the large jewel on the left shoulder-piece of the high priest's vestment — the left side is the side near the heart, as with the tefillin — gleams in such a way as to be visible to all present, this judgment of God proves the prophetic claim legitimate. In like manner, the gleaming of the twelve precious stones on the breast pocket of the high priest's vestment signals to Israel's chief military leader a happy outcome of the battle to be waged by his troops in a defensive action. Whether he may wage an offensive war is decided by the oracular stones, the Urim and Thummim, to be found in this breast pocket.

The description of the high priest's vestment is given in the Torah (Exodus 28). The function of the various precious stones as instruments of divine oracles is portrayed by Josephus, who was the son of a priest (*Antiquities* 3.214-18), just as in our new Mosaic text from the Qumran finds. Only, Josephus has erroneously ascribed to the stone on the right shoulder-piece of the vestment the function that actually accrues to the one on the left.

Josephus expressly observes that, "some two hundred years" before the composition of his portrayal — presumably he is referring to the violation of the Temple in December of 167 B.C. — the gleaming of the precious stones, and therewith this manner of oracle, had ceased. In the Mosaic text from the Qumran finds, however, the continued efficacy of the oracle of the jewels is still completely taken for granted. Accordingly — and on many other grounds — the work was beyond any doubt composed in pre-Essene times.

Ordinances

Composed in a different style from this Mosaic work is a legislative book customarily designated as the *Ordinances,* of which two or three copies were found in Cave 4. In the fragments still preserved we find a reaction to the increase in the Temple tax at the time of Ezra (Neh. 10:33-34) and the directive to adhere as ever to the prescription of the Torah that the half-shekel contribution established by Exodus 30:11-16 and 38:26 be paid only once in one's lifetime. The concrete life situations of the other ordinances of this work constitute an open question. In terms of content, at any rate, pre-Essene relationships are presupposed. The style and details of the terminology, however, speak for not too large a temporal distance from Essene beginnings.

Owing to the pitiable state of their preservation, the remains of other Hebrew paraphrases of Pentateuchal material — the so-called *Pseudo-Moses* texts and the legal material coming to us principally from the finds in Cave

4 — have not as yet been adequately investigated. But there can hardly be anything only of Essene origin here. Most or all of it comes from earlier times.

The Genesis Apocryphon

The same is true for an Aramaic *Genesis Apocryphon*. This work reproduces, in the style of popular wisdom, the content of the biblical book of Genesis and thereby embellishes especially the history of Israel's forebears. For instance, there is a portrayal of the matchless beauty of Abraham's wife Sarai. Roughly the first half of this work is fragmentarily preserved in a scroll from Cave 1 made toward the end of the first century B.C. Unfortunately, the iron content of the ink has extensively corroded the leather, so that even the portion of the text that has been preserved can only be partially deciphered.

The *Genesis Apocryphon* may originally have extended at least to the conclusion of the story of Abraham in Genesis 25, or even further. Very fragmentary manuscripts from Cave 4, which likewise were composed in the Aramaic language and contain material dealing with Jacob in a similar style, are for the most part as yet unpublished. There is nothing, however, to indicate Essene authorship. Only because *Jubilees* was known to the author of the *Genesis Apocryphon,* and the appearance of the latter tends to be dated in the second third of the second century B.C., is the *Genesis Apocryphon* thought to have originated only in Essene times. Probably, however, it comes from as early as the third century B.C. and has freely used *Jubilees* — already available at that time, just as was the Hebrew Genesis — for a popular rendition in the Aramaic vernacular of the beloved Genesis material. It may have been a book of edification that was not studied in Qumran at all but was kept in the library only as a master manuscript for copies.

The New Jerusalem

Likewise composed in the Aramaic language is an extensive description of the New Jerusalem that God has readied in heaven. The presentation is based on Ezekiel 40–48. The picture of this New Jerusalem as a city ready and waiting in heaven corresponds to the one in the Revelation of John in the New Testament (Revelation 21). But the author of the latter, the Christian seer John (Rev. 1:1-2), was certainly neither known nor used by the author of the work now known from the Qumran finds. John expressly emphasized that he "saw no temple" in this New Jerusalem (Rev. 21:22). In the description of the New Jerusalem offered by the Qumran manuscripts, however, the portrayal of the Temple — just as in Ezekiel — is a principal part of the work.

How important this description of the New Jerusalem was to the Essenes is shown by the fact that, of at least six copies, only two come from Cave 4, but one each from Caves 1, 2, 5, and 11. The two oldest manuscripts were prepared in the period between 100 and 50 B.C. But there is nothing in the language and content of this work to indicate Essene authorship. Probably it is a matter of one of those Aramaic apocalypses that — like the Astronomical Book and the Book of the Watchers — appeared in the fourth or third century before Christ.

The Angelic Liturgy

Conditions in the heavenly world are also portrayed in another work written in Hebrew, one that the Essenes especially prized. It is called the *Angelic Liturgy* or the *Songs of the Sabbath Sacrifice*. For thirteen consecutive Sabbaths — one-fourth of the year — we read a detailed description of which of the classes of angels is responsible for the heavenly worship service on a given Sabbath; which hymns, prayers, and blessing formulas are prescribed for the day; what liturgical vestments the angels wear; and how their divine service gloriously unfolds in the brilliance of the heavenly light. The work was composed under the inspiration of Ezekiel chapters 1 and 10 especially. The structure is pretentious theological filigree, all of it artfully composed around the sacred number seven, which is the most frequently applied concept here. The central, seventh Sabbath is the high point of the internal structure.

Eight manuscripts of this work come from Cave 4 and another from Cave 11. One copy of this work was also found in the ruins of the fortress of Masada, which was destroyed in A.D. 74. The oldest of these manuscripts was produced in the period between 75 and 50 B.C., the two most recent between A.D. 20 and 50, among the latter the one from Masada. It hardly comes, as is usually assumed, from the stacks of the Qumran library but is one of the copies prepared in Qumran for the Essenes living in the cities and villages of Judea. The fact that it was found in Masada shows that Essenes too sought refuge there, but not especially the inhabitants of Qumran.

In the structure of their Sabbath worship, the Essenes surely allowed themselves to be influenced by what they learned from the *Angelic Liturgy* to be happening simultaneously in heaven. Indeed, they imagined the heavenly angels themselves as invisible participants in their own prayer services. But the *Angelic Liturgy* was composed in the Temple at Jerusalem as early as the fourth or third century B.C. The language and style of this work point quite clearly to a structure of worship from that earlier time steeped in the wisdom tradition and poetic style out of which some of the biblical Psalms also arise. Its origin in the worship of the Jerusalem Temple of pre-Essene times has been very impressively demonstrated in several publications by the Cologne Judaica specialist Johann Maier. The Essenes valued this traditional work especially highly.

Wisdom Texts

The linguistic and cultural background of the *Angelic Liturgy* will become even clearer once the numerous wisdom texts from Cave 4, which are partially preserved in fairly large fragments, are finally published in their entirety. At least four copies of one of these wisdom books were found in Cave 4, all of them rather old, three of them coming from the period between 150 and 125 B.C., and the fourth appearing shortly thereafter.

The new wisdom writings from the Qumran finds betray a strong pedagogical engagement. However, this finding is no indication that we are dealing in particular with influences of Greek or Hellenistic pedagogy, which acquired stronger influence in Palestine from the second century B.C. onward. Rather, this pedagogical thrust is characteristic of the entire wisdom literature of the ancient Near East itself. It is verifiable in manifold fashion for Egypt from the beginning of the second millennium B.C. and for Mesopotamia from some five centuries later. In Judaism, too, an upbringing toward a happy, successful way of life had always been the main goal of a sapiential education. Then a training in piety grew in importance, as we see it in the new wisdom texts especially. None of the contents of these new finds requires a date of authorship later than the fourth or third century B.C. The Essenes highly prized these old wisdom books but, apart from one or two possible exceptions, did not themselves compose them.

Other New Works

In all probability pre-Essene as well is a work in the tradition of Joshua, of which there are at least two manuscripts and from which one passage, presented as an old citation of tradition, appears in an Essene collection of quotations composed around 100 B.C. (4Q175 *Testimonia* 21-30). Several *Pseudo-Jeremiah* and *Pseudo-Ezekiel* works, whose manuscripts come from Cave 4 alone, may also be pre-Essene.

More difficult is the problem of works dealing with questions of cultic purity. Some of them may be fairly old, others first composed by Essenes. It is frequently of further help here to observe whether passages from the Torah are introduced with citation formulas. Findings of this kind could suggest the Essene authorship of such a work.

Other pre-Essene works that are new to us from the Qumran finds furnish us with hymns, prayers, and liturgies from the worship conducted in the Jerusalem Temple, commentaries on the Old Testament, revelatory writings, earlier stages of the book of Daniel and other biblical works, as well as books dealing with the Flood, Noah, Joseph, and other events and personages, especially of the Pentateuch. A great deal of further research will have to be conducted before these texts, so fragmentary throughout, can finally become meaningfully located in the literary and cultic history of ancient Judaism. Most of these materials come from Cave 4, although some are from the other caves as well.

Let us specifically indicate only two other kinds of older texts, both of which had become especially important to the Essenes: certain calendrical works and various versions of the *War Rule*.

Calendrical Works

Of surely pre-Essene origin are calendrical tables for the weeks of service in the Temple, according to the traditional 364-day solar calendar, of the twenty-four priestly families. The number of different manuscripts, at least nine, some of which were prepared only in Herodian times (40 B.C. to A.D. 68), clearly evinces the Essenes' ongoing interest in these old orders of worship. The Essenes were obviously prepared to participate once more in the sacrificial worship in Jerusalem. As a prerequisite, however, the old 364-day solar calendar would have to be put into effect once again in the Temple. But this had not come to pass by the time the Temple was destroyed in A.D. 70.

At any rate, the Essenes kept unaltered the old order of the twenty-four priestly families that was given already in 1 Chronicles 24:7-18. Each of these priestly families was to perform the worship service in the Temple throughout one week. With the termination of the Sabbath — the high point of the service week — that family was replaced by the next priestly family. In the old solar calendar, each year had exactly fifty-two weeks. With the completion of only forty-eight weeks, the second of the yearly service cycles came to an end. Thus, the next service cycle began four weeks earlier each year than it had in the year before until, after six years, the starting point was reached once more. This system made sure that the respective seasons of the Temple year would not be celebrated by the same priestly families year after year, especially the great festivals of pilgrimage, when the priests' income was especially high. Instead, a rotation was installed, so that income was distributed in equal measure to each of the various families.

This system, worked out for a fair distribution of the priestly income from the service of worship, was certainly not invented only by the Essenes.

It harks back to the first beginnings of the Second Temple, which was dedicated in the year 515 B.C., and had been laboriously negotiated at that time by the priestly families amidst sharp rivalry. Older lists of the priestly families in the biblical tradition also show that many of the originally participating families had to withdraw and that others took their place. But when 1 Chronicles was written in the fourth century B.C., this system, with the families named there, was now firmly established and indeed with exactly the same concept of distribution to which the Essenes faithfully held.

There is no indication whatever that these priestly-service lists had any function in the Essenes' own praxis of worship — for example, that members of Essene communities belonging to such and such a priestly family observed special assignments in "their" service week. In this respect the Essenes were simply the guardians of tradition, waiting for the old calendar system to be reestablished in the Temple at Jerusalem.

The War Rule

Clearly identified up until now is only one work of pre-Essene authorship that the Essenes not only handed on but developed and further shaped. It is an ordinance for the future final battle to be waged between the forces of light and darkness, between good and evil, in heaven as on earth. Accordingly, it is designated the *War Rule.*

Of the various versions of this work, which was unknown before the Qumran finds, there are at least ten manuscripts in all. One scroll, produced toward the end of the first century B.C., and containing two versions of this work (1QM), is in large part still preserved. The core of the *War Rule,* however, actually arose in the time of harshest religious repression — in the years just after 170 B.C., near in time to the completion of the book of Daniel (164 B.C.), but composed in another circle of transmission.

The book of Daniel stands in the wisdom tradition without any special cultic or priestly interests. The *War Rule* is also characterized by biblical materials, especially by the presentation of Israel during its forty-year wandering in the wilderness as found in the Pentateuch. Alongside this material we have the concepts of the Holy War as found in Joshua and Judges. However, the battle of the end time is expanded in this futuristic book and is led by priests, in the style of the conquest of Jericho as Joshua 6 presents it. The priests direct all of the events of the battle with trumpet calls, assisted by Levites blowing horns.

From the viewpoint of its foundational ideas, the *War Rule* portrays more a cultic event than an actual war. The enemy lines are breached — like the walls of Jericho of old — not so much by force of arms as, essentially, by the mighty, concerted trumpet blasts of the priests. Still, the strategic leadership of the individual divisions of the army and their subgroups is incumbent upon nonpriestly officers of all ranks. Their supreme commander is the "Prince of the Congregation," who is ultimately responsible for the reliable performance of the detachments of priests. Standing over the entire battle event is God, whose four mightiest archangels intervene in favor of Israel.

In the pre-Essene foundational composition of the *War Rule,* the "Prince of the Congregation" was only the ranking army commandant. He had no other function whatever than his formal position at the pinnacle of the military pyramid. No activities of his own were expected of this leader.

Only in a later, Essene version of the *War Rule,* found in manuscript 4Q285, is the "Prince of the Congregation" also presented — with express reference to Isaiah 10:34–11:1 — as the Davidic Messiah. True, he is also a member of the priestly line. But he is now personally involved in military actions and jointly responsible for judicial jurisdiction. In this capacity he hands down the death sentence as well.

One of the isolated fragments of this manuscript offers a glimpse of a phase of the coming drama of the end time. The matter at hand is the killing of an especially mighty person. Another fragment shows that this will occur not in battle but in the execution of a judicial sentence to be pronounced by a court, with the assistance of the messianic "Prince of the Congregation." After the execution of the sentence, the high priest will once more go into action and cause the events of the battle to continue, to whose victorious course the person now executed had obviously been a powerful obstacle.

It is not the Messiah whose future execution is portrayed here, but a mighty opponent of the people of Israel. Owing to the loss of text, the manner of execution can no longer clearly be established, but it is to be painful. Nevertheless, a crucifixion is not anticipated. The term introducing the portrayal of the execution is not the one used especially for "crucify," but the general one for "put to death."

This fragment is currently shown on television and ballyhooed through the press. It is supposed to prove that the Qumran texts present a "crucified Messiah." The context of war, in which "Jesus" appears here, is supposed to show that the Messiah was a member of the insurgent Zealots and poles apart from the peace-loving figure presented in the New Testament. Meanwhile this fragment is touted as chief documentary evidence for the notion that the Qumran finds call the Church's picture of Jesus into question so radically that the Vatican was obliged to do everything possible to prevent its publication.

All of this is sheer nonsense. The text is distorted, the immediate context is disregarded, and a manuscript that clearly comes from pre-Christian times is invoked for questions concerning Jesus. Furthermore, in all available versions of the *War Rule* from Qumran it is always guaranteed from the outset that Israel and its priestly as well as "worldly" rulers will ultimately triumph over all enemies. Neither here nor anywhere else in all pre-Rabbinic Judaism is the possibility ever entertained that the coming Messiah can be killed. The special element in the Essene version of the *War Rule* consists simply in the fact that it makes the future "Prince of the Congregation" into the royal Messiah. It has not anticipated his being killed in the coming battle of the end time.

The Essenes' Own Writings

Some forty works, at most, from the Qumran finds were composed by the Essenes themselves. In many cases the fragments of them that are still preserved are of course so small that little can be made out of them. For this reason only the most important works whose Essene origin is beyond all doubt will be mentioned here. They show us what special interests the Essenes actually had over and above the study of the Torah, the Prophets, and other writings received from tradition. Further, they afford us our first glances into the history of the Essenes, into their piety, their organizational circumstances, and their confrontations with other groups of the Judaism of that time. Incidentally, they are all composed in the Hebrew language — not a single one in Aramaic or of course Greek. This finding reflects the Essenes' claims to an elite training in the interest of the sacred tradition of Israel, which did not accommodate itself in missionary fashion to the lowlands of the Aramaic vernacular.

The Directive of the Teacher to Jonathan *(4QMMT)*

From the Essenes' founding phase, around 150 B.C., we have a letter that the Teacher of Righteousness sent at that time to the political leader of Judea, Jonathan the Maccabee. The aim of this letter was, first, to win over Jonathan and his military following of up to ten thousand men to the union of all Israel that the Teacher was founding at that time and that would henceforward be called the "Essenes" — that is, the "Pious Ones." Second, this letter was intended to move Jonathan to renounce the office of high priest at the Jerusalem Temple, which he had taken by force shortly before, and to confine himself in the future to the performance of his political tasks.

The historical effect of this letter is reported to us by a commentary on the biblical Psalms from the first century B.C. Here, in the context of a continuing verse-by-verse commentary, Psalm 37:33 is quoted:

The wicked man spies on the just
  and seeks to slay him.
The Lord will not leave him (the just) in his power
  nor let him be condemned when he is on trial.

The interpretation of this passage from the Psalms begins with the words, "Thereby [the] wicked [priest] is meant, who has [spied] on [the Teache]r of Righteous[ness in order to] murder [him on account of weal]th and [on account of] the directive the latter had sent to him" (4QpPs³ 1-10 iv 7-9).

The "wealth" referred to is the Temple treasure, which Jonathan as high priest — "Wicked Priest" is a pun on this title — had at his disposal. The wealth at hand in the Temple can be surmised from the *Copper Scroll.* Jonathan had probably confiscated Gentiles' deposits and assets acquired by unlawful means from the Temple bank (1QpHab 8:10-13) and used them to finance his military undertakings (cf. 1 Macc. 10:21!). The possibility of gaining access to this source of money for himself could in fact have been Jonathan's main motive in taking over the office of high priest. The written "directive" cited in the *Commentary on the Psalms* as a second reason for Jonathan's — failed — attempt on the life of the Teacher of Righteousness was, historically, none other than the letter we now have at hand.

The Qumran finds have given us six fragmentary copies of this letter. The oldest comes from the end of the second century B.C. In research this letter is called 4QMMT^(a-f) because all six copies (a-f) come from Cave 4 and because one part of the letter gathers together prescripts of the Torah as *miqṣat ma'ăśēh hat-tôrâ,* "some of the practices (commanded as compulsory in) the Torah." In *The Dead Sea Scrolls Uncovered,* by Eisenman and Wise, the fragments of this work are joined together in a way that is unjustified from a number of points of view. Further, the corpus of the letter is arbitrarily divided into two parts, which are misleadingly titled "Letters on Works Reckoned as Righteousness" (pp. 180-200). The actual meaning and utterly real purpose of the composition of the letter are completely concealed.

Unfortunately, nothing remains in the six fragmentary copies of the first third of this originally rather detailed letter. It must have begun with a reference to the names of the sender and the addressee, which can now be identified only from the commentary on Psalm 37:32-33. This so-called prescript was certainly once followed, in conformity with the style of letter-writing in vogue at that time, by a proemium or introduction containing friendly, obliging terms and good wishes to the addressee.

The first substantial subject in this letter is the old priestly 364-day solar calendar, with the exact dates of all Sabbaths and feast days listed. Obviously it is listed with the demand that it once more replace the 354-day lunar calendar introduced at the Jerusalem Temple by the high priest Jonathan, the calendar still in use in Judaism today. The textual content still preserved for us begins with the last sentences of the calendrical part of the letter.

There follow a full twenty prescriptions from the Torah said to be violated by current practice in the Temple, for which violations the high priest Jonathan is held responsible. And so the addressee is confronted with the blessings and curses of the bygone times of the kings, with the warning that, as political leader of the people, he must henceforth be guided especially by the examples of David and Solomon. Through this reference the addressee is emphatically required to renounce his office as high priest. Not even David and his successor ever claimed it for themselves, but confined themselves to their royal office. First — according to the understanding of the biblical tradition in the second century B.C. — David had installed Zadok, son of Ahitub, as high priest for service to the Ark of the Covenant, and then David's son and successor Solomon had made Zadok high priest of the newly erected Temple in Jerusalem (2 Sam. 8:17; 15:24-29; 1 Kings 2:35). The Teacher of Righteousness was of the lineage of Zadok, which in postexilic times provided the high priests of the Jerusalem Temple. Jonathan the Maccabee, on the other hand, was of the simple priestly family of Jehoiarib (1 Chron. 24:7), whose members traditionally had no right to the office of high priest.

The conclusion of the letter begins with the emphatic observation that all of the letter's contents — especially, then, its criticism of Jonathan's claim to the office of high priest and his concrete conduct in that office — stand in full accord with the requirements of the Torah and the biblical books of the prophets, including the Psalter composed by King David himself. In other words, the letter is in full accord with the sacred tradition that both parties acknowledged as authoritative. Finally come warnings to the addressee and the demand that, for his own sake and Israel's, he submit unreservedly to the instructions of this letter.

The addressee's reaction to this letter was the failed attempt on its sender's life (4QpPs[a] 1-10 iv 8; 1QpHab 11:2-8) — the crassest possible manner of spurning all the demands cited. In particular, the 354-day lunar calendar remained in force as long as the Jerusalem Temple stood. Thus the breach between the Essenes and the sacrificial worship of the Temple, performed according to the dates of this lunar calendar, was definitive and irreparable. The last, failed attempt to patch it over had been the *Directive of the Teacher to Jonathan,* which we now come to know for the first time from the Qumran finds. Here is the most important document concerning the rise of the Essenes. Without its help, we could scarcely have surmised what was concretely played out at that time.

The Hymn Collection Hodayot

From the Qumran finds come quite a number of scrolls containing collections of hymns. The most important of them is a master manuscript from Cave 1, which originally contained some thirty-five hymns and was composed toward the end of the first century B.C. (1QH). It comprised twenty-eight columns of text, each with from forty-one to forty-two lengthy lines. The beginning and end of the scroll are severely damaged, but they can be partially completed from fragments of six parallel manuscripts from Cave 4. This collection of hymns is usually called the *Hodayot,* "Songs of Praise," since many of the hymns begin with *'odekah 'adonai,* "I praise you, O Lord." Actually this lengthy manuscript is composed of a number of smaller hymn-collections, which also existed individually.

The seventeen hymns of the middle part of this manuscript — columns 1–11 in the editors' numbering — were composed by and large by the Teacher of Righteousness himself. They reflect his personal destiny, his claim to be the only legitimate high priest one day in the future, and they praise God for his goodness and fidelity in all that occurs.

The other hymns in this collection come from the hand of Essenes, who thank God for his gracious dealings with the community itself, praise his mercy, and celebrate his knowledge. For all of this they thank the gift of the Holy Spirit. All of these hymns were composed back in the second half of the second century B.C., as, apart from their content, the oldest manuscripts of partial collections show. They are the principal document of the Essenes' spiritual piety, their picture of human beings and of God, and their struggle for a deeper insight into God's unfathomable plan of salvation for the entire world.

Community Rules

A master manuscript from Cave 1, produced around 100 B.C., contains four different community rules. The first has an appendix in the form of a literarily independent didactic piece on the Two Spirits. We have the first two community rules in several other, parallel manuscripts from other caves as well; we have no other manuscript at all of the latter two rules.

This long manuscript originally had at least twenty columns of text, with twenty-six to twenty-nine lengthy lines of text. The first thirteen columns have been preserved almost in their entirety; five other columns are quite fragmentary; and the conclusion has been destroyed without a trace. The only part of the title on the verso of this scroll is the beginning: "The Community Rule and (more) of [. . .]" And so we do not know what the Essenes themselves called the further parts making up this combination of texts.

All five individual texts of this scroll were composed back in the second half of the second century B.C., therefore before the founding of the Qumran settlement. From start to finish, they are concerned only with the Essenes in general, not with any particularities of Qumran — contrary to what is still ordinarily assumed in scholarship today simply because the manuscript published as early as 1951 and 1955 came from the original Qumran library. Meanwhile, there is a parallel manuscript (4QS^e) as many as two to three decades older than 1QS 5–9.

The Rule of the Community *(1QS 1:1–3:12)*

The first work of this scroll is called, according to the testimony of the title on the back of the scroll and a formulation in the second sentence of the text, the *Rule of the Community*. Its text fills columns 1:1–3:12. It deals essentially with the agenda for the annual festival of the Renewal of the Covenant, which regarded especially the induction of new members and the new distribution of ranks to each individual member in a framework of the three classes of priests, Levites, and simple Israelites. This yearly feast was always celebrated "in the third month" (see 4QD^a 18 v 17-18), probably at the Feast of Weeks celebrated on the fifteenth day of the third month, our Pentecost today.

The introductory part of this agenda formulates the basic requirements of the members of the Essene community, and of new candidates in particular. The agenda proper first lists the praises of God and his saving works to be recited by priests and Levites in the entrance liturgy, and then supplies the wording of a confession of sin on the part of those assembled, the priest's blessing, the Levites' curse, and a prophylactic self-curse on the part of the festival participants in the event of their turning rebellious. Individual parts of this liturgical formula are answered by the assembly with "Amen, Amen," whereby they declare themselves to be in agreement with the content of these texts. The conclusion deals with the establishment of rank, and with the question of what sort those persons are who disdain entry into the Essenes, and of what sort those who prove ready to join.

The *Teaching on the Two Spirits* (1QS 3:13–4:26)

Affixed to the agenda is a didactic piece, the *Teaching on the Two Spirits*. It is surely of Essene origin and influenced by Babylonian Judaism. The *Teaching on the Two Spirits* stands in columns 3:13–4:26 of the scroll, but is missing after the *Rule of the Community* in copies from other caves. Only one other manuscript from Cave 4 (4QS^c) also contains it.

This didactic piece posits the thesis that God created the entire world from the beginning in equal parts of light and darkness. This concept comes to mind from an observation of nature. In summer the days are long, while in winter they are short. But on the average the year is divided equally into light and darkness. The *Teaching on the Two Spirits* has transferred this phenomenon of nature to the entire world order, especially to the powers holding sway in creation and to the persons who are exposed to their activity. Everything consists here partly of light, partly of darkness — in basic principle, half and half, like the solar year, but in concrete cases with differentiated weighting, as the longer and shorter days obviously demonstrate.

Another Qumran text, the so-called *Horoscope* from Cave 4 (4Q186), concretely demonstrates, without detriment to certain differences in detail, how the Essenes conceived this creation-like distribution as applying to human nature itself. Every person has nine qualitative parts. The most righteous person of all is eight parts light and one part darkness. With the next category of persons the ratio stands at 7:2. Then come 6:3 and 5:4. With 4:5, the predominantly evil start. But even the most dreadful sinner, with a quotient of 1:8, is still one part light, however small a part.

This basic distribution of the world into light and darkness, good and evil, righteousness and sin, was established in God's plan before the beginning of all creation — along with each human being's special destiny, from the outset, wherever he or she was to be born. No one, however strenuously one might strive, can become better or worse than has been determined by his or her immutable makeup, fashioned to the standard of all creation.

At the coming end of the ages, when God appears for the Last Judgment, stock will be taken of all that has occurred until that moment. God will observe that both basic principles have held absolutely equal sway until then; thus, his plan for creation will have flawlessly attained its goal. Then God will annihilate everything that was determined predominantly by the principle of darkness. From among the predominantly good, God will make a selection and, through the working of his Holy Spirit, will make over these righteous ones, with the result that, for the first time, there will be one-hundred-percent good persons, so to speak, by way of a proportion of 9:0 of goodness. They will be so righteous as never to be able to sin. Thus, a misfortune like the Fall in Paradise (Genesis 3), which had been the burden of every human being until then, will never be able to recur. The proclamation of this future new creation is an essential purpose of the *Teaching on the Two Spirits*.

The title of this didactic piece rests on the fact that the presentation does not limit itself to a description of the distribution of the world in general and human beings in particular into light and darkness, but at the same time places both realms under the influence of good and evil angels. True, the assignments of the latter are limited to maintaining the stability of the twofold structure of being, as established by God, throughout the course of the ages. The history of this two-spirit teaching in terms of the history of religions is supplied by the more than 3,000 Assyrian and Babylonian divinities, good and evil, which exiled Mesopotamian Judaism reconsecrated into hierarchies of angels and integrated into the biblical view of creation. The strongly dualistic world-principle itself goes back to ancient Iranian influences.

To the stark dualism and the light-darkness terminology of the *Teaching on the Two Spirits* correspond analogous findings in the pre-Essene *War Rule,* but these features have no parallels in the texts demonstrably composed by Essenes. Accordingly, it is to be assumed that the Essenes adopted this didactic piece unchanged from older tradition. Some of the congregational hymns of the *Hodayot* collection are influenced in concept and terminology by the *Teaching on the Two Spirits,* but not those that were written by the Teacher of Righteousness. In the corpus of the Qumran writings, the *Teaching* has found a good place as an appendix to the *Rule of the Community,* since it renders the latter's conclusion plausible: it corresponds to God's creative will that only certain persons are ever disposed to enter the Essenes, while others, despite the best of personal intentions, never make it.

The Manual of Discipline *(1QS 5:1–11:22)*

The next part of this scroll, columns 5:1–11:22, is a combination of organizational prescriptions for the community of the Essenes, prescriptions that had been developed in the first decades of their existence. Older bodies of law, of pre-Essene communities, are acknowledged still to be immutably valid (1QS 9:10-11). These latter dealt, for example, with regulations for Sabbath observance and the calendar of festivals, for problems of cultic purity, for marriage and inheritance law, for land ownership and tithing, and for many other areas of law. That had all already been satisfactorily regulated in pre-Essene communities and, to the minds of the tradition-oriented Essenes, stood in no need of revision. Therefore all of these subjects are missing from the specifically Essene rule in 1QS 5:1–11:22, which is limited substantially to new circumstances of an organizational and disciplinary kind.

On the other hand, in the present text we do have the *Manual of Discipline* in the latest stage of its development. The beginning of the text in 1QS 5:1 is already transformed from the original version, in order to fit it to the new context (1QS 1–4 + 1QSa + 1QSb). A number of penalties are now doubled — for instance, from a one-half-year exclusion from community functions to exclusion for an entire year. The original conclusion, with its regulations for the priestly families' weeks of service in the Jerusalem Temple, as an older manuscript from Cave 4 still offers it (4QS^c), has been replaced by a regulation for the daily times of prayer and by a sample hymn for the prayer service (1QS 9:26–11:22). Of this latest version of the text, other copies of the *Manual of Discipline* were made, partly on the basis of our preserved master manuscript.

With regard to content, the *Manual of Discipline* begins as the agenda does in 1QS 1:1–3:12. At the beginning, by way of a preamble, stand certain basic definitions (5:1-7). The next matters taken up are the oath sworn upon entering the community and the prohibition of any contact with non-Essenes in religious affairs (5:7-20), the annual revision of the members' respective ranks within the community (5:20-25), and the obligation of mutual admonition in the event of misconduct (5:25–6:1). There follow regulations for local gathering, in all places of the country, at prayer services, meals, and deliberative gatherings (6:1-8). As is still the case in Judaism today, so also among the Essenes a worship service could take place only when a group of at least ten religiously mature men — in today's terminology, a *minyan* — were present (cf. Exod. 18:21, 25). With the Essenes, a priest always had to preside, which the Pharisees and later Rabbinic Judaism no longer held to be necessary.

The *Manual of Discipline* also offers rules of procedure for deliberative gatherings, as well as for the admittance procedure for new members, which must be conducted at least every three years (6:8-23). It concludes (6:24–7:27) with a comprehensive book of penal law, in which (evidently frequent) kinds of misbehavior are listed with the applicable penalties. The latter range from pain of death in case of blasphemy to the minimal penalty of a ten-day exclusion from all community functions, for example, for the transgression of interrupting another's speaking during an official gathering (7:9-10).

Besides temporary exclusion from community functions, the repertoire of sanctions includes the curtailment of daily rations. That is, when anyone upon entering the community is proven consciously to have failed to contribute his full personal fortune to the community coffers, punishment consists in a one-year exclusion from the ritual immersions, together with a curtailment of rations by one-fourth during that time. Finally, finding of judgment in a penal case is to be determined by a court, which must always be composed of three priests and twelve laymen (7:27–8:4).

To this original corpus of the *Manual of Discipline,* a number of additional materials are successively appended. First there are two passages in which the Essenes present themselves as the true Temple of God on earth, with the priests as its Holy of Holies. Only in the Essene community, and no longer in a Jerusalem Temple now desecrated by a false calendar ordinance, does that expiation for the whole country take place which according to the Torah is to be performed especially on the Day of Atonement (8:4-10; cf. Leviticus 16). There follows a note prescribing that neophytes in their third year have access, above and beyond the biblical writings, to all of the doctrinal and legal corpora of the Essenes without exception (8:10-12). The next note appended here is the one with the citation of Isaiah 40:3, a passage possibly appealed to partly with reference to the founding of the Qumran settlement (8:12-15; see above, pp. 54-55).

Further appendices are missing from the oldest copy of the *Manual of Discipline* (4QSᶜ). At issue in these appendices are regulations for the duration of exclusion in case of intentional or negligent transgression, not of the Essene statutes and rules, but of the Torah; the unreserved acknowledgment of the Essene prayer services and the pious conduct of life of all members as a fully valid substitute for the offering of sacrifice in the Jerusalem Temple; as well as the exclusive responsibility of the priests for legislation, questions of property, and the admittance of new members together with concerns of property rights. This last was especially difficult when one member of a family entered the Essenes while his father, blood brother, or other persons entitled to a share in the family possessions did not. In this case a clear division of goods must be introduced, since Essenes' property must never be "mixed" with that of others. All of these additional regulations must, as is observed in conclusion, remain unchanged and in force until such time as a new prophet like Moses, or the High Priest and royal Messiah of the coming time of salvation, with their special prerogatives, can make changes in what will have been valid until that time (8:15–9:11).

These particularly late additional regulations are followed by two passages listing necessary qualifications and concrete assignments for members of the Essenes in leadership functions. These regulations had already appeared in the older version of the *Manual of Discipline* (4QSᵉ) as independent additions, while the concluding comprehensive regulation of prayer times, accompanied by a sample hymn (1QS 9:26–11:22), is still missing there, or else a regulation for the service weeks of the priestly families in the Temple at Jerusalem is in its place. Of course, this turned out to be superfluous in the final version of the *Manual of Discipline,* once the Essene prayer services and the pious lifestyle of all of their members together had now been firmly established in the latest additions as a fully valid substitute for the worship service in the Temple.

The *Manual of Discipline,* then, with its regulation of organizational problems and its clear demonstration of the genesis of its literary formation, affords valuable concrete insights into the early community life of the Essenes even before there was a Qumran settlement. Granted, this work never became a full-fledged "Community Rule," however much the later additions to the original *Manual of Discipline* show a tendency to present it as such.

The Essenes' Oldest Congregational Rule (1QSa)

The oldest actual congregational rule of the Essenes is quite concise. It stands in columns 12 and 13 of 1QS, and comprises only fifty-one lines of text. Later it was no longer used; at any rate, no further example can be identified in the Qumran finds. The grounds for this may lie simply in the fact that the much more comprehensive *Damascus Document,* composed around 100 B.C., replaced it and rendered it superfluous. For us, however, it is of priceless value, since here we have, in concentrated form for the first time, the ideas that guided the Teacher of Righteousness in founding the Essenes, his organizational priorities, and the future expectations that he had over and above what we know from the hymns in the *Hodayot* collection that he himself composed.

The great importance of the *Rule of the Congregation* frequently goes unrecognized in Qumran research. The main reason for this is that it begins with the words, "Now, this is the Rule for the entire congregation of Israel during the end time." The concept "end time" — or "the end of the days," as it translates literally — is often mistakenly taken to refer to the coming beginning of the time of salvation, when the Messiah will finally have come, whom the conclusion of this congregational rule already views as a participant in Essene community functions. Accordingly, this work is looked upon as a sketch of a congregational rule for the coming messianic time of salvation.

In reality, however, the Essenes regarded themselves from the outset as living in the last epoch of history before the Last Judgment and time of salvation and designated this entire epoch — were it to last a full century or even longer — "the end time." The very content of this text completely contradicts the picture of a congregation of a *future* time of salvation, since there are still problem figures, such as "fools," to whom no offices are to be entrusted, or impure persons and those with physical defects, who must be excluded from the prayer services and deliberative assemblies. In the time of salvation, on the other hand, the Essenes expected there to be no more such imperfect human beings at all — nor therefore any need for the requirements of the regulations listed here.

This text was surely conceived as a binding congregational rule for its author's *present* time. This present time placed especially high demands on the purity of the cultic congregational life, of course, since it was also, as the "end time," the last epoch in history before God's Last Judgment, an epoch in which the evil in the world raged more terribly than it ever had before. Adequately to arm the cultic community of Israel against the influences of evil was indeed precisely a special purpose of the composition of such a rule.

The opening sentence of the *Rule of the Congregation* actually runs on somewhat further than cited above. In its entirety, it reads: "Now, this is the Rule for the entire of congregation of Israel, during the end time, for its (community) gatherings." After an intermediate section securing the leading role of the priests of the lineage of Zadok for all concerns, the text continues:

> When they come, they shall assemble all those who come, even unto infants and wives, and they shall read in their [hearing a]ll of the statutes of the Covenant (the Torah received by Moses on Sinai) and shall instruct them in all its precepts, that [henceforward] they may no longer stray in their [errors] (i.e., sins of ignorance).

The preamble of the *Rule of the Congregation* thereby seizes upon the very words of the prescription of Deuteronomy 31:9-13 to summon, every seventh year, on the occasion of the Feast of Tabernacles, *all Israel,* and "to read" them "this law" — which was understood in the second century B.C. to mean all of God's directives in the entire Torah — "in their hearing . . . so that they may hear and learn to fear the LORD your God and to observe diligently all the words of this law (vv. 11-12).

The reference to the Feast of Tabernacles and the seven-year time period are missing in the Essene *Rule of the Congregation.* Instead, the Essenes here understand themselves as the permanent representatives of the whole of Israel, supplying ongoing instructions to the entire people of Israel — "even unto infants and wives" — regarding the commandments of the Torah. How this looked in practice — who participated in the common study of the Torah, in what manner women and children would be taught the commandments that applied to them, or how children would be schooled — is not detailed in the *Rule of the Congregation.* Nor does the voluminous production of manuscript scrolls ultimately necessary for this broad educational work come into view as yet. But the principal purpose of the foundation of the Essene union is clear, as is the fact that it was not only open to all Jews, but was from the outset intended for all of the pious in the whole of Israel.

The individual components of the *Rule of the Congregation* can be quickly listed. First comes the requirement of instructing all young persons in the "Book of Meditation." The formula is from Psalm 1:2: ". . . but delights in the law of the LORD and meditates on his law day and night." What is meant here is nothing other than a penetrating study of the Torah. This is followed by regulations concerning the age at which men are sufficiently mature to take on various duties. For full membership in the Essenes, for example, and for beginning a family, one must be at least twenty years old. To hold offices such as that of a judge or administrator, one must be at least thirty years old, always presupposing the corresponding personal qualities. This is followed by prescriptions for the functions of the Zadokite priests and the Levites, for the three days' sanctification before each meeting of the judiciary councils, as well as before entering military service, for the personal composition of the supreme leadership council, and for meetings and offices of excluded groups of persons.

The conclusion of the *Rule of the Congregation* (1QSa 2:11-22) is a special instruction in the event that the Messiah should come — his appearance on the scene was obviously expected in the near future — and take part in the Essenes' community functions. Despite his unquestionably lofty rank, the Messiah must cede precedence on these occasions to the simplest priest, in every regard. After all, the Messiah is of the lineage of David, and the latter is only of the tribe of Judah, not of the higher-ranking priestly tribe of Levi.

The danger of an absolutely fundamental misunderstanding of the concluding passage in the *Rule of the Congregation* is frequently heightened by the temptation to fill two lacunae in a highly problematic manner so that an additional figure, a "messianic High Priest," is introduced into the text. Daring interpolations of this sort are contradicted, however, by the last sentence in the document. There, directly appended to the portrayal of the course of a meal, we read: "and in accordance with this statute (the fundamental preeminence of the priest over the Messiah) they shall act at each me[al when] at least ten m[en are gat]hered." It is not a unique "messianic banquet" that is portrayed, then; rather, the cultic rank of the Messiah is being established in general, even for a gathering in the smallest local congregation. The High Priest would still take precedence over the Messiah. The problem addressed here could only arise for the many simple priests all over the country. Precisely to them must the Messiah be expressly subordinated, in order that the preeminence of all that is priestly — and this as a matter of principle — might remain intact in the future as well.

The Rule of Blessings *(1QSb)*

In time of origin as in area of interests, the *Rule of Blessings* (1QSb) is a twin of the early-Essene *Rule of the Congregation* (1QSa) and is directly intended to complement the latter for the liturgical configuration of prayer services. It once filled columns 14–20 of 1QS, but is only comparatively fragmentarily preserved. Just as in the case of the *Rule of the Congregation,* there is no other copy of the *Rule of Blessings* from the Qumran finds.

The *Rule of Blessings* supplies the full wording of four blessing formularies. First we find a blessing of all of the pious of Israel, extending over eighteen lines of text. There follows a blessing of the High Priest as the highest representative of Israel, with fifty-three lines. Then comes a blessing of the Zadokite priests, with fifty lines of text. Finally we have a blessing of the Messiah to come. Of this last formula only the first ten lines of text have been preserved; originally, however, it too may have comprised some fifty lines.

The blessing formulas for the pious, for the high priest, and for the Zadokite priests are broadly developed versions of the Aaronite blessing in Numbers 6:24-26. These blessings also appear — less extensively developed, to be sure — as formulas of blessing and curse in the agenda for the annual festival of the renewal of the covenant at the beginning of the new year (1QS 2:2-9).

Owing to the presence of the blessing of the Messiah here, it is customary in Qumran scholarship to regard the whole *Rule of Blessings* as a fictive, anticipatory sketch for the messianic time of salvation. As with the *Rule of the Congregation,* however, this is to put the cart before the horse. Beyond any doubt, we are dealing with a blessing ordinance actually practiced in the present, which ritually invokes the presence of the Messiah in order to stand in the shadow of his power. He was already present in the prayer service by virtue of the blessing pronounced over him, although his actual coming was still in the future.

Of equal importance is the fact that the *Rule of Blessings* was surely composed during the lifetime of the Teacher of Righteousness. It was precisely he, then, to whom the blessing of the high priest referred. The Teacher may have devoted his utmost attention to the composition of precisely this blessing formula, in its smallest details. Accordingly, this blessing formula reflects not only the more general attributes of the office of high priest, but the Teacher's utterly personal understanding of his office as well.

However one may regard the political and personal backgrounds of the *Rule of Blessings,* at all events it is an especially important document for the early Essene understanding of the offices upon which it bears.

The Damascus Document

The last of all of the rules that the Essenes prescribed for themselves is the *Damascus Document.* Its name is based on the fact that its text repeatedly mentions a "new covenant in the land of Damascus." Widespread opinion holds the organization thus named to be identical with that of the creators of the document. In a passage from this work, however, it is expressly established that during the some forty-year interval between the demise of the Teacher of Righteousness — an event already past — and the "emergence of the Messiah from Aaron and Israel," expected in the future, no members of the "new covenant in the land of Damascus" are to be received into the Essenes (CD 19:33–20:1, in tandem with 20:13-15). All further references to the new covenant in the Qumran texts unambiguously also show that it was not identical with the Essenes.

On the other hand, the work ordinarily referred to as the *Damascus Document* ends with the sentence: "Behold, [this is] the totality of what has been found as the last midrash of the Torah." The "last midrash of the Torah" — in Hebrew, *midraš hat-tôrâ ha-'aḥărôn* — is nothing other than the proper title of this work, which — as in the case of *Jubilees,* so highly valued by the Essenes — is cited once more at its conclusion. *Midrash,* in the Qumran texts, is a technical term for the exposition of the biblical writings. "What has been found" denotes, among other things, the Essene *halakah* — the totality of those norms and rules of behavior that have been formulated in their own legislation as interpretations of their findings in the Torah.

The *Damascus Document* is a very extensive work. The best-preserved manuscript from the Qumran finds (4QD[a]) originally comprised thirty-two columns, each with twenty-five lines of text. In Caves 4, 5, and 6, ten fragmentary copies have been found. At least one other must have reached the Karaites from Cave 3 in the Middle Ages (see above, pp. 69-71). The copies discovered in the Karaite synagogue at Cairo at the end of the last century, which have preserved approximately one-half of the original content of the text, is called the *Cairo Damascus Document.* "CD" is the siglum with which this work is generally cited today.

The *Damascus Document* is so extensive because it includes many earlier congregational and disciplinary rules, especially a number from pre-Essene times, rules that previously had been simply referred to as still in force. As its very title at the end of the work expresses it, the *Damascus Document* is a comprehensive presentation of all of the Essenes' postbiblical legal regulations. At the same time, the author claims that it is the ultimately valid version of all of these materials, after which there can be no more. In order to bolster his claim, the author has introduced and interspersed his work with a number of sapiential warnings and overviews of history.

As we see from the passage on the cessation of admitting members of the new covenant in the land of Damascus, together with the context of that passage, the *Damascus Document* was completed shortly after the death of the Teacher of Righteousness. Other calculations on the part of the Essenes concerning the course of history indicate that the Teacher's demise is to be dated in the time around 110 B.C. Thus the *Damascus Document* may have been produced around 100 B.C. At that time the Essenes expected the end of the world to occur in 70 B.C. When it did not come on time, problems arose, and we shall examine them in our treatment of the *Commentary on Habakkuk* (see below, pp. 128-29, 131). In any case, the Essenes never again composed a congregational rule. Instead, for all future time, they were ruled by the prescriptions of the *Damascus Document.*

All of the extant copies of the *Damascus Document* — the oldest being from the period 75-50 B.C. — are written in large format and with care. Of the older agenda for the celebration at the turn of the year (1QS 1:1–3:12), and of the *Manual of Discipline* with all of its additions (1QS 5:1–11:22), after the great master manuscript composed around 100 B.C. there are only small-format reproductions, mostly of individual parts. The officially recognized work that was generally studied and that served as the foundation of judicial decisions was, for all future time, the *Damascus Document.*

It would take us too far afield to detail the entire content of this extensive work. About one-half of its textual content — including the most important passages — can easily be gleaned from any edition of the Qumran texts, inasmuch as this work has been generally available since the publication of the Cairo fragments in 1910. The most important things the unpublished fragments from Cave 4 have to add to this content are further sapiential admonitions, marriage laws, prescriptions dealing with purity, instructions for handing down a judgment of leprosy, regulations for the administration of land and for tithing, and a revised version of the old *Manual of Discipline* (1QS 6:24–8:4). The details are of the highest concern to professionals, but are otherwise of scant interest. The important thing is that, in its fundamental concept as in so many parts of its content and formal peculiarities, the *Damascus Document* is an early form of the Mishnah, which Rabbinic scholars fashioned three centuries later (ca. A.D. 200). Here we find connections — definitely including historical ones — that have as yet attracted little attention.

Scholarly Treatises on Scripture

As early as the close of the second century B.C., the Essenes began to prepare scholarly scriptural treatises on individual parts of the Bible or on thematic questions. In order to distinguish these from their commentaries, which expound on the individual writings of the biblical prophets in textual order — even, at times, verse by verse — they go by the name "thematic midrashim." Admittedly, until now only three works of this kind have been reconstructed, from fragments still preserved, extensively enough to make it worthwhile to examine such works more closely.

The Melchizedek Midrash

Of the *Melchizedek Midrash* only thirteen rather small fragments have been found, in Cave 11. In combination they yield the remnants of three successive columns of text from the middle part of the original scroll. Only in the second of these columns can twenty-five lines of text be reconstructed extensively enough to be evaluated for content. Because the figure of the high priest Melchizedek plays a special role in it — a figure familiar to Bible readers from Genesis 14 and Psalm 110:4, as well as from the New Testament letter to the Hebrews — the entire work is usually named for him.

This work originally comprised more than ten columns of text. If the text of 4Q180, published in 1968 by John M. Allegro, is a parallel manuscript of the same work, then its proper title reads, "Exposition on the Periods of History that God Has Made." Another manuscript of this work could be 4Q181. The fragments preserved from the latter probably come from the conclusion of a manuscript, and 4Q180 surely from the beginning of another. It remains questionable, however, whether these three different manuscripts are to be regarded as representing the same literary work. At all events, manuscripts 11Q13 and 4Q180 come to us from around the middle of the first century B.C., while manuscript 4Q181 was composed some one-half century later.

The extensively reconstructed column of text from 11Q13 published by Émile Puech in *Revue de Qumran* (1987) deals with the tenth and last epoch of world history. Each of the epochs in question probably comprises ten "jubilees" — 490 years — as in the ten-week doctrine of the Enoch literature (*1 Enoch* 91–93). The reckoning of time surely begins — as it still does in Judaism today — with the creation of the world. According to the presentation in *Jubilees,* which the Essenes especially valued, half of this world history had gone by when Joshua, in the year 2450 after the creation of the world, led the people of Israel through the Jordan into the Promised Land. Perhaps the Essenes calculated otherwise and saw themselves already near the beginning of the tenth epoch when they composed their Melchizedek text. According to the Enoch chronology, by the end of the second century B.C. they were only in the eighth epoch of world history as a whole.

The first week of years of the tenth and last epoch of world history is portrayed by the *Melchizedek Midrash* as a great "Year of Release," in which Melchizedek fulfills the promise of Isaiah 61:1 that "release" will be proclaimed to prisoners. This act is interpreted to be a general amnesty of the pious in Israel for all of their sins thus far committed. The conclusion of the tenth epoch consists in a "Day of Atonement" (Lev. 25:9), on which Melchizedek proclaims the "Year of Favor from the Lord" announced in Isaiah 61:2 and presides over the Last Judgment in the form of a judgment of punishment upon all of the evil in the world. This "day" also comprises a week of years. Finally, the "comfort" of "all . . . who mourn in Zion" (Isa. 61:2-3) consists in the comprehensive enlightenment of the pious concerning all of the past epochs of world history, so that now these faithful ones will finally understand why all of the suffering and wandering from God's ways that have afflicted Israel throughout history could not have been circumvented.

Melchizedek, in this text, is a celestial redeemer with divine traits. As priest he forgives sins; as royal judge he presides at the Last Judgment. The role of the messenger at his side "who brings glad tidings" (Isa. 52:7) remains questionable: for one thing, this messenger is dubbed "Spirit-Anointed," and for another the herald of salvation for the sorrowing. Whether it is a matter of two distinct figures here, or of one only, is rendered by the extensively deteriorated state of the contextual parts of the manuscript as difficult to decide as their relationship with Melchizedek. Perhaps as "Spirit-Anointed" the messenger fulfills these heraldic roles as well, just as he had been the messenger in Isaiah 61:1. In any case, what is presented here occurs only at the conclusion of the tenth epoch of the world — in the remote future, then. Thus, the heraldic figures characterized as messianic in these works certainly have nothing to do with contemporary relations at the time of the composition of the *Melchizedek Midrash.*

The Midrash on the End Time (Florilegium)

Only the last epoch of history is envisaged in this scholarly treatise on scripture, which was probably composed toward the end of the reign of the Jewish Queen Alexandra Salome (76-67 B.C.). The Pharisees are criticized especially harshly and vehemently in this work. But they had first come into political favor under Queen Alexandra and were currently in their heyday, the only such time before that of the Rabbis.

This midrash originally comprised some eighteen columns of text and consisted of two main parts. The first main part is a reproduction, with commentator's annotations, of Moses' blessing upon the twelve tribes of Israel (Deut. 33:6-25). Here the tribe of Joseph is passed over in silence and therefore purposely excluded from Israel, inasmuch as the Essenes — as many of their texts show — identified the part of Joseph's tribe called Ephraim with the Pharisees, and the other part, Manasseh, with the Hasmonean ruling house and the Sadducees. Appended to the first main part is a quotation from 2 Samuel 7:10-11, which is interpreted as referring to the tribe of Judah and to the Essenes: here is the true temple of God on earth, which God shields from all evil. Then follows a quotation from 2 Samuel 7:11-14, which is taken as referring to the Davidic Messiah, of the house of Judah, who was expected to come one day for the redemption of Israel in the company of the high priest of the time of salvation.

The second principal part of this work is an eclectic reproduction of the Davidic Psalter (Psalms 1–41), which introduces further quotations from other biblical books as well. This part serves concretely for the polemic against the Pharisees in particular and the Hasmoneans and Sadducees in passing. Their wicked works are evaluated as a sign that the last epoch of history before the Last Judgment is now nearing its end, which end will bring with it the triumph of the Essenes over all of their opponents.

There are at least three manuscripts of this work, all prepared in the second half of the first century B.C. and published by John Allegro in 1968. Manuscript 4Q174 supplies six beginnings of columns of this fragmentarily preserved work. The fragments of manuscript 4Q177 can be combined with five consecutive and textually almost completely reproducible columns of the original middle part of the entire work. The middle section follows almost immediately, in terms of content, the textual content of 4Q174. The sparse fragments of manuscript 4Q178 come from the last third of the entire work, probably from both concluding columns. This is the finding of Annette Steudel's dissertation, which she completed in 1991 and published in 1994.

The Midrash on Genesis

The *Midrash on Genesis* is a scholarly treatise on the book of Genesis. As far as we can still determine, it dealt exclusively with individual figures of the first book of the Torah. There is only one manuscript of this work, 4Q252. Preserved are the upper parts of four consecutive columns of text, probably from the end of the scroll. Of the first of these columns, we have the last one to three words of lines 1-7; of the fourth column, the first one or two words of lines 1-3. Of the second column, lines 1-5 are intact, while lines 6-7 are fragmentarily preserved; and of the third column lines 1-4 are intact, lines 5-7 fragmentarily preserved.

The text preserved in the second column begins with a quotation from Genesis 36:12, which mentions Esau's grandson Amalek. Then we read: "He it is whom [King] Saul had [only] smitten, [but not destroyed, but who ultimately will be destroyed], in accordance with what [God] had said to Moses: 'At the end of days, I shall [forever] extinguish the male lineage of Amalek under heaven [i.e., on the whole earth]" (cf. Exod. 17:14). Then, introduced with the words, "The blessing of Jacob," begins an enumeration, with commentary, of the twelve sons of Jacob according to Genesis 49:3-27. Here statements are quoted with which Abraham, Isaac, and Jacob have praised or blamed themselves and thereby the twelve tribes of Israel. The promise of the future Messiah from the house of David is linked — in a commentary on Genesis 49:10 — with Judah. This is all that has been preserved.

Scholarly writings refer to this work as *Patriarchal Blessings,* since Allegro had so named it, on grounds of the textual content of the third column alone, in his publication of the work in 1956. The complete text of the work is to be found in *The Dead Sea Scrolls Uncovered,* by Eisenman and Wise, under the heading "A Genesis Florilegium" (pp. 77-89). However, it is questionable whether the material is appropriately reproduced. Only the *ends* of lines 1-7 of their "column 3," and the further text of "columns 4–6," belong to this *Midrash on Genesis*. All that follows could be text from another manuscript. The latter has perhaps been prepared by another scribe, and at all events is completely different from the midrash in content. It does not quote passages in Genesis, but is a free reproduction of the Genesis text, in textual order, with special interest in the calendar dates of what is reported, like *Jubilees* with its insistence on the early-priestly, 364-day solar calendar. Like *Jubilees,* this other work is probably of pre-Essene origin. It probably has nothing whatever to do with the thematically oriented *Midrash on Genesis*.

Commentaries on the Prophets

When the Teacher of Righteousness founded the pan-Israelite union of the Essenes around 150 B.C., he and his followers were firmly convinced that they were living in the last phase of the history of the world, just before the last judgment of God and the dawn of the time of salvation. They regarded salvation as so near that, in their oldest congregational rule (1QSa) and in the liturgical *Rule of Blessing* (1QSb), they implicitly understood the coming appearance of the Messiah from the house of David as almost already realized.

A special insight on the part of the Teacher of Righteousness consisted in the concept that nothing that God had once had the biblical prophets commit to writing had ever referred to situations of those prophets' own time. From the outset, all of it had been God's solemn pronouncements for the last phase of history — precisely that time, then, in which the Teacher of Righteousness was living. Accordingly, in the hymns of the *Hodayot* collection that he himself composed, he applied numerous statements of the prophets to his own destiny and that of his followers. The same concept is already present in his *Directive to Jonathan* (4QpapMMT[e] 2 i 7, 9; 2 ii 6). In reading the biblical books of the prophets, he and his followers found the events of their own time directly reproduced.

This understanding of the Prophets, which the *Commentary on Habakkuk* from the Qumran finds expressly presents as having been conceived by the Teacher of Righteousness (1QpHab 2:7-10; 7:4-5), had enormous consequences. It marked the Essenes throughout their existence. John the Baptist, Jesus, and early Christianity adopted it, of course considering their own time as the phase of history to which the ancient pronouncements of the biblical prophets referred. The writings of the New Testament contain a plethora of examples.

Before the Teacher of Righteousness conceived this view, no one understood the biblical books of the prophets in this current meaning. The prophetic declarations were always referred to the remote future. One awaited conditions that had been expressly announced by the prophets to be only a matter of the future. That one lived in the very time foretold by the prophets was the notion of the Teacher of Righteousness that proved to be of the greatest consequence.

When the Teacher of Righteousness died a natural death from old age around 110 B.C., his expectations of an imminent Last Judgment and time of salvation, like the coming of the Messiah, had not been fulfilled. Among those he left behind, this set in motion thought processes that led to a new orientation. If the biblical prophets had foreseen and described the entire last phase of world history in detail, then data could surely be found in their books from which the actual duration of this phase, and the precise time of the Last Judgment, could be extracted.

The Time of the Last Judgment

The *Damascus Document* (CD 1:5-8), composed around 100 B.C., and other works of the Essenes show the conclusions to which they then came. They interpreted the 390 years of Ezekiel 4:5, during which the house of Israel was to have borne a heavy burden of guilt, as applying to the period from the beginning of the Exile (587/6 B.C.) to the moment of the murder of the high priest Onias III (170 B.C.). The fact that the Essenes' calculation was off by twenty-seven years is irrelevant. They shared this mistake with one of the best Jewish historiographers of the time, Demetrius (end of the third century B.C.), who had likewise calculated the span of time between the beginning of the Exile and his own time as twenty-seven years shorter than we hold to be correct today. In terms of what was known at that time, the date concluding the 390-year period was precisely 170 B.C. Only later historical scholarship has corrected it.

The Essenes now combined the number 390, from Ezekiel 4:5, with the seventy weeks of years — 490 years — from Daniel 9, and determined the moment of the approaching Last Judgment to be the year 70 B.C. Thanks to the prophets, at last they could be sure why God had not begun the Last Judgment before, in 170 B.C., and long since blotted out all evil from the world.

A further result of these calculations on the part of the scripture scholarship of the time was that the thirty-eight years of the people of Israel's further wandering in the desert after the departure from Egypt until the death of all "soldiers," according to Deuteronomy 2:14, was referred to the "some forty years" that must pass between the date of death of the Teacher of Righteousness and the year 70 B.C. (CD 20:13-17; cf. 19:33–20:1). Thereby the entire

future existence of the Essenes until the Last Judgment and the time of
salvation corresponded to Israel's forty years' wandering in the desert from
the departure from Egypt until the entry into the Promised Land. The destiny
of Israel's desert generation of long ago must now be reflected in the Essenes'
own further destinies, until the Last Judgment.

When the Essenes calculated the moment of the coming Last Judgment
in this fashion, the latter was admittedly still three decades away. But this
new knowledge immediately sparked activities of which no one had thought
until then.

For one thing, the Qumran settlement was now planned and built, in
order to intensify the study of the Torah and the Prophets by way of the
production of writing scrolls — quite literally "in the desert." Insofar as
possible, all of the many thousands of Essenes living at that time had to receive
adequate opportunity to acquire exact knowledge of the will of God as revealed
in the Torah and the Prophets and to direct their daily lives accordingly, in
order to be found blameless at the coming Last Judgment. And all Israel had
to receive the opportunity to do as they.

Second, there now arose a new literary genre that had not existed before
and whose basic concept was the application of the declarations of the biblical
prophets to the individual events of the last phase of world history, together
with the extraction, from these holy writings of tradition, of the precise
destinies of everyone involved in this last phase of history, in the Last Judgment, and in the time of salvation.

The writings that appeared in this fashion furnish us with the text of
individual biblical books of the prophets reproduced word for word in individual passages, or verse for verse with interpretations appended. Accordingly, these works are designated "commentaries." The interpretative passages
usually begin with the Hebrew word *pesher,* "interpretation," "exposition."
Hence these works are also called *peshar îm,* "interpretative books," and their
manner of setting forth Scripture the *"pesher* method."

The Essenes composed eight commentaries of this kind on the Prophets.
In some cases we have two or three manuscripts of the same work. But the
scrolls are so thoroughly fragmentary that not even a small piece of text is
preserved twice. The reason for this is usually that — as in the case of the
second *Commentary on Isaiah,* or the *Commentary on the Psalms* — from
three scrolls with the same textual content we shall have, from one, fragments
of the first part, from another, fragments of the middle, and in the third case
only such as come from the conclusion of a scroll.

Granted, the opinion is widespread today in Qumran research that the
sixteen manuscripts of such commentaries from the Qumran finds have come
from sixteen different works. These manuscripts are all taken to be "auto-
graphs" — manuscripts for which the author and the scribe are the same

person. The paleographical dates of these manuscripts would then be the dates of composition of the corresponding works.

However, this opinion is demonstrably erroneous. Many of the manuscripts of the commentaries on the Prophets contain corrective additions, which interpolate things the scribe has originally overlooked, or textual omissions, which have come about from the fact that the copyist has mistakenly jumped from one word in the text to a similar word in the text that follows, omitting to transcribe the intervening material. These are altogether typical mistakes on the part of a copyist, just as they are today with almost anyone transcribing a text. Furthermore, there is manifold evidence of a formal kind — for instance, misunderstood marginal notes in the original — that clearly show that the manuscript that we have today is a copy, and not the original. Finally, peculiarities of content show that the multiple copies that we have of commentaries on a given book of the prophets all come from the same work. There is only one exception: two different commentaries on the book of Isaiah were written.

One of the two manuscripts of the older *Commentary on Isaiah* is from the beginning of the first century B.C. All of the other manuscripts of commentaries on the Prophets were composed between 80 and 30 B.C. It is frivolous, therefore, for authors like Barbara Thiering or Robert Eisenman to misuse these old commentaries as special evidence of events of the time of John the Baptist, Jesus, or early Christianity. All of the contemporary references that these commentaries have to offer are to the century between 170 and 70 B.C. Only the commentaries on the books of the prophets Hosea, Nahum, and Habakkuk include later events, until about 50 B.C.

The First Commentary on Isaiah

The Essenes' oldest commentary on the Prophets deals with the book of Isaiah. It was composed around 100 B.C. The various passages of the commentary also contain numerous quotations from other books of the biblical prophets, identifying them each by name. This shows that the expository method of the pesharim was developed from that of the midrashim, in which we so frequently find the same thing. None of the later commentaries seems to contain this sort of cross-reference to the prophetic writings. The two manuscripts in which this work has been fragmentarily preserved are 4QpIsaiah^c and 4QpIsaiah^e.

This *Commentary on Isaiah* addresses a special problem. The union of the Essenes had been founded around 150 B.C. by the Teacher of Righteousness as the sole legitimate representative of all of Israel. It never surrendered this absolute claim. But after half a century of existence, the Essenes were confronted with the fact that they had been able to induct into their organization only a small portion of the Judaism of the time, and that in the three decades remaining before the Last Judgment things would not be very different. Eighty-five percent of all Jews lived, as before, in Mesopotamia, Syria, Egypt, and other parts of the world. They showed no interest whatever in returning to their homeland and entering the Essenes. Even in the land of Judea, from which so many had emigrated, the Pharisees, the Sadducees, the political potentates, and substantial parts of the rest of the population were just as little prepared to become members of the Essene union.

From a strictly quantitative standpoint, therefore, the Essenes' claim to represent the whole of Israel was seriously in question. But the text of the book of Isaiah testified that this was precisely what God had foreseen for the last phase of world history and that the Essenes were indeed still on the right path.

Passage for passage, this commentary presents substantial parts of the book of Isaiah, in the course of which it demonstrates, in all specificity, that all of the parts of Judaism existing in the world around 100 B.C. are mentioned therein — the Essenes themselves, as still the sole true representatives of Israel, as well as those who opposed God's will: the Pharisees, Sadducees, rulers, and all of the various groups of Judaism abroad. The latter have accommodated their lifestyle to pagan habits and must therefore be condemned in the Last Judgment just as all hardened sinners in the heartland of Judea.

Basically, this *Commentary on Isaiah* is an apologetic work. It uses the most extensive, and at that time the most important, of all of the books of the prophets in order to justify, through findings in its text, the absolute claim of the Essenes to be still the only legitimate representatives of all of Israel, and to defend that claim against all self-doubt springing from the resistance of most Jews of their time. The Essenes were never missionaries. But they had expected God to lead to them at least the greater part of Israel before the Last Judgment took place. What God had revealed through the prophet Isaiah for the last phase of history now showed that he had had other plans. Not only heathendom, but also the majority of all of Israel, had irrevocably laid itself open to God's angry punishment, namely, annihilation in the coming Last Judgment.

The Second Commentary on Isaiah

Another commentary on Isaiah appeared shortly before the year 70 B.C. It is fragmentarily preserved in manuscripts 4QpIsaiah[a,b,d]. Its interests are completely different from those of the older *Commentary on Isaiah*. The *end* of the last phase of world history was now just approaching. The work addresses, in its series of biblical starting points, those passages of the book of Isaiah that in some special way seemed to explain the immediate situation of the present.

The fragments that have been preserved refer especially to the imminent final struggle with the enemies of Israel, and to the Messiah who would then be victorious. The presentation is closely akin to that of the version of the *War Rule* reworked by the Essenes and invested with messianic import (see above, pp. 103-4). Other passages refer to the coming Last Judgment and to the Pharisees. The latter are twice characterized as being the current leaders in Jerusalem. Historically, the first time this occurred was during the reign of Queen Alexandra Salome (76-67 B.C.), and it was from the very beginning of her reign that they were in favor. This work therefore certainly appeared during the time between 76 and 70 B.C. Finally, some parts of this work praise the Essenes as still the sole true cultic center of the twelve-tribe people of Israel, whose triumphal recognition throughout the world is now imminent.

The Commentaries on Micah and Zephaniah

Of the commentaries on the books of the prophets Micah and Zephaniah, we have two scrolls each, in both cases one exemplar from each of the two Caves 1 and 4. But the remnants of all four scrolls are extremely small. Still, they make it evident that in these two commentaries on the Prophets the biblical text was not cited and commented on verse by verse, but in larger blocks of text, which otherwise occurs only in the two commentaries on Isaiah that appeared before the year 70 B.C. Just as in the latter works, the passages of commentary are usually relatively short here.

In terms of content, we can still conclude from the scanty fragments at hand that the *Commentary on Micah* has applied the predictions of this prophet partly to the Teacher of Righteousness and his personal opponents in the past, and partly to the Essenes and the imminent Last Judgment. The *Commentary on Zephaniah* seems to have concerned itself especially with God's punitive judgment upon those inhabitants of Judea who kept aloof from the Essenes.

The Commentary on the Psalms

Neither commentary on Isaiah has quoted and commented upon the entire text of that extensive biblical book, but rather, taking the text in its canonical order, has selected those passages whose presentation would serve its particular interests. The rest was passed over.

The author of the *Commentary on the Psalms* proceeded in like fashion. We have three copies of this work: 1QpPsalms and 4QpPsalms[a,b]. The surviving fragments of this work show that the author has begun with Psalm 37 and then moved on immediately to Psalm 45. Psalms 60, 68, and 129 follow, perhaps with others in between and after. This work, too, surely appeared before the year 70 B.C., probably as early as the reign of King Alexander Jannaeus (103-76 B.C.), who was hostile to the Pharisees.

The interpretations of this *Commentary on the Psalms* move on three temporal planes. The presentations of the Teacher of Righteousness and both of his main opponents, the "Wicked Priest" Jonathan and the "Liar," refer to the past. The portrayals of the Pharisees, the Sadducees, and the political rulers usually have reference to the present. In the future lies the appropriate punishment of all of these miscreants at the Last Judgment. A further principal interest concerns the Essenes themselves. They are described in their present fidelity to God, and their reward for this in the coming time of salvation is — especially in the exposition of Psalm 37, a psalm of salvation — richly portrayed.

Thanks to this work, we know that seven groups belonged to the Essene union around 150 B.C. who had returned from the surrounding pagan world to the Holy Land (4QpPs^a 1–10 iv 23-24). We also learn that the *Directive* once composed by the Teacher of Righteousness was actually addressed to the high priest Jonathan and that it provoked the latter to an attempt on the life of its sender (4QpPs^a 1–10 iv 8-9), of which the more immediate circumstances are later portrayed in the *Commentary on Habakkuk* (1QpHab 11:4-8). The end of the forty-year term between the death of the Teacher of Righteousness and the Last Judgment in the year 70 B.C. stands at some distance, since "all godlessness" — that is, all of the outrages occurring under pagan influences — must yet be effaced from the Holy Land without a trace (4QpPs^a 1–10 ii 6-8). In the coming Last Judgment, far from being called to account, the Essenes would constitute God's jury in judgment over the rest of the world (4QpPs^a 1–10 iv 11-12, in similar fashion to the Apostle Paul's later expectations for the Christians (1 Cor. 6:1-3; cf. below, p. 208).

The Delay of the Last Judgment

The year 70 B.C. went by without the awaited Last Judgment having recognizably begun. Alexandra Salome continued to rule undisturbed, and the Pharisees were doing nicely. The Essenes were somewhat perplexed. Their exposition of the books of the prophets, and their reckoning therefrom of the length of time before the Last Judgment, just had to be correct. Or had they perhaps miscalculated? For that matter, had God changed his plans?

The *Commentary on Habakkuk,* composed about 50 B.C., addresses this obvious but highly irritating fact with the observation that "the last phase of time is extended, and indeed far beyond all that the prophets have communicated" (1QpHab 7:7-8). Two reasons are cited that could be the riddle's solution. For one thing, "the mysteries of God are wondrous" (7:8); so God's ways, which are not accessible to the capacities of human knowledge, have to be considered. For another thing, from Habakkuk 2:4a it could be deduced that God intended to "double" the burden of sin of the wicked, in order to render their sentence irrevocable in the imminent Last Judgment (7:15-16). Obviously this required a suitable additional length of time, so that there might be sufficient space for sin (cf. Rom. 6:1-2). Even though "the extent of the last time draws on beyond due measure" (7:7, 12; cf. Matt. 24:45-51; Luke 12:42-46), nevertheless "all determinations of term planned and set by God" must "occur as God in his mysterious wisdom has immutably established them" (7:12-14).

Once the calculated time preceding the Last Judgment had expired, considerations of this kind motivated the Essenes to intensify their investigations into the Prophets, in the hope of learning the grounds for the delay and justifying the accuracy of their interpretative concept. The results of these efforts that have come down to us consist in three further commentaries on the Prophets. They differ from the previous works of this kind in three respects.

First, the prophetic writings in question are now quoted verse by verse and, partly, provided with very detailed interpretations, which until now had been the case only with the *Commentary on the Psalms*.

Second, the prophetic writings are now actually handled in their entirety, rather than by way of a selection of certain passages. Proof that the predictions of a given prophetic book, for the last phase of world history, had now actually been fulfilled verse by verse, was proof at the same time that the Last Judgment and the beginning of the time of salvation could no longer be far off.

Third, these prophetic writings are now examined for the first time with a view to whether they indicate events that have actually occurred only *after* the year 70 B.C. Such occurrences receive the commentary that they have taken place "in very recent times" — meaning that something that had been concretely announced by a particular prophet could simply not have come to fulfillment at an earlier point in time.

The Commentary on Hosea

Even the small fragments that have been preserved of two manuscripts of a commentary on the book of Hosea, 4QpHosea[a,b], show that the content of this work referred to the Sadducees, to the false praxis of worship being conducted at the Jerusalem Temple, and to the Hasmonean rulers who were responsible for that false praxis. Also in view are the Pharisees, who have allowed themselves to be seduced into giving support to such error. But their power in the state, which they had enjoyed during the reign of Queen Alexandra Salome (76-67 B.C.), has now been shattered.

The partial verse Hosea 5:14a — "For I am like a lion to Ephraim" — is extensively interpreted in this commentary, to the effect that the high priest currently in office "has dealt a heavy blow" (4QpHos^b 2:2-4) to the evil Ephraim. "Ephraim" in the Qumran texts is a stereotypical designation for the Pharisees. The high priest here can only be Aristobulus II (67-63 B.C.), who had driven the Pharisees from the Sanhedrin, the central political body of Judea, and thereby deprived them of their political power. Inasmuch as Aristobulus II was deposed by the Romans in 63 B.C. and brought to Rome as a prisoner, while the *Commentary on Hosea* presupposes him to be in office, and since the overthrow of the Pharisees is presented as having occurred "in very recent times," this work certainly appeared during the tenure of the high priest Aristobulus II.

The Commentary on Nahum

From Cave 4 we have barely one-half of a scroll containing a commentary on the book of Nahum. It is the only commentary in whose preserved parts the names of persons occur. Thus, we learn here that, in the time between Seleucid ruler Antiochus IV Epiphanes (175-164 B.C.) and the first occupation of Jerusalem by the Romans (63 B.C.), Judea was spared occupation by hostile powers.

The only danger during that period arose when, around 90 B.C., internal political enemies of the Hasmonean King Alexander Jannaeus (103-76 B.C.) invited the Seleucid King Demetrius III Eucaerus (ca. 95-87 B.C.) into the country with his troops, in order to overthrow the hated Alexander. Alexander was completely crushed. When Demetrius III thereupon sought to use the favorable opportunity to occupy the city of Jerusalem as well, Alexander Jannaeus's internal political enemies changed sides, and the Jews of Palestine joined forces to drive the Seleucid king out of the country. But revenge for the abortive plan to overthrow the ruler did not long delay. At the victory celebration in rescued Jerusalem, Alexander Jannaeus had 800 of his internal political enemies arrested and crucified alive.

All of this is reported in detail by Josephus (*Jewish War* 1.88-98; *Antiquities* 13.372-83). Through the *Commentary on Nahum* we learn for the first time that Alexander Jannaeus's internal political enemies — as well as those crucified — were primarily Pharisees (4QpNah 3–4 i 2-8). The Pharisee Josephus had been too ashamed to confide this to his readers.

Apart from the above, the *Commentary on Nahum* primarily offers criticism of the political authorities of Judaism, as well as of the Sadducees and Pharisees. Their fall from power under Aristobulus II likewise recurs (4QpNah 3–4 iii 6-8). What is new is that the enemies of Israel, known as Kittim, are no longer the Seleucids and the Ptolemies, as they have been in all earlier Essene works through the second *Commentary on Isaiah,* but instead, for the first time, the Romans.

In the *Commentary on Nahum,* as an event "of very recent times," the fact is emphasized that the *kingdom* of Israel that had endured until now has been done away with (4QpNah 3–4 iv 3). The reference is unmistakably to the arrest and deportation of Aristobulus II (63 B.C.), who had united the offices of high priest and king in his person. His successor as high priest was Hyrcanus II (63-30 B.C.). But there was no longer a king of the Jews. Thus, the *Commentary on Nahum* was written very soon after the year 63 B.C.

The Commentary on Habakkuk

Last of all of their commentaries on the Prophets, the Essenes composed the one on the book of Habakkuk. Here the unexpectedly long span of time between the term calculated for the Last Judgment (70 B.C.) and the time at which the author was writing is expressly noted and reflected on (1QpHab 6:12–7:17). It also appears, however, that the complete fulfillment of all of God's predictions through the prophet Habakkuk had required more waiting. Part of Habakkuk 2:8a — "Because you despoiled many peoples all the rest of the nations shall despoil you" — is taken as referring to the plundering of the Jerusalem Temple by the Romans "in very recent times" (54 B.C.; 1QpHab 9:2-7; cf. Josephus, *Jewish War* 1.179; *Antiquities* 14.105-9). The *Copper Scroll* from 124 years later enables us to estimate the wealth that the Jerusalem Temple usually held (cf. above, pp. 72-74).

The *Commentary on Habakkuk* was composed very soon after this occurrence of the year 54 B.C. The only scroll still preserved with the text of this work — but preserved practically in its entirety — 1QpHab, is at least a third-hand copy and comes itself from the time around 50 B.C. The Romans had been in the country almost a decade by the time this work was written. They are presented here very knowledgeably and in great detail — much more precisely than in the previous *Commentary on Nahum.* They are considered God's instrument for the punishment of the wicked in Israel. The *Commentary on Habakkuk* regards them not with hostility, but pays their might the tribute of unconcealed admiration. In no way whatever did the Essenes of that time regard the Romans as *enemies* to be fought.

Now as before, the *Commentary on Habakkuk,* already published in its entirety in 1950, is one of our main sources of information on the Teacher of

Righteousness and the closer circumstances of his founding of the Essene union about 150 B.C. But there are also references to the author's own time, in addition to his presentation of the Romans.

The most interesting finding of this kind is the fact that, listed here as the main groups of Palestinian Judaism along with the Essenes — as "apostates" from the Essenes — are the Pharisees, the New Covenant, and the Sadducees (1QpHab 1:16–2:10). The order in which these groups are listed may correspond to the respective number of members of these competing groups at the moment of composition of the *Commentary on Habakkuk*. At all events, last named are the Sadducees, who were politically influential but notoriously few in number. One of the principal reproaches against them in the *Commentary on Habakkuk* is that they recognize only the Torah as the authority of divine revelation (cf. Josephus, *Antiquities* 18.16), and not the Prophets, although "God has set forth therein [in advance] what is coming upon his people Is[rael in the last phase of history]" (1QpHab 2:9-10). This is what the Teacher of Righteousness, under the influence of divine inspiration, had determined at one point (2:6-9), and his special authority was precisely that of the biblical prophets, and then the basis of all Essene commentaries on the prophetic books through the *Commentary on Habakkuk*.

The Romans

The commentaries on the Prophets composed after the year 70 B.C. make it clear why the Essenes wrote no more works of this kind after the *Commentary on Habakkuk*. The basis was a second rethinking with respect to the term of the Last Judgment, such as had been undertaken earlier, after the death of the Teacher of Righteousness about 110 B.C., with its consequent modification of the imminent expectation, maintained until then, of the Last Judgment (cf. above, pp. 123-24).

The *Commentary on Hosea,* which appeared between 67 and 63 B.C., had been content to present events occurring only after the year 70 B.C. as indispensable for the complete fulfillment of the predictions of a particular prophet. The same thing was done by the authors of the commentaries on Nahum and Habakkuk. To these authors, their most important finding here was that the Romans, who had come into the country only in 63 B.C., through certain of their actions — such as the deposition of King Aristobulus II, or the plundering of the Jerusalem Temple — had been necessary for the complete fulfillment of the predictions of these prophets. At the same time, it was clear to these authors, more or less incidentally, that the prophets Hosea, Nahum, and Habakkuk had patently proclaimed the Romans generally as God's last instrument of punishment for Israel before the Last Judgment.

Until then, the Essenes had always relied on their old view of the book of Daniel, which appeared in 164 B.C., according to which view the fourth and last foreign rule before the Last Judgment and the dawn of the time of salvation was the rule of the Seleucids in Mesopotamia and Syria, as well as that of the Ptolemies in Egypt. Now it turned out that the old interpretation of Daniel used until now must have been mistaken. The authors of the commentaries on Nahum and Habakkuk had not felt another foreign supremacy over Israel, after the Seleucid and Ptolemaic rules, to be a basic problem. Rather, they regarded the coming of the Romans more pragmatically, instead of as occurring for the complete fulfillment of the announcements of these two prophets. But now it became clear that Roman rule over Palestine was not to be a short-term episode of a few years, but, obviously, one of longer duration.

And so the Essenes arrived at a new understanding of the book of Daniel. Now they interpreted the fourth and last empire as the *Imperium Romanum*, whose further duration was perhaps at first open-ended. But the preparation of new manuscripts of Daniel in Qumran around the middle of the first century A.D. is a clear indication that the Essenes, by then at the latest, were interested in a general, broadened exegesis of Daniel that would specify the date of the end of the *Imperium Romanum* — and therewith the term for the Last Judgment and the dawn of the time of Israel's salvation — to be A.D. 70. But no other Qumran text has been preserved that might show how the Essenes' new orientation, after the composition of the *Commentary on Habakkuk*, concretely materialized. We can only observe, negatively, that the Essenes never again composed a commentary on the Prophets that is available to us. It is likewise striking that all of the manuscripts from the Qumran finds of commentaries on the Prophets date from no later than 30 B.C. Further interest in these works therefore seems to have been relatively low.

A Congratulation to King Alexander Jannaeus (4Q448)

We have a genuine autograph from the Qumran finds in the form of a small, square sheet of leather with a side measuring some 18 centimeters. Only the right half, containing the first part of the text, has been preserved. This manuscript, 4Q448, was published in the spring of 1992 by Esther and Hanan Eshel with Ada Yardeni, and partially appears also in *The Dead Sea Scrolls Uncovered*, by Eisenman and Wise (text 50, pp. 273-81, and plate 25). On the upper portion of this sheet of leather, someone wrote in about 90 B.C. a short psalm of praise that comes from pre-Essene times. By another hand from the same time, on the lower portion of this sheet of leather, a text has been added that, in the style of the commentaries on the Prophets, applies the declarations of this psalm to King

Alexander Jannaeus (Jonathan or Yannai) and heartily congratulates him on his victory over Seleucid King Demetrius III.

We are dealing with the same historical occurrence that is later mentioned in the *Commentary on Nahum* as well (see above, p. 130). An Essene living in Qumran obviously wished to give expression, by dedicating the psalm in this way, to his joy that King Alexander Jannaeus had preserved the city of Jerusalem, and the Temple, from the assault of the pagans. The interior political collapse of the hated Pharisees may also have been a happy event for the author of this congratulatory text.

The Essenes' criticism of the Hasmonean rulers had always been restricted, as the Teacher of Righteousness' *Directive to Jonathan* (4QMMT) has already shown, to the complaint that these rulers held the office of high priest at the same time. As political potentates they were criticized only if they also transgressed the Torah in the exercise of their political office. A glorious triumph over Israel's enemies, however, unreservedly overjoyed even the Essenes.

Even the material preparation of this congratulatory text makes it clear that it was prepared for sending, with a fastening for the strings with which the little leather scroll was to be secured. But obviously an individual Essene could not directly apply to the King in this way. For this he needed the approval of the local council and senior officials.

In the Qumran council, however, other advice evidently prevailed. Presumably there were a number of reservations, since, at his victory celebration, Alexander Jannaeus had had persons crucified alive. But the Torah knows crucifixion only as a shameful additional punishment for transgressors who have already been executed (Deut. 21:22-23). True, in cases of national betrayal, as was the case here, death by crucifixion might be permissible by way of exception (11QT 64:6-9). But it may be that opinions of the Essenes in Qumran at that time were divided, whether the conception represented in the *Temple Scroll* was acceptable, or whether all 800 persons crucified alive were to be considered as national traitors in the strict sense. At any rate, this congratulatory document did not even reach the pan-Essene leadership body, but was brought as an original document to join the records of the Qumran archive, which found its way to Cave 4 in A.D. 68.

A Calendar with Days of Commemoration

Most calendrical works from the Qumran finds come from pre-Essene times and were only further developed by the Essenes. Until now there has been only one clear exception to this general finding: a text of which we have fragments of two manuscripts, 4Q323 and 4Q324. Eisenman and Wise have made them partially available in their *Dead Sea Scrolls Uncovered* (text 24, pp. 119-27, with plate 8 showing certain fragments).

This text lists, in customary fashion, the weekly dates of the entry into service of the twenty-four priestly families. At the same time, as usual, those traditional festivals are also named that occur during the individual service weeks. But there is a new element here: a series of additional days of commemoration, whose precise occasion, however, is only sporadically ascertainable owing to the extremely fragmentary context of the references as a whole.

Today's Jewish calendar also contains such additional days of commemoration, which have been celebrated since the second century B.C., for example, the festival of Purim, or Hanukkah. But these festivals, introduced by the Hasmoneans, were rejected by the Essenes, as is shown by their absence in the Essene calendars and the absence of the book of Esther, the basis of the Feast of Purim, from the holdings of the Qumran library.

The new Essene days of commemoration relate, as far as the fragments we have offer any clear information, to events connected with the reign of Queen Alexandra Salome (76-67 B.C.), with the high priest Hyrcanus II (76-67, 63-30 B.C.), and with the first Roman governor for Syria and Palestine, Aemilius Scaurus (63-62 B.C.). Their names appear in the text without negative suggestions. But it is no longer recognizable whether the two massacres that took place during Aemilius Scaurus' tenure (cf. Josephus, *Antiquities* 14.54-79), or the "arrival" of Queen Alexandra at a locale no longer identifiable, gave the Essenes occasion for lasting joy or enduring sorrow. Either is possible.

The only thing certain is that this calendar presupposes at least the tenure of the governor Aemilius Scaurus, and therefore must have been written only after 62 B.C. The older of the two copies we have, on the other hand, dates from as early as the time between 50 and 30 B.C., when Hyrcanus II was in office. This calendar therefore has nothing to do with the time of Jesus.

A List of Official Reprimands

The fragments — unfortunately very meager — of manuscript 4Q477 were first published by Eisenman and Wise in *The Dead Sea Scrolls Uncovered* (text 49, pp. 269-73, and plate 24). This manuscript is from the last third of the first century B.C. It is a list of Essenes, by name, who have been reprimanded for various kinds of misconduct (see above, p. 32).

The type of misbehavior is recorded case by case. But there are no data on any sanctions, such as short-term or lengthy exclusion. Therefore it is certainly not a protocol of judicial sentences. And terminologically, there is no reference to "punishment"; rather, throughout, the reference is to "reprimands" by the competent Essene authorities. It concerns the same sort of "fraternal correction" that we find later in Christian communities as well (Matt. 18:15-18). The first transgressions, which did not as yet call for a sanction, were officially recorded, in order for it to be legitimate to punish the one named upon evidence of another case of the same kind. It may be that this is a list of Qumran Essenes in particular.

Conclusions

Our survey of the original Qumran library holdings that have been preserved for us and whose content is accessible yields a clear picture. The great majority of the manuscripts offer the text of biblical writings or other works of the pre-Essene tradition. Only relatively little writing is clearly of Essene origin.

This picture resembles the one in early Christianity. In extent, the Christian Bible consists overwhelmingly of writings of the Old Testament, which the early Christians themselves eagerly copied and to which they constantly referred. Even if we add to the writings of the New Testament all of the extracanonical material that appeared during the first hundred years of Christianity — until around A.D. 130, then — this new Christian corpus is still considerably smaller in number and extent of works than all that the early Christians adopted and still held in high regard, together with certain further Jewish traditional writings — for example, the Enoch literature — as their Old Testament.

This finding is all the more remarkable in view of the fact that the Christians spread fairly rapidly throughout the ancient world and thereby developed very heterogeneous interests, as is documented by, for instance, the fourfold form of the Gospel tradition in the New Testament. Despite basic homogeneous interests, regional differences arose that occasioned different works of the same kind, increasing the total number of new writings. By contrast, the Essenes remained restricted to Judea, were substantially more homogeneous than the Christians, and had nothing of their missionary impulse, which had an influence on the number of the Pauline letters. The Essenes were primarily interested in the Torah and the Prophets. Regarded from this perspective, it is rather amazing how many different works the Essenes composed in the first hundred years of their existence in addition to all that had been handed on to them.

The proportion of specifically Essene writing in the totality of the Qumran finds surely appears small only to those who have grown accustomed to the notion that everything new for us today from the finds comes from the Essenes, probably even from the inhabitants of Qumran alone. This opinion has been widespread from the beginnings of Qumran research; in fact, up to the present it is the dominant one.

The proponents of this view hold only the writings of the Bible, along with the Old Testament Apocrypha and Pseudepigrapha that were already known to us before the Qumran finds, as pre-Essene. All other works from the Qumran finds are regarded by them to have appeared only from the middle of the second century before Christ onward. Only in those few cases in which the age of one of the manuscripts that have been preserved, or — as in the case of certain proto-Daniel works — when literary criticism forces them to go back to pre-Essene times, do they hesitantly submit to the inevitable.

If we turn the question the other way around and ask which of the writings that are new to us today from the Qumran finds can actually be proved to have been composed by the Essenes themselves, we get a completely different picture. Then only those relatively few works are left whose greater number has been presented in this book as unambiguously of Essene authorship.

Whichever basic view one embraces, it is still surprising that, among all the rich Qumran finds, there seems to be not a single Essene work that we can prove to have been composed only after the middle of the first century B.C.

In the case of each of the last-cited findings — the calendar with its additional holidays and the list of reprimands of individual persons — a composition only after this date, if only relatively soon thereafter, can admittedly not be excluded. The still unpublished archive materials from the Qumran library — contracts, business accounts, and lists of persons — surely come in part only from the first century A.D. Nor is it to be excluded that some of the still unexplored fragments from the Qumran finds come from works that were composed only after the middle of the first century before Christ. But there is no likelihood whatever that there will be many.

As far as can be established until now, the *Commentary on Habakkuk,* composed shortly after the sacking of the Temple in the year 54 B.C., is the last literary work that the Essenes ever produced. From that time forward, they concentrated essentially, perhaps even entirely, on the biblical writings, on other works of pre-Essene tradition, and on writings of their own that they had already produced, studying and copying these again and again, but neither revising their contents nor expanding or abridging them.

The number of copies of these works from the Qumran finds that were prepared only in the Herodian period, and even later, is surely an indication of which works the Essenes especially busied themselves with in the years that followed. But even this finding permits conclusions concerning only the special interests of the few inhabitants of Qumran. By the very nature of things, it remains unknown which works were at the same time copied for the great mass of Essenes throughout the country, and how many copies were made. The Essenes living outside Qumran may to some extent have had entirely different areas of interest from those of the inhabitants of Qumran.

Finally, one further consideration is especially important for an overall evaluation of the manuscript materials from the Qumran finds. That consideration emerges from the insight that Qumran was by no means the "headquarters" of the Essenes. Qumran was simply the principal place of their manuscript production beginning around 100 B.C.

Apart from manuscripts for particular study interests of individual inhabitants of Qumran, it goes without saying that only such literary works and other texts reached Qumran that were to be reproduced in a number of copies for the general use of the Essenes in the cities and villages of Judea. Necessarily missing here, therefore, are any other writings that the Essenes may have produced.

Examples of the latter might be petitions on the part of a local Essene congregation to their central administration — probably in Jerusalem — the responses that these might have received, records of local courts as well as of the highest court of the Essene union, the annual new catalogue of members indicating the current ranks of all individuals, the property register of the Essene land office, accounts of income and expenditures on the part of the numerous budgetary offices — in a word, everything that a well-ordered administration customarily produces. Surely not all such things were ever sent to Qumran for multiple copying. Accordingly, they are missing from the Qumran finds, as were literary productions of individual Essenes whose more general propagation was not considered necessary.

Rich as are the Qumran finds, the proportion of writings — especially literary writings — to which we can have any access at all in this connection is limited. The other side of the coin, of course, is that the absence of writings of this kind constitutes a massive, and ultimately absolutely irrefutable, indication that Qumran was never the "headquarters" of the Essenes.

CHAPTER SEVEN

The Essenes

Ancient Reports concerning the Essenes

According to the presentation of the Jewish historian Flavius Josephus, there were four significant groupings in the Judaism of Palestine around the middle of the first century B.C. The Essenes had a good 4,000 members, the Pharisees a good 6,000. The Sadducees and the Zealots — the latter being a group that had broken away from the Pharisees at the beginning of the first century B.C. — numbered only a few hundred members each. The Essenes and the Sadducees were mainly concentrated in Jerusalem and surrounding Judea, while half of the Pharisees, and most of the Zealots, inhabited Galilee.

These groups of Palestinian Judaism were not, as one often reads, mere "movements" or "currents." They were close-knit organizations, with carefully regulated procedures for the admittance of new members. Today we would call them religious parties. There were at that time no secular parties as we have them today.

According to the calculations of Israeli economist Arye Ben-David, in his *Talmüdische Ökonomie (Talmud Economics)* (Hildesheim and New York, 1974, pp. 41-48), there were at that time some 6.5 to 7 million Jews worldwide. Some 1 to 1.25 million of these lived in Palestine. The at most 12,000 total members of the four significant religious parties would therefore have made up only about one percent of the Palestinian population at that time. Of course, 12,000 would have been the number of adult men only, so that we should have to add in, statistically, a wife and three to five children for each man.

But even a proportion of these groups, in the overall population of around six percent, looks at first to be a relatively insignificant number. We imagine the proportions in the Palestinian Judaism of that time as being like ours in

139

today's Germany, where the majority of all the inhabitants belong to one or other Christian church. But one is Jewish simply on grounds of having been born of a Jewish mother, not by having been admitted to a particular religious organization.

The religious organizations of Palestinian Judaism at that time — unlike Christian churches today — were elite groups. Similarly, our political elite are organized into parties. Total membership in all parties of the Federal Republic of Germany is about 2.4 million. That is only three percent of eighty million inhabitants, and this despite the fact that women are also members of our parties. Thus, comparatively speaking, the membership of only one percent of the overall Jewish population of Palestine in the four religious parties — counting men only — is by no means small.

The various sympathies on the part of the general population for the different parties in our country are revealed primarily at election time. There was no corresponding sympathy-barometer in ancient Judaism. The varying degrees of respect for the four religious parties among the general population — later called 'am ha-'areṣ, "people of the land," or "simple folk" — is shown especially by the entry of new members, as well as by the kind of reports we have of these elite groups.

Most informative, in this regard, is Josephus' report on the three most important groupings in the second book of *The Jewish War*. First, the extensive paragraphs 119-61 portray only the Essenes and praise them as the most exemplary of all Jews. Only the concise paragraphs 162-66 are thereupon devoted to the Pharisees and Sadducees, with the latter being rather belittled and criticized. When we stop to consider that Josephus himself was a Pharisee, the way he presents the Sadducees is understandable. But then his preference for the Essenes is doubly striking. Just so, of course, the Jewish philosopher of religion Philo of Alexandria, a contemporary of Jesus, repeatedly presents in his works the "more than four thousand" Essenes as the best of all Jews, and recommends them to his readers as an example of true piety. Finally, the fact that the Jewish population of Palestine designated this group as "Essenes," in the sense of "the truly pious," shows what great respect they enjoyed at that time.

Evaluations of the Essenes Today

The Essenes' particularly high esteem as the most praiseworthy representatives of Jewish piety on the part of their Jewish contemporaries is diametrically opposed to the picture that Christians today have of them. The principal cause of this is the simple fact that Pharisees and Sadducees are repeatedly mentioned in the New Testament, and even one of Jesus' disciples is identified as a former Zealot (Luke 6:15; Acts 1:13), while the Essenes are never mentioned. Christians therefore think of the Essenes as a very nebulous entity that in Jesus' time must have been rather insignificant and probably led only a marginal existence.

Far from altering this picture until now, the Qumran finds have reinforced it. True, there have always been researchers who have ascribed the scrolls from the caves to the Essenes. But at the same time, they have assumed that Qumran was the historical place of origin, and ever the center, of pan-Essene life. Pliny's report in particular, which relegates the "Essenes" to the Dead Sea (see above, p. 58), has had a permanent effect: it has given rise to the supposition that Qumran was the Essenes' main center. But even the most generous interpretation of the archaeological finds will not yield a number of persons living there and in the near vicinity greater than 150-200. It was therefore assumed that this was the size of the original kernel of the Essenes. Only later, we hear, were there a few Essenes in the cities and villages of Judea as well. The total number of well over 4,000 Essenes, as given by Philo and Josephus, was held to be wildly exaggerated. To our very day, many scholars regard the archaeological discovery of Qumran as the sole realistic standard for the actual number of Essenes in the time of Jesus.

And so the Qumran finds have had the strange effect — in scholarship as among the public in general — of shrinking the great religious party of the Essenes down to a tiny cluster of religious eccentrics and of banishing them to the remote desert on the Dead Sea. This approach is said to render the silence of the New Testament plausible with respect to such a tiny marginal group in Judaism at that time. But it completely fails to do justice to the reports of Philo and Josephus about the Essenes: the Essenes' remote Qumran settlement was regarded by neither author as worthy of any mention at all.

Some scholars have therefore been consistent enough to go one step further and deny any connection of the Qumran finds with the Essenes at all. At Qumran, they tell us, a small, otherwise completely unknown Jewish sect existed and left the scrolls that have been found there. As for the Essenes themselves, there has never been anything but the completely exaggerated reports of ancient authors like Philo and Josephus. Other than that, the Essenes have left no trace of their one-time existence.

The approaches that we have just presented are unfortunately the dominant ones until today. Even recognition of the fact that the Qumran settlement was erected only around 100 B.C., instead of a half-century earlier, with the founding of the Essenes, is only slowly making its way among the scholars of our day. At the same time, the opinion is once more gaining ground that, therefore, the Teacher of Righteousness founded the Essenes only around 100 B.C. The fact that the manuscripts of specifically Essene works, such as the

Rule of the Community (4QS^e), are older than this date, and that many internal indications in the Qumran texts require a substantially earlier date for the founding of the Essenes, is simply ignored or arbitrarily distorted. In particular, the declarations of the pesharim concerning the "Wicked Priest" as a personal adversary of the Teacher of Righteousness, far from being applicable to the Hasmonean king Alexander Jannaeus, who reigned around 100 B.C., can only refer to the Maccabean ruler Jonathan (152-143 B.C.).

The idea that the Qumran settlement came into being only after the death of the Teacher of Righteousness, so that he never lived there himself, is still rather foreign to the great majority of scholars. The far-reaching consequence that the early Essene works — especially all of the community rules — were therefore composed not for the Qumran settlers especially but for *all of the Essenes* everywhere in the country has until now been drawn by only very few scholars.

These indications of discrepancies — especially between the reports of Philo and Josephus regarding the Essenes and the view of the Qumran finds still so widespread in scholarship today — serve here only to explain the multiplicity of current approaches to evaluating the Scrolls and the original significance of the Essenes. Even among Qumran scholars, there is far from any generally accepted conceptual model, not even with those who regard Qumran as an Essene settlement. This state of affairs explains to a very large extent the widespread perplexity surrounding the Qumran finds and their significance for an understanding of Jesus and early Christianity.

Notwithstanding the diffuse spectrum of opinion still prevailing in scholarship today, let us here sketch the picture of the Essenes as it presents itself when (a) the Qumran discoveries are regarded as Essene, (b) the reports of Philo and Josephus are evaluated as substantially accurate, and (c) all of this information is inserted into the picture of ancient Judaism that the other sources offer. The panorama of all of this actually leads to a convincing picture of the whole that is intrinsically plausible.

The Rise of the Essenes

Until the beginnings of the second century B.C., the Judaism of Palestine was a very homogeneous entity. In the center was the Temple at Jerusalem. Worship here was ensured by the priests and their assistants, the Levites. At the pinnacle of the whole stood the high priest, who, if at all possible, was to be of the very ancient priestly lineage of Zadok. He was also responsible for the administration of this Jewish mini-state, regardless of what foreign power held political hegemony at the moment. After the Babylonians, these were the

Persians, then the Ptolemies, and finally, from the beginning of the second century B.C., the Seleucids. These all left the Jews the traditional practice of their religious exercises and seldom interfered with the internal affairs of Judea.

We have a clear picture of the Palestinian Judaism of the time in the historical work of the Chronicler, written in the fourth century B.C., in the form of the biblical books of 1 and 2 Chronicles, Ezra, and Nehemiah. The last biblical witness to this era is the sapiential book of Sirach. It culminates in the presentation of the high priest Simon, his wise incumbency, and his exemplary cultic practice (Sirach 50). All of these works show the picture of a hierarchically well-ordered world obliged to the Israelite and Jewish traditions.

The Essenes adopted precisely these traditional presentations of a hierarchically well-ordered Israel in the Holy Land and continued it despite all obstacles. They understood themselves not as innovators, but as guardians of tradition. The only things that had changed around the middle of the second century before Christ were the more general circumstances of the time. The main cause of this was the Hellenization of Palestine.

An early witness to Hellenistic influences on Palestinian Judaism is the sapiential book of Ecclesiastes (Qoheleth), probably composed in the third century B.C. Here conflicts still lie on the lofty plane of philosophical education. Beginning in 175 B.C., however, in dramatic steps, Hellenization led to the worst religious disaster that Palestinian Judaism every experienced between the Exile of the sixth century B.C. and the destruction of the Temple in A.D. 70. It reached its absolute climax in the year 167 B.C.

Here we can only indicate a limited amount of data that clarify events of that time, knowledge of which will facilitate our understanding of the rise of the Essenes. Incidentally, the most lasting impressions of the circumstances of that time are offered by the biblical book of Daniel, composed in 164 B.C. We have a presentation of contemporary events down to the year 160 B.C. in 2 Maccabees and, parallel to this, in 1 Maccabees, which covers the period to the year 134 B.C.

Basic for a historical evaluation of these sources has always been Jewish scholar Elias Bickermann's *The God of the Maccabees.* A comprehensive treatment of the decisive circumstances from the beginning of the Hellenization onward is at hand in *Judaism and Hellenism,* by Martin Hengel. Klaus Bringmann's study, *Hellenistische Reform und Religionsverfolgung in Judäa (Hellenistic Reform and Religious Persecution in Judea)* supplies a more extensive explanation of individual elements of the situation of the time.

The Hellenization that invaded Palestine on the heels of Alexander's campaign of the years 336-323 B.C. was first of all a general cultural influence, comparable in many respects to the massive Americanization of Europe since the end of the Second World War. The Greeks, their philosophical education, their way of rearing children, and their lifestyle were regarded as the exemplary, modern ones, which caused what had until now been customary to be regarded as provincial and outmoded. In particular, the Judaism of the cities, and Jerusalem most of all, inclined more and more toward Hellenism. Core obligations of the religion of the ancestors, such as circumcision, observance of the prescriptions for purity of worship and the dietary taboos, sacrificial offerings, and Sabbath observance, became increasingly regarded as unimportant. Goals such as striving for a philosophical education, for the Greek masculine virtues, or for athletic success in international competitions replaced them. A societal reform that would remove old obstacles and usher in a modern lifestyle became the most urgent goal of the progressive-minded.

The accession to the throne of King Antiochus IV Epiphanes, Seleucid overlord of Judea, in the year 175 B.C., gave the already Hellenized Jews the starting signal. They had been hoping for the young king's support for their own plans for reform. Nor was such support now withheld. The high priest Onias III, an enemy of the reform, was deposed. His brother Jesus — in Greek, Jason — took his place. Out of respect for the new ruler, and as an expression of the new lifestyle, one of the quarters of Jerusalem was renamed Antiochia. One of the first acts of the high priest Jason upon taking office was the erection of a gymnasium in the area just below the Temple. Now there was a sports stadium here, where men and boys competed mostly in the nude. The effect that such events in the Holy City — held often enough on the Sabbath — must have had on those who held traditional attitudes is easy to imagine. But even the priests neglected their worship duties in the Temple in order to be able to participate in or watch the competitions (1 Macc. 1:11-15; 2 Macc. 4:7-17).

Jason, the new high priest, was in any case of Zadokite descent. But in the year 172 B.C. a simple priest of the family of Bilga purchased the office of high priest. His Jewish name is unknown, but in good Greek he was called Menelaus. One of his first acts in office was the murder of Onias III in 170 B.C. in the Syrian asylum-sanctuary at Daphne. After all, in principle it was unheard of that a high priest who had come to his office and dignities legitimately might be deposed. Anyone who became high priest remained in office until the end of his life. That made Onias III Menelaus' permanent competitor, and in the eyes of pious Jews he was still the only legitimate high priest of Israel. His murder solved this problem. The Essenes later made the date of this murder the beginning of the last, hundred-year phase of world history before God's Last Judgment (cf. above, pp. 123-24; cf. also Dan. 9:25-26; 11:22; 2 Macc. 4:30-38).

In the year 169 B.C., Menelaus permitted King Antiochus IV, who was constantly in financial difficulties, to plunder the Jerusalem Temple of absolutely everything of value. Even the gold mountings of the entrance gates were dismantled. By reason of this violent contribution of Menelaus to the king's coffers, the latter became a firm partisan of the former's power (1 Macc. 1:20-28; 2 Macc. 5:11-21). In 168 B.C. Menelaus had religious laws passed to the effect that worship according to the Torah, the circumcision of male infants, and observance of the Sabbath became punishable by death (1 Macc. 1:41-53; cf. 2 Macc. 6:1, 5-6). Let us imagine that, one day, the Pope in Rome were to decree the execution of all Catholics who in the future would assist at Mass, own a Bible, have their children baptized, or refuse to work on Sunday. That would be the end of the Roman Catholic Church. As Jewish high priest, Menelaus decreed and implemented exactly what would correspond to that.

Menelaus' Hellenistic modernization reached its climax in 167 B.C. The worship of the Jewish God that had prevailed until then in the Jerusalem Temple was abolished and replaced by the worship of the Greek god, Zeus Olympius. The priestly 364-day solar calendar was replaced by the pagan 354-day lunar calendar, of Babylonian origin, which Judaism still uses today. Obviously this calendar — implemented as part of high priest Menelaus' reform measures — did not contain a single one of the Jewish festivals prescribed in the Torah. Instead, the supreme feast day in this new calendar was the annual birthday of King Antiochus IV, whose surname, Epiphanes, means "God appearing on earth." In December of 167 B.C., on the birthday of the pagan Epiphanes, the practice of this new order of worship began. Thereupon its recognition was implemented throughout the land. Priestly deputations moved from place to place with portable altars, compelled the Jewish inhabitants to take part in the new worship, and followed up on the observance of the new prescripts at regular intervals (1 Macc. 1:54-64; 2 Macc. 6:2-4, 7-11).

It scarcely comes as any surprise that, faced with such events, the pious among the Jews of Palestine left the country in droves. The last straw was the religious legislation of 168 B.C. that made a lifestyle according to the Torah impossible in this country. The shameful desecration of the Temple through the worship of a pagan god, and the abolition of the Jewish festivals, was catastrophic for any attachment to the holy places. There was no remedy but to flee before the might of Menelaus and his minions, who were effectively supported by the Seleucid forces of occupation.

Many a pious Jew went underground. Many went to the remote mountain areas or the desert of Judea. But tens of thousands moved with their families into bordering countries, settled there, and formed associations for the purpose of ensuring social continuity among the emigrants and facilitating a pious lifestyle.

This was the beginning of the formation of organizational groups in those segments of Judaism that had lived in Palestine until now but had emigrated. Among those who fled to the regions east of the Jordan — to

Gilead, Perea, and Nabataea — the organization having the most members was that of the Hasidim, the "Pious." It can no longer be determined exactly how many new Jewish organizations sprang up at that time in the countries that surrounded Palestine. However, there were at least seven (cf. 4QpPs[a] 1–10 iv 23-24; cf. also 1–10 iii 1-2; CD 4:2-3; 20:22-25).

Further developments are portrayed in 1 and 2 Maccabees. Menelaus' enterprise — to obtain the recognition of the new worship in the country by force — led not only to emigration, but also to resistance at home. In the small locality of Modein, a priest named Mattathias and his sons, henceforward to be known as the Maccabees, refused to offer the pagan sacrifice. With his own hand, Mattathias slew the first inhabitant of the place who showed readiness to do so. Then he fled to the mountains with his sons and there founded an armed resistance group (1 Macc. 2:1-28; cf. 2 Macc. 5:27; 8:1-7).

The Maccabean resistance was joined by hundreds, then thousands, of volunteers. A crucial feature of the attitude of the pious who remained in the country was that they did not fight on the Sabbath. The Seleucid occupation forces soon learned this and, precisely on the day of the Sabbath rest, massacred their defenseless victims without encountering any opposition (1 Macc. 2:29-38). Egypt and Syria employed a similar strategy in recent times when they launched their surprise attack on the State of Israel in October 1973 precisely on Yom Kippur, the highest of Jewish holy days, because they reasoned that they would find the enemy largely defenseless and easily overwhelm them. The pious in the country who had ties with the Maccabees were divided on this question. Some held that, while one might not attack the enemy on the Sabbath, a dogged defense posed no problem. The others, basically, placed the value of piety above the value of their own lives and allowed themselves to be cut down on Sabbath days without offering any resistance.

The Maccabees and their troops fought on the Sabbath. They put the Seleucid occupation forces more and more on the defensive and secured footholds in several places in the country. At the end of 164 B.C. they succeeded in penetrating the city of Jerusalem, putting an end to the worship of Zeus Olympius and restoring the traditional worship of the God of Israel. Otherwise, things remained about the same. Menelaus was still high priest. The Maccabees concentrated on dealing the Seleucid forces of occupation telling blows everywhere in the country. King Antiochus lost his life in Mesopotamia in the course of his attempt to sack a temple there. His son, Antiochus V Eupator (164-162 B.C.), granted the Jews in Palestine freedom of the traditional practice of their religion once more. But the opportunities for this religious practice remained restricted.

In the year 162 B.C., Menelaus died. The Seleucid government installed as his successor a simple priest named Eliakim — in Greek, Alcimus. The Hasidim who had organized east of the Jordan sent a delegation of their representatives to him to negotiate concerning the new order of worship. Alcimus had all of the members of this delegation whom he could lay his hands on, sixty in number, killed (1 Macc. 7:13-18; cf. 2 Maccabees 14), which exacerbated the antipathy prevailing until now between the exile groups and the Temple.

The Tenure of the Teacher of Righteousness as High Priest

In the year 159 B.C., Alcimus died. What happened then to the office of high priest cannot be deduced from contemporary sources. 2 Maccabees ends with the year 160 B.C., just before Alcimus' death. 1 Maccabees, which is favorable to the Hasmoneans, abstains on principle from naming any predecessors to Jonathan the Maccabee, who became high priest in 152 B.C., except Alcimus. Onias III, Jason, and Menelaus go unmentioned. The historian Flavius Josephus had only 1 Maccabees as a source for this time. And so he made a virtue of necessity and stated, in accordance with the state of his sources, that for seven years there had been no high priest in Jerusalem (*Antiquities* 20.237; cf. 13.46).

But in terms of the way things were at that time, this is altogether impossible. In 164 B.C. the Maccabees had reintroduced, along with the traditional worship, the annual observance of the Jewish feasts in the Temple. The highest holy day is Yom Kippur, the Day of Atonement, which simply cannot be observed in conformity with the Torah without a high priest, as long as the Temple exists (Leviticus 16). Furthermore, in 157 B.C. the insurgent Maccabees had concluded a peace with the Seleucids, so that the country was calm now, and there could be no grounds for doing without the annual celebration of the Day of Atonement or the high priest, who was absolutely necessary for that celebration.

Only with the Qumran finds have the informational lacunae in that which history had so far handed down been filled. They show that, before he founded the Essene union, the Teacher of Righteousness must have been high priest at the Jerusalem Temple, and this as the immediate predecessor of Jonathan the Maccabee, who occupied the office of high priest in the year 152 B.C. On the other hand, whether the Teacher of Righteousness was the immediate successor of the high priest Alcimus, who died in 159 B.C., or acceded to his office only at some later point during these seven years, is still unknown.

The most important pieces of evidence for the thesis that the Teacher of Righteousness was a functioning high priest in Jerusalem are his titles. His customary designation as "The Teacher of Righteousness," in Hebrew *môrê haṣ-ṣedeq,* literally means, "The [Only] One Who Teaches Right [according to the Torah]." This is a traditional title of the high priest, which designates him as the highest doctrinal authority in Israel. The same holds for the designation of this figure as *môrēh hay-yaḥîd* ("The Unique Teacher") and *dôreš hat-tôrâ* ("The [Highest-Ranking] Interpreter of the Torah"). Just as the high priest Simon in Sirach (Sir. 50:1), so also does he bear the title *ha-kôhēn* ("The Priest [Par Excellence]"), which places him at the pinnacle of the Temple worship in Jerusalem.

Over and above this, a number of passages in the Qumran texts show that the Teacher of Righteousness did not somehow lay claim to the rank of high priest without ever having been invested with this office, but that he had been the actual holder of the office, before being expelled by Jonathan. Thus his fate was the same as that of Onias III, who was deposed in 175 B.C. and who at that time fled to Syria, or as that of his son Onias IV, who after his father's murder (170 B.C.) briefly exercised the office of high priest in Jerusalem but was expelled by Menelaus. Onias IV fled to Egypt and there erected the Jewish temple at Leontopolis, which the Romans closed in A.D. 73. Without antecedent exercise of the office in Jerusalem, Onias IV could by no means have founded this temple sheerly on the basis of a claim to the succession. To his claim to the succession he coupled his actual past exercise of the high priesthood, in order to lay claim to a continued investiture in that office. The Teacher of Righteousness, however, proceeded otherwise when driven from office. He founded not a temple in safety abroad, but the Essene union.

The Founding of the Essene Union

In the year 157 B.C., a peace was struck between the Seleucids and the leader of the Jewish troops, Jonathan the Maccabee. The latter moved his headquarters to Michmash, twelve kilometers north of Jerusalem. There was nothing for him in Jerusalem; that city still remained under Seleucid control. We might remark that Jonathan owed his decisive victory (157 B.C.) over Seleucid field commander Bacchides in the vicinity of Bethlehem in part to the support of two Bedouin tribes of the Judean desert (1 Macc. 9:66). One of these was that of the *Odomera* — the very Taʿamireh who still live today in their ancient tribal region and who between 1947 and 1959 discovered the most important manuscript caves at Qumran.

The page turned for Jonathan as Alexander Balas made a claim on the throne of the Seleucids and arrived in Acco (Ptolemais) with quite a strong contingent of troops. In his distress, Seleucid King Demetrius I Soter (162-150 B.C.) turned to the Maccabee Jonathan for military support. Jonathan consented and in return received the right henceforward to reside in Jerusalem. As he entered the city, a significant number of the inhabitants fled before this feared potentate.

No sooner had Jonathan brought the city under his power, however, than he changed parties and offered his support to Alexander Balas. His reward consisted in Alexander's naming him to the office of high priest. Now Jonathan the Maccabee had consolidated all power in his own person. As military dictator with powerful troops and as a friend of his patron Alexander (Seleucid king, 150-145 B.C.), who had just been victorious in his struggle for the throne, he was now absolute political ruler in Judea and its neighboring regions. As high priest he was at the same time the highest religious authority of Judaism, at least according to his own claim. But that claim did not remain uncontested.

As Jonathan seized the office of high priest in the autumn of 152 B.C., his ousted predecessor, the Teacher of Righteousness, succeeded in fleeing Jerusalem. He found asylum in Syria, and this with the New Covenant in the Land of Damascus (CD 7:18-20). There he felt safe from Jonathan.

As high priest in Jerusalem, the Teacher of Righteousness had been the supreme representative of the covenant of election that God had once struck with his people on Sinai. In the traditional understanding of his office, he remained this as long as he lived. To his way of thinking, the usurper Jonathan had no right to it whatever. In his own view, God's covenant with Israel had withdrawn from Jerusalem with the Teacher of Righteousness, where both dwelt in exile. Now it embraced only those Jews who had remained faithful to their high priest, now driven from office, or who would turn to him in the future. This appears in all clarity in pronouncements of the Teacher of Righteousness himself (1QH 2:21-22, 28; 4:23-25; 5:8-9, 23; 7:6-10, 18-25).

Decisive for all that was to happen was that the Teacher of Righteousness did not wait to see how things would develop and who would turn to him in the course of time as the ongoing representative of all of Israel. Instead, he seized the initiative shortly after his flight into exile. He made contact with all of the other groups and organizations of Judaism that had formed during the time of persecution in the regions around Palestine. In his mind, God would first have to gather together in the Holy Land the scattered parts of Israel before the Last Judgment expected shortly could take place and the time of salvation begin. The Teacher of Righteousness was firmly convinced that these events would soon make their appearance and that God had chosen him personally, the only legitimate high priest of all Israel, as his instrument of destiny and as the responsible representative of this undertaking. Time was pressing hard, and the tasks to be performed in the few years remaining before the Last Judgment were enormous.

The Qumran texts contain all manner of detailed information concerning much of what occurred at that time, even concerning the persons involved. Numerous priests, among them those who were of the distinguished lineage of Zadok, and ranking functionaries of the Temple administration, who had fled into exile with the Teacher of Righteousness, formed his staff of co-workers. On the other hand, confrontations of manifold varieties arose. A number of the members of the New Covenant declined to return to the Holy Land; in their view, God had definitively abandoned the Temple and the Land to perdition, and the salvation of Israel was henceforward to be awaited in exile among the pagans. A number of the Hasidim who had previously emigrated to the regions east of the Jordan, though some of them had now returned, rejected the claim of the Teacher of Righteousness as lifelong holder of the office of high priest. Their opinion was that the sacrifices required by the Torah in the Jerusalem Temple must be offered even under current conditions without the Teacher of Righteousness necessarily returning to his original office and installing the 364-day solar calendar once more. These were the two most important problems facing the exiled groups of the time.

But the main problem for the Teacher of Righteousness was posed in the Holy Land itself. When he had succeeded in bringing rather large parts of the various exiled groups under his authority and in preparing them for their return to their homeland, he now, as the high priest so many recognized, addressed his authoritative directive to Jonathan, urging the latter for Israel's sake to renounce the office of high priest and confine himself in the future to his political leadership in the country (4QMMT). But Jonathan rejected this admonition and reacted with his abortive attempt to remove his dogged rival by murder (4QpPs^a 1–10 iv 7-9; 1QpHab 11:2-8).

In spite of all such problems and difficulties, the Teacher of Righteousness nevertheless managed at that time to motivate seven of the exiled groups (4QpPs^a 1–10 iv 23-24), wholly or in their majority, to return home to the Holy Land, and he succeeded in uniting them organizationally into a union that claimed to be, de jure, pan-Israelite. Many who had remained in the country also entered it. Thus arose the largest religious organization in the Palestinian Judaism of that time.

Aside from insignificant splinter groups, there now remained only three others, each of them substantially smaller than the Essene union. First, there were members of the New Covenant in Damascus who were unwilling to return. Second, there were those among the Hasidim who were henceforward to be known as "Pharisees" ("Schismatics"). Third were those who remained loyal to Jonathan's priesthood at the Jerusalem Temple. The elite of this last group later joined together into an independent organization and were called "Sadducees," since it was members of the distinguished lineage of Zadok who were the leaders among their ranks as well. As a result of this unification operation by the Teacher of Righteousness, which had succeeded in large measure but not completely, henceforward there were three religious parties in Judea: the Essenes, the Pharisees, and the Sadducees.

A fourth entity in the country were Jonathan's troops, who stood under him as their supreme commander. To be sure, from the standpoint of religious politics they were neutral. But in internal secular politics they were the strong right arm of their ruler, who at the same time was the high priest in Jerusalem recognized by the Seleucid king, and they stood as an insurmountable obstacle to any possible attempt on the part of the Teacher of Righteousness to bring once more under his own authority the worship of the Jerusalem Temple. Thus, the accomplishment of the Teacher of Righteousness' unification operation ultimately was wrecked on the shoals not of internal Jewish divergences in doctrinal positions, but of circumstances of political power, which left no room for change with such scanty political power as accrued to the Teacher.

From the outset, there were never any Essenes outside of Judea. True, the Teacher of Righteousness undertook preparatory initiatives from his place of exile in Syria. There he received delegations from the various exiled groups. From his place of exile he traveled to groups who raised difficulties, for example, to the Hasidim (1QpHab 5:8-12; cf. 2:1-3). He was still abroad at the time of Jonathan's assassination attempt (1QpHab 11:2-8), when the latter had received his warning that he must renounce the office of high priest. But the founding of the Essene union took place not in the region of exile but, altogether intentionally, in the heartland of Judea (cf. 4QpIsa^d 1:1-8). After all, the Teacher's constitutive concept in founding his Essene union was that, under his aegis as high priest, all Israel should be together in the Holy Land, and there and nowhere else should await in unity the coming of the imminent Last Judgment of God upon the world.

So far the Qumran texts have not revealed whether the Teacher of Righteousness, in the course of his preparatory initiatives, also made contact with the Jews in the wider world, especially with those in Mesopotamia and Egypt. Conceptually, in any case, they were included in his overall picture, as is later evident from the first of the two commentaries on Isaiah (see above, pp. 125-27). At all events, for the Teacher of Righteousness it was decisive that ultimately there could only be an Israel within the boundaries of that Land which was God's special possession and into which, after the death of Moses, Joshua had once led the people of Israel.

The founding of the Essene union within Judea by the Teacher of Righteousness took place twenty years after the murder of the high priest Onias III (CD 1:9-11), therefore around 150 B.C. The place at which it occurred is unknown. In no case was it Qumran, since the settlement there sprang up only a half-century later.

More important, and still capable of being precisely established, are the organizational circumstances prevailing on the occasion of the founding of the Essene union. The members of the various exiled groups who returned to the country ordinarily moved back to the places in which they had lived before, where they had land, dwellings, or nonexiled relatives of their extended families. And so, members of different exiled groups were mingled in the several localities in which they now lived once more. Those who had remained at home could also enter the union. The only normative consideration was that, in order to be able to form a local organizational unity, there had to be in each locale at least ten adult men and among them at least one priest.

The overarching principle of organization was, on the one hand, of a formal kind. All of the local groups were regarded as organic parts of the union. They stood directly under the authority of the Teacher of Righteousness and his directive powers alone. A central leadership organ, subordinate to him, in which priests of the lineage of Zadok had the final say, coordinated and administered the larger union. The Essene union taught no special doctrines, although the Teacher of Righteousness applied the declarations of the biblical books of the prophets to his own time and circumstances.

The Essenes' highest authority was the Torah, whose normative interpreter in all questions of doubt was the Teacher of Righteousness alone. The Teacher had also determined that, within the Essene union, the various corpora of laws that had come into being among the exiled groups would remain in force, of course after critical review, revision, and complement in individual cases. For example, the Essenes took over from the New Covenant in the Land of Damascus its laws for property administration and its Sabbath ordinance. Only in the course of time did further, complementary bodies of law arise among the Essenes. The author of the *Damascus Document* finally and definitively put together, around 100 B.C., everything that was to have abiding validity for the Essenes over and above the biblical writings.

On the other hand, the Teacher of Righteousness was not satisfied with a purely formal principle of union of the hitherto scattered parts of Israel under his authority. From the beginning, he demanded that each individual qualify personally, as well, for membership in this pan-Israelite union. Accordingly, the formal act of foundation was immediately followed by a period within which all future full members had to prove themselves to be authentically pious Jews through a study of the Torah and the Prophets, a corresponding lifestyle, and finally, an entrance examination.

Subsequently, out of this special process of qualification of all members there arose the three-years' admittance procedure of the Essenes. At the beginning, these measures had the effect of delaying the materialization of the Essene union for some time after the formal act of foundation. Later, a consequence of the rigid admissions procedure was that the number of the Essenes always remained substantially smaller than would have corresponded to the sympathy for them among the population. But, finally, it was precisely through this demanding entry procedure that the Essenes became a scholarly elite in Judea of a sort that had never before existed on so large a scale (see also below, pp. 266-68).

The Further History of the Essenes

The union of the Essenes was certainly, from its foundation onward, the most numerous religious group in the Judean heartland of Israel. By the grace of the Seleucids, however, the office of high priest remained in the hands of the Maccabean Jonathan, and the Jerusalem Temple was in his power. The Sadducees were integrated into this power structure. The Pharisees had compromised with it. The broad mass of the Jewish population, finally, were glad that the times of religious repression and military confrontation in the country were over. Generally, then, relations were accepted as they happened to be. The Essenes were paid their due respect, but the claim of the Teacher of Righteousness to have the only answers to the needs of all Israel was mostly ignored, and instead the population took part in the government-approved, and to that extent official, Temple worship.

The decisive act for further development occurred in September of the year 140 B.C. Three years earlier, Jonathan had fallen into the hands of the Seleucid commander Trypho, was abducted, and was killed by him. Jonathan's successor was his brother Simon. Simon compelled the last Seleucid bastion of Palestine, a fortress inside Jerusalem, to surrender. By doing this he definitively delivered the country from all foreign rule and attained that for which the people had struggled for so long and for which many of them had sacrificed their lives. Simon made use of this triumph of a quarter-century of Maccabean military action to strike an internal political pact.

Simon had a decree approved by the Temple priesthood, by the official delegates of the people, by the representatives of the distinguished families of the country, the Jewish nobility, and by the representatives of the individual localities, who were called the "Elders." This decree was accepted in a public assembly of the people at Jerusalem and immortalized on bronze tablets in the outer court of the Temple. It specially provided that, by reason of the services rendered to the nation and to religion by the Maccabees, Simon be confirmed in his offices as political leader and high priest "forever" — thus including his successors in his dynasty — "until a trustworthy prophet should arise" (1 Macc. 14:41). Consequently, only an authority such as Moses himself, who could add to the Torah laws of equal validity that might reserve the office of high priest to descendants of Zadok not mentioned in the Torah, could now, according to this edict, make any changes in the Hasmoneans' sphere of power.

The Teacher of Righteousness, whose competence, even in terms of his own claim, was limited to the interpretation of the Torah already at hand, was thereby excluded from the area of internal politics. His influence was now definitively restricted to the Essenes and their narrower circle of sympathizers among the people. From the viewpoint of religious politics, this was the most serious defeat that he had had to accept since his expulsion from his office by Jonathan twelve years before. At the same time, the office of high priest that Jonathan had occupied by force was now so overwhelmingly regarded as belonging to the Maccabees by right that the competing claims of the Teacher of Righteousness, politically speaking, were as good as finished. Obviously neither he himself, nor the Essenes, ever accepted this standpoint. But from Simon's perspective, the danger of competing claims had been adequately conjured away, and his own pretension to lordship sufficiently secured.

How difficult it was at first for Simon to win wide acceptance of his self-decreed claim to the office of high priest on behalf of the Hasmonean rulers is shown by the fact that even his son and successor John Hyrcanus I (134-104 B.C.) was urged by the Pharisees to renounce the office of high priest and content himself with his political hegemony; and only Hyrcanus I managed to be accepted by the Sadducees as a member of their organization of priestly elite (Josephus, *Antiquities* 13.288-96). His father Simon, and the latter's brother Jonathan, both already superiors of the Sadducean priests where service in the Temple was concerned, were always refused this. But the Essenes maintained neutrality with respect to secular politics. Although the Teacher of Righteousness did not die until around 110 B.C., nowhere in the Qumran texts is there to be found a special polemic against Simon or John Hyrcanus I as high priest.

Typical of the relationship of the Essenes with the Hasmonean hegemony, a relationship now distant but relaxed where secular politics was concerned, are the circumstances accompanying the appearance of the first Essene to be cited in general history. His name was Judas, and he held forth in the lecture halls of the Jerusalem Temple daily before a great throng of eager Essene students. One day in the year 103 B.C. he had a piece of bad luck. That morning he had prophesied that, on the same day, Antigonus, a brother of the current high priest and king, Aristobulus I (104-103 B.C.), would be murdered "in Strato's Tower." "Strato's Tower" was the designation used at that time for the distant city of Caesarea on Palestine's Mediterranean coast. Imagine Judas the Essene's consternation, then, as he beheld, after having uttered his prophecy, the said Antigonus striding through the Temple court as alive as he could be. He could scarcely meet death in Caesarea on the same day. But what a relief for this Essene and his pupils when, shortly thereafter, the report sped through Jerusalem that Antigonus had been murdered, and murdered in a dark alley of the city of Jerusalem that was likewise designated "Strato's Tower."

Flavius Josephus reports this event in order to celebrate the Essenes' special gift of prophecy (*Jewish War* 1.78-80). But at the same time his report shows how taken for granted it was, even then, that the Essenes should constitute an accepted presence in religious politics at the very center of Jerusalem. Although it was never sent, the congratulatory letter from an Essene of Qumran addressed to *King* Alexander Jannaeus, after the latter's internal political triumph around 90 B.C., shows the same acceptance of prevailing circumstances (see above, pp. 133-34).

Far more painful for the Essenes than their relationship with the leadership of state was the growth in numbers and increasing influence of the Pharisees in the country. The latter had dismantled the traditional preeminence of the priests within their organization, admitted laity among their Scripture scholars — a heavy assault on the exclusive competence of the priests as jurists — and propagated an exposition of the Torah that was satisfied with a minimalist interpretation of its words. Therefore it could be much more easily accepted by the broad population of Judea than the Essenes' stricter exposition of the Torah. The Essenes reproached the Pharisees for their lightening of the observance of the Torah, calling them *dôršê ḥălāqôt* ("seekers after flattery"), thereby castigating their invitation to an all too lax practice of religion.

An example of what was meant was that the Pharisees — like the Rabbis, later — held that it was lawful for an uncle to marry one of his nieces, since the Torah did not expressly forbid this. The Essenes, on the other hand, pointed out that the Torah forbade an aunt to marry one of her nephews (Lev. 18:13), which, to their way of thinking, must be applied to all structurally analogous family relationships. So they reproached the Pharisees for their "whoredom" and their "shaming of the sanctuary" (CD 5:7-10). We witness a similar polemic ourselves when, for example, persons who support abortion rights are characterized as "murderers" without their ever having actually committed a murder. Only different understandings of law can give rise to such reproaches. The polemical vocabulary comes mostly from the rigorist camp.

Different interpretations of the Torah had already in the beginning led a number of Hasidim to oppose the efforts of the Teacher of Righteousness to establish a pan-Israelite union (1QpHab 5:9-12). This opposition in turn led to their constitution as an independent organization in the form of the "Pharisees." The Qumran texts show that these divergences in terms of law continued to exist and that on individual points they developed further. On the interpretation of the Torah, the legal positions of the Essenes coincided to a very large extent with those of the Sadducees. The gap between the latter two groups prevailed essentially on *political* grounds. The Pharisees, by contrast, gradually developed into *religious* competitors and adversaries of the Essenes in the Judaism of Palestine. The rift between the two groups grew ever deeper. The Pharisees were unconcerned by the competition between the Maccabee Jonathan and the Teacher of Righteousness when it came to their respective claims on the office of high priest, and despite the 354-day lunar calendar established by Jonathan, they took part in the sacrificial worship of the Jerusalem Temple without voicing any criticism. At the same time, they also had better chances of sharing political power and increasing their influence.

The Pharisees seem to have achieved this influence on a large scale only during the beginning of the reign of Alexander Jannaeus (103-76 B.C.). Their attempt to overthrow the latter failed, however, and ended in the crucifixion of many of their representatives. During the reign of Queen Alexandra Salome (76-67 B.C.) the Pharisees were again in favor. In particular, they became a significant presence in the Sanhedrin at that time. But the king and high priest Aristobulus II (67-63 B.C.) once more stripped them of their power. From the standpoint of religious politics, then, the Pharisees no longer played a leading role when the Romans assumed political power in the country in 63 B.C.

It is difficult to ascertain how the Essenes behaved during all of this time. The only major activity of theirs that can be firmly established was of a purely religious kind, and an altogether internal affair: the founding around 100 B.C. of the Qumran settlement for the large-scale production of writing scrolls. The Essenes' own works from this time show them as a unitary, closed organization that stood aloof from the Pharisees and the Sadducees. They continued to regard the Sadducees as an established factor in the interplay of political power.

It is striking that, in contemporary works of the Essenes, the first Hasmonean ruler, Jonathan, is very sharply criticized, but not one of his successors comes under attack. Only four of these later Hasmonean rulers are recognizably mentioned in the Essene writings at all. These are, first, Alexander Jannaeus (103-76 B.C.), whose designation as "Lion of Wrath" pertains only to the political part of his double office, his status as king. Here it is emphasized that he has rescued the country from pagan attack and has crucified those responsible for the uprising — especially Pharisees. Both of these deeds were highly useful from the perspective of the Essenes. The other side of his double office, his high priesthood, comes in for no mention, and therefore for no criticism. Of Queen Alexandra Salome (76-67 B.C.) and her son Hyrcanus II, who was simultaneously invested with the office of high priest, we learn only that certain of her deeds occasioned the insertion of corresponding memorial days in the Essene calendar (4Q323 and 4Q324). Whether these deeds gladdened or saddened the Essenes is no longer recognizable, owing to the loss of manuscript context in these passages. King Aristobulus II (67-63 B.C.) is mentioned as "high priest" (4QpHosea^b 2, 3), because in this capacity he led the Sanhedrin, from which he drove the Pharisees. Only the fact itself — highly advantageous to the Essenes — is noted. Here too any criticism of the person holding the office of high priest is absent.

Even in Jonathan's case, the Essenes' criticism is limited to his occupation of the office of high priest. A hundred years after the events, the *Com-*

mentary on Habakkuk acknowledges that "when he first arose" — that is, as political leader of the Maccabean insurrection from the death of his brother Judas in 160 B.C. to his entry into Jerusalem in 152 B.C. — he "had the best reputation" (1QpHab 8:8-9). The *Directive of the Teacher to Jonathan* (4QMMT) positively confirms him as Israel's leader after the example of such kings as David and Solomon. Jonathan is criticized in the Qumran texts exclusively as the "Wicked Priest" who has arrogated to himself the office of high priest in contravention of law, who despite express instructions not only has not restored it to the Teacher of Righteousness, but has actually attempted to murder him, and who has confiscated for his own use property of the Essenes in the country (4QpPs^a 1–10 iv 7-10; 1QpHab 8:9-13; 9:8-12; 11:16–12:6, 9-10). None of his successors is reproached in any Essene work for anything comparable.

This finding yields two conclusions with particular certainty. On the one hand, the Essenes remained politically unharmed after the death of Jonathan. On the other hand, neither did the Essenes undertake to effect a change in political relations in the country, either by force or by subversion. A kind of truce prevailed. This is true not only for the time after the death of the Teacher of Righteousness around 110 B.C., but already for the three decades immediately preceding, when Simon and John Hyrcanus I were high priests and political rulers in Jerusalem.

The Teacher of Righteousness himself, as far as we can tell, had desisted from his current polemic against the Hasmonean rulers in the course of time and had finally limited himself to the expectation that, at the beginning of the coming time of salvation, God would prepare an end of the Hasmonean rule and instead cause a new ruler to rise up, descended from David, the royal "Messiah of Israel." Like King David, he would naturally have to belong to the tribe of Judah and not — like the Hasmonean rulers, as Aaronite priests — to the tribe of Levi. The independent, superior claim to rule on the part of the priestly tribe of Levi was still personally embodied in the Teacher of Righteousness as high priest. When he died without any legitimate successor in his office, the Essenes began to expect that, at the beginning of the time of salvation, besides the "Messiah of Israel," God would appoint a "Messiah of Aaron" who in their view would again, if possible, be a member of the priestly line of Zadok.

As with all Jews of the time, so also with the Essenes, the father's line was the only standard of descent that determined one's membership in a given tribe of Israel. No one, then, could be a member of both the tribe of Levi and the tribe of Judah. Future high priests, from Levi, and kings, from Judah, would therefore necessarily have to be *two different persons*. But the Hasmonean rulers in no way fulfilled these requirements. They were descendants neither of Zadok nor of David and even went so far as to combine both offices in one person.

But this state of affairs evidently did not lead to any ongoing polemics from the side of the Essenes. The reason was that they kept their gaze focused on the commencement of the approaching time of salvation. Only this could restore a situation in which the identity of the rulers would be in conformity with the will of God. Until then, there could never be any high priest or king in Israel at all — only the Essene union, open to all Jews. Their "government" consisted in authorities of the *past* — namely, the books of the Torah and of the Prophets, including their interpretation once authorized by the Teacher of Righteousness. The priests and overseers who led the union in the *present* administered this legacy and watched over its observance in keeping with tradition, but they had no right to be high priests and kings in Israel or to acknowledge such as legitimate. On the basis of the Essenes' messianic concept, it was necessarily reserved to the *future* that there would be high priests and kings in Israel. And this future could only begin with the coming Last Judgment of God.

The Essenes' messianic expectations are usually considered only from the viewpoint that the Essenes implicitly criticized the status quo and placed their hope in the future, which unfortunately had not yet materialized. But this view ignores the day-to-day political effects of such a concept of the future. These effects emerge from the very notion that only the coming time of salvation could once more bring a legitimate high priest and a ruler of the royal house of David. The effect of this concept of the future was reinforced by the notion that God's Last Judgment was to take place at the beginning of the coming time of salvation. Until then there was no question of the presence of these savior figures. Finally, this concept was fine-honed by the notion that the Last Judgment simply could not occur today or tomorrow, but only at a future term long since determined by God himself.

God had revealed this fixed term through the biblical prophets. The Essenes had at first counted on the year 70 B.C.; then they had recognized their error and, on the basis of a new exegesis of the book of Daniel, had established that the Last Judgment would come only in A.D. 70 (see above, pp. 123-25, 128-29, 132-33).

From this very precise concept of the future it necessarily followed that there could not be another lawful high priest or Jewish king until A.D. 70. The Hasmonean ruler, King Herod, or high priests like Caiaphas — whoever exercised cultic or political authority in Jerusalem — were basically of no importance. The Essenes tolerated all of these ruling figures, like the foreign rule of the Romans, with indifference. If the acts of those in power were to the benefit of national interests, or to the benefit of the Essenes, then that was a happy circumstance, while the opposite was aggrieving. In case of doubt, such personages were to be regarded as instruments of God's punishment for the sinfulness of the people. The qualities that would be normative for Israel's future salvation could not be possessed by any of these figures.

This firm concept of the future must also have had the consequence that the appearance on the scene of John the Baptist and Jesus around A.D. 30 was of no importance to the Essenes. The Baptist's proclamation that the Last Judgment and time of salvation was imminent contradicted the Essenes' date of A.D. 70. Jesus could not possibly be the awaited Messiah; entirely apart from his crucifixion by the Romans, he simply came four decades too soon. The Essenes had better information.

The scrolls from the Qumran library evince a heightened interest on the part of the Essenes in the biblical book of Daniel the nearer the year A.D. 70 approached. This book was the chief foundation of the Essenes' calculations for the term of the Last Judgment and the beginning of the coming time of salvation. Now it was even more eagerly copied and studied than before.

The last Essene of that time whose name we know was called John. In A.D. 66, the revolt of Palestinian Judaism began against Roman rule in the Holy Land. True, that was still four years before the calculated end term. But this close to the expected end of the Roman rule, an active preparation for the imminent turn of events might be useful.

The Essenes were obviously divided over the question of whether to wait patiently for the act of God or participate actively in its preparation. Flavius Josephus reports that, during the insurrection, it was Essenes especially who in admirable fashion typically accepted torture and death at the hands of the Romans without giving up their faith, but also without offering physical resistance (*Jewish War* 2.152-58). This attitude corresponds to that of those devout individuals who preferred to allow themselves to be cut down without resistance rather than to desecrate the Sabbath by self-defense. Other members of that same group had at that time assigned their own lives and the lives of their families a higher value than that of the Sabbath observance, and, when need arose, took up arms even on the Sabbath (see above, pp. 145-46).

Just so, there were now Essenes who actively participated in the uprising against the Romans. Some finally lost their lives at the mountain fortress of Masada as their resistance to the Romans collapsed in A.D. 74. Of the Essene by the name of John, Josephus reports that he had taken over the high command of the insurgents for the toparchy of Thamna, together with the cities of Lod, Joppa, and Emmaus on the coastal plain of Judea. Thus he was, so to speak, one of the colleagues of the Pharisee Josephus, who for his part became supreme commander of the insurgents in Galilee (*Jewish War* 2.562-68). The Essene John fell that same year, A.D. 66, during an attack on the city of Ascalon (*Jewish War* 3.9-21).

There is no evidence for the favorite assumption that, as one of the high commanders of the insurgents, this John no longer belonged to the Essenes. His very designation as "the Essene" belies such an assumption. The congratulatory letter addressed to King Alexander Jannaeus had already showed emotional commitment on the part of an Essene to Israel's national interests, especially when what was at stake was the defense of Jerusalem and Judea from foreign, pagan rule. The only thing striking about the Essene John is that he did not remain passive, as did most Essenes, but took an active part in the uprising. The calculated imminence of the end term could have been decisive here.

The course of the history of the Essenes during the some 120 years between the composition of the last literary work of theirs that has come down to us — the *Commentary on Habakkuk,* created shortly after the plundering of the Temple in 54 B.C. — and the revolt against the Romans in A.D. 66, can be established only very sporadically. We have none of the Essenes' own works from this long period of time. The reports of Philo of Alexandria and Flavius Josephus, at any rate, present the Essenes as a continuously present and numerous force throughout this whole time. Otherwise we learn of only two individual Essenes, whom Josephus mentions on account of their prophetic, visionary gift — as he mentions the Essene Judas, who taught in the Temple in 103 B.C. Both are mentioned in connection with rulers. Only in the case of one of the two do further conclusions become possible.

After the death of King Herod, his son Archelaus was ethnarch of Judea and Samaria (4 B.C. to A.D. 6). Shortly before the report reached him that he was to go to Rome and answer to Caesar Augustus and be deposed, he had a dream that no one could interpret aright. Only an Essene named Simon, brought under safe conduct, found the solution to the puzzle of the dream. Ten ears of grain eaten up by cows signified the imminent end of Archelaus' now ten-year rule. Five days after this accurate interpretation came Augustus' messenger (*Antiquities* 17.345-48). Thus an Essene stepped once more into the light of history.

Of King Herod (37-4 B.C.) Josephus reports that he held the Essenes in the highest esteem, and that he even exempted them from taking the oath of loyalty that he required of all of his other subjects, although in the case of the Pharisees it was not imposed by force. As the basis for this impressive favoritism, Josephus adduces a report whose credibility he himself had doubted, he admits, but of which, for lack of other information available to him regarding Herod's patronage of the Essenes, he was unwilling to deprive his readers.

An Essene named Menahem, so the tale goes, once encountered the boy Herod on his way to school, greeted him, to the boy's utter stupefaction, as "King of the Jews," and prophesied a happy reign for him. Later, when Herod actually became king, he sent for this seer of the future, Menahem, and asked him how long his reign was going to last. After some hesitation, Menahem identified his prospects: "At least twenty to thirty years." Thereupon, we hear, Herod dismissed him with a handshake and from then on granted the Essenes their privileges (*Antiquities* 15.368-79).

Difficult as it may be to explain its historical genesis, the fact of the Essenes' favored status in the time of King Herod is historically credible, and scholars are fond of combining it with three other pieces of data. Their point of departure is Pliny the Elder's dubious opinion that the Essenes lived mainly on the Dead Sea — that is, in Qumran. Further, in the course of his presentation of the Jewish War, Josephus furnishes us with a very thorough description of the city of Jerusalem at the time of its siege at the hands of the Romans, and mentions a "Gate of the Essenes" in the southwest part of the city wall (*Jewish War* 5.145). From this it is readily concluded that a quarter of the city here was principally inhabited by Essenes.

The reconciliation of these two seemingly contradictory pieces of information — after all, the Essenes can only have lived *either* in Qumran *or* in Jerusalem! — becomes possible in light of Josephus' report on the devastating consequences of the earthquake of 31 B.C. (*Jewish War* 1.370-79), which archaeological research has shown to have sorely affected Qumran as well (see above, pp. 56-57). From the combination of these data it is then concluded that "the Essenes" left Qumran after the terrible earthquake and moved to Jerusalem, where King Herod provided them with shelter in the vicinity of what would henceforth be known as the Gate of the Essenes. When their patron Herod died, most of the Essenes returned to Qumran, we are told, restored the settlement, and lived there until its destruction in A.D. 68. Thus the end of the Qumran settlement coincided with the end of the Essene community.

This reconstruction, currently in such favor, is extremely questionable in all of its component parts. Only a fraction of the fully 4,000 Essenes who lived in Josephus' time can have lived in Qumran, or even in Jerusalem. The Jerusalem wall in which the Gate of the Essenes was to be found already existed when the union of the Essenes was founded around the middle of the second century B.C. There is no reason why, even at that time, the Essenes living in Jerusalem — among whom, for example, were the Essene Judas, who taught in the Temple in 103 B.C., and his pupils — had not been concentrated in their own quarter in this area. Their especially strict prescriptions of ritual purity may have required this from the outset.

We do not know why it was only sometime after the earthquake that the Qumran settlement was so extensively restored that scroll production in quantity could begin once more. In any case the library, with its master manuscripts, was still in Qumran after the earthquake. In the meantime, numerous scrolls were prepared, and surely the agricultural installations between Qumran and Ain Feshkha were not completely neglected. A move of *all* Qumran Essenes to Jerusalem in consequence of the earthquake, and their return to Qumran in consequence of the death of their patron Herod, is neither demonstrable nor a very likely historical assumption.

Nevertheless, the question remains how the Essenes' status as a favored group during King Herod's long reign, to which Josephus testifies, may have worked out in practice. We may seek a solution in two different areas.

First, we could consider the possibility of Essene participation in the Sanhedrin. The Sanhedrin met under the presidency of the high priest or his representative. It consisted of the three factions, priests, nobility, and Scripture scholars. Each of these factions held twenty-three seats. There were members of these three societal groups among the Essenes as well. It would therefore be theoretically conceivable that, in Herod's time, the Essenes were somewhat as strongly represented in the three factions of the Sanhedrin as the Pharisees had been in the time of Queen Alexandra Salome (76-67 B.C.). Their reservations in principle when it came to the legitimacy of the functioning high priest and the non-Davidic kingship of Herod must not have had a generally excluding effect on this level of religio-political collaboration — somewhat as, today, parliamentary factions can meet under the presidency of persons whose party membership is at odds with that of other members of the parliament. The picture suggested by later Rabbinic literature of a Sanhedrin under permanent Pharisaic domination until the destruction of the Temple is surely not very likely historically. At the same time, historical data are too scarce to take us beyond the simple conceivability of an Essene dominance in the Sanhedrin. Still, such a hypothesis is worthy of discussion as an antithetical model to one-sided views of another kind.

Or, second, we could start with the supposition that the Essenes energetically cooperated in the restoration and expansion of the Jerusalem Temple begun in 20 B.C. by King Herod. In particular, the extensive use of one of the two copies of the *Temple Scroll* from the Qumran library — both prepared in Herodian times — as well as many of the details of the construction work (completed in A.D. 62) that are in conformity with its standards, provide evidence in this direction. The thought also suggests itself that the Essenes may very well have been interested in providing the legitimate high priest, the "Messiah of Aaron," who would appear only at the beginning of the time of salvation (A.D. 70, according to their calculations), with an appropriate edifice for the implementation of the duties of his office. One need not go immediately so far as to suppose that, ninety years before this date, the Essenes persuaded their patron Herod to take such a mighty building project in hand. The king could have done that altogether on his own. But the fact is that the Essenes certainly did welcome this undertaking, and perhaps cooperated assiduously in its execution.

There is nothing more, essentially, that one can add to the history of the Essenes for the time up to the destruction of the Temple. The subsequent activities of this mighty religious power are sketched below (pp. 266-68). And so we finally arrive at the question of what ideas and values stamped the Essenes from within and constituted their essential peculiarity in the Judaism of the time.

The Peculiarities of the Essenes

The texts from the Qumran finds that are demonstrably of actual Essene authorship show, in all clarity, that the Essenes stood on the ground of their received biblical tradition more unwaveringly, more consciously, and more massively than any other portion of Judaism at that time.

In the center of the Essenes' doctrinal orientation stood the covenant that God had once made with the people of Israel at Sinai. The literary embodiment of the divine covenant of Sinai, the standard for all else beside, was — for the Essenes as for all Jews, even to our own day — the Torah revealed to Moses, that is, the Pentateuch, in the form of the five books of Moses. This Torah was actually God's salvific gift to Israel — the foundation of every teaching, especially in the area of ethics, and therefore of what the Rabbis later called halakah. More powerfully and more unwaveringly than all other parts of the Judaism of the time, the Essenes understood — in terms of biblical tradition! — the actualization of the salvation of Israel revealed in the Torah as bound up with Israel's presence in the Holy Land as God's altogether special, private territory upon earth.

On the basis of the standards of the Torah and of the rest of biblical tradition, the most important installation of the Holy Land for the Essenes was the Temple of God in Jerusalem, with its priesthood, its sacrificial offerings ordained by God, and its other cultic celebrations. In conformity with the demands of the Torah, the people of God assembled around the Jerusalem Temple were strictly divided hierarchically into priests, Levites, simple Israelites, and proselytes or persons born pagan who had come over to Judaism. At the pinnacle of their cultic hierarchical system — in conformity with the Torah — stood the high priest. In accord with other biblical tradition, he had to come from the priestly lineage of Zadok and remain in office as long as he lived, or as long as he was physically able to carry out his office. Apart from a strict adherence to this hierarchical order, or outside the Holy Land, Israel's existence in conformity with the Torah was, to the mind of the Essenes, impossible.

The Torah alone also formed the basis for the Essenes' entire corpus of laws. It provided them with their prescriptions for purity, holiness, tithing, social relations, and all other areas of ethics. Here the only difference between the Essenes and their Jewish contemporaries was that the former were stricter on some points. They refused to accept any watering-down of the tradition, any tendentious accommodations to changing times and circumstances, or especially to any pagan influences — not even norms independent of the received written Torah, such as later gained a foothold in the course of the tradition that the Rabbis regarded as the "oral Torah."

The Essenes' prayer services followed the Temple ritual, and their community meals followed prescriptions of the Torah for the festivals of pilgrimage celebrated in the Temple. In their time, the Essenes were altogether the strictest observers of the religious heritage of the Fathers — conservative to the marrow of their bones, averse to all foreign influences, and desirous of no manner of innovation. Their chief interest was exclusively the consistent practice of the Torah in all of its components, and the following of its prescriptions even under the most adverse circumstances of life.

The only new doctrine of the Essenes vis-à-vis the tradition was the discernment on the part of the Teacher of Righteousness that the content of the prophetic books of the Bible bore on the Essenes' own time as the last epoch of history before the Last Judgment and time of salvation, so that the demands of God contained in the Prophets must also have direct relevance for the present. However, neither the Teacher of Righteousness nor the rest of the Essenes regarded the prophetic writings as being in competition with the Torah. Rather, the prophetic books were oriented toward the Torah and, in case of a possible divergence of interpretations, always subordinate to it.

Independent authorities of equal rank alongside the Torah were never recognized by the Essenes. Accordingly, not a single apocalypse — or any new writing invested with the authority of revelation — was composed by the Essenes. All that had come to the Essenes from tradition as "secret knowledge" — apocalypses, the *Angelic Liturgy,* the *Teaching on the Two Spirits,* instructions for exorcism, and sapiential writings — were regarded by them simply as aids to a more profound penetration of the mysteries revealed by God through the Torah and the Prophets, never as being of equal value with the central corpus of divine revelation, or even as being in competition with the latter. The Essenes used these works, insofar as they seemed to them to be in conformity with the Torah.

At the foundation of the Essene union lay the attempt to bring together in the Holy Land all that remained of the traditional twelve tribes of Israel, and to unite them. The solitary goal of the Essenes' rigorous induction procedure was to gain general recognition of the importance of tradition in the form of the Torah and the Prophets. Anyone wishing to be a true Jew had to come to know this core content of tradition as extensively as possible and take it to heart in one's practical lifestyle.

The Essenes as God's People Israel

From the outset, then, the Essenes never regarded themselves otherwise than as the sole legitimate representation of the twelve tribes of Israel as a whole in the current age. Their union was *'am 'ēl,* the "people of God," and *'ădat yiśrā'ēl,* the "[whole] community of Israel." Their annual plenary assembly, at the Feast of Weeks, our Pentecost, was a concrete representation of the *qĕhal yiśrā'ēl*, the "assembly of the people of [all] Israel," just as each of their daily worship assemblies for prayer services and community meals was understood as a community "assembling of the people." A sign of this communal element was that the worship assemblies were always held, in all places where there were Essenes, at exactly the same time of the day.

Each of the local Essene groups was also an integral part of the ideal Temple of God on earth, "built by human beings," with the priests as the Holy of Holies, and with the rest of Israel as the rest of the Temple installation — all of whom were to perform for the entire Holy Land the prescribed expiation as long as the false ordinance of worship was being practiced at the Jerusalem Temple. Ideally, of course, the Ark of the Covenant, with the Torah revealed of old on Sinai, stood in the Holy of Holies of the Jerusalem Temple; but the Essenes also called themselves the "House of the Torah" — that Temple, then, whose heart and core was the Pentateuch that had been entrusted to the priests for special safeguarding (cf. Num. 1:50, 53). Finally, the Essene priests, with the Zadokites at their head, embodied — as the *bĕrît 'ēl*, the "covenant of God," together with the Torah entrusted to them for appropriate exposition — the earthly representation of the old order of God on Sinai.

The Essenes' internal organizational structure corresponded to that prescribed for the whole of Israel in the Pentateuch. In conformity with the order of encampment prescribed for the tribes of Israel in Numbers 1–2, the Essenes divided themselves into "camps," determined men's minimum age for participation in worship as that of the completion of their twentieth year, and regulated the special status of priests. In the framework of this order of encampment, the Essenes followed Exodus 18:21-22 and formed organizational subunits of 1,000, 100, 50, and 10 men entitled to perform worship. The respective leaders of these subunits also functioned as judges.

It would take us too far afield to present the Essenes' whole organizational and administrative structure in detail. The most important consideration is that, from beginning to end, they based it on standards given in the Torah, and this in terms of the whole of Israel, not of an association that would be, even de jure, only part of Israel. In their own self-understanding, the Essenes were not a special association within Israel; they simply represented the *whole of Israel*.

What was new with the Essenes over against the biblical tradition was only their designation of God's people Israel as *yaḥad,* in the sense of "association" or "union." This designation of Israel, absent from the terminology of the Bible, takes account of the fact that, at the point in time of the founding of the Essenes, the greater portion of the people of Israel were scattered throughout the world, and only a small minority lived in the Holy Land. Accordingly, now for the first time the reunification of all of the scattered parts of Israel in a union of the whole people of God in the Holy Land became an essential, constitutive feature of Israel.

The dispersion of Israel into geographical areas outside the Holy Land had of course begun as early as the fall of the Northern Kingdom of Israel in 722 B.C. In this case the population had for the most part moved to Mesopotamia. Through the deportation and flight of inhabitants of the Southern Kingdom of Judah — 597, 587, and 582 B.C. — the dispersion was reinforced. Through the mass emigration of pious Jews during the religious persecution begun in 170 B.C., it became almost the general situation of Israel. Thus, on the one hand, the union of the Essenes was a restoration of relationships prevailing before the year 722 B.C.; on the other hand, after more than a half-millennium of the majority of Israel being dispersed, it was something altogether new.

The decisive thing is that the Essenes' union was neither an interest group formed for recalling to the Holy Land those parts of Israel living in the Diaspora, nor an association formed for some special purpose within Israel. Rather, it was the *unification of all Israel in the Holy Land.* Those who persisted in declining this union thereby definitively closed themselves off from Israel and from the salvific people of God, spurned the covenant of God made on Sinai, and abandoned the foundation of the Torah, which had inextricably bound up salvation for Israel with Israel's existence in God's Holy Land.

The Calendar

There were numerous calendrical systems in the ancient Near East. The three most influential still define our daily lives today. These were also the three that, from the time of the Exile of the sixth century B.C., claimed validity in Judaism: the ancient Egyptian solar calendar, the Babylonian lunar calendar, and the Israelite seven-day week with the Sabbath as its close and climax.

The Solar Calendar

We owe our calendar today to the Romans. This is evident from the Latin names of the months: September, October, November, and December were once the seventh, eighth, ninth, and tenth months, respectively, of a year that began with March. This spring month has its name from the god of war, Mars, under whose protection the Roman legions would move on to new campaigns after their winter respite. The months that come next owe their names to the Roman divinities Aprilis, Maius, and Juno. July is dedicated to Gaius Julius Caesar, August to his successor Gaius Octavius Augustus.

It was none other than the latter Caesar who reformed the old Roman calendar, establishing the winter solstice as the beginning of the year, and adding one day to the old last month of the year, February, every four years in order to even out the calendar with the natural solar year. An even more exact match with the solar year of 365.2422 days was achieved by Pope Gregory XIII in 1582, with the determination that, thrice in the course of every four-hundred-year period, the extra day would not be added. Ten superfluous days that had accrued since Caesar's time were canceled: October 4, 1582, was immediately followed by October 15. And so the Julian calendar became our Gregorian calendar of today.

Caesar owed the basis of his reform of the old Roman lunar calendar to the Egyptians. From time immemorial, the Egyptians had had a solar year of exactly 365 days, divided into twelve months of thirty days each, with five additional festival days at year's end. The commencement of the year had originally been the high-water time of the Nile in mid-July. But since this year was too short by one-fourth of a day, the official beginning of the year slowly shifted through the previous periods of vegetation, until, after a "Sothic period" of 1,461 slightly too short years, the original starting point was reached once more. Only in the third century B.C. did the Egyptians postulate the additional day every four years, which Caesar first concretely introduced. The Egyptians followed their 365-day solar calendar from, at the latest, 2772 B.C. onward.

When the Babylonian king Nebuchadnezzar had the Temple in Jerusalem destroyed in 587 B.C. and crushed an uprising against his governor Gedaliah in 582 B.C., many Jews, among them the prophet Jeremiah, fled to Egypt. Until then the Israelites had had no comprehensive calendrical system of their own but had mainly practiced the seven-day week, and had bound the New Year empirically to the observation of the first new moon in the spring. Now they adopted the profane ancient Egyptian calendar, which therefore was not a matter of religious obligation for them, at the same time modifying it in a way that implicitly allowed the Israelite seven-day week determinative significance.

From the Egyptian calendar the Jews adopted at that time the division of the year into twelve months of thirty days each. Of the five additional days at the end of the year, however, they kept only four, adding them to the third, sixth, ninth, and twelfth months. Thus, each year consisted of 364 days of exactly 52 weeks, each quarter having 91 days and exactly 13 weeks. The first day of the year, in this innovative Israelite calendar, was always a Wednesday, the fourth day of the week, since God had called into being the sun, moon, and stars as the starting points and determining factors of all calculations of time only on the fourth day of his creation of the world (Gen. 1:14-19). Since God had obviously created the moon as a full moon, and not a new moon, the first year of creation must have begun with a full moon. Further, the spring equinox was regarded as the natural beginning of the year, since from then on the sun increasingly ruled the greater part of the day.

This calendar was perfect in itself. Its basis was the solar year that dominated in nature. And every quarter year began with the day of the full moon, when an additional day was granted to the last phase of the moon in the previous month. In the first year of this calendrical order, the weekly service of the twenty-four priestly families ended for the second time four weeks before the close of the year, when the next service cycle began at once. After six years, in which the beginning of the twenty-four-week cycle always occurred four weeks earlier than in the previous year, the seventh year always began once more with a week in which the same priestly family was responsible for service as at the beginning of the first year. Within each six-year period, each priestly family had twice had its service on the high feast days prescribed in the Torah, on which the priests' income was especially lavish. Thus, this priestly oriented calendrical system assured distributive justice. After exactly forty-nine of such six-year cycles, the point of departure was finally reached at which the beginning of the natural year and the beginning of the 364-day year coincided: owing to the difference of 1.2422 days, 294 years of the calendar corresponded almost exactly to 293 natural years.

The unavoidable difference between the calendrical and the natural year was evidently taken into account with the explanation that the godless power of evil in the world prevented the sun from completing its yearly cycle, in accordance with the order of creation, punctually within 364 days. There was never any attempt to even out this calendrical system with the natural year by adding days, weeks, or months. On the contrary, relevant texts repeatedly insist that each year has exactly 364 days, no more and no less. The inner harmony of this calendrical system, its implicit seven-day or Sabbath principle, proclaimed so clearly that what was at issue was the primeval divine order of the cosmos (cf. Gen. 2:1-3), that any consideration to the contrary must be left out of account.

In all probability it was this calendar system that Jewish returnees from Egypt brought to Jerusalem when the edict of King Cyrus of Persia permitted their homecoming in 538 B.C., and that regulated the order of worship in the Jerusalem Temple after its rebuilding and its dedication in 515 B.C. The strongest evidence for this is the fact that even the latest source of the Pentateuch — the so-called Priestly document, prepared only after the beginning of the Exile, and probably in Palestine — presupposes this Egyptian-Jewish calendar and regards it as normative.

This fact is clear in the final Priestly form of the Pentateuch, not only where the length of life of the primeval sage Enoch as the great expert in astronomy is given as 365 years (Gen. 5:23) — Egypt was the "father" of this calendar — or the duration of the Flood as exactly one solar year (Gen. 7:11; 8:14). But besides, as early as 1953 the leading expert in the investigation of this calendar, Annie Jaubert, established that throughout the Pentateuch, the principle is observed that — presuming this calendar! — the Patriarchs are never represented as traveling on the Sabbath. Finally, in the Priestly account of creation each day is expressly presented as consisting, first, of its daytime half, then of its nighttime half (Gen. 1:5, 8, 13, 19, 23, 31). This presupposes the beginning of the day with sunrise, in the morning, as was customary in Egypt, not with the evening, as would have corresponded to the lunar-oriented Babylonian calendar system (see below, p. 202).

Further, even longer time-calculations — those of the ages of the world — show that, regarded in terms of the Torah, this calendar alone corresponded to God's plan of salvation. If, with the author of *Jubilees* in the third century B.C., we reckon the part of world history presented in the Torah in units of forty-nine solar years, the result is that, from the creation of Adam to Israel's entry into the Holy Land under the leadership of Joshua, exactly fifty such periods had passed: 2,450 years (*Jubilees* 50:4). That was also five cycles of 490 years each, whence the author of the Ten-Week Apocalypse of *1 Enoch* deduced his speculation that the entry of Israel into the Holy Land marked the halfway point in a world history of 4,900 years in all (*1 Enoch* 93; 91:12-17).

In our own context, these examples will suffice to show in particular how generally and obviously this Egyptian-Jewish 364-day solar calendar served Palestinian Judaism after the Exile in the sixth century B.C. as the basic orientation of its worship and religion. Probably it was uninterruptedly the official standard calendar at the Jerusalem Temple until the year 167 B.C. This does not mean that it was not finally perfected by way of many a compromise in its early history. But, beginning in the fourth century B.C. at the latest, its inevitable deviations from the natural year were taken for granted, in the same way as in old Egypt with its Sothic periods, or as in Islam, where the beginning of the 354-day year constantly rotates through the natural year.

The Essenes knew that this 364-day solar calendar had been unknown to the Israel of the age of the kings. Only to those who had survived the annihilation of the state of Judah at the beginning of the sixth century B.C. had God revealed this calendrical ordinance. It was therefore not a simple further development of ancient Israelite traditions, but was new and independent vis-à-vis the latter. But only those who remained true to this calendrical and cultic ordinance, revealed to Israel in exile, henceforward had any part in life. Those who spurned it and followed another calendrical order were thereby excluded from all the life force of Israel (CD 3:12-17).

The Lunar Calendar

The other ancient Near Eastern calendrical system, which in modified form still partially determines our calendar today, is the Babylonian lunar calendar. We still calculate the date of Easter according to the phases of the moon, which therefore also determine the dates of Lent, in one direction, and the Feasts of the Ascension, Pentecost, and Corpus Christi in the other. Accordingly, Easter Sunday fell on March 31 in 1991, April 19 in 1992, April 11 in 1993, April 3 in 1994, and April 16 in 1995. Industry, politics, administration, and school holidays must live with these fluctuating dates, as well as with the fact that no year can ever begin with the same day of the week as the previous year, since the ancient Israelite division of time into strict seven-day weeks, which we have likewise adopted, fails to fall neatly into our 365- or 366-day year.

Each cycle of the phases of the moon — from full moon to full moon, or from new moon to new moon — lasts 29.5306 days. The Babylonians, for whom the calendar was ruled by the moon god Shin, began each day with its nocturnal half and divided the year into twelve months having, alternately, thirty or twenty-nine days, for a total of 354 days in the year. In order to balance their calendar with the natural year, they added an extra month after every second or third year — seven times in the course of a nineteen-year cycle — as well as extra days at the end of months in which the natural delay in the date of the new moon made this necessary. The months and years always began with the new moon — not, as in the solar calender system, with the full moon.

The Babylonian names for the months — Nisan, Iyyar, Sivan, Tammuz, and so on — found in today's Jewish calendar, along with the latter's full agreement in basic concept with the Babylonian calendar, show the origin of the Jewish calendar. The only possible question is when Jews adopted it, as well as when and why it became Judaism's official calendar. Christians took it over from the Jews later, although in an altered form.

The assumption is usually made that, even in the last phase of the Kingdom of Judah, Israel followed the Babylonian 354-day calendar, just as the deported Jews must have in their Mesopotamian exile, and the returnees from there must have done in Jerusalem after Cyrus' edict of 538 B.C. Thus, we are told, this calendar obviously determined worship at the Jerusalem Temple as well, after its restoration and its dedication in 515 B.C. Actually, however, there is not a single piece of evidence for this customary view.

When the Babylonians became the political superpower of the Near East toward the end of the seventh century B.C., their lunar calendar was not only basic for the entire greater empire, but was the only calendar available in this region for the designation of long periods of time, the dating of documents, and the unambiguous determination of important interregional events. Once the Persian king Cyrus took power (538 B.C.), and his son Cambyses (521-486 B.C.) organized the new greater kingdom into a single administrative unit, this calendrical ordinance was in force internationally, to the most southerly reaches of the kingdom ruled by the Persians — all the way to upper Egypt. Thus, Darius II (423-404 B.C.) had orders given in 419 B.C. even to the inhabitants of the Jewish military colony at Aswan that they begin the celebration of Passover and Unleavened Bread on the fourteenth day of the month of Nisan. Until then, obviously, they had known only the imperial calendar, but not, as yet, this Jewish festival. Besides, this is the only documentary evidence from pre-Maccabean times that Jews can have been guided in their practice of worship by the Babylonian lunar calendar. With regard to procedures in the Jerusalem Temple at this same time, the finding in question says nothing whatever.

By way of an analogy with calendrical procedures in Judea at that time, we may invoke the calendrical situation in today's state of Israel. Newspapers, business and private letters, often even private documents, are dated according to days, months, and years of a calendar that was once only Christian, but that today is international. Often, in everyday life, the year 1996 is used instead of the year 5756 — or the year 5757 that begins on September 16 — since the creation of the world. At the same time, for all religious matters, such as the dates of festival days, the only calendar used is the traditional Jewish lunar one.

In similar fashion, during Babylonian, Persian, and Seleucid times, not only in the Diaspora but also in Palestine and in Jerusalem, in all internationally oriented areas of administration, commerce, correspondence, and so on, the Jews used the dates of the Babylonian lunar calendar — which in no way implies that this was the official calendar of the Jerusalem Temple and thereby the basis of an orientation in worship.

The first demonstrable introduction of this Babylonian calendar at the Jerusalem Temple was at the hands of the high priest Menelaus in the year 167 B.C. To be sure, as a purely pagan calendar it had no Sabbath, nor a single traditional Jewish festival. Only when the Maccabee Jonathan took office as high priest in 152 B.C. and — for the sake of his internationally oriented interests of politics and power — promulgated this calendar once more at the Jerusalem Temple, was it integrated with the seven-day week and the Jewish festivals.

How un-Jewish this 354-day lunar calendar was in its origin is perhaps shown most clearly by the problems it posed for the Rabbis. It contradicted other elements of their tradition, and even the Torah itself. Neither the beginnings of the months, nor the beginning of the year, fit the ancient Israelite seven-day week. Festival dates repeatedly fell on the Sabbath, so that it had to be decided on a case-by-case basis whether it was the Sabbath or the festival day that was to be observed. Although all work is forbidden on the Sabbath, and the Rabbis were very careful not to allow the slightest activity in any way resembling work, the activities — likewise prescribed — of preparation for a festival on the following day occasionally required the violation of the Sabbath precept.

One need only study the books and learned treatises that have been composed, since Rabbinic times, on the peculiarities of this Jewish lunar calendar, still in use today, in order to understand very quickly why the Essenes rejected it and — despite all problems with the natural year — doggedly held to the 364-day solar calendar of their Palestinian Jewish tradition. Only the latter calendar was as Jewish as possible, if the seven-day week with its crowning point, the Sabbath, is implicitly to be the supreme measure of all things. The internal commensurability of this solar calendar with the phases of the moon in every three-year cycle only counted as further evidence for the rectitude of this basic orientation. Otherwise the moon had no function at all in the 364-day solar calendrical system, either for the regular beginning of each year with a full or new moon, or for the date of any festival. Were one, instead, to orient oneself basically by the phases of the moon, all of the divinely willed order in the world would be thrown into total confusion (*Jubilees* 6:28-38, esp. 6:36; cf. our Easter dates!).

The book of *Jubilees,* which is surely pre-Essene, had already insisted that the sun alone must provide the basic orientation of all calendrical order (*Jubilees* 2:9-10). It also offers a foundation that goes beyond all specific calendrical questions: only the sun can rightly divide light and darkness.

In the *Teaching on the Two Spirits* from Qumran (1QS 3:13–4:26), this basic division of the world is further developed by way of a theology of creation. When God created the world, he measured out equal shares of light and darkness, good and evil, truth and falsehood, righteousness and wickedness — exactly half of each with respect to the pair in which it occurs, although within the individual works of creation now one, now the other side weighs more heavily in the balance. The average proportion of sunlight and nocturnal darkness throughout the year, however, is exactly one to one. But only an orientation to the duration of the solar year can do justice to this fundamental ordering of creation. Lunar years, with their sometimes 354 days, sometimes 383 or more, never yield equal portions of light and darkness, and on this basis alone are antagonistic to the divine order of creation.

The Rivalry of the Two Calendars

From 152 B.C. on, the Essenes continuously followed only the 364-day solar calendar of Israel's exilic tradition. The Sadducees, as well, regarded it as the only correct one, but in Temple worship, out of political considerations, they practiced the lunar calendar that had become official, just as the Pharisees did.

Again and again in their writings, the Essenes bitterly criticized the abandonment of the calendrical order that was consonant with creation, and they saw in this one of the principal reasons for the punishments that God allowed to come upon his people. But as the Essenes lacked the political power to remedy these untoward circumstances, only the coming Last Judgment could pave the way for a return to the old calendrical order. Until then, Palestinian Judaism would continue to follow two irreconcilable calendars, by way of which the Essenes were sharply divided from the other Jews in the cities and villages of Palestine.

Similar rivalries prevail in Christianity. For example, the Roman Catholic Church celebrates Christmas on December 25, while the Russian Orthodox Church annually honors the birth of the Lord on — in terms of the dates of the Gregorian calendar today — January 7. Where, in Russian or Ukrainian locales, there are both Roman Catholic and Orthodox churches, Christians always celebrate their high festival at different times. Where Catholic and Orthodox faithful live together in mixed neighborhoods, this is a deep cleft in a common life that is otherwise harmonious. Things were no different with the Essenes in Palestinian Judaism.

But this calendar dispute probably antedated the Essenes' appearance on the scene of Palestinian Judaism. As early as *Jubilees,* as well as in the *Astronomical Book of Enoch* (composed in the third century B.C. at the latest), it is emphatically stated that only a solar year of, consistently, 364 days corresponds to the creative will of God. This kind of apologetics can be mounted only against other Jews, who at that time already followed the lunar calendar not only in their business affairs, but precisely in their religious practice as well. Presumably these were especially the Jews of the Diaspora in Mesopotamia, who had been there since 722, and in greater numbers since 587 B.C., and of whom only a small proportion had taken advantage of Cyrus' edict of 538 B.C. and returned to Palestine. They had probably adopted the Babylonian calendar very early and had integrated with it the seven-day week along with the dates of the Israelite feast days.

Thus, there had probably been two distinct parts of Judaism, each following its own calendar, since the sixth century B.C. The influence of Babylonian Judaism on the motherland may have led to confrontations in the Jerusalem Temple as to the correct calendrical order as early as 538 B.C., but especially in the time of Ezra (middle or end of the fifth century B.C.). Still, until now there is no evidence for the use — even temporary — of the Babylonian lunar calendar for the official orientation of worship in Jerusalem in pre-Maccabean times.

Accordingly, works of Palestinian Judaism such as *Jubilees,* or the *Astronomical Book of Enoch,* are to be valued as early witnesses to the solid establishment of the calendrical order of worship and the defeat of attempts at the time to introduce changes in the Jerusalem Temple. On the other hand, against this background it becomes understandable why the introduction of the lunar calendar — by the high priest Jonathan in 152 B.C. — did not meet with general resistance. Jonathan had not invented a new calendar, but only made a regional calendar already practiced in the Judaism of the time that of the Jerusalem Temple as well. The peculiarity of the Essenes consisted in their rejection of this change and in their remaining imperturbably loyal to the tradition of worship of the Jerusalem Temple.

Sacrifice in the Jerusalem Temple

The heart of worship at the Jerusalem Temple consisted in the sacrifices of animals, food, and drink that were offered on the altar of burnt offerings on the Sabbath and on the occasion of religious festivals. These sacrificial offerings were linked to certain occasions whose dates were determined by the calendar of worship.

The validity of these sacrifices, therefore — their acceptance by God — depended not least of all on their being offered at the correct moment. The corresponding prescriptions of the Torah are to be found especially in Leviticus 23 and Numbers 28–29. Leviticus 23:37-38 in particular requires a basic distinction between the ritual of sacrifice on Sabbath days and that performed on the festival days. The celebration of both rituals on the same day was — strictly speaking — excluded by the Torah.

The sacrificial prescriptions in the Torah form a solid system. That system might be broadened, but it could not be changed in its foundations. If a calendrical order was practiced that allowed a feast day to fall on the Sabbath, that calendrical order desecrated not only this particular Sabbath but the entire system, and thereby the sacrificial procedure of the Temple essentially and generally. All sacrifices offered within the framework of this faulty cultic ordinance were then not performed in accordance with prescription, and were as null in their effect as if they had simply never been offered.

The Essenes never criticized the sacrificial worship prescribed in the Torah, let alone rejected it. The lunar calendar introduced by Jonathan, however, was regarded by them as having the effect that no sacrifices consonant with the Torah could ever be offered. Had the Essenes nevertheless continued to participate in the sacrificial worship conducted in the Jerusalem Temple, their own sacrifices would have been null and void as well. At the same time, the Torah inexorably demanded that the prescribed sacrifices indeed be offered. Accordingly, the Essenes had no choice but to offer these sacrifices independently of the Temple worship in Jerusalem, and to boycott the latter as long as it was practiced on the basis of a false calendrical order.

The Essenes' boycott of the failed Jerusalem sacrificial worship corresponded at the same time to an instruction from God, through the prophet Malachi, for the last epoch of world history before the Last Judgment — an epoch particularly exposed to the power of evil: All who would remain true to God's covenant made at Sinai must "no longer tread the sanctuary in order to kindle fire [offer sacrifice] on its altar in vain, but [instead] must be those who 'keep the door shut' [remain aloof from the falsified sacrificial worship], with regard to which God himself has said, 'Oh, that one among you would shut the temple gates to keep you from kindling fire on my altar in vain' (Mal. 1:10)" (CD 6:11-13).

The alternative — to follow the example of the high priest Onias IV, who a few years before had erected an independent Jewish temple in Leontopolis, in Egypt, and there was conducting a sacrificial practice — was rejected by the Teacher of Righteousness, surely partly because he expected the Last Judgment within a short while, so that the falsified order of worship in Jerusalem would be abolished in any case. Thus, he was concerned only with measures to be practiced over a short intermediate time. The possibility that the provisional measures might have to be in effect for centuries occurred to no one at first.

The Essenes took their orientation in the situation at hand from indications from God such as his word through Solomon: "The sacrifice of the wicked is an abomination to the Lord, but the prayer of the upright is his delight [Prov. 15:8; ". . . is as a pleasing sacrifice" in CD11:21]" (CD 11:20-21). "Instead of the flesh of burnt offerings and the fat of slain offerings, the prescribed sacrifice of the lips [liturgically correct prayer services] will be accounted as an adequate odor of sacrifice and perfect conduct [a manner of life in conformity with the Torah], as well-pleasing [to God], a freely offered sacrifice," which will "atone for [all] guilt through the transgression [of God's commands] and the [other] sinful deeds, and [win God's] benevolence for the [Holy] Land" (1QS 9:4-5; similarly, 1QS 8:6-7, 9-10).

The appropriate place for these alternative sacrificial offerings was the Essene union of the whole of Israel as the Temple of God in the Holy Land. The Essenes' daily local prayer services, liturgically correct according to the pattern of the Temple ritual, and their manner of life conducted in strict accordance with the Torah, were valid as an adequate equivalent for all of the sacrifices prescribed in the Torah. But the Essenes never appealed to individual elements of their liturgy or particular areas of their life practice as exact equivalents of specific sacrifices. Rather, their entire liturgical and ethical practice took the place of the sacrifices on the Temple altar. Accordingly, the

Essenes always had to do justice to the special norms of purity and holiness that were provided in the Torah for the service of worship in the Temple — even stricter for priests and Levites than for simple Israelites. Only thus was God's acceptance of these substitute sacrifices guaranteed.

The Qumran texts clearly show that the Essenes neither participated in the sacrifices offered on the altar of the Jerusalem Temple, nor continued to offer the prescribed sacrifices of animals, food, and drink anywhere outside the Temple. This finding coincides with the data given in Philo's and Josephus' reports concerning the Essenes. On the other hand, the Essenes may have continued to offer, in the Jerusalem Temple, sacrifices not bound up with dates on the calendar of worship — for example, sacrifices at the birth of a child or upon fulfillment of a vow.

Otherwise, the Essenes' boycott of the Sabbath and festival sacrifices involved no general shunning of the Jerusalem Temple. The Temple was still the central dwelling place of God on earth amidst Israel. The Essenes taught there and made sacred gifts for the building as well as for its elegant appointments. Like all Jews, they paid the half-shekel Temple tax, although not annually but only once in a lifetime, in accordance with Exodus 30:11-16. Like all Jews, the Essenes, too, always prayed facing the direction of the Temple. The longitudinal axis of the assembly hall in Qumran faces the Temple; and the strikingly sharp ascent of its floor points precisely to the Holy of Holies in Jerusalem, only 26 kilometers away as the crow flies, and lying 1,080 meters higher than the floor of the assembly hall. Only in the case of those sacrifices whose offering on Sabbath and feast days was regulated by the calendrically falsified order of worship did the Essenes shun the Temple and substitute other things.

Apart from the annual slaughtering of the Passover lambs on the fourteenth day of the first month, the Essenes' only slaughter of animals for purposes of ritual worship was the slaughter and burning of the red heifer in conformity with Numbers 19:1-10. The ashes of this heifer served for the production of water of purification, which everyone needed who had come in contact with the dead. This ritual was bound neither to a fixed calendar date, nor to the participation of the high priest, nor to a burnt offering. Nor was it a sacrifice in the proper sense. Thus it could continue to be practiced by the Essenes without any problem in terms of detriment to the elements of their boycott.

The Community of Goods

Those who became members of the Essenes brought not only their persons, but all of their property as well, to the union of all Israel. Thus arose the style of community of goods that was characteristic of the Essenes. How this community of goods was conceptualized, and how it functioned, has been learned for the first time only thanks to the Qumran finds — concrete, individual regulations and the actual terminology used by the Essenes being previously unknown.

The property brought along by persons entering the union, which thereby became the property of that union, is usually designated in the Qumran texts indifferently as *hôn*. More specifically, the terms *kôah* and *da'at* are used (as in 1QS 1:11-12). They are included in the concept *hôn*.

The term *hôn* denotes, comprehensively, a person's entire financial resources — a person's material property as well as bodily and mental strength, including the use of all of this, and therefore including the profits from it. Only in terms of its core does *hôn* mean material property, like plots of land, houses, fields, vineyards, plantations, gardens, workshops, stores, slaves, cattle, money, or other things of value, including any inheritance rights — in a word, all of a person's property, immovable and movable. An essential part of this material property is its profit and income — therefore whatever a person gains from property in various ways, through personal use, rent, lease, or sale.

Kôah, in economic terms, is one's own physical ability to work, including the profit therefrom, for example through the selling of one's labor or other services. *Da'at* is mental skill as the essential foundation of the material profit of artisans, traders, lawyers, scribes, teachers, physicians, or other representatives of callings whose proper capital is precisely specialized knowledge.

Consequently, the power to work and technical knowledge were regarded by the Essenes as components of one's personal resources in terms of fortune just as surely as material property was, and this from the viewpoint of the profits accruing to them.

But those who wished to enter the Essenes were permitted to hand over their fortunes, and their claims to any resulting interest or profits, only after undergoing a year's probation and passing an examination at the termination of the year. And so the fortune that had been brought in was first booked and administered in the candidate's personal account, in case — through the candidate's death, unsuitability for the union, or decision to withdraw — a full membership (after at least three years of preparation) did not finally materialize. Only if and when full membership was granted to the candidate did the Essene union become the unrestricted proprietor of what the candidate had originally brought (1QS 6:13-23), to remain such for all time, even if after this point in time the full-fledged member left the union, was excluded, or died without personal descendants. Of course, all of this held only for rights of ownership to the fortune that the candidate had brought. Rights of possession and use are simply not addressed here. In legal terms, these rights belong in an altogether different category.

How the Essenes' community of goods was conceptualized, and on what material and religious presuppositions it rested, becomes clear only if we take into account its biblical foundations. In this respect, too, the Essenes' exclusive concern was to remain true to biblical tradition and to continue strictly to follow its standards. Therefore we must know the points of departure specified for Israel in terms of property rights, especially in the Torah, if we are to understand the Essenes' special regulations.

In the biblical representation, the Holy Land never was and never became the property of the people of Israel. Rather, from the outset and for all time the land and its inhabitants were the property of their God YHWH (e.g., Leviticus 25, esp. vv. 23, 55). This God had chosen for himself the people of Israel languishing in slavery in Egypt, delivered them from their distress, and led them into his own land, a land previously unknown to Israel (Numbers 13). In this rich and prosperous land of God's, "flowing with milk and honey," he had assigned the twelve tribes of Israel, their clans, and their individual families, very definite regions of the land to be inhabited and cultivated — from whose produce they could live richly and thus become a great and mighty people (Numbers 32–36).

Legally, God had always transferred to the Israelites their respective regions as *naḥălâ* — in permanent lease, as it were, or for purposes of usufruct: as possession, but not as property. The people's tribal, clan, or family rights of possession were to be bequeathed to their children and their children's descendants. The proprietor of the entire land always continued to be God, and God's unassailable title of ownership implied two basic demands that were to remain forever valid for Israel, and to which the Essenes, in concrete legal relations in the milieu of their founding, sought to do justice with their community of goods.

For one thing, in establishing the covenant of Sinai, and concretely in the Torah as the document of that covenant for Israel, God had bound the existence and continued habitation of the chosen people in the Holy Land to their following of the instructions of the Torah in every respect. The Torah, in turn, bound all salvation for Israel to Israel's presence in the Holy Land. The Torah threatened every Israelite who failed to hold to this with punishments extending to the death penalty — indeed, for the case of rebelliousness on the part of the whole people of Israel, expulsion from God's land, which was equivalent to the withdrawal of Israel's material existence; after all, there was no land of God in exile. The one kind of demand of God as proprietor of the Holy Land on Israel as its possessor was therefore the inexorable duty of obedience to the landlord, whose principal instrument of governance was the Torah with its binding standards for blessing and curse.

Second, as proprietor of the Holy Land God had a claim on a share of its yield. Basically the land's yield belonged to him part and parcel. But he had stipulated in the Torah that this yield should be for the benefit of those who produced it. Only small shares thereof, if always of the best, should be offered to the owner of the land — not for his own maintenance, since God needs nothing, but as a ritual expression of the acknowledgment of the prevailing relations of ownership. Materially, the shares of the yield of the Holy Land, sacrifices, and other cultic gifts offered to God were therefore overwhelmingly destined once more for the benefit of the Israelites. Here, for one thing, the personnel who performed the worship, and for another, those parts of the population of Israel without income, as well as other elements in need of social support and their neighbors in the Holy Land, were appropriately taken into consideration.

In Israel's early, mainly agricultural times, God's share in the produce of the Holy Land consisted of the firstfruits of all that the land brought forth. Here the birth of a first male child was very soon compensated by the offering of an animal, reflecting the presentation of the sacrifice of Isaac by his father Abraham in Genesis 22. Later, offerings of money were made. In nature, God's claim was paid in the form of the firstborn males of cattle, sheep, and goats, as well as the annual firstfruits of the grain fields, vineyards, and olive groves, later also of the date palm, the fig and other fruit trees, and of the products of the garden.

The offering of these firstfruit sacrifices occurred cumulatively, on the occasion of three annual festivals of pilgrimage, whose dates coincided with the various harvest times, and in which all of the men of Israel who were able to worship were to be together in the Jerusalem Temple. These festivals were that of the barley harvest, that is, the Feast of Unleavened Bread combined with Passover, in the spring; the Feast of Weeks, celebrating the wheat harvest, seven weeks later; and in autumn, the Feast of Booths (Tabernacles) for the firstfruits of the agricultural products that ripened later. Parts of the sacrificial gifts were then offered on the altar of the burnt offerings. Further parts went to the priests and Levites, who as worship personnel possessed no shares of the Holy Land of their own and therefore were indirectly to share in its yield. Most of the sacrificial gifts that were brought, however, were consumed after their ritual offering by the pilgrims of the festival themselves, in the spacious outer court of the Temple. The sacrificial banquet lasted seven days at the Feast of Unleavened Bread, eight days at the Feast of Booths, and at the other feasts usually only one day.

The basic order of sacrifices presented corresponds in its essence to the circumstances of the end of the time of the kings, therefore toward the end of the seventh century B.C. The prehistory of this pattern, which in Israel's Northern Kingdom took a different form from that of the Southern Kingdom of Judah with its Temple in Jerusalem, is still partially recognizable in the various component traditions of the Torah and in other biblical writings. A truly unified picture is just as little available from these various traditions as it is from the further formation of this system in the historical work of the Chronicler, or in the text of the *Temple Scroll* from the Qumran finds, both of which reflect relations around 400 B.C. There were always manifold interests at work, which in the framework of this system wanted to establish new festivals, increase the shares of the priests and Levites, include additional harvests, reinforce the Temple monopoly, or deposit parts of the cultic gifts in their places of origin everywhere in the land. Available sources still reveal only partial aspects of such centuries-long struggles, and not their factual relations at any particular point in time.

It is all the more important, therefore, to observe the tendency, already visible in the time of the kings, to gather the manifold sacrificial offerings in the paying of tithes, independently of the dates of the pilgrimage festivals. The Torah itself contains various models of this sort alongside the sacrifices that are linked to dates. Actually, however, the tithing system is a system in competition with the feasts of pilgrimage. Its rise originally had cultic, political, and social causes, but its significance grew when the 364-day calendar came to determine the order of worship in Jerusalem at the end of the exilic period.

Until the destruction of the Northern Kingdom of Israel in 722 B.C., there had been three great state sanctuaries — erected and maintained by the kings — in Jerusalem, Bethel, and Dan, along with numerous high holy places and private establishments of worship maintained by well-to-do Israelites everywhere in the country. The large number of these places of worship provided numerous priests and Levites with adequate income opportunities. The destruction of the Northern Kingdom, which was larger in area, left most of them, if not to be deported, at least without their daily bread. The reform of the Judean kings Hezekiah (716-687 B.C.) and Josiah in 622 concentrated in the Temple in Jerusalem all of the worship that remained to Israel, liquidating all other places of worship still in existence. But in Jerusalem, the old established priestly families, especially the Zadok line, enjoyed the highest authority and income privileges. Only a part of the priests and Levites from other sanctuaries, who had become penniless, could therefore be integrated into the service of worship in the central sanctuary, and they were underprivileged there also.

The so-called Levite tithe was probably introduced this early. It was to be contributed annually, according to Numbers 18:20-32; according to Deuteronomy 14:28-29 and 26:12-15 the term was to be only every three years. Ten percent of the total contributions were to be paid to the Levites and to the priests. The texts cited show very clearly that from the outset it was a matter of social-welfare contributions. Their yearly collection may have been introduced at the beginning of the time of the Second Temple.

The latest tithe to be introduced at this time is surely the corresponding priestly tithe (Num. 18:8-19; Deut. 14:22-27; 26:1-11), in which the other, until now cultic, contributions from the agricultural produce of the Holy Land were combined. The traditional festivals of pilgrimage retained their meaning as cultic high points, but henceforward, as the *Temple Scroll* shows (11QT 13–29), the sacrifice of animals, not bound to any dates of the year, acquired supreme importance for all calendrically determined festivals in the Temple. The agrarian sacrifices, on the other hand, could essentially be paid as tithes, independently of the dates of the cultic year, whenever the natural year provided the opportunity.

Thus, from an originally agrarian orientation of the offering of sacrifices at the three great pilgrimage festivals (cf., e.g., Deuteronomy 26), a system finally emerged in which, at all festivals, the sacrifice of animals in the Temple became the most important consideration. Furthermore, instead of the first-fruits of the barley, wheat, grapes, or olive harvest, available of course only at the right moment in the season, now at every feast, indeed at the daily sacrifice or *Tamîd,* the products available throughout the year in the same form were offered (flour, wine, and olive oil) — in merely symbolic quantities, it is true, compared with the amount of the tithe.

Contributions from the agricultural harvests were also no longer made for the special advantage of those priestly families expressly performing the Temple service at the time of the payment, but rather, ever new determinations of distribution ensured that they went to the priestly families given the right to this income. Whether the parts of the animal sacrifices, of slaughters performed at home, and of bread to which the priests were entitled were paid as tithes or as extra payments, can no longer be clearly established. At all events they were a solid source of income for the priests and their families.

The transition to the overall system of tithes that were independent of the time of year makes it understandable why the 364-day solar calendar, which gradually departed from the course of the natural year, could be relatively problem-free in terms of the practice of Temple worship, without it being necessary to insert appropriate extra weeks or months in order to even out the calendar with the natural year. The feasts of the cultic year now had mainly a ritual meaning. Practically, most sacrificial gifts were replaced in terms of the tithing prescriptions of these feasts.

Of course, the uncontested basis for the collection of all of these cultic gifts, as for any sharing in these products, continued to be in postexilic times as well the habitation of the Holy Land and its agricultural use. Judaism at that time was not yet a religion of the Book that would have included by virtue of equal title all persons around the world who were Israelites by origin and who guided their lifestyle according to the Torah. It was a religion of the Temple, oriented toward God's covenant with Israel, that covenant being firmly attached to the Jerusalem sanctuary, and it was a religion existing exclusively within the boundaries of the Holy Land (e.g., 11QT 59:1-13). Only *this* land's harvests were required in worship. Of course it could be questioned what concretely counted as "harvest of the land," and on what basis in property rights the obligation of the tithe in particular rested.

The point of departure for all further observations is the incontestable fact that, according to the biblical witness, the Jerusalem Temple never entered into YHWH's rights of ownership of the Holy Land as his representative or replacement. It had no real estate of its own beyond the outer walls of the Temple courts. As early as the time of the kings, parts of the land had come to be the property of the kings. At any rate, the city of Jerusalem, as the "City of David," was independent of Israelite tribal areas. The old Northern Kingdom had belonged almost entirely to pagans since 722 B.C. In postexilic times, the pagan overlords regarded the old royal possessions in Judea, too, as their property and leased it out for the benefit of the state treasury. They did the same with other lands that they had expropriated or forcibly acquired. The little that remained of the Holy Land to the Jews was legally regarded as the private property of the pagans. Thus the Holy Land as an entity against which cultic gifts could be legally assessed basically no longer existed at all.

In this situation, the Essenes conducted themselves in the middle of the second century B.C. in accordance with the biblical tradition. Just as their union did its best to join the scattered *people* of Israel together again in the Holy Land, so also should the dismembered *land* of Israel itself, distributed among so many private owners, be lawfully restored once more to God as its true proprietor.

The rededication of these property rights to God was not possible all at once, although practically the entire Holy Land was regarded as simply God's property. Had it been attempted, Gentiles, and Jews not living according to the Torah, would, as proprietors of parts of the Land, automatically have been included in the system of cultic gifts. But that was completely out of the question, owing to the purity and holiness prescriptions concerning all cultic gifts. The only way that remained was an ambitious, large-scale procedure by which the eligibility for worship of all Israelites living within the boundaries of the Holy Land would be investigated, and the private property only of those who proved to be blameless from a religious standpoint would be restored to God as the true proprietor of the Land.

Little by little, over the course of time, the entire land along with its inhabitants could in this way become God's property once more, especially if plots of land and fields were to be bought up from pagans and godless Jews, or appropriated for God as unlawfully acquired goods. More important than the quantitative proportion of the whole land obtainable at a given time, however, was the *qualitative* side of the matter: that the Holy Land should come into existence once more in Palestine at all, and should be gathered together legally as the property of God alone.

It is of the highest importance that the Essenes never planned to make themselves proprietors of the Holy Land. They simply acted as God's fiduciaries. The terminological accuracy of our language is evinced, for example, in the fact that as receiver of the fortune of a new candidate, the Essene union expressly designated itself *yaḥad 'ēl,* the union of *God* (1QS 1:12). God himself therefore became proprietor of the fortune being signed over. The board of the Essene union's real estate and property administration for the entire Holy Land was called *'ăṣat ḥibbûr yiśrā'ēl,* the "Israelite Cooperative Council" (CD 12:8). We learn of its existence only because it alone had the right to confiscate pagan property in the Holy Land. It is likewise revealing that the business of this panel was not to administer Temple affairs, but to function as an independent organ. Thus, the Temple now would function not as fiduciary in matters of material property, but only as receiver of certain *yield* from property.

The designation "Israelite Cooperative Council" further shows — as we likewise know from numerous other texts in the Qumran finds — that the community of goods of the Essene union was basically conceptualized as a pan-Israelite enterprise. Only because parts of Israel in the Holy Land, among them those holding political power, declined membership in this pan-Israelite union did the community of goods remain factually restricted to the organization of the Essenes. However, the concept of the community of goods was intended not for an exclusive group within Palestinian Judaism, but for the *entire people of God in the Holy Land.*

Those parts of Palestinian Judaism that, from 150 B.C. onward, remained aloof from the Essene union never strove for a similar comity of goods, but continued to orient themselves in various ways to rights of private property.

As early as the second century B.C., the Hasmonean rulers began to take possession once more of nearly the whole territory of the old twelve tribes of Israel, and to annex to their kingdom even bordering Gentile areas like the northern part of Idumea, the old Edom, and land east of the Jordan. All pagans whom they met in this expansion were either Judaized, if they chose to be, or put to death. Thus the Hasmoneans created a rich source of gifts for the Temple over which they ruled; nor were they particularly concerned with the actual purity and holiness of the circles of persons whom they now controlled, the manner in which the individuals had acquired their property, or how the contributions from that property arose. The important thing was that all individual Jews in this kingdom contribute their obligatory cultic gifts, which partly reached the Jerusalem Temple, to redound to the benefit of the personnel officiating at worship there, but partly — especially in the form of the old Levite tithe — reached the state treasury, including the public social-welfare offices.

Further-reaching perspectives were opened by the lunar calendar, with the Jewish festivals integrated into it — the calendar that Jonathan introduced at the Temple in 152 B.C. On the basis of this international calendar, the Jewish Diaspora outside Palestine could for the first time be included in the system of cultic gifts. The best opportunity for this was in the Temple tax, which, according to Exodus 30:11-16, all Israelites had to pay after the completion of their twentieth year. Included in this system of obligatory contribution were now those Israelites, too, who did not live in the Holy Land. The connection of the cultic gift with living in the Holy Land was deduced, at best, from the context of the Pentateuch, and not from the isolated evidence of a passage in the text, which alone was determinative for the Pharisaic expository method of the time.

Thus, as early as the beginning of the first century A.D., Philo of Alexandria reports it as an old, obvious custom that the Temple tax was collected in Egyptian Judaism as well and carried to Jerusalem every year on a fixed date by a delegation. If we accept corresponding information from Flavius Josephus and the Rabbinic tradition, then we must conclude that, from Hasmonean times Jews worldwide, from Rome to Mesopotamia, were included in the obligation to pay the Temple tax. They brought it to Jerusalem especially on the occasion of the three pilgrimage festivals — for example, Mesopotamian Jews at the Feast of Booths — and they took these opportunities to send to Jerusalem also other sacrifices prescribed by the Torah, or else corresponding monetary contributions. Here the connection of the cultic gifts with Israel's existence in the Holy Land is, in principle, completely surrendered — indeed, any connection of the gifts with right of ownership is finally renounced. Instead, the decisive thing now was one's personal membership in Israel as a worldwide people of God — the governing connection is to the Torah, instead of to existence in the land of God.

The Pharisees proceeded in like fashion. They demanded especially the exact observance of the purity and tithing precepts of the Torah, included every last garden vegetable in the calculation of that obligatory tithe (Matt. 23:23; Luke 11:42), and kept their personal possessions separate from those of other Jews. Especially in the case of agricultural yield, they regarded it as unnecessary for them to make up the tithe in case the farmer had not delivered it or it was doubtful whether he had. The Pharisees practiced community possession, however, only in the way that it was practiced in all synagogue communities, especially in the common possession of houses of prayer and schoolhouses.

Only by the Essenes was the tradition fully observed, or restored, of an Israel united in the Holy Land as the sole recipient of all of the salvation promised in the Torah. This end was served by the gathering of all property rights in their community of goods. But obviously the individual Essenes continued to be the personal possessors, with all traditional rights, of all that they had transferred to the "union of God" in terms of proprietorship. Essene farmers continued to cultivate their fields, vineyards, or orchards, and they and their families continued to live on the yield. Essene hired hands, service personnel, artisans, dealers, and other representatives of occupations whose capital consisted in skill, proceeded in the same way. Among members of such professions numbered especially priests and Levites with their families. As long as they practiced their profession, their proceeds, too, were under obligation of the tithe. At the same time, they and their families could live well on what was due to them from the sacrificial gifts or tithes of the other Israelites in the Holy Land.

Since the tithe had basically been intended for Temple worship, but the Essenes had from the beginning boycotted the sacrificial worship in the Jerusalem Temple because of the calendrically falsified order of worship there, the application of the tithe, in the meantime, until the restoration of the regular sacrificial worship, naturally had to be devoted to something else. The portions traditionally assigned to the personnel in charge of worship, of course, still benefited those priests and Levites who had become members of the Essene union. Additional sacrificial gifts from cattle farming and grain farming — therefore from the traditional priestly tithes — were applied by the Essenes essentially for their community meals, while the gifts from trade and professional income (the traditional Levite tithes) were applied especially for social purposes.

Obviously these were only basic principles. One could also derive an allocation of the tithe for special purposes from many other regulations pertaining to sacrifices and giving in the Torah. For example, the highest administrators of the Essenes were certainly prevented by the duties of their offices from also exercising a trade or profession by which they might gain their daily bread. But whether only persons were selected for leadership positions whose income from their own fortunes would suffice to maintain them, or to what extent they were compensated from the common treasury, we do not as yet know. There must have been some source for the enormous financial means that were necessary for the building and use of the Qumran settlement, together with the agricultural installations at Ain Feshkha. Did all of this materialize through the donations of well-to-do members, or was the surplus of the various community treasuries applied for these purposes? The Qumran texts, composed for the purpose of communicating far different things, unfortunately provide us with no information about this.

At any rate, it is certain that this type of community of goods placed the Essenes in a far better economic position than can be presupposed for the rest of the Jewish population of Palestine. The Essenes were not materially poor, but relatively rich! The cause of this relative wealth was the principle of internal economy that the type of community of goods practiced by the Essenes necessarily entailed, since the requirements of ritual purity and holiness extensively limited imports. For example, the Essene laborer bought his bread from an Essene baker, certain that the latter's flour came from the harvest of an Essene farmer who, for his part, had already paid the obligatory tithe on the yield of his harvest. Just as did the Pharisees, the Essenes spared themselves the expense of paying an extra tithe just to make sure it had been paid. In addition, however, all the income from the tithes remained in their own domain. What Pharisees and other Jews contributed to the Jerusalem Temple within the framework of the priestly tithe — to cultic personnel not of their group, therefore — served the Essenes to satisfy their own needs and spared them funds that otherwise would have been necessary. As for the Levite tithe, part of which would otherwise have gone to the cultic personnel at the Jerusalem Temple, and part to the general social-welfare fund and the state treasury, it was available in its entirety to the Essene union for its own social services.

Finally, the ethical rigorism of the Essenes sharpened their members' awareness of obligation not only with regard to the honesty of their tithing — the biblical sources themselves bemoan a lack of fidelity concerning these gifts — but also with regard to the economic use of their personal resources, their material possessions as well as their professional capabilities. When pious persons, conscious of their obligations, consider these resources and capabilities as gifts of God, they strive as earnestly as possible to increase their yield (cf. Matt. 25:14-30; Luke 19:12-27). For the Essenes, the contribution of their erstwhile private property to the "union of God" meant nothing less than its reacquisition as a gift from God.

The profits that the Essenes reaped thanks to their type of community of goods were at any rate so great that they were the only Jewish organization of their time to be able to afford to include nonmembers in their charitable system (*Jewish War* 2.134). This bears mentioning here mainly because the impression is often conveyed in the literature that the Essenes' renunciation of property drove them into personal poverty, asceticism, or even death by starvation. The diametrical opposite is the case. Precisely because of their manner of community of goods, there was no organized group in ancient Judaism as prosperous as the Essenes.

True, the Essenes called themselves the "congregation of the poor" (4QpPs^a 1–10 ii 10; iii 10). But with this designation they denoted only their poverty before God in the sense of the biblical piety of the poor, as the Psalter, for example, has it. Economic circumstances, on the other hand, come into view when the "Wicked Priest" Jonathan is reproached for unlawfully having "robbed the wealth of the poor," namely, the actual estate of the Essenes (1QpHab 12:9-10). At issue here are government measures regarding property rights, measures that redounded to the detriment of the Essenes, prejudicing their property — perhaps the confiscation, to the benefit of the state, of real estate to which Essenes laid claim — but not the deprivation of the socially poor by the wealthy of society. The one especially "robbed" by the Wicked Priest in this case was God. Otherwise the affair would by no means have been mentioned in a religious text such as the *Commentary on Habakkuk*.

Philo, Josephus, and Pliny the Elder themselves mistakenly assumed that the Essenes' community of goods was a community of *possession*, which excluded any private possession. Thereby they created a completely over-drawn picture of the relationships in question. Accordingly, the scholarly literature often sees the Essenes on analogy to the later, Christian monastic orders, in which there is no private possession. Actually, however, the Essenes' community of goods was expressly confined to the members' *rights of owner-ship* as the basis to be appealed to for the fulfillment of duties of contribution. With their possessions, the Essenes might even engage in trade, for example selling to other Jews the surplus of their grain harvests, or even selling to pagans the products of their workshops. Their ownership, on the other hand, was basically inalienable.

Whoever recklessly misappropriated community property had to make restitution in terms of the same value, or, alternatively, be excluded from community prayer services and meals for two months (1QS 7:6-8). As a general rule, in question here was movable property, such as a rented donkey that had simply disappeared, or community goods such as tithes whose trans-port had been carelessly entrusted to outsiders. Because it was often reasonable in such cases to suspect intentional theft on the part of others, in order to escape punishment the Essene who had been entrusted with the object in question had to swear that it had been actual theft. If this oath turned out to be perjured, not only the person taking the oath but all persons who had kept silent about the truth were punished with the even heavier sanction for perjury (CD 9:10-12). From a legal viewpoint, it is informative that the person in question was designated only as a *ba'al*, "possessor, holder," of the lost item, not as its proprietor. In Hebrew a construction with *hāyâ lô* could have served for the latter: "It was his property." But the legal proprietor, in all cases of this kind, was the Essene union.

The nice examples that Philo and Josephus adduce for the reality of the Essene community of goods actually belong in an entirely different category. According to their reports, any Essene who was traveling might lodge with any other Essene free of charge — that is, have free room and board for the night — and even receive new clothing or sandals if the condition of his own made it seem appropriate. This was nothing but a continuation of the hospi-tality that the Torah had already recommended be shown by every Israelite to his fellow. Customs of this kind have nothing to do with the Essene community of goods. Wonderment that the Essenes should practice such hospitality as a matter of course — however limited it might be to their fellow members — only goes to show how far the traditional norms of the ancient Israelite rights of guests had fallen out of use in the rest of Judaism. Many synagogue communities did the same, it is true. But in their time the Essenes turned out to be a shining example of the kind of Judaism that knew how to be generous in granting traditional hospitality to their fellows.

The Essenes' corresponding social legislation was nothing but the materialization of what had developed in postexilic times out of the old Levite tithes. The Levites themselves had nothing whatever to do with it any longer. They had long since been adequately cared for socially with contributions for the worship personnel of the Jerusalem Temple. These contributions came to the descendants of Levi along with the priests. The actual recipients of the Levite tithes had become, even in pre-Essene times, those socially underprivileged portions of Judaism that, in the biblical formulations, had only been included in the Levite tithes but not intended as its exclusive beneficiaries.

The concrete form of the Levite tithe around the middle of the second century B.C., and the manner in which it was built into the concept of the pan-Israelite community of goods in the Essene union, is shown, with all of the clarity that one could wish, in the relevant legislation. The main evidence is the passage in the *Damascus Document* 14:12-17. Following the terms of this legislation, social contributions were collected and administered by the Essene property administrators, although not by themselves personally; these contributions were allocated or paid out to the needy by independent personnel of the judiciary.

The acquisitions of the social fund resulted from the duty of making contributions out of income from all financially compensated services and professional or vocational activity, in the amount of the yield of "fully two [working] days per month" — in principle, then, ten percent, but monthly now, and no longer merely annually. This rough percentage emerges from the fact that, according to the 364-day solar calendar, the first month of the year, for example, always had only 8 working days, the second 25, the third and fourth 26 apiece, and so on. In the course of the entire year, 52 Sabbaths and 32 other feast days were days of rest. The remaining 280 days in the year were working days, for an average of 23.33 working days per month. One tenth of this figure would be 2.333 days. Hence the very rough standard of "fully two [working] days per month."

Payments from the social fund belonged by right to all Essenes who were regarded as socially "injured" — namely, as socially weak and therefore in need of support, or as of scanty means in terms of possessions and therefore in need of social promotion. In all, nine different kinds of those thus in need of support are named. The first six had already belonged to the classic clientele of social assistance in preexilic Israel, while the remainder were included only in postexilic times. The nine are (a) anyone lacking land or property; (b) those needing support owing to impoverishment; (c) those unable to earn a living owing to age or (d) physical handicap; (e) Israelites imprisoned or enslaved by pagans who have been ransomed; (f) brides whose families are unable to provide the obligatory dowry. The omission of widows and orphans is striking here. Evidently these groups were now adequately cared for under family law and were no longer, as once was the case, the main beneficiaries of social measures.

New categories vis-à-vis ancient Israelite tradition are, first, (g) "young men for whom employment is [economically] unavailable"; in this case it is probably a matter of financial aid for training in a trade, by which the beneficiary was helped to ply a trade of his own, to marry, and then to support himself together with his family through the income from his trade. Such assistance in acquiring training presupposes a spectrum of trades and professions that was by no means available as yet in overwhelmingly agrarian ancient Israel.

The next category bears on (h) contributions for the basics of someone's professional or industrial life — for example, for rent payments, or for the basic expenses of getting a store, workshop, transport business, or the like, started. Whether means of this kind were granted as lost contributions, or as repayable credit but without interest, remains an open question.

The last designation reads, (i) "And no member's house may be removed from their control." This cannot be a matter of payment to a third party of mortgages on the possession of a house by members, since in this case it would not be the social fund, but the property administration that would be responsible. In the case of social assistance, "his house" can only mean a member of the Essenes together with this person's family members.

Actually, then, it is a matter of redemption from a third party's claim to one's work — therefore liberation from so-called "debtor's slavery." The latter was customary in the Judaism of that time. It arose, for example, when a farmer, after a failed harvest, was in need of means to feed his family or to be able to buy seed grain, and it was possible to cancel the debt acquired to this end only through the hired work of family members. Any Jew who was a member of the Essenes had, according to this statute, the right to impose the burden of the discharge of his obligations on the social fund. Hence there were no "slaves" among the Essenes, but only "free," which fact Philo and Josephus especially celebrate (Philo, *Every Good Man is Free* 79; Josephus, *Antiquities* 18.21). The possession of male and female non-Jewish slaves, on the other hand, went without saying (CD 11:12; 12:10-11; cf., e.g., Exod. 20:10, 17; Deut. 5:14, 21).

Besides, the Essenes were forbidden to found business establishments in common with outsiders or with excluded Essenes, or together with such to engage in business with a third party. The Essenes regarded this sort of collaboration in business as an impermissible "mixture of property." Permissible, on the other hand, although subject to approval in each case, were trade relations on the part of individual members with outsiders, even with pagans. Of course, pagans could not be sold any produce of the land, which came under the tithe and were therefore counted as "sanctified" — nor any "pure" farm animals or birds, since it could not be ruled out that the buyer would offer these to pagan gods.

Further, trade with outsiders might be practiced only "from hand to hand"; thus, for example, no mutual long-term delivery contracts were made. The pagan usually offered money, or wares that were not produced in Palestine's domestic production, like papyrus scrolls from Egypt, metals, spices and incense from Arabia, lumber and textiles from Syria, supplementary grain from Asia Minor or Egypt in case of failed harvests, and so on.

Internal trade, on the other hand, was unrestricted in the Essene union. The widespread picture of the Essenes' community of ownership as a community of possessions, and of the concentration of everything Essene into the little Qumran settlement, has unfortunately had the effect that this area has not yet received the attention it deserves.

As far as possession was concerned, the individual Essenes and the enterprises conducted by them were altogether independent. Out of one's personal income, one paid everything necessary for living, including rent, lease, or business costs such as wages or the cost of buildings. The circumstance that every Essene, wherever possible, bought bread from an Essene baker, wine from an Essene vineyardist, and clothing from an Essene draper, tailor, or cobbler helped the various industries to guarantee their business and sales. All articles of clothing sold by Essenes corresponded to the Torah's prescriptions of purity. Meat from the Essene butcher was guaranteed to have been slaughtered in accordance with ritual prescriptions. In no sandal sold by an Essene shoemaker was any pigskin sewn. The only thing forbidden in the Essenes' domestic trade was profiteering. Probably fixed prices, as well, partially favored an exchange of goods over payments of money.

Ritual Baths, Prayer Services, and Ritual Meals

At sunrise, at midday with the sun at its zenith, and at sunset, all full members of the local groups of Essenes gathered for common prayer services. Their ritual followed the Temple liturgy. At the opening of their liturgies, priests had the ritual trumpets sounded. The prayer ritual required repeated prostrations in the sight of God. The direction in which the Essenes faced during prayer, as with all Jews of their time, was that of the Holy of Holies in the Jerusalem Temple (cf. pp. 175-76). The recitation of hymns was mostly reserved for the more complex services of the Sabbath and festival days. Readings from Scripture, customary in synagogue communities, were never practiced at Essene prayer services.

A common breakfast is never mentioned. At noon, and in the evening, the prayer service was followed by a common ritual meal, shared by all participants, in the assembly hall. These were abundant meals, with warm food, and fruit juices to drink — also wine, on the occasion of festivals. The order of seating at these meals strictly followed the internal hierarchy established annually at the covenant renewal ceremony, with the basic ranking of priests, Levites, other Israelites, and proselytes. Strictly obligatory was the presence of a priest, who held the precedence and, at the commencement of the meal, recited the blessing over the food and drink. Otherwise, silence reigned. Reading and liturgy were absent at the meal, as well. To conclude the meals, the presiding priest pronounced a prayer, at least according to Josephus' information (*Jewish War* 2.131). This is not expressly mentioned in the Qumran texts, as something that goes without saying.

The food and drink for these communal meals came from the natural produce belonging to priestly tithes, as well as from purchases, after what was due the priests, Levites, and their families personally had been divided off from the priestly tithes as a whole. However, because the Torah prescribed for the pilgrimage festivals that priests and Levites were to be included in the pilgrims' sacrificial banquet in the Temple area even after the performance of the sacrificial rites, the Essenes required — above and beyond all liturgical requirements — that at least one priest partake of the meal. His presidency was a consequence of his hierarchical precedence. Since, in practice, receipts from the priestly tithes were no longer bound to the ritual year and its festivals of donation, but were distributed over the year according to the various harvest seasons, daily community meals were held instead of the festival meals to be celebrated on such and such a date. During the times of the year without a harvest, it was disputed whether to apply to ritual meals the stores of natural produce at hand, or the ready cash that also came in regularly as part of the priestly tithes.

The Torah provided that only Israelite men of ritual age (twenty years completed and upward) were permitted to take part in the ritual meals in the Temple on the occasion of pilgrimage festivals, and then only if they were free of physical handicaps and were in a state of ritual purity. Accordingly, admitted to the Essenes' community meals were only full members who were free of handicaps — no women, and no minors. Also excluded from participation, however, were full members who temporarily found themselves in a condition of ritual uncleanness — for example, after sexual relations, or after the death of a family member — or who, on grounds of misconduct, had to keep their distance from the ritual community for some days, weeks, months, or even years. Until they were readmitted, they had to say their obligatory prayers privately and take their meals in the circle of their families. Thus, they temporarily lost the advantages of community board, nor was any replacement forthcoming from that community.

It is especially important to notice that the Essenes regarded the common prayer services, along with the meals that followed them, as ritual events in the sense of the Temple ritual. It was insufficient for participation, therefore, merely to have just completed the several days' rites of purification prescribed by the Torah in case of sexual intercourse or contact with the dead. Instead, immediately before entering the assembly hall, each participant also had to take an immersion bath, which in the Temple was prescribed only for priests about to perform service, but which the Essenes made a matter of obligation for all members equally, even for the prayer services at sunrise.

The corresponding bathing installations might be integrated into the assembly buildings, as in the Temple, provided they stood directly at the entrance to the hall, as in the Qumran settlement. In this respect we find something similar with Muslims today. In front of Eastern mosques are grooved channels built into the ground, along with benches, faucets, water conduits, and drains, where perfectly clean Muslims, who have just stepped out of the bathtub at home, can perform the ritual purifications prescribed by the Qur'an before they enter the mosque.

It was no different in ancient Judaism. Only, the Essenes prescribed these ritual purification procedures for each of their daily ritual gatherings, and instead of the cleansing only of hands, feet, and forehead, a ritual immersion of the entire body was required. That one first had to be physically clean was self-evident to the Essenes as well. The performance of the baths of immersion was a ritual obligation, not a bodily cleansing, nor did it have anything to do with forgiveness of sin.

The Essenes' erection of special places of assembly was only an interim solution of necessity, until such time as a worship in the Jerusalem Temple should be restored that would be in conformity with the Torah. All of the liturgical ceremonies traditionally prescribed for the Temple worship, the prayers that accompanied the sacrificial ritual, and the common meals of those participating, found their substitutes in suitable spaces in the Essenes' private homes or in buildings constructed ad hoc for these purposes.

Once the Essenes possessed such spaces, they naturally used them also for their council meetings, judiciary sessions, common readings from Scripture, and instruction — that is, they used them as schools and community houses at the same time. But these further uses were not bound to "prayer houses" (CD 11:22). They could just as well take place in other private houses or, to some extent, even in the sacred precincts, as is shown by the example of the Essene Judas, who taught his pupils in the Jerusalem Temple in the year 103 B.C.

The coming into being of the Essene houses of prayer had nothing to do with spatial distance from the Jerusalem Temple, unlike the appearance of synagogues in Galilee or in the Diaspora. The purpose of their foundation was exclusively to make it possible to celebrate the Temple worship despite the adverse conditions for which the Maccabee Jonathan was responsible as high priest in the year 152 B.C., especially through his introduction of the lunar calendar as the official Jerusalem order of worship. The Essenes renounced only sacrificial altars and the offering of the altar sacrifice *in natura,* especially since the Torah had expressly limited the performance of an actual sacrificial rite to the central place of worship (Deuteronomy 12), that is, to the Temple in Jerusalem.

Marriage, Family, and Upbringing

The Essenes are often presented as generally celibate. Nowhere in the Qumran texts, however, is there the slightest reference to celibacy. It would never occur to anyone who read these texts without preconceived ideas that the Essenes might have been hesitant with regard to marriage, let alone renounced it. How is this contradiction to be explained?

In ancient Judaism, a man's intentional renunciation of marriage was regarded as a serious transgression of the Torah. After all, God's very first command, for all human beings, on the sixth day of creation, was, "Be fruitful and multiply" (Gen. 1:28). In Judaism this command was always understood as the foundation of all human beings' obligation to marry. In all traditional Jewish literature, only one rabbi is known not to have married, because he held the study of the Torah to be more important than taking care of a family of his own. Ordinarily such misconduct was heavily criticized as a grave transgression of God's order of creation (Babylonian Talmud, *Yebamôt* 63b). Corresponding to the case of the rabbi we have Jesus' words concerning "eunuchs for the sake of the kingdom of heaven" (Matt. 19:12), by which he may have particularly wished to defend his own celibacy. Both cases are rare exceptions in ancient Judaism. Nothing of the kind can be cited for the case of the Essenes.

Nevertheless, the Essenes offered adequate occasion for being regarded as living celibate lives. There are essentially three different such considerations, which, however, have nothing to do with celibate intentions.

Pious Jews go to their synagogues every Sabbath, and they do so as a family. That the women, once inside the synagogue, withdraw into a side area or to a gallery above, and only the men constitute the worship service, is invisible to the outside observer. The Essenes actually went to their assembly houses thrice daily. But no one ever saw a woman accompany them into the hall, not even for the preparation of the meal. Thus, in public, the Essenes appeared to other Jews of Palestine as a purely male society.

Even in ancient Judaism, boys were usually regarded as of age for religious purposes, and thereby capable of marriage, with the completion of their thirteenth year. Since the founding of a family also called for economic, and often professional, independence, they usually married only when they were sixteen or seventeen. The Essenes, however, required, in principle, the completion of the twentieth year as a prerequisite for religious majority and marriage. And so young Essene men were still living in the single state for years, when their contemporaries had long since married. That was striking and was regarded by other Jews as a general reserve with regard to marriage.

The third reason for the notion that the Essenes practiced celibacy was the most important and in this context the most operative. The Essenes permitted a man to marry only once, instead of requiring only monogamy, which was the only restriction elsewhere in ancient Judaism (where, for that matter, polygamy was still allowed in principle).

As early as 400 B.C., more severe standards were established by Jerusalem priests. Even the king was forbidden to have more than one wife; only after her death might he marry another (11QT 57:15-19). The Essenes followed an even stricter interpretation of the Torah. Following the judicial legislation of the time for the solid establishment of the facts of a case, they even adduced three passages in the Torah as proof of the requirement of lifelong single marriage for all men (CD 4:20–5:2).

Taken by itself, Genesis 1:27 could be very easily understood in the sense that, from the beginning, God had created humanity in two sexes, "partly male and partly female." Read in conjunction with Genesis 2, however, according to which at the beginning of humanity Adam and Eve had been created by God as two individual persons, Genesis 1:27 was interpreted generally in the sense of "a man and a woman." The Essenes understood this primordial doubleness still more strictly, as "basically in pairs." For them — according to God's order of creation — every man and one, very specific woman belonged to each other for life.

The second witness in this sense for the Essenes was the narrative of the Flood, according to which Noah — the exemplary righteous person — and his sons entered and left the ark each with one wife, therefore strictly in pairs (Gen. 6:18; 7:7, 13[!]; 8:16, 18; 9:1, and, correspondingly, 1:28). Thereby was established a binding norm for all further humanity, which according to the biblical presentation is of course entirely sprung from Noah: humanity's existence in pairs, fundamentally in a single marriage, as a matter of principle.

The third proof is Deuteronomy 17:17, which actually reads merely, "And he [the king] must not acquire many wives for himself" — therefore especially is King Solomon, with his "seven hundred wives of princely rank and three hundred concubines" (1 Kings 11:3), not to be emulated. But the Essenes understood the corresponding Hebrew expression in Deuteronomy 17:17 as "no plurality of wives": even the King, in their opinion, was permitted to have only one wife during his lifetime.

But now the Essenes' lifelong single marriage — alone admissible, because grounded through the Torah's triple testimony, but also an inescapable requirement of every man by virtue of the order of creation — had considerable consequences in one's practical life. Every man was to marry as soon as possible after the completion of his twentieth year. The bride, who was usually sought out by the man's father — in accordance with preparatory negotiations with the bridal family — was just twelve years old, in the custom of the time, or only a little older. Now she must bear a child year after year, as many boys as possible, do the housework as well, help with the farmwork, and, in her "free time," weave wicker baskets and foot mats and produce wool and cloth, as was expected of women in the course of "housework."

Given these exhausting living conditions, and the fact that women this young had in no way yet acquired the physical resistance of adults, it is no wonder that so few of them reached an age of more than twenty-five. Many died prematurely of puerperal fever, or — not least because of their weakened constitution — from other diseases, were sickly, or were unfruitful, which could be grounds for divorce and so of a return of the no longer useful woman to the family of her origin. Men, on the other hand, were so often older than sixty years that the Essenes expressly established that, after reaching this age, no one might any longer exercise a public office, since then "his spirit" is "in decline" (CD 10:7-10; cf. 14:6-8).

Even when the wife died early, or when the marriage was childless, no Essene was permitted to acquire another woman, neither a wife nor a concubine. Owing to women's abbreviated longevity, the time during which an Essene was married lasted on the average certainly no more than ten years. On that account, most Essenes were unmarried indeed, but not as lifelong celibates — rather either because they had not yet reached the late age at which Essenes married, or because they were widowers or divorced. Before and after the time their marriages lasted, they lived with their families, but without the possibility of a second marriage.

Relations in the Essene groups in the cities and villages of Palestine were of course not as extreme as in the Essene Qumran settlement. As the cemetery finds show, the men in Qumran died on the average at about age thirty. Hard working conditions, as well as trying climatic conditions, certainly contributed considerably to these early deaths. Only some ten percent of those working in Qumran lived there with their families (see above, p. 48). Many others will not have expected their wives and children to live in Qumran or Ain Feshkha, but will have left them home and visited them there occasionally. Therefore we must not regard the extreme conditions of Qumran as representative of Essene circumstances in general.

Together with the fact that Essenes everywhere gathered in their community houses for prayer and meals several times a day, and on all of these occasions the men were alone together, the late marriage age and single marriages, with their consequently high quota of unmarried, encouraged the widespread conception that the Essenes essentially lived without marriage. Josephus himself, who knew Palestine so well, portrayed them thus. According to his representation, the Essenes did not reject marriage on principle (*Jewish War* 2.120-21), but only a few of them actually lived with wives (2.160-61), whom they did not allow to participate in their worship gatherings (*Antiquities* 18.21).

This realistic view of relations among Essenes was exaggerated by many other Jewish authors, like Philo of Alexandria, into an ideal of general celibacy. They sought to demonstrate to their pagan readers that the much maligned Judaism could show forth, in the form of so great a "school of philosophy" as that of the Essenes, a community that paid homage to the ideal of celibacy, which could always be accepted along with the Pythagoreans, who in this respect were so much admired by the Greeks as a shining example. Pliny the Elder similarly exaggerated relations in Qumran on the basis of a report given to him by certain Jews (see above, p. 58).

Today the Qumran finds demonstrate the concrete presuppositions that gave credibility to this idealistic picture. They also show that in reality all Essenes, in the faithful following of the divine order of creation, had to marry.

Nevertheless, the old reports of the Essenes' celibacy on principle continue to shape opinion. At the beginning of Qumran research, it was frequently supposed that the Essenes living in Qumran in particular were indeed celibate, while those dwelling elsewhere in the country were usually married. Since the discovery of women's graves in the Qumran cemeteries, the notion of a celibacy on principle has been transferred instead to an "inner circle." As evidence, the especially high norms of priestly purity and holiness among the Essenes are cited, which for all who actually held to them would have necessarily excluded a married life.

The starting point of such interpretations is the fact that the Essenes regarded themselves provisionally — until the traditional calendar and order of worship would be once more installed in Jerusalem — as the Temple of God on earth.

Accordingly, their daily assemblies and their whole lifestyle always had to meet the demanding norms of purity and holiness that traditionally applied to priests, Levites, and other Israelites during participation in the Temple worship. Now, if all Essenes were, so to speak, constantly engaged in worship, would not marriage, whose principal end is the procreation of children but which nevertheless necessarily involves a polluting sexual activity, be generally out of the question for them?

This view is completely overdrawn for four main reasons. First, in the Torah reproduction as a commandment of creation has precedence and superiority over all commands having to do with worship. Second, according to Leviticus 15:18 sexual intercourse renders its subject unclean only for one day, and not for a longer period of time. Third, the Essenes had so ordered their married life that sexual intercourse was confined to a wife's fertile years, and even during this time was practiced only rarely, so that the cultic impairment was altogether minimal. Fourth and last, it is anything but demonstrable that the Essenes had internally different norms for purity and holiness. Rather, all of these norms held for all full members in the very same way.

How did Essene marriages look in practice? Young men permitted to marry the children, practically, to whom they were engaged only after the latter had had three successive regular menstrual periods without side effects. Further, the Essenes had to abstain from sex during the seven-day period that began with the onset of menstruation, during which time, according to Leviticus 15:19, the woman was accounted unclean. This observance had the further effect that copulation occurred precisely at the high point of the woman's fertility. If a pregnancy resulted, any further sexual intercourse was forbidden according to Leviticus 12:4-5 until at least thirty-three days after the birth of a boy, or sixty-six days after the birth of a girl. Even in that case, the resumption of menstruation had to be awaited. If it did not resume, there could be no further sexual intercourse.

In order to have intercourse, Essenes living in Jerusalem had to leave the city and seek out quarters elsewhere (CD 12:1-2). This determination shows indirectly how relatively seldom sexual intercourse must have been practiced, and that it was practiced only for the procreation of children. The personal cultic defilement of those engaging in it was tolerated for the sake of the higher goal, but the Holy City had to be spared.

The prescriptions of the Torah were rigid in any case; in addition, they were broadly interpreted. Thus, during an average of at most ten years of married life an Essene would have sexual intercourse no more than some twenty times, and the number of days on which he was ritually unclean on these particular grounds was just as few. Much more often, ritual uncleanness in practice probably occurred through involuntary nocturnal ejaculations of semen, which, according to Leviticus 15:16, rendered its subject unclean for the same period of time as did intercourse. Only castrated men could have lived up to the special purity and holiness norms that are hypothetically postulated for the Essenes' "inner circle" or "elite leaders"; but castration excluded its subject from ritual worship lifelong (Lev. 21:20; Deut. 23:2). And so the hypothesis so often and so confidently advanced that some Essenes, at least, must have practiced lifelong celibacy is void of any plausibility. In contrast, one should keep in view that the high priest especially, as the highest ritual officeholder, *had* to be married if he wished to practice his office and needed at least one male offspring in order to bequeath that office.

If an Essene's wife died in her all too early years, traditionally there were wet nurses, and male and female maintenance persons who looked after the household and reared the children. With the completion of their tenth year, boys began to be instructed in everything that adults wishing to become Essenes had to learn more solidly during their minimum three years' admissions procedure. At twenty years of age, the "birthright Essene" could become a full member and marry (1QSa 1:6-11).

Entry, Legislation, and Exclusion

The Essenes' three-year-minimum entry procedure before attaining full membership is clearly attested by the Qumran texts as well as by the reports of ancient authors, and it is the surest proof that the inhabitants of Qumran were Essenes. No other group of ancient Judaism had such an extensive entry procedure.

Wives, as well, were members of the Essenes, although of course with fewer rights and with a limited participation in ritual activities. In any case, on religious and economic grounds Essene men married, if possible, only virgins from Essene families. These girls' instruction in matters of the Torah probably began with the completion of their tenth year, just as with the boys; but it ended with marriage, soon after completion of their twelfth year. Their religious education was terminated on the occasion of first access to the ritual bath, which was incumbent on wives especially after menstruation and child-bearing before they were permitted sexual contact with their husbands.

In the case of the entry of outsiders into the Essenes, first access to the ritual immersion after the first year of probation was bound up with the transfer of all of their personal property to the Essene union. This property was listed in a special account until full membership was conferred (see above, p. 177). Probably the procedure was the same with wives. But since they could never become full members, their dowry and whatever else they had brought by way of property or inheritance rights remained their personal property all of their lives.

In case of divorce or the death of the husband, this property then served for a woman's continued material security. This was important not least of all because the one-marriage principle of course ruled out remarriage for widows and divorced women, and therefore being cared for by a new husband (cf. 1 Cor. 7:10-11). At the same time this procedure with regard to property rights explains why widows are not mentioned in the Essene catalogue of customary social cases (CD 14:12-17).

For all kinds of problematic legal cases, the Essenes had their own internal judicial system overseen by a number of legal officers and courts. It corresponded fairly extensively to relationships that are later evinced in the case of Jewish Christian communities (Matt. 18:15-17; cf. 5:23-24).

The mildest kind of punishment for a fault was personal admonition by a single fellow-Essene. It was reserved for *unconscious,* minor transgressions. The reprimand of the transgressor had to take place before sunset on the same day as the observed misbehavior. Its purpose was to prevent a repetition of the fault. There was no provision for penalties in such cases.

If it was a matter of serious misconduct, or if the culprit proved recalcitrant, the reprimand was to be made in the presence of witnesses and officially reported to the competent court, so that an injunction could be handed down against a repetition of the fault. In all cases of *conscious* transgression of the Torah or of Essene statutory norms deriving from the Torah, the courts were responsible from the outset in any case. Depending on the seriousness of the transgression or the number of witnesses, the local courts could either leave it unpunished and only issue an injunction against its repetition (cf. above, pp. 135-36), or they could impose a sentence. If the accused refused to admit guilt or alleged that the penalty was excessive, then the case was transferred to the central court of the Essenes, for decision by the supreme authority, from which there was no appeal.

The Essenes' local courts consisted of four priests or Levites and six regular Israelites, although in some cases judgments could be rendered by a smaller number (CD 10:4-10). The highest court always had twice that number of regular Israelites, twelve, and in addition, three priests (1QS 7:27–8:4). But there were also cases in which decisions were handed down jointly by a "plenary assembly" at least a hundred members strong, among whom in the earlier years the Teacher of Righteousness as high priest had reserved to himself all competence to hand down decisions, or among whom special plenary powers were granted to the Zadokite priests.

The punishments imposed by these courts were first of all those prescribed in the Torah for particular offenses. Over and above these — or in some cases as alternatives to them — were fixed catalogues of sanctions ranging from temporary curtailment of the culprit's rations at community meals, to temporary exclusion from all ritual community events as well as from collaboration in the various councils, to exclusion for life.

Full exclusion seems also to have begun to be imposed by the Essenes especially as a substitute for all or some death sentences and their execution. For them, organizational exclusion was worse than death. After all, it meant the complete and irrevocable exclusion of the accused and his family from eternal salvation (cf. Heb. 6:1-8; 10:26-31; 12:15-17). The Essenes were strictly forbidden any contact with excluded persons. In serious cases — such as doing business with an excluded person — the Essene in question was expelled and had to renounce without compensation all of the property values that he had brought with him at his entry into the Essene union.

The basis of the Essenes' judicial decisions was first and foremost the Torah, supplemented by the corpus of acknowledged statutes that appears at the conclusion of the *Damascus Document,* in the form of older versions along with 1QSa and 1QS 5–9. These statutes were regarded as flowing entirely from the Torah and as basically standing in harmony with it — similar to the valuation of the Mishnah and the Talmud in later, Rabbinic Judaism. Older sources of law from pre-Essene times, such as the *Temple Scroll* or *Jubilees,* were used by the Essenes in the shaping of their own statutes, it is true, but they had no "canonical" dignity of their own and therefore could not be appealed to as acknowledged bases of judicial decisions.

Most of the cultic, economic, and civil or organizational regulations of the Essene statutes as well as the demands contained in the *Directive of the Teacher to Jonathan* (4QMMT), and practically all regulations of the sort that the Rabbis later designated halakah and that we today call ethics, were in no way "invented" out of whole cloth by the Essenes themselves. Almost all of their legal and ethical regulations represent the acceptance, for continued use, of what had already been developed in the postexilic Judaism of Palestine, in pre-Essene times — especially by priests of the Jerusalem Temple — in their concrete application of the Torah and the formation of certain of its regulations. Much of this has become known to us for the first time through the Qumran finds and therefore is often regarded as specifically Essene. Actually, however, it had already been the common property of Palestinian Judaism previously, or at least had been the prevailing doctrinal opinion of the Jerusalem priesthood and accordingly the common traditional heritage of all groups that formed from the middle of the second century B.C. onward.

Manifold research would be necessary in order to shed more light on the individual traditional traits of Essene legislation. Symptomatic of the general state of our findings, however, are two very different, rather broad results.

In 1922 a celebrated study by the Jewish Talmudic scholar Louis Ginzberg first appeared under the title *Eine unbekannte jüdische Sekte.* The book was privately published at first but went through several reprintings and in 1976 was finally issued in a revised, English version by a New York firm with the title *An Unknown Jewish Sect.* The book represents a very detailed investigation of everything that was known at that time about the *Damascus Document* in relation to Rabbinic tradition. The author came to the conclusion that the "sect" investigated by him — the Qumran finds prove that it was the Essenes — was essentially of a *Pharisaic* nature.

More recent research, on the other hand, especially on the part of Jewish scholars, shows that many of the Essenes' judicial regulations coincide with rulings that were later classified by the Rabbis as specifically *Sadducean.* In reality, this traditional material — still often considered "sectarian" today — came extensively from the Essenes, the Sadducees, and the Pharisees *jointly.* The Essenes just held to the sacred tradition more strictly than did others.

The Teachings of the Essenes

According to Jewish understanding, religious doctrine has essentially to do with those organizational, juridical, and ethical requirements that have already been presented here. What Christians designate as theology, for Jews belongs largely to the area of private philosophical speculation and has no religious dignity. What counts is religious *practice,* not dogmatics.

Accordingly, nearly everything left to present here was not the Essenes' teaching in the proper sense, but a series of *guiding ideas* that were more or less self-evident to them, but concerning which one could often have a different opinion, usually without such differences being ascribed any essential importance.

The basic teaching of the Essenes was Torah piety. This implied, as it did with all Jews, faith in the one God, beside whom there are no other gods, who had created heaven and earth, who had chosen the people of Israel and led them out of slavery in Egypt, who had made his covenant with them on Sinai, and, finally, had led them into the Holy Land. It is simply in their strict connection of all salvation for Israel to its *presence in the Holy Land* that the Essenes are to be distinguished from many of their Jewish contemporaries. The Essenes regarded Jews living in the worldwide Diaspora as rejected by God unless they returned to the Holy Land before the Last Judgment. Likewise, the Essenes believed that all of those Jews within the Holy Land who failed to follow the will of God revealed in the Torah with that clarity and earnestness which characterized the Essenes themselves were about to be struck by God's punishment in the Last Judgment. Outside the pan-Israelite union of the Essenes in the Holy Land, there could ultimately be no salvation, neither for Jew nor for Gentile.

This rejection, so characteristic of the Essenes, not only of everything pagan but also of everything within contemporary Judaism that was irrecon-

cilable with obedience to the Torah, gave the Essenes their exceptional position. This place was neither sectarian nor dissident; it was merely characterized
by the consistent preservation of the main current of Jewish tradition, as that
stream had developed over the first four centuries since the Exile. In this
sense, the Essenes' only teaching was a Torah piety according to tradition.
Even in the title "Teacher of Righteousness," the main point is that its bearer
must be concerned with the preservation and observance of the Torah piety
that had been handed down, together with its cultic associations.

       During the first four centuries since the Exile, Palestinian Judaism had
of course absorbed manifold cultural and religious influences that preexilic
Israel had not yet known, but which for the Essenes belonged to the firm rock
of received tradition. In most cases it must have been those returning from
the Diaspora who brought such innovations along. Some examples from the
Egyptian Jewish Diaspora would be the new order of worship according to
the 364-day solar calendar, introduced at the Jerusalem Temple as early as the
sixth century B.C.; the elaboration of the books of Jeremiah and Baruch; or
the introduction of a Jewish-priestly version of the Hymn to the Sun of
Akhenaten (Amenophis IV, 1372-1355 B.C.) into the biblical Psalter (Psalm
104). From the Babylonian Jewish Diaspora, the elements introduced in
Palestine by returnees from there were especially the sciences of cosmology
and astronomy; the apocalypticism that was linked to these; ancient Iranian
dualism; and a determinism to the effect that the whole history of the world
and humankind, including the personal destiny of each individual, had been
immutably established from the beginning.

Angels and Demons

The Qumran finds show the influence of surrounding cultures on Palestinian
Judaism partly in the form of pre-Essene writings, partly in the extension of
these at the hands of the Essenes. The conveyor and mediator of the corresponding scientific materials was essentially the *maśkîl* — the "scholar" —
a new kind of officeholder among the postexilic worship personnel. His
principal task, however, was not the service of worship at the altar of sacrifice,
but the teaching of wisdom. The latter consisted not only in transmitting
knowledge to a group of students, but also in the professional application of
such knowledge, for instance in exorcism, the most widespread method used
in the healing of the sick at that time. The "scholar" was not a priest, but
usually a Levite.

       In modern terms, the professional field of a Jewish scholar of this sort
would be, in the broadest sense, angelology — the teaching on angels. In
preexilic Israel, angels appear only very sporadically, for instance when God

himself, with two "men," visits Abraham (Genesis 18); or when two male strangers are guests of his brother Lot (Genesis 19); or when Jacob wrestles with an angel who stands for God himself (Gen. 32:23-31). In postexilic times, by contrast, all of God's activity in heaven and on earth, until the time of his coming intervention at the Last Judgment, was basically thought of as only mediated. The mediating powers between God and the human being — for good as well as evil — were the angels.

From the viewpoint of the history of religions, Jewish angelology absorbed thousands of primary and secondary divinities, primarily Canaanite, then especially Assyrian-Babylonian; ranged them in hierarchical groups with differentiated areas of competence; and subjected them to God as his servants or instruments. There were two hierarchies, corresponding to the old Iranian dualism — the good angels, with the "Prince of Light" at their head, and the evil, led by the "Angel of Darkness." In principle the two hierarchies had equal numbers of angels, and each hierarchy was as powerful as the other (1QS 3:17–4:1; cf. 4:15-26).

In order to render this kind of angelology intelligible in its main traits, three of its groupings may be cited, the archangels, the angels of worship, and the demons.

The Essenes had already received a doctrine of four archangels, also called "angels of the presence," since they alone of all creatures stood in God's presence at the highest point of all heaven and received their tasks directly from God. The highest-ranking of these four was called *Michael* ("Who [else] is like God?"). As guardian angel and warrior against God's enemies, Michael was especially responsible for the people of Israel and would be active in the coming Last Judgment. In the second place stood *Gabriel* ("Strength of God"), responsible for all revelations of God as well as for their interpretation in the case of apparitions in dreams. In the New Testament, he reveals to the priest Zechariah the birth of John the Baptist (Luke 1:19), and to the Virgin Mary the birth of Jesus (Luke 1:26); in the Qur'an, he conveys the messages of Allah to Muhammad. Third place was held by *Uriel* ("Light of God"), who was responsible for the hosts of the heavenly lights and therefore was also called *Sariel* ("God's Supreme Commander"). With his myriads of lower angels, he was to see that all of the stars in heaven followed their regular courses and to take care that the sun and moon be laden with the correct proportions of fire at their daily rising. Accordingly, Uriel was also responsible for the zodiac and the horoscope. The fourth of the group was *Raphael* ("God Heals"), lord of the realm of the dead and of the resurrection of the dead, also responsible for all healing of the sick through prayer and exorcism. Through these four supreme powers God directed events in the world according to his creative will.

The angels of worship, symbolized in ancient Israel by the cherubim

on the Ark of the Covenant in the Holy of Holies (Exod. 25:17-22; cf.
1 Kings 6:23-28), represented God at the Temple worship; brought the
sacrifices, hymns, and prayers of the worshiping community into God's
presence; and in the other direction, mediated God's blessing for Israel.
Jacob's ladder, in Jacob's dream at Bethel (Gen. 28:10-22), illustrates in an
especially beautiful way the function of these angels in the act of worship.
Scholars of the Jerusalem Temple worship in pre-Essene times composed
the *Angelic Liturgy*, whose content is based on the correspondence of the
earthly with the heavenly, a correspondence guaranteed in turn by the
presence of the angels in earthly worship. The Essenes accepted these ideas
from their tradition and extended them. Not least of all for this reason, their
prayer services had to offer the highest degree of ritual purity and holiness;
their services had to be free of the presence of women and any other
impurity, because only thus was the presence of the angels at these services
guaranteed. According to a still unpublished Qumran text, God has his
angels, whom he can send forth everywhere; but we have no one whom we
might send forth from us to God in heaven; however, the presence of the
angels in our ritual assemblies guarantees that our deeds, prayers, and
hymns will be borne up to God and that we shall receive his blessing.

The demons were the bad angels. They, too, had been created by God
(1QS 3:15–4:1) but had subsequently gone their own ways (Gen. 6:1-4), and
even before the Flood they had become the mightiest power in the world
opposed to God. Their headquarters was thought to be likewise in heaven, as
is illustrated by Jesus' words, "I watched Satan fall from heaven like a flash
of lightning" (Luke 10:18; cf. John 12:31; Rev. 12:7-12). The plunge of the
angel of darkness from heaven signals the imminent end of the power of evil
in the world.

For the Essenes, who usually called him *Belial,* and for the tradition that
preceded them, Satan with his hosts was a power that influenced everything
heavenly and earthly. His cosmic might was best recognizable from the fact
that he managed year after year to have the course of the sun lag behind the
364-day calendar that was faithful to creation, by 1.25 days, as well as to
darken the face of the sun or the moon on occasion, or make stars shoot down
from the firmament. On earth, the bad angels wrought all of the disturbances
of the order of creation — catastrophic floods as well as sweltering droughts;
hailstorms and failed harvests; devastating wars; human sin; deformities,
illness, and suffering; all need and death.

Human beings could do little against this power of evil. Their principal
tool was the power of God, which was exercised through the good angels.
But human beings could intervene to a limited extent. Especially owing to
the pre-Essene Enoch apocalypses, the main groups of the bad angels were
also known, as well as the name of their leader. Therefore it was known which

angel was individually responsible for which diseases, types of bad weather, and so on. One who could seize evil by name had it in his power, and through an appeal to a higher-ranking power on the opposite side, for example that of an archangel along with the host of those under his authority, could ban the evil — make it incapable of activity. In this way one could heal the sick, avert a threatening storm, or bring rain over the parched earth.

The science of exorcism, tabooed in ancient Israel, became familiar to Jews of the Diaspora in Mesopotamia and Egypt, and they developed it in Palestine as early as the Persian era (sixth to fourth century B.C.). The Essenes adopted this set of tools in the form of special knowledge that had come into existence before their time, developed it further, and applied it in practice. Hence their reputation as outstanding scientists and physicians. The broader population also turned to them in a variety of needs.

Our enlightened world no longer puts much stock in rain-making or healing the sick by prayers of conjuration. But in the world of the Essenes, other perspectives and standards still held. Piety will necessarily show itself precisely in its practical effects. No one would have attended to Jesus' words about the "Kingdom of Heaven," that is, the Reign of God on earth, had such words not been related to concrete deeds of might on the part of God in the presence of Jesus, as recorded in the New Testament Gospels (cf., e.g., Matt 12:28; Luke 11:20).

The Essenes regarded the teachings concerning the angels that they had received as especially important secret knowledge that was not to be revealed. Only those who had become full Essene members might be initiated into it. The revelation of angels' names to outsiders was reckoned as one of the especially weighty transgressions (*Jewish War* 2.142), punishment for which was contained by anticipation in the self-curse of the entry oath (1QS 2:11-18) and which entailed exclusion for life if discovered.

End Time, Last Judgment, Messiah, and Time of Salvation

Even before the Essenes had come into being, broad circles of Palestinian Judaism were firmly convinced that the end of the age was near. We see it, for example, in the biblical book of Daniel, which appeared in 164 B.C., or in its contemporary composition, the *War Rule* from Qumran. The only new thing was that the Teacher of Righteousness was the first to relate the biblical books of the prophets to events in the present end phase of world history. His starting point was that he was personally to experience God's Last Judgment and the beginning of Israel's time of salvation. When he died, around 110 B.C., the Essenes began to expect the onset of these events at first for the year 70 B.C. and then, from the middle of the first century B.C., for A.D. 70 (see above, p. 133). Thus, the Essenes always lived in the expectation of the end of current conditions, but only in certain phases of their history did they live in *immediate* anticipation of the changes they awaited. Usually their orientation was shifted to a relatively distant time — to reliably calculated moments in a remote future assigned for the Last Judgment and the time of salvation, indeed, even beyond the life expectancy of all of those on the present scene.

Holding a special place in the Essenes' orientation to the future was their expectation of the Messiah. The form in which this expectation was current in the time of Jesus (the awaiting of an *individual* figure in the *future* — if possible, a descendant of King David — who would rule Israel with justice and annihilate its enemies) was not yet common in pre-Essene times. Probably it first arose during the lifetime of the Teacher of Righteousness, who was at any rate familiar with it and who made it binding on the Essenes.

Messiah means "the anointed one." In particular, senior priests of sanctuaries, and kings, were anointed in ancient Israel on the occasion of their induction into office. In postexilic times, correspondingly, the high priest was anointed. At the end of the sixth century B.C., the prophet Zechariah referred to the current high priest, Joshua, and the Persian governor, Zerubbabel, as "the two anointed" of God (Zech. 4:14). Here a priestly and a royal "Messiah" were not awaited for the *future;* rather, specific, identifiable persons of the present were ascribed the special quality of being anointed by God himself. The high priest Joshua had of course already been duly anointed at his induction into office, but not the Persian governor Zerubbabel. This ritual act of anointing was, however, by no means to be belatedly performed in Zerubbabel's case; rather, he was reckoned as anointed through God's Holy Spirit.

Likewise, the Persian King Cyrus was called *mĕšîhô,* "his [= God's] anointed," or "the Messiah" (Isa. 45:1). After all, it was doubtless the Spirit of God himself who inspired Cyrus to issue the edict of 538 B.C. that was so extraordinarily favorable to Israel. Later, the biblical prophets, whose calling by God was reckoned retroactively as their induction into office, were also regarded as "Spirit-anointed." Accordingly, the biblical prophets are repeatedly designated as *mĕšîhâw,* "his [God's] anointed," in the Qumran texts as well (1QM 11:7-8; CD 2:12-13; 6:1; 4Q521 2 ii 1, 8, 9).

The messianic predictions of the biblical writings bearing on the future were, in the pre-Essene Judaism of the second century B.C., interpreted as referring not to individual figures, but collectively to the people of Israel as the future agent of salvation. So the "one like a son of man" who would be sent by God in the future to rule the world is Israel as the "holy people of the Most High" (Dan. 7:13-14, 27). The entire people of Israel as a collectivity is the corresponding referent of the prediction of the "star . . . from Jacob" and the "staff from Israel" (Num. 24:17-19) in 1QM 11:6-7 (context!). Indeed, Israel even praises its exaltation into the company of the angels in the first person singular, in 4QM^a 11 i 11-18. Here we have a continuation of biblical perspectives and formulations found especially in the Servant Songs of Second Isaiah (Isa. 42:1-9; 49:1-6; 50:4-11; 52:13–53:12). None of these collective references has anything at all to do with the expectation of individual messianic figures. In fact, they exclude it for the time of their formulation, since they contain no polemics against an individual messianism.

The two oldest pieces of evidence from ancient Judaism for the expectation of a future royal messiah as an individual figure are his place in the hierarchical order at community events (1QSa 2:11-22), and the blessing to be pronounced over him, of which we have only the beginning (1QSb 5:18-27).

When the Teacher of Righteousness, with his *Directive to Jonathan* (4QMMT) around 150 B.C., attempted to enlist him for the pan-Israelite union, he expressly approved of Jonathan's continuing to rule politically in Israel. This practically excluded a simultaneous expectation of a royal messiah as the legitimate ruler in Israel. Probably only Jonathan's harsh rejection of the *Directive* provided the Teacher of Righteousness with the occasion to condemn now, as well, the political side of the double office of this usurper and instead to place all hope in a future royal messiah. Tradition insisted that, as political ruler in Israel, the messiah would have to be a descendant of King David and therefore, like David, belong to the tribe of Judah and the family of Jesse, whose home was in Bethlehem of Judea (2 Sam. 7:8-16; Isa. 11:1-5; Mic. 5:1-3; cf. Matt. 2:6). Priests like Jonathan, as descendants of Levi, could never be of the correct lineage anyway (cf. also Heb. 7:11-14).

At the same time, the Teacher of Righteousness too was, as a priest, of the tribe of Levi. Indeed, in postexilic times the high priests from the Zadok line — reckoned as "Levitical" — had governed Jerusalem and Judea politically as well. But they never laid claim to the office of king. Should there one day be a legitimate king in Israel again, he could scarcely be a priest, but rather would have to be a non-"Levitical" descendant of David. The Teacher could at most tolerate a political rule along with himself — even a priestly one, if necessary — provided this ruler laid no claim to the office of king. Or else he would have to be descended from David, but then he would not be a priest.

The Teacher of Righteousness could by no means await a new, future high priest, a "Messiah from Aaron." After all, he was still — despite his arbitrary removal from office at the hands of the usurper Jonathan — the sole legitimate high priest of all Israel, chosen for life.

But when the Teacher of Righteousness died around 110 B.C. and calculations of the time of the Last Judgment revealed that there were still "some forty years" (CD 20:15) to pass before the end of days, the Essenes dispensed with choosing a successor and instead expected the future to bring a priestly messiah in addition to a royal messiah. That meant nothing else but that, at the beginning of the time of salvation, as "Messiah from Aaron," a legitimate high priest would once more lead worship in the Jerusalem Temple and that beside him would stand as "Messiah from Israel" a king of the lineage of David. *Above* both of them would be a "Prophet like Moses" through whom God would introduce new laws to complete the Torah (1QS 9:11; 4Q175 *Testimonia* 1–20). Until then, Essene legislation had to remain immutably frozen in the stage of development it had reached by about 100 B.C., as the *Damascus Document* presents it.

Accordingly, messianic figures are mentioned several times in Essene texts, in the concluding passages dealing with legal matters, where it is established that the precepts listed earlier must enjoy immutable validity until the entry into office of the said messianic figures (1QS 9:10-11; CD 12:23–13:1; 14:18-19; 19:33–20:1; cf. 19:10-11). Portrayals of a messianic time of salvation, or descriptions of the activity of the future savior figures, are never connected with admonitions of this sort.

Only in relatively few Essene texts is the royal messiah expressly honored in terms of Nathan's prophecy in 2 Samuel 7:8-16 as the coming representative of the Davidic kingship in Israel, as the "star" or "staff" of Numbers 24:17, or as triumphant in the coming final battle of Israel against its pagan oppressors (1QSa 2:11-21; 1QSb 5:18-27; CD 7:19-21; 4QpIsa^a 2–6 ii 10-29; 4Q174 *Florilegium* 1:10-13; 4Q252 *Patriarchal Blessings* 3:1-5; 4Q285 *War Rule* 6 1-10; 7 1-5). This picture corresponds in all essential traits to the one offered in *Psalms of Solomon* 17, which is usually regarded as Pharisaic and as dating from the period between 50 and 30 B.C. The Qumran texts show that this picture of the royal messiah was developed especially in the course of an Essene reworking of the *War Rule,* which raises the question of how the Essenes conceived the Last Judgment and the transition to the time of salvation in the first place.

With regard to the Last Judgment, the Qumran texts present various kinds of scenarios simultaneously and without mutual connections. A hymn presents the end in terms of the whole earth melting away in a lava-like, fiery glow, while the righteous are amazingly snatched from this cosmic catastrophe (1QH 3:19-36). The life of individuals like the Wicked Priest Jonathan can end in a sulfurous pool of fire (1QpHab 10:5), or else in places of everlasting darkness. The Last Judgment can also be represented as a refiner's furnace from which the righteous emerge purified like gold or silver, while everyone else dissolves without a trace. It is also conceived as a court of arbitration, somewhat as in Matthew 25:31-46, in which all human beings who have ever lived appear before God's judgment seat and go either to eternal life or to eternal damnation. Finally, there is also the notion that at the Last Judgment all Israel — or the Essenes as Israel's representative — sit on judgment seats alongside God to judge all other persons while they themselves are not judged at all (4QpPs^a 1–10 iv 10-12; cf. Dan. 7:13-14, 26-27; *1 Enoch* 62:12; 1 Cor. 6:2).

In the *Melchizedek Midrash* the "Day" of Judgment lasts seven full years. In the *War Rule,* the end drama is a forty-year undertaking, in the course of which Israel conquers the rest of the world and thereby completes the transition to the time of salvation. Whichever of these viewpoints one may adopt, the Essenes conceptualized the transition from the unsaved present to the time of salvation not as an event that would create fully new relations overnight, but as a more or less protracted process, whose end would finally bring the everlasting time of salvation that is to be unimpaired by any evil.

The central future place of salvation was, for the Essenes, the earthly Jerusalem surrounded by God's Holy Land with an exclusively Jewish population. All who would remain in neighboring lands after the Last Judgment were also to serve the Creator of heaven and earth in the Jerusalem Temple worship. More beautiful and spacious than anything ever built by human hands, a Jerusalem long since prepared in heaven by God would descend, with the Temple in its midst, to be served by those priests and their descendants who had remained faithful to God through all of the chaos. The entire process of worship, with its sacrificial offerings and its festivals of pilgrimage, would then finally proceed once more in conformity with the Torah. The natural year would once more correspond to the 364-day solar calendar of creation, because the power of evil in the world that had delayed the sun's course would be definitively annihilated.

Alongside such thoughts of the restoration of earlier conditions, especially those at creation, the Essenes also imagined the time of salvation as a new beginning through a new act of creation by God. Thus, God would make a new selection of those who had received a positive evaluation in the Last Judgment, remaking them into a new humanity now stamped by the Holy Spirit alone and hence incapable of sinning again (1QS 4:20-23); or else transfer the whole world until now, through an act of new creation, into a mode of existence that would now be immortal (1QH 13:11-12). Such conceptions are to be found in the same Essene writings right alongside other notions. But they are not representative of different stages of development or circles of transmission. "Unity of doctrine" prevailed among the Essenes, it is true, in the organizational, legal, and ethical spheres, but not in the areas of messianism and eschatology.

The Resurrection of the Dead

From their grave sites alone at the Qumran settlement, it is evident that the Essenes believed in the resurrection of the dead. In their tradition, this faith is incontestably expressed in Daniel 12:2. Previously it is found as early as the Enoch literature and *Jubilees*. In 4Q521 2 ii 12, God is celebrated as the one who "makes the dead [once more] alive," and in the same work (7 6) as the one who in the future "will make the dead of his people [Israel] [once more] alive." But the best proof that the Essenes actually shared the conceptions represented in these works — perhaps entirely as received tradition — remains their manner of interment. They no longer, as in ancient Israel, "gathered to the fathers" those who had died — that is, buried them in the family grave, with its characteristic common pit for the bones of all who came there. Rather, the Essenes always buried their dead in deep *individual graves,* where they awaited the resurrection intact.

The Essenes expected the resurrection of all deceased Israelites at the beginning of the coming Last Judgment, just as Paul expected at the Lord's parousia the resurrection of all Christians who had fallen asleep (1 Thess. 4:16). The New Testament notion that especially righteous figures like Abraham, Moses, or Elijah were long since with God in heaven (Matt. 8:11; Mark 9:4; Luke 16:23; cf. 23:43) was completely foreign to the Essenes. The reason for this was not only that, when it came to the resurrection of the dead and everlasting life, they always envisioned a destiny that all the pious of Israel could only experience *in common;* rather, it had its foundation mainly in the fact that the idea of *heaven* as a possible realm of salvation for human beings was always foreign to them.

Even in New Testament times, there were Christians who could conceive of everlasting life only in a spatially different world, distinct from an earthly one — only in *heavenly* community with God (John 14:1-3; cf. Luke 16:19-31; 23:43). For the Essenes, on the other hand, the place of the blessed after the resurrection was Paradise, the Garden of Eden portrayed in Genesis 2–3, here *on earth.* The Apostle Paul thought of Paradise as being on the third level of a seven-story heaven (2 Cor. 12:2-4). But for the Essenes, it lay in a pleasantly cool area to the north of Palestine, which was often very hot — namely, in the East Turkish region of the sources of the Tigris and the Euphrates, at the foot of Mount Ararat. Those buried at Qumran gazed in this direction, and it is here that the Essenes expected to enjoy in the future all of the delights that God had once intended for Adam (1QH 17:15; 1QS 4:23; CD 3:20; 4QpPs^a 2:9-12; 2:26–3:2), which, however, he had for the time being forfeited for himself and his descendants through the Fall.

A messianic savior figure was not needed for access to this realm of salvation. The God of Israel, the Essenes believed, would "by his own hand," so to speak, raise from the dead those who had died in faithful service to him (4Q521 2 ii 3).

CHAPTER EIGHT

John the Baptist

Was John the Baptist in any way involved with the Essenes? Was he close to them, or even an Essene himself? Was his baptism an adoption and continuation of Essene rites? These are questions that scholarship has concerned itself with for centuries, but reliable answers to them have become possible only with the Qumran discoveries.

True, Flavius Josephus repeatedly refers to the great importance attributed by the Essenes to their ritual immersions (*Jewish War* 2.129, 137-38, 149-50, 161), but he never connects them with a desert. In the New Testament tradition, however, "the desert" is the characteristic place of John the Baptist's entry upon the scene (Mark 1:2-6; Matt. 3:1-4; Luke 3:2-6; John 1:23). And granted, Pliny the Elder had already written his report on the Essenes by the Dead Sea (see above, p. 58). Still, no one knew where between Jericho and En Gedi they could have lived, and Pliny's reference to "palm trees" as their only neighbors called to mind an idyllic oasis rather than a place in the desert.

Accordingly, many regard the Essene settlement at Qumran with its baths, discovered four decades ago, as the long-missing link among the various traditions. This locale was indeed inhabited by Essenes at the time of the Baptist's activity, and it did indeed lay in the desert, only some sixteen kilometers distant as the crow flies from John's place of baptism at the lower course of the Jordan. It has been extremely tempting to make connections. The Baptist's strange clothing and his diet (Mark 1:6; Matt. 3:4) could be indications that he was an expelled Essene; Josephus reports that expelled Essenes were allowed to accept no food prepared by others (*Jewish War* 2.143). Since Josephus likewise informs us that the Essenes had reared other people's children (*Jewish War* 2.120), the puzzle of Luke 1:80 seemed at last to have been solved: if from his childhood to his appearance on the public scene John had lived "in the desert," the Qumran settlement was made to order as the place of his upbringing.

211

Other possible connections between John the Baptist and the Essenes are suggested by the content of the Qumran texts. Thus, we now have the appeal by both John and the Qumran writings to Isaiah 40:3, with its call for the preparation of a highway in the desert (1QS 8:12-16; Mark 1:2-3; Matt. 3:3; Luke 1:76; 3:4-6; John 1:23); the expectation by both parties of the Last Judgment as imminent and now at hand; both sides' call to "conversion"; or the distance kept by both from the sacrificial worship of the Temple.

The very number of these parallels or possible connections often counts as clear evidence that there was a historical connection between John the Baptist and Qumran, however this connection may have presented itself concretely.

The fanciful development of a possible connection by Barbara Thiering, who identifies John the Baptist with the Teacher of Righteousness and makes him the abbot, as it were, of the Qumran monastery (see above, pp. 28-29), has now been clearly shown by Otto Betz and Rainer Riesner, in their *Jesus, Qumran and the Vatican,* to represent unfounded speculation.

The other connections, which are altogether worthy of discussion, can be satisfactorily dealt with only when preceded by an attempt to gain a comprehensive picture of the Baptist and his activity from the sources still available to us — a concise report by Flavius Josephus and the Gospels of the New Testament — and to relate this picture to the Qumran discoveries and other Essene traditions.

The Activity and Personage of the Baptist

According to Josephus' report (*Antiquities* 18.116-19; cf. Mark 6:17-29; Matt. 14:3-12; Luke 3:19-20), the Jewish tetrarch Herod Antipas, who from 4 B.C. until his banishment to Lyons in A.D. 39 was "quarter prince" over Galilee and Perea — parts of the kingdom of his father, Herod the Great — had John the Baptist executed at Machaerus, his stronghold high in the mountains east of the Dead Sea. This stronghold lay at the remote southern end of Perea, on the east side of the Jordan. Somewhere near the center of Perea, opposite Jericho, was the place "in the desert" where John attended to his work of baptism "across the Jordan" (John 1:28; 10:40).

The place name *Bethany,* "Boathouse" (John 1:28), refers to the ferry traffic crossing the Jordan there. Later textual witnesses supposed this application of the name Bethany — which otherwise in the New Testament always refers to a village on the Mount of Olives near Jerusalem, "House of Invalids" (Mark 11:1, 11; 14:3; Matt. 21:17; 26:6; Luke 19:29; 24:50; John 11:1, 18; 12:1) — to be erroneous and inserted in its place a locality seven kilometers further to the south of "Boathouse": *Beth-Abara,* "Place of Crossing." Others changed it to the name of the Judah-Benjamite border town lying five kilometers west of the place of baptism in the direction of Jericho, *Beth-Araba,* "Desert House" (Josh. 15:6, 61). Both interpretations are actually inappropriate.

The region on the east bank of this ferry route was also called *Aenon,* "Area of Many Fountains," on account of its abundance of springs. Since this location seemed to coincide with Bethany (John 1:28), the Gospel of John itself erroneously regarded another place of the same name — near Salim on the west-bank region of Decapolis, that is, in the province of Samaria — as a further site of John's baptism (John 3:23, 26).

Finally, for the Christian pilgrims streaming to John's site of baptism from the fourth century onward, it became increasingly difficult — dangerous, in fact, owing to marauding Bedouin — to cross over to the east bank of the Jordan in this region. Christian places of worship in honor of the Baptist were by this time arising on the opposite, west bank of the Jordan. They are already marked there on the earliest map of Palestine, a floor mosaic dating to around A.D. 565 in a church at Madaba, a village east of the Jordan. In fact, John the Baptist was never active west of the Jordan.

Besides, Aenon of the many springs, near Bethany, belonged precisely to the desert. The Hebrew concept *midbar,* customarily rendered as "desert," designates a landscape not of dunes and desolation, without flora, but only one ill-suited for farming and therefore regularly used as pastureland.

At all events, only because John's place of baptism was on the east bank of the Jordan in Perea, and thus within the jurisdiction of Herod Antipas, could Antipas have the Baptist, whom he found disagreeable, arrested and put to death without opposition from the other side of the river. There is no doubt whatever of this geographical datum. Indeed, it is at the same time the most important starting point for an understanding of the activity of John the Baptist as a whole.

At the place where John baptized, an old trade route crosses the Jordan, stretching from Jerusalem through Jericho into the region east of the river. At low water, fords, and at other times ferries, provided the means of transporting a great deal of traffic in persons and goods every day, just as occurs today with the Allenby Bridge — which lies just a little to the north — between Jordan and the Palestinian West Bank. Here, John could mightily prick the conscience of all those Jews he caught making business trips on the Sabbath; those who as toll collectors on the border demanded more than they were entitled to; or those who as soldiers busied themselves with their own enrichment through military action in the neighboring territory (cf. Luke 3:10-14).

John did not spare from criticism even his own sovereign, Herod Antipas. He publicly denounced Antipas' marriage to a relative, which violated the

Torah, and thereby indirectly signed his own death warrant (Mark 6:17-29; Matt. 14:3-12; Luke 3:19-20).

John's criticism of his religiously impure Jewish contemporaries reached its climax in his outright revilement of them as a "brood of vipers": God would more likely raise up the broken stones lying around to be "children of Abraham" than allow "children of the devil" such as these to profit from the rich store of blessings of their forbear Abraham in the imminent Last Judgment (Matt. 3:7-9; Luke 3:7-8). Everlasting damnation awaited them shortly, unless they "converted" in time.

John's choice of location for his call to "conversion" was of course scarcely the most evident one for the effectiveness of such intensive public activity. Had he only been concerned with reaching a large audience, he could just as well have come forward on the west side of this crossing, where he would also have been safe from arrest by the minions of the object of his criticism, Herod Antipas. Indeed, he would have reached far more of the Jewish public whom he deemed so deserving of criticism in the lecture halls of the Jerusalem Temple, or indeed on any street corner of Jerusalem or other Palestinian city, moving from place to place or following the trade routes across the country to the Mediterranean.

Had John been primarily concerned with having sufficient water for his baptisms, Lake Gennesaret, the areas of the sources of the Jordan, or many of the streams in the country that flowed all year long, would have afforded him all he needed. Finally, even in Jerusalem, or in the wealthy city of Jericho, there were enough private and public baths in which baptism would have surely been less fatiguing than in the searing summer heat on the banks of the Jordan. Why, then, did John baptize precisely "in the Jordan River" (Mark 1:5-9; Matt. 3:6; cf. Luke 3:3; 4:1; John 1:28; 10:40)? Why not in a thronging city instead of "in the desert"?

The actual background for John's peculiar choice of location is revealed by biblical tradition alone. John had chosen as the place of his entry upon the public scene precisely that location, opposite Jericho, where Joshua had once led the people of Israel across the Jordan into the Holy Land (Josh. 4:13, 19). His choice of the *east bank* of the Jordan as the place of his activity, then, corresponded to Israel's situation immediately *before* the crossing of the river. Thus the Baptist's public appearance was analogous to Israel's life, after the flight from Egypt, "in the desert," before the entry into the Promised Land, where only in the future would everything that God had once promised his chosen people through Moses on Mount Sinai become a reality.

In a kind of symbolic, prophetic manipulation of signs, John was thereby placing the people of Israel at the transition to the future time of salvation, corresponding to that of the desert generation of Israel that had indeed already been promised salvation, but whose members had to perish before their children could reach the sacred goal. Mere membership in the posterity of Abraham, Isaac, and Jacob — merely belonging to the chosen people — in no way guaranteed them a personal share in salvation (cf. also 1 Cor. 10:1-13; Heb. 3:1-4, 13; John 6:30-35, 47, 51). Hence John's condemnation of all of his impure Jewish contemporaries as eternally damned "children of the devil."

The Baptist demanded of each and all an immediate "conversion" to the will of God as revealed of old on Mount Sinai. He required a blanket renunciation of the way in which persons had conducted their lives up to this time. No longer could a readiness to preserve unbroken in the future all of the prescriptions of the Torah rescue each individual from impending doom. Now it was a question of a corresponding lifestyle that would include the prescribed prayers, rules of fasting, and concern for the needy neighbor (cf. Mark 2:18; Matt. 9:14; Luke 3:11; 5:33; 11:1; cf. also Jesus' Sermon on the Mount, Matt. 6:1-18).

Unlike Israel's desert generation, of whose first members none but Joshua and Caleb were to reach the Holy Land, the equally guilt-laden and sinful Israel of John's generation could still be saved, and this was what was special about the Baptist's view — a view that has been of such importance in religious history for Christians, Mandeans, and Muslims. For John himself, it was primarily a prophetic mission from God that had called him to the desert east of the Jordan and made him all Israel's last chance in the face of imminent annihilation in the coming Last Judgment.

The analogy of Israel's present to the situation of its bygone desert generation was symbolized by John the Baptist in his actual personal appearance. In Bedouin fashion, as a typical desert-dweller he wore a camel's hair cloak with a leather belt and ate grasshoppers, with wild honey for dessert (Mark 1:6; Matt. 3:4). This way of life had nothing whatever to do with an ascetic habit distinguishing him from the comparatively almost sensuous "glutton and drunkard" Jesus (Matt. 11:18-19; Luke 7:33-34). Grasshoppers fried in olive oil taste like French fried potatoes. Like wild honey, they are a delicacy. Only inhabitants of the desert could allow themselves such a rich daily fare, just as farmers and city dwellers won their staples from the produce of the arable land. While cultivated persons normally wore clothes of linen or wool, John symbolized the situation of Israel's wanderings in the desert with his no less elegant camel's hair cloak, whose leather belt was worth every bit as much as other persons' cloth sashes.

But John had no intention of playing the cultural critic and propagating the lifestyle of the Bedouin as a universal ideal, an alternative to the usual lifestyle. Never did he recommend anything of the sort to his followers. He only wished to place the present in the twilight of Israel's desert generation — in altogether personal fashion — in the style of a prophetic manipulation of signs. At the same time, his clothing was consciously intended to recall that of the prophet Elijah (2 Kings 1:8; cf. Zech. 13:4). The appearance of the prophet John clearly expressed the elements of tradition that converged in his entry upon the scene.

Jesus himself asked his Jewish contemporaries whether they had gone out to John "in the wilderness" to gape at a reed swaying in the wind, or someone dressed after the fashion of courtiers in royal palaces. The antithetical relationship of these two images to the Baptist's lifestyle and appearance would be even more clear if "waving fields of grain" and customary "clothing of the cultivated" had been cited as a contrast. Still, both rhetorical questions are to be answered with an unambiguous "By no means!" and ultimately serve to prepare the way for the third question, which now expects a positive answer: "Why then did you go out [to the desert] — to see a prophet? Yes, [a prophet indeed, but] I say to you: you saw something more than [just] a prophet!" (Matt. 11:7-9; Luke 7:24-26).

Prophet, at that time, meant a person who proclaimed a future event. A true prophet was recognized by virtue of the factual occurrence of what he had predicted. John the prophet's particular prediction of the future consisted in his proclamation of God's Last Judgment and the beginning of the time of salvation for Israel as altogether imminent. The imminence of these events was comparable, in the graphic expression of the Baptist, to the situation in which someone has now picked up an ax to fell a tree, or has now come to the threshing floor with winnowing fork in hand to separate the grain from the chaff (Matt. 3:10, 12; Luke 3:9, 17). The "one mightier than I" for whom John is completely unworthy to perform even the lowest of slavely duties and who will shortly "baptize . . . in the Holy Spirit and fire" (Matt. 3:11; Luke 3:16; cf. Mark 1:7-8; John 1:26-27, 33) was, for the historical John the Baptist, neither Jesus nor any messianic figure, but none other than God himself, whose forerunner and pioneer John regarded himself.

John's function as herald and pioneer is frequently considered to have been attributed to him only in Christian tradition, since in the Gospels it serves to emphasize the Baptist's inferiority to Jesus. The principal instrument of the Christian interpretation of the figure of the Baptist is frequently thought to be the citation of Isaiah 40:3, which appears on the lips of the Baptist only in the latest of all of the Gospels (John 1:23) as a reference to a preparation of the way *for Jesus,* rather than merely a statement *concerning John,* as in the earlier Gospels (Mark 1:2-3; Matt. 3:3; Luke 3:4-6). Of course, it is rarely taken into account that the same scriptural reference is present in Zechariah's Benedictus, which is apparently free of all Christian interpretation and is a hymn created by followers of the Baptist to the latter's praise (Luke 1:76). But even more important for an understanding of the historical Baptist is the appeal to Isaiah 40:3 in Malachi 3:1, where any suspicion of an original Christian influence is completely out of the question.

Neither Josephus nor the New Testament transmits a report of John's calling, such as is characteristic for the Old Testament prophets (Isaiah 6; Jeremiah 1; Ezekiel 1–3; etc.). The evangelist Luke sensed this lack and attempted after the fact to fashion a report of John's calling as a prophet (Luke 3:2-6) from the traditional material available to him (Mark 1:2-4 and Luke 1:5-25, 59-79). Apart from this obviously purely literary presentation by Luke, however, there is no such report in the Baptist tradition.

If we read the last chapter of the last book of the biblical prophets, however, we see from beginning to end practically the same set of motifs as were characteristic and typical of John's appearance and proclamation. From the perspective of John's time, the chapter reads exactly like the history of his personal calling. Here, already, are the motifs of judgment by fire and of conversion (Mal. 3:2-7, 19) — even the basic motif of his graphic images of the ax laid to the root and of the chaff being winnowed (Mal. 3:19ab). Even the distance maintained by the Baptist from the sacrificial worship of the Jerusalem Temple has its clear parallel here (Mal. 3:3-4, 8-10; cf. chaps. 1–2). Finally, it was not the Christians who first made John the "messenger of the covenant," but his well-known prophetic "call narrative" (Mal. 3:1), which at the same time forced upon him the role of Elijah as the last admonisher to come immediately before the "great and terrible day" of the Last Judgment of God himself (Mal. 3:23-24; cf. Mark 6:14-15; 8:28; 9:11-13; Matt. 11:14; 16:14; 17:9-13; Luke 1:17; 9:19; John 1:21, 25).

This reference to Elijah in his prophetic "call narrative" had a further, normative significance for John. According to 2 Kings 2:1-18 the prophet Elijah had come from Jericho and had crossed the Jordan dry-shod at precisely that place where the people of Israel, under Joshua's leadership, moving in the opposite direction, had once entered the Holy Land. It was only on the east bank of the Jordan that "a flaming chariot and flaming horses" appeared — and Elijah, conveyed by the chariot, "went up to heaven in a whirlwind" (2 Kings 2:11).

True, Malachi 3:23 does not name a particular place where Elijah would return. But it would be reasonable to expect the place to be that of his assumption to heaven. In any case this would be an obvious explanation for why John, with his manner of dress and diet, besides symbolizing the desert, was demonstrating peculiarities of Elijah: John's emergence was at the same time the promised return of Elijah.

Of course, had John wished to present himself only as the returned Elijah, it would have been altogether sufficient for him to appear, at the beginning of his work, at the place of Elijah's assumption and then wander about the Holy Land calling for Israel's conversion. Neither his remaining in this place nor even his baptizing in the Jordan is understandable in terms of his role as Elijah. His "call narrative" had imposed that role upon him, however, and significantly influenced John's function as fulfiller of salvation for Israel (Mark 9:9-13; Matt. 17:9-13) — perhaps even making him for Jesus in this regard as well, "a prophet indeed, and something more" than just another prophet (Matt. 11:9; Luke 7:26). Finally, however, what was decisive for John was his local connection with that place where Israel had once stood before its entry into the Holy Land.

If we regard the book of Malachi, especially its third chapter, as the call narrative of the prophet John — or, strictly neutrally, as the normative basis of orientation for his appearance on the scene — then the motif of the desert, so characteristic of the Baptist, is missing. But John's well-attested appeal to Isaiah 40:3 was probably in the picture from the beginning, as the decisive background for an understanding of Malachi 3:1 (cf. 3:22).

The only thing missing now is the baptizing that was such a salient characteristic of his exercise of his mission. Baptism presents itself neither in Malachi nor in any other biblical source. True, one could like Paul appeal to the cloud and the crossing through the sea at the moment of Israel's flight from Egypt (1 Cor. 10:1-2). But even then it would be a baptism by God himself, and not by a human figure. Of just as little help is the frequent reference to the healing of the Syrian military commander Naaman by way of his immersion in the Jordan (2 Kings 5:1-19); it was not the prophet Elijah who had sent him there, however, but his successor Elisha, who actually stayed at home and did not function as the baptizer of Naaman; and, finally, Naaman's sevenfold immersion in no way prefigured John's rite of baptism.

Indeed, until John's appearance, neither in Judaism nor in the world around had anyone baptized other persons. True, there was a plethora of ritual purifications, including the immersion of the entire body to that effect. But each person performed these rites of purification completely independently, without the cooperation of a baptizer. John was the very first to immerse others.

Subsequently Jesus may have adopted this baptismal rite and practiced it independently — he himself, and not only his circle of disciples (John 3:25-26; 4:1-3). At any rate, this would be the simplest explanation for the appearance of Christian communal baptism (cf. Matt. 28:19). After all, the latter was practiced from the outset not as a ritual bath of purification performed by the individual independently, but as a being baptized (1 Cor. 6:11; Rom. 6:3; etc.) by other Christians (1 Cor. 1:14-16; Acts 8:38; 10:48; etc.), as is still customary in Christian churches today, without this astonishing characteristic of the baptismal rite having seemed to a single one of the New Testament writers to need explanation. To trace it back to John the Baptist is therefore the most obvious way to explain its origin. In fact, in the absence of other indications concerning the emergence of this rite, this explanation is ineluctable.

This is far from establishing, of course, what meaning the baptizing of other persons had for John himself. For him it was certainly bound up with the forgiveness of sins. John saw the imminent Last Judgment as a fiery catastrophe that would annihilate all who until then had not heeded his call to conversion and had had themselves baptized by him. But simple conversion, and a sinless way of life henceforward, did not suffice. There remained the problem of the burden of sin accumulated until then, frequently over the course of decades. But according to the Old Testament, no human being can grant forgiveness of sins, neither a priest nor a prophet, neither the Messiah nor the most righteous or holiest of all the pious, but always only God (cf. Mark 2:7).

Accordingly, neither did John the Baptist forgive anyone's sins, and Josephus expressly emphasizes this in his appraisal of John's work (*Antiquities* 18.117). Nevertheless, the forgiveness of sins was closely connected with his baptism, as the reports of the Gospels testify (Mark 1:4-5; Matt. 3:6; Luke 1:77; 3:3). Otherwise it would scarcely be understandable that, from the outset, one of the principal meanings of Christian communal baptism was the forgiveness of sins (1 Cor. 6:11; Rom. 3:25; 6:1-23; etc.). But while Christian baptism, in the sacramental act itself, effects the discharge of all previously committed sins, John's baptism was only *unto* the forgiveness of sins. It was the warranty — likewise sacramental — that *God himself,* in the future Last Judgment, would not charge the baptized with sins committed up to the time of baptism. This guarantee assured them unhindered access to the future realm of salvation through their preservation from annihilation in the fiery Judgment, despite all of their as yet unforgiven sins of the past.

Owing to the significance of his baptism, contemporary Jews called John and his followers, somewhat derisively, "the Preservers" — in Aramaic, *nāṣrên,* or, with the article, *nāṣrâyâ* — in Greek transliteration, *nazarēnoi* or *nazōraioi.* The better to distinguish his name from many similar names, Jesus was therefore called by many the "Nazarene" (Mark 1:24; 10:47; 14:67; 16:6; Luke 4:34; 24:19), or the "Nazorean" (Matt. 2:23; 26:71; Luke 18:37; John 18:5, 7; Acts 2:22; 3:6; 4:10; 6:14; 22:8; 24:5; 26:9), which originally referred not to his coming from Nazareth (the interpretation of many Bible translations in the passages cited), but to his coming from the circle of the Baptist or his membership in it. "Preservation" from annihilation in the coming Last Judgment was John's special salvific stamp, his baptism its visible side. Therefore, this John was called, the better to distinguish him from many other persons of the same name, the Baptist. Never before had there been anyone who performed a baptismal rite.

As in early Christian communal baptism, so even with John, the total immersion of the candidates symbolized death, the extraction from the waters of their newly attained state of salvation. The Baptist acted as God's representative — as priests do in public worship, for example in a blessing imparted in the course of that service.

In Judaism, of course, one cannot *become* a priest, for instance through the attainment of certain professional knowledge. Rather, one *is* a priest from birth on, namely as son of a father belonging to the tribe of Levi, that is, as a descendant of Moses' brother Aaron. Jews today whose last name is Kohn, Kuhn, Cohen (in Hebrew, *kōhēn,* "priest"), Katz (medieval abbreviation for *kāhēn ṣedek,* "genuine priest"), or Levy usually come from the ancient Israelite priestly families, whose male members in Jesus' time numbered more than ten thousand.

Especially in John the Baptist's case, it is historically beyond any doubt that he was of priestly birth, corresponding to what we read of his father Zechariah and his mother Elizabeth in Luke 1:5-25 and 1:39-79. John's quality as a mediator, stemming from his priestly origin, was certainly the decisive component of his active role in his baptisms, which made him, as ritual representative of God, the Baptist, and the baptisms performed by him an efficacious sacrament. God guaranteed through his priestly representative in the act of baptism his revocation of punishment for previous sins in the coming Last Judgment.

From these points of departure it also becomes clear what far-reaching symbolic significance his baptisms precisely in the Jordan had for John (Mark 1:5, 9; Matt. 3:6, 16). John did not lead the people of Israel *through* the Jordan into the Holy Land, as Joshua once had (Joshua 3–4). Instead, he led them *to the border* of this crossing. The coming realm of salvation, seen symbolically, lay on the other side of this boundary, on the other bank. The Jordan symbolized for John the barrier of the imminent Last Judgment, a barrier that otherwise could not now be transcended and that could be crossed only in the future (cf. the "eschatological reserve" in Paul's understanding of baptism in Rom. 6:4). But baptism "in the Jordan" was at the same time, in symbolic anticipation of the situation at the Last Judgment, the defeat of that situation for the baptized, with the Baptist himself being the guarantor of the coming transition or crossing.

The concrete, priestly, sacramental mediation of the transition from an otherwise inescapable deadly fate for Israel into the realm of future salvation was the center of the Baptist's effectiveness, his prophetic interpretation of the present, and his announcement of the meaning of that present for the future. As Jesus himself said, with John the Baptist it was a matter of more than a prophecy — at its core it was an efficacious mediation of salvation. The sole guarantor of this mediation, for the totality of current Israel, was John the Baptist.

The Baptist is frequently presented as a mere prophet of the Judgment, his baptism seen one-sidedly as a symbol of *death,* and the Jordan regarded simply as a convenient natural place for baptism. Actually, however, the Jordan symbolized for John precisely the transitional situation of the crossing. The aspect of *life* dominated his act of baptism, and Israel's *time of salvation* stood just as clearly before the eyes of the Baptist as the Last Judgment did. The Baptist's double pronouncement, characterizing God as baptizer both in Spirit and in fire (Matt 3:11; Luke 3:16), keeps both aspects equally in view. In Josephus' appraisal of John, the aspect of bringer of salvation is actually uppermost.

The fact that almost only the judgment side of the Baptist's proclamation is transmitted in the New Testament is to be explained by the fact that the evangelists present the salvation side of the event mainly in connection with Jesus. In this sense, Jesus is not only consciously contrasted with the Baptist as the fulfiller of John's prophecy concerning the conditions of salvation (Matt. 11:2-6; Luke 7:18-23); but according to the presentation of the Gospels the time of salvation actually begins in immediate connection with Jesus' baptism by John (Mark 1:9-11; Matt. 3:13-17; Luke 3:21-22; cf. John 1:29-34), if indeed not with the very birth of the Redeemer (Matthew 1–2; Luke 1–2).

Owing to these Christian interests of faith and therefore of presentation, a rather one-sided picture of John the Baptist emerges from our principal New Testament sources. However, this picture contains enough elements to render the original comprehensive picture recognizable at least in its principal traits. According to the latter picture, the sacramental baptism in the Jordan was John's most important mark; the twofold character of his prophetic announcement of judgment and salvation was the interpretation of that baptism; and the totality of current Israel was the reprobate community addressed by him, for whom his baptism offered the last remaining access to salvation.

Connections to the Essenes?

It is tirelessly repeated in books and in the media, as being one of the principal results of the Qumran finds, that the latter show not only that the Essenes were "Christians before Jesus," but in particular that "Qumran already had baptism." As a bridge between these — alleged — Qumran finds and Christian baptism, John the Baptist is usually pressed into service. Did his baptism come from Qumran?

Actually, almost the only relationships between John's baptism and the Qumran finds are *differences*.

(1) For John, the ritual of baptizing other persons had a fundamental significance. This rite constituted the figure of the Baptist and made baths of immersion into baptism. At Qumran, as in all of the rest of Judaism, there

were instead only baths of immersion, which each person performed without the assistance of another, never a rite similar to baptism and never including the figure of a baptizer. (2) For John, the performance of his baptism had sacramental significance. He warned of the annihilation impending in the Last Judgment and opened the doors to the coming time of salvation. The purification baths of immersion in Qumran — just as in all of the rest of Judaism — were, by contrast, by no means of a sacramental sort; they served only ritually, for the materialization of cultic purity. (3) John baptized in a very particular place, on the east bank of the Jordan. The Essenes, on the other hand, performed their immersions not only in Qumran but wherever they lived, in hundreds of fonts expressly installed for this purpose. Neither the Jordan in general nor John's place of baptism in particular had any real or symbolic meaning for the Essenes' immersions. (4) When John baptized a person, it was a one-time event in that person's life. The Essenes performed their self-immersions several times daily. (5) John's baptism guaranteed the forgiveness of sins in the coming Last Judgment. The Essenes' baths of immersion, by contrast, were never connected with the thought of the Last Judgment or with the mediation of the forgiveness of sins. (6) For John, baptism sealed the execution of a conversion. For the Essenes, as well, conversion meant strict obedience to the Torah, but it was primarily concretized in a return from the Diaspora and entry into their union. No conversion motif was ever bound up with their immersions. (7) The Essenes allowed candidates to participate in their immersions only after a one-year probationary period. With John there was no obligatory waiting period. (8) The Essenes admitted to their immersions only full-fledged members of their union, or candidates who had already seen much of their waiting period. John, instead, baptized all who came to him, regardless of their organizational membership, and without inducting those baptized by him into any organization of his own.

The only thing John's baptism and the Essenes' baths of immersion had in common was their ritual use of water for immersion. But this was a very common rite in the Judaism of the time, which the Essenes only practiced more often than did other Jews. Precisely in this respect, the one-time character of John's baptism was the exact opposite of Essene practice.

Actually, John the Baptist and the Essenes were strong competitors. Both sides claimed, each for itself, that it alone could safeguard Israel from annihilation in the coming Last Judgment — the Essenes through entry into their union, John through his baptism. Each way to salvation excluded the other. Nor did these ways have anything else in common in their starting points, other than being directed toward the whole of Israel.

On closer examination, none of the alleged points of commonality or connection between John the Baptist and the Essenes or Qumran fares any better than does baptism.

The preparation of a way for God in the desert, according to Isaiah 40:3, led John into the region of Israel's old wandering in the desert east of the Jordan. The Essenes, by contrast, while the founding of the Qumran settlement may have led them to the west-Jordan desert of Judah, ultimately prepared for God's coming by the study of the Torah and the Prophets in all of the places where they lived (1QS 8:12-16; cf. 9:17-21).

Both sides awaited the future Last Judgment of God and the dawn of the time of salvation. In the case of the Baptist, there is no doubt whatever that he expected it in the near future, within a few years at the latest. For the Essenes, by contrast, when John the Baptist began his work, A.D. 70 had long since been firmly established as the date of the end, on the basis of their calculations from the data of the book of Daniel (see above, p. 130). Entirely apart from the different dates on each side, an orientation to a date three or four decades off surely cannot qualify as an imminent expectation and therefore resemble the Baptist's announcement in this respect.

The two sides differed with respect to the sacrificial ritual in the Jerusalem Temple. For the Essenes, the orientation of the Jerusalem order of worship to the 354-day lunar calendar was the main cause of their rejection of the sacrificial ritual performed there. Of John the Baptist, on the other hand, it is not known that he criticized calendrical matters. His father Zechariah must have accepted the Jerusalem order of worship, if the announcement of the birth of a son reached him through the archangel Gabriel precisely during his offering of incense in the Temple (Luke 1:8-22). The transmission of this material by disciples of the Baptist even shows indirectly that their teacher never polemicized against the sacrificial worship in the Jerusalem Temple in the fashion that the Essenes did. The criticism of abuses in worship found in Malachi 3:3-4, 8-10 may, it is true, have given the Baptist occasion to censure carelessness in the practice of worship and in the paying of tithes, and to demand of those involved a praxis according to the Torah in this respect as well; but there is no corresponding tradition. The distance taken by the Baptist from Temple worship can only be explained by the fact that he made the salvation of the future for all Jews basically and exclusively dependent on his baptism in the Jordan, and altogether disregarded the annual Day of Atonement of the Temple worship as an institution for the forgiveness of sins for all of Israel, although the Torah calls for it (Leviticus 16) and John himself was a priest.

The Baptist's dress and diet were a planned prophecy in signs, through which John presented himself as a typical figure of the desert and at the same time as one corresponding to Elijah. The factual background here was not only his typological orientation to the bygone desert generation of Israel, but also the preparation of a way for God in the desert according to Malachi 3:1 and Isaiah 40:3 (cf. Mark 1:2-3; Matt. 11:10; Luke 7:27). His manner of dress and diet had nothing whatever to do with emergency help for expelled Essenes.

True, the way from Qumran to John's baptismal station on the Jordan can be managed in a five-hour walk. But this relative geographical proximity has no importance whatever. These two places lay in completely different worlds. Qumran, like the whole desert of Judah, belonged to the Holy Land, outside of whose borders, according to the mind of the Essenes, there could be no manner of service to the God of Israel. But John the Baptist had quite intentionally selected as the place of his public appearance the outer desert, on the threshold of the place of entry into the Holy Land, in order to prepare the people of Israel for the coming entry into the Holy Land — namely, for Israel's time of salvation after the Last Judgment — on the other side of the Jordan. His place of baptism was not a branch of Qumran, where the same things could happen as at Qumran, but the location of an entirely independent enterprise of a unique kind.

And so, as the last possibility of a connection between John the Baptist and Qumran, we have Luke 1:80, concerning the maturation of the boy John in the desert. This information, however, is not independent but has been taken from the source material that the evangelist had available and given a new form in order to bind disparate material together. Thus, Luke has proceeded here in his presentation of the Baptist in the same way as he has proceeded for his presentation of Jesus, for which his sources were similarly problematic.

The source material that Luke possessed for his presentation of Jesus ended for Jesus' childhood with the prophecy of Anna (Luke 2:36-38). Jesus was then only a few days old (Luke 2:21-24). The connecting source available to Luke, the Gospel of Mark, offered as the next occurrence in Jesus' life his baptism by John (Mark 1:9-11). At that time Jesus was, according to Luke's calculations, "about thirty years of age" (Luke 3:23). That is a difficult "dark phase" for a biographer to tolerate in the life of the principal figure of the biography. Luckily, however, Luke possessed in a separate tradition the story of the twelve-year-old Jesus in the Temple (Luke 2:41-50). By inserting that, he could to some extent bridge over the intermediate time. With redactional notices (Luke 2:39-40 and 2:51-52), whose individual component parts he removed from the contextual material and rounded out with general features of Jewish piety, the evangelist did his best as an author to create further connective links.

Luke proceeded no differently with John's biography. In this case his source material ended with Zechariah's Benedictus (Luke 1:67-79), on the eighth day of the young Baptist's life (Luke 1:59-66). But neither the Gospel of Mark nor any other source material available to Luke offered any material to fill the likewise "about thirty years" that must have passed until the Baptist's public appearance (Luke 3:1-18) and the baptism of Jesus, who was almost of the same age as John (Luke 1:36, 39-58).

The only help for the evangelist's biographical interests was the creation of the redactional note, Luke 1:80. The text of Mark 1:2-4 was demonstrably understood by Luke to the effect that John lived "in the desert" (Luke 3:2) "until the day when he made his public appearance in Israel" (Luke 1:80). Before, there was only the eight-day-old "child" John (Luke 1:59-66). An intermediate scene of this child with his elders, as had been transmitted in the case of Jesus (Luke 2:41-50), was unknown to Luke. Thus, with all brevity, he had "the child" grow up "in the desert," where he would have to be for the beginning of his presentation as baptizer (Luke 3:1-3). All further components of the note in Luke 1:80 are customary pious manners of presentation (cf. Luke 2:40, 52).

Where that desert is to be found in which John is supposed to have grown up Luke has described negatively at best. For him it did not lie in the "region of the Jordan," at any rate, where John went only after his calling (Luke 3:3). Anyone taking Luke 1:80 as historical would therefore have to rule out Qumran, strictly speaking, as a possible place of John's upbringing. Actually what we have in both cases are historically worthless constructions on Luke's part.

John the Baptist was neither an Essene nor a spiritual pupil of the Essenes. Were he ever to have made the effort to walk over to Qumran, as a non-Essene he would have been denied entry, and at best provided with enough food and drink for the long walk back.

But a true prophet remains where God has put him in any case. That, for John, was the place on the east bank of the Jordan opposite Jericho, until Herod Antipas had him arrested there and executed at Machaerus. Geographically and spiritually, for the Baptist Qumran lay in another world.

The Significance of the Qumran Finds

Without the Qumran finds it would have been simply impossible to present John the Baptist and his activity as has been done here, or adequately to grasp his dissimilarity from the Essenes. The sources already known to us before the Qumran finds would not have been sufficient. In reflection on the Qumran finds until now, the question whether John the Baptist was an Essene or could have received a basic impulse from the Essenes for his activity naturally stood in the foreground. Here the result is clearly negative. But the entirely different question is still open as to what new knowledge the Qumran finds and their evaluation have brought us in general for Palestinian Judaism in the time of John — knowledge that is important for our understanding of the Baptist and his activity and that, as background for his views, can even shed a certain amount of light on his person.

First, the Qumran finds show us how important for the Essenes, from the beginning onward, was concentration on the Holy Land with its biblical boundaries. Such a massive orientation to the boundaries of the Holy Land on the part of postexilic Jews was not known until recently. But the symbolic force of John's place of baptism presupposes precisely this kind of clear awareness.

The Teacher of Righteousness had made, for all of Israel, access to salvation dependent upon entry into his Essene union. After him, John the Baptist was the first to see, for all of Israel, a single opportunity for salvation, this time through his baptism.

True, the Essenes did not live constantly in the imminent expectation of the Last Judgment. But they were conscious of its coming, and they oriented themselves to it as did no other group in Palestinian Judaism. Without this work of preparation on the part of the Essenes among the broader population, the spontaneous mass effect of the Baptist's proclamation of the Judgment would scarcely be comprehensible.

The manifold representations of the Last Judgment in the Qumran texts (see above, pp. 208-9), especially that of judgment by fire in 1QH 3:29-34, constitute an important background for an understanding of the Baptist's metaphorical figures for the Last Judgment.

The temporal juxtaposition of the Last Judgment and the beginning of the time of salvation, so characteristic of John, has abundant biblical foundation, it is true. But through the Qumran texts, especially 1QS 4:18-23, as well as interpretations in the midrashim and the commentaries on the Prophets, it has provided access to substantially clearer contemporary modes of representation.

The view, inaugurated by the Teacher of Righteousness and propagated through numerous Qumran texts, that the writings of the biblical prophets referred not to those who had come before but to the Essenes' own time as the epoch immediately preceding the Last Judgment, came to bear upon John the Baptist in a special way. Witness his appeal to Malachi 3 as his call narrative, together with the implicit reference to Isaiah 40:3.

Obedience to the Torah — demanded most strictly at that time by the Essenes — was in the same way the foundation of the Baptist's call to conversion, including the criticism of his Jewish ruler's marriage contract, which cost him his life.

The basic connection of the forgiveness of sins for Israel to an institution that had distanced itself from the sacrificial worship of the Jerusalem Temple — with the Essenes, to their union as substitute and representative of the Temple, with John, to his baptism in the Jordan — is without analogy in the rest of ancient Judaism.

All of this background for an understanding of John has only been opened up through the Qumran finds. But in the very similarities, characteristic differences emerge as well. As a priest John the Baptist could have been aware — as later the Jerusalem priest Flavius Josephus was, or perhaps even more so than Josephus — of much that the Essenes taught even without having heard the Essenes themselves. But much more important is the fact that most of what the Qumran texts contain was characteristic of all of Palestinian Judaism at the time — the fact that it is only we who, through the Qumran finds, have finally received knowledge of it.

The Essenes doubtless completely rejected John the Baptist and mentioned him in none of their works. Nevertheless, today it is precisely the Essene Qumran texts that in manifold respects open anew to us the activity and person of the Baptist.

CHAPTER NINE

Jesus

The first scholar of modern times to link Jesus with the Essenes was Johann Georg Wachter, in his two-volume work written in 1713, *De Primordiis Christianae Religionis (The Beginnings of the Christian Religion)*. For example, Wachter attributes Jesus' ability to work miracles to training by the Essenes. Since then, each century has generated a multitude of equally fanciful, occasionally multivolume works on the obviously enticing subject, "Jesus as an Essene" — to the point of the publication of allegedly longmissing Essene texts written in part by Jesus himself, which, however, turn out to be products of the twentieth century.

Meanwhile, the speculations about Qumran that spring up in such luxuriance from the fertile soil of Essene manuscript fragments have become the favorite fodder of those sheep who wish to continue grazing on this abundantly blooming meadow. On the German book market, a heightened interest on the part of readers in matters Essene never materializes unless the title of the book includes the word "Jesus," even when Jesus scarcely plays any role at all in the content of the book, as in the German edition of the book by Baigent and Leigh and the one by Eisenman and Wise. The few partial sentences and single words from the Qumran finds that they cite, taken out of context and often enough ignorantly interpreted to boot, suggest, in such contrived works, connections that have never historically existed. Seeming similarities are so stylized that they yield clear correspondences. Besides all this, the "Jesus" of such books is a contrived figure concocted of little mosaic stones that have come together coincidentally — like their patchwork quilt, sewn with such hasty needle, of alleged truths about "Qumran" or "the Essenes." Practically none of this has anything to do with ancient realities.

Unfortunately, all efforts to bring reliable material about Jesus before our eyes are beset with manifold difficulties. Just a few centuries after Jesus'

life on earth, four evangelists, in distant Syria, Asia Minor, or Rome, composed, as best they could on the basis of transmitted material still available
to them, presentations of the earthly life of Jesus. These presentations were
adopted by the Church and placed in its canon. They are the only sources
from which it is still possible to extract reliable information about Jesus. Here
the Church has always been conscious that it is only through the fourfold
form of the Gospel, with all of the differences in the presentations, that it is
possible to lay hold of Jesus.

The representation of the evangelists in church art continues to make
use of the symbols with which the church father Jerome depicted those writers
around A.D. 400, when he adopted various biblical symbols (Ezek. 1:10; Rev.
4:7) to correspond to the different texts of the beginning of their works.
Because of Jesus' family tree at the beginning of his Gospel, Matthew is
symbolized by a human being. Mark, owing to his opening presentation of
the Baptist as one crying in the desert, becomes a lion. Luke's opening scene
is one of Temple sacrifice offered by Zechariah, and so Luke is a bull. John,
with his lofty theology — "In the beginning was the Word" — is symbolized
by an eagle. The same variety holds for the conclusions and for the other
content of the Gospels. They are not susceptible of being meshed together
into a fully unitary overall picture.

For centuries, the diverging presentations of Jesus contained in the
Gospels have been compared, in order to discover what might go back to
Jesus as core material and what is to be ascribed to later development. Despite
all efforts, only on a few questions do we have a scholarly consensus. Indeed,
today there are almost as many conceptualizations of the "actual" Jesus as
there are scholars involved in the search for him.

From the rich offerings of this supermarket of opinions about Jesus,
every dilettante chooses according to taste. For every remotely possible
Qumran and Essene comparison, the Gospels are bound to have something
or other that matches what someone or another among the countless researchers has ascribed to his or her "genuine" Jesus — if well-founded
opinions are sought at all and an uncritical self-service in the Gospels does
not completely predominate. But this sort of cafeteria procedure proves
nothing.

Hence it is incumbent upon all of those who want to express an opinion
on the significance of the Qumran finds for understanding Jesus, first, to
supply information on how, according to their particular analyses, Jesus presented himself in his time, at least to the extent that this bears on the question
of connections with Qumran and the Essenes. One cannot simply look at the
Qumran finds and then look at the Gospel tradition and spontaneously claim
that everything comparable in the two relates Jesus to Qumran. The proper
procedure is just the other way around: one ought to ask whether material

supposedly applicable to Jesus, on his side, is clearly available in the Qumran finds as well.

Owing to the manifold form of the Gospel traditions, many New Testament scholars today are admittedly skeptical of the possibility of clearly establishing any claims about Jesus. This can be done, however, if one appeals not to sporadic elements of the Jesus tradition, but to the core content of what the Gospels have transmitted as the principal data of his life on earth and have related to it as to his utterances. If this is done thoroughly and carefully, it immediately becomes clear whether connections existed between Jesus and the Essenes.

The Reign of God

Aside from his crucifixion by the Romans, Jesus' baptism by John is the best-attested fact of his entire life on earth, and therefore the best starting point for all further questions about that life. Only as someone who had been baptized by John did Jesus begin his public activity as presented in the Gospels. Never did Jesus stand aloof from the Baptist. On the contrary, he unmistakably emphasized his abiding importance for all times (Mark 9:9-13; Matt. 11:7-11a; 17:9-13; Luke 7:24-28a).

Faithful to these preliminary data, all of the Gospels have solidly and positively included John the Baptist in their presentations of Jesus, and this not only with regard to his person, but with regard to the core elements of his proclamation as well. Therefore we can draw the conclusion that Jesus personally endorsed, without reservations, the Baptist's self-understanding and his perspective on the future, and — just as did others who had been baptized by John — expected the Last Judgment as well as the time of salvation in the immediate future. In particular, the imminence of the end of current conditions, as proclaimed by John, probably excluded basic changes in position for each of those baptized by him.

It is all the more surprising that, at the center of the Jesus tradition, a concept appears that is completely absent in the Baptist's proclamation — namely, the *Reign of God*, or, in the expression used by the Gospel of Matthew, the *Kingdom of Heaven*. Only later is its announcement placed on the lips of John, in order to present the Baptist's proclamation as in basic agreement with that of Jesus (Matt. 3:2; cf. 4:17; and Mark 1:15). But the Baptist himself never used the concept of the Reign of God. Also, the context of events in which the Jesus tradition concentrates on the concept — the expulsion of demons and a series of parables (e.g., Mark 4; Matthew 13; Luke 13:18-21) — has nothing whatever to correspond to it in the tradition of the Baptist.

In relationship to the preliminary data directly concerning the Baptist, therefore, that which took form in Jesus' proclamation as the Reign of God must have been something altogether new. This new element had the effect of creating Jesus' relative independence from John, as attested in the Gospels. It is also the reason why Christianity became an independent religion — neither a simple extension of the activity of the Baptist, nor only a further shaping of other religious starting points already available in the Judaism of the time.

Jesus was a Jew obviously, and Christianity was originally an inner-Jewish phenomenon. There is no point whatever in making these indubitable conditions indirectly questionable. Inescapably, however, Christianity developed from premises that go beyond what was already at hand in the Judaism of Jesus' time. But the first to have introduced a decisively new element in this respect was not Paul, who is frequently reproached with distancing Christianity from Judaism. It was Jesus, with what he called the Reign of God.

Strangely, almost no one today ever asks about what occasioned Jesus' adoption of a message so independent of that of the Baptist and, simultaneously, decisively conditioned the appearance of Christianity as a new religion. Scholars are most often satisfied with describing the many different ways in which Jesus speaks of the Reign of God, pursuing the possible meanings of his parables, or investigating the possible meanings of Jesus' claim, present in all of the Gospels, that he himself is the ruler in the Reign of God (see below, p. 249).

Undercurrents of centuries-old psychological models of explanation are still at work here. For example, some suggest that Jesus discovered supernatural powers within himself — or was impressed by the mass effect of his proclamation and its power of suggestion — and therefore in the course of time arrived at the conviction that he was the Messiah, the Son of God, or the Son of Man. On this view, he regarded the Reign of God — present or still future — as the realm of messianic rule that would be in conformity with his own picture of it (see *Psalms of Solomon* 17), unless indeed it could be rendered actual by his preaching (through the speech event of his parables). The significance of John the Baptist for all of Jesus' activity, a significance so strongly emphasized by Jesus himself, is, strangely, completely neglected in all such constructions and discussions. At best, the Baptist's proclamation of judgment is occasionally used as a negative foil for Jesus' announcement of salvation.

Considered historically, there are only three possible ways of explaining the emergence of Jesus' special proclamation of the Reign of God after his baptism by John. Either (1) Jesus experienced an *independent call* that made him the prophet of the Reign of God; or (2) the language used by others in his *religious environment* was so extensively marked with discourse concerning the Reign of God that Jesus could make himself understood best through the use of this concept; or (3) *events* eventually occurred that went beyond what the Baptist had formulated, which were interpreted by Jesus as happenings closely connected with the Reign of God. Only the Gospel tradition and the sources from Jesus' religious surroundings — the latter being considerably broadened by the Qumran finds — enable us to decide which of these possible explanations corresponds to reality.

(1) Even the earliest of the four Gospels portrays Jesus' experience of an *independent call,* and this as he emerged from the water precisely at his baptism by John (Mark 1:10-11). But there is nothing here about the Reign of God, whose prophet Jesus is supposed to be from now on. Rather, Jesus' identity as Son of God is endorsed as grounded in the Spirit and the will of God, and the baptismal situation is presented as the effective moment of its coming into force, as demonstrated immediately by Jesus' temptation in the desert, the first test of his identity as God's Son (Mark 1:12-13).

The other evangelists have preferred to present Jesus' divine sonship as actually verified from his mother's womb (Matt. 1:18-25; Luke 1:26-38), or indeed from before the creation of the world (John 1:1–3:18), so that for them the events in connection with the baptismal situation have lost the character of a call vision. Not least among the reasons for the possibility of these changes was that the calling portrayed by Mark as a personal experience of Jesus was not a personal report by Jesus in the first-person singular, but an outside report in the service of theological interests and without even the naming of any witnesses.

Historically regarded, Mark's presentation poses insurmountable difficulties. Had Jesus had the experience of a prophetic calling of his own at his very baptism by John, he would have become, almost at the same moment, a disciple of the Baptist and a prophet independent of the Baptist. Then Jesus' own declarations concerning John's unique importance — why should he be said to be the greatest person who ever lived (Matt. 11:11a; Luke 7:28a)? — and all of the efforts of the evangelists to downgrade him to a mere forerunner and preparer of the way, would be altogether incomprehensible, even apart from numerous references to Jesus' membership in the Baptist's circle of disciples (for example, his designation as a Nazarene or Nazorean), or, for that matter, to his having been baptized.

Furthermore, Jesus can have had no *later* experience of a calling, some time after his baptism. The relatively spare tradition that we have received concerning the Baptist, and the tendency of early Christianity to see that it stood in second place to that of its central figure, Jesus, make it understandable that in the case of the prophet John no further call report should have been received. As for the scope of the Jesus tradition in the Gospels, on the other hand, at least a trace of such a striking event as the later experience of a calling would necessarily have been received; not to mention that no Christian would have raised objections to accepting and passing on a report about a calling of Jesus by God himself as the herald of his Reign.

Thus, there is no way around the datum that there never was a special experience of a calling of Jesus to which his independent discourse on the Reign of God can be traced.

(2) As for Jesus' *religious environment,* at last it can be proved, on the basis of the Qumran finds, that Jesus did not owe what he said about the Reign of God to the Essenes. Speculations currently in favor again, like the one that Jesus surely spent several years in Qumran, since many of the statements in the Sermon on the Mount are similar to finds in the Qumran texts, are of no help in this case either. In the Qumran texts, the Reign of God — or God's royal rule — occurs as rarely as in the Old Testament and other pre-Christian Jewish literature. Besides, in these cases what is at issue is almost exclusively the everlasting heavenly lordship of God over the whole world since the creation of that world and unto all eternity, without essential references to current events in heaven or on earth.

Only seldom in pre-Christian Judaism do we find so much as the expectation that the Reign of God will be established worldwide in the future. When such references are made — as in the book of Daniel (Dan. 2:31-45), or in the contemporaneous *War Rule* from Qumran — it is political entities, such as the kingdoms of the Babylonians, Persians, Seleucids, or Romans, who have subjugated Israel, whose power shall be broken in the future as they give way to the Reign of God. The two characteristic aspects of the Jesus tradition — that the Reign of God abolishes the rule of Satan in the world, and that it is already presently becoming effective in seed, are to be found neither in the Qumran texts nor in other Jewish literature, at least where these surely stem from pre-Christian times.

At this point we must reach out further, in order to escape the reproach that we are too fixated on a certain concept, at the expense of broader opportunities for an understanding of our topic. It is necessary, therefore, to inquire into God's intervention in events of the world in general. Christians, after all, like to imagine that God has to intervene constantly in events of the world, as soon as God's will is contravened somewhere. In the Judaism of Jesus' time, however, other conceptions prevailed.

Jews of that time — including the Essenes — generally held to the notion that all of God's active dealings, in heaven as on earth, were confined to the past and the future. In the past, God had created the world, led the people of Israel out of Egypt with his own hand, gave the Torah to Moses on Mount Sinai, and finally, on earth, through his Spirit, confided to the prophets what they were to write in their books, including the threat of banning Israel from the Holy Land were his people not to keep the covenant of Sinai. This occurred for the last time with the prophet Malachi, at the close of the sixth century B.C. To him God entrusted the last instructions for the future. Only in this future, prophesied by Malachi himself, would God actively intervene once more in world affairs — namely, he would usher in the Last Judgment, annihilate all that is godless in the world, and establish his mighty rule without any competition. In the meantime, God does not directly intervene in world events, but governs them only indirectly, through angels, through the revelation of his will of old, and through his revelation of all future events in the books of Moses and the Prophets, which books are available on earth. God also rules, indirectly, through the establishment of systems of governance such as the successive foreign rules over Israel as ongoing punishment meted out to the ever sinful people of God.

Only God's indirect activity on earth, in the time between the last biblical prophet of the past and the coming Last Judgment, features in the Qumran texts, although some of these texts are often interpreted otherwise. For example, hymns composed by the Teacher of Righteousness celebrate God's protection of their composer from his enemies and express his divine endorsement as the representative of God's covenant, thereby providing for the continued existence of the people of God (1QH 2–9). The case is the same with a later Qumran text that declares God himself to have chosen the Teacher of Righteousness, and to have appointed him to establish the holy community of the reunited people of God on a continuing basis and to lead them in the way of justice (4QpPs^a 1–10 iii 15-17). This is indirect governance of earthly events and preservation by God, as it is also variously portrayed in the books of Maccabees, and not the active victory of God's power on earth as henceforward the sole determining force.

Only in connection with the coming Last Judgment did the Essenes, like all Jews, expect a renewed creative activity of God on earth, through the effective power of his Holy Spirit (1QS 4:18-23). True, community hymns from the Qumran finds especially praise God in a variety of ways for having enabled human beings, even in the present, through the gift of the Holy Spirit, to attain to insights that are closed to the natural human spirit (1QH 1, 12–18). But this represents neither an anticipation of the coming gift of the Spirit at the Last Judgment (Joel 3:1-5; cf. Acts 2:17-21), nor an immediate intervention of God in the heart of earthly human beings, but rather the experience of heavenly enlightenment through the presence of angels in the community worship assemblies, as well as through the study of the revealed Scriptures — the Torah and the Prophets — whose revelatory content includes the gift of the Holy Spirit (cf. Ps. 119:18). By virtue of their anointing of old by God's Spirit, the Old Testament prophets, through their writings, are the true "messiahs" of the present, until the future Last Judgment (cf. above, p. 206).

Neither Essene notions of God's activity nor data from the Old Testament or known from elsewhere in the Judaism of the time can have brought Jesus to speak of the Reign of God in the way that he did. There must be more behind it than simply a manner of speaking that went beyond the Baptist's formulations. It must be something whose own dynamics made Jesus independent of the Baptist. The religious environment did not give it to Jesus in advance.

(3) The only realistic explanation for the materialization of Jesus' discourse on the Reign of God therefore remains: sometime after his baptism by John, *events occurred that Jesus witnessed,* events that he regarded and testified to as immediate divine activity in the present — activity that he interpreted, for his part, as "the Reign of God."

The expression used by Jesus in his Aramaic mother tongue, *malkûtā' dĕ'ălāhā',* depending on the context, can mean *the Reign of God* (as distinguished from other reigns at hand), *the Rule of God* (in the sense of its active supremacy over other powers), or *the Realm of the Rule of God* (in the sense of God's already conquered realms in the heavenly world, on earth, and in the underworld). It is difficult, then, to find a single translation that will fit all cases.

The simplest thing to do would be to retain the expression, *Reign of God,* with the awareness that Jesus usually used it to mean the current supremacy of God's governance, although at times what he meant was the realm of God's rule as already taking shape as a result of that supremacy; relatively rarely did he use the expression to denote the opposition of God's reign to other existing reigns, and when he did he used it not in the sense of a political opposition to the Roman Empire, but as the antithesis of the reign of Satan's rule, which had prevailed until then. When the expression *kingdom (reign) of heaven* is on Jesus' lips, it usually means precisely what we have just defined — not a realm beyond this world, but the victory of the rule of heaven (God's rule), especially in the earthly realm.

The conceptual background for Jesus' discourse on the Reign of God is illuminated most powerfully in his declaration, "I watched Satan fall from the sky like lightning" (Luke 10:18; cf. John 12:31; Rev. 12:7-12). Thus, God has cast Satan from his erstwhile center of power in the heavenly world and has already begun to bring about the supremacy of his sole rule throughout the world. From now on, the power of evil, which has prevailed since the Fall, must give way to the mightier power of God (cf. Mark 3:23-27; Matt. 12:25-29; Luke 11:17-22).

The miracle reports of the Gospels show how the victory of God begun in heaven is extended on the earth. All of these wonders are presented as performed by Jesus. Yet there are striking differences.

Jesus is occasionally presented as a wonder-worker filled with divine power, for example, in the healing of the woman with a hemorrhage (Mark

5:25-34), by his walking on the water of the Sea of Galilee (Mark 6:45-52), or at his changing of water into wine (John 2:1-10). Much more often, however, Jesus appears simply as a *mediator* of heavenly, divine power, even though this is usually only incidentally or indirectly clear from the representations transmitted.

Even after Jesus' first miracle, of which Mark informs us, those present do not ask, "What manner of astounding person is this, who has such miraculous powers?" (cf. Mark 4:41), but "What does this mean?" (Mark 1:27), as if it were not the wonder-worker who was important, but a mighty deed independent of him.

In the fashion of the man of God Elisha (2 Kings 4:42-44), Jesus satisfied the hunger of thousands of persons with a few loaves and fishes (Mark 6:30-44; 8:1-9; John 6:5-13). But what happened is not that the feelings of hunger on the part of all present miraculously disappeared because they ate a tiny bit of food. Rather, at the end of the meal there was much more left over than had been available in the first place, without Jesus' adequately multiplying the small quantity of available food before the beginning of the distribution. It was a heavenly miracle on earth, in connection with Jesus, not a wonder worked through the power contained within Jesus.

God's activity is even more clear in the miracle of the healing of the sick, when, for example, Jesus heals a paralytic and those present praise not him, but God (Mark 2:12). The person delivered from a whole legion of demons should not be thankful to Jesus, but should report to his family at home what God as "the [only] Lord in his mercy has done for you" (Mark 5:19). Often Jesus also heals the sick through a simple gesture (Mark 1:31), or with a supplementary demand (e.g., Mark 1:41-42; 5:41-42). In all of these presentations, Jesus proceeds not like the Jewish healers of his time, who wrought their cures with wonder medicines, ointments, the laying on of hands, or prayers (cf. also James 5:13-18); Jesus only mediates the power of God, who is the actual wonder-worker.

To messengers from the Baptist, who are to ask Jesus whether he is the one proclaimed to be coming, Jesus pointed to "what you hear and see: the blind recover their sight, cripples walk, lepers are cured, the deaf hear, the dead are raised to life, and the poor have the good news preached to them" (Matt. 11:4-5; cf. Luke 7:22). The context shows that these indications are supposed to confirm Jesus as the one announced by the Baptist. Still, he makes his reference almost as someone not personally involved in the present events, whose author in the background seems to be God himself. Luke has felt this problem, and has had Jesus quickly accomplish certain miracles still in the presence of the Baptist's messengers (Luke 7:21). But why had the traditional material received by Matthew and Luke not already presented these wondrous occurrences unambiguously as Jesus' personal activity?

God's activity in wondrous events around Jesus becomes clearest in the expulsion of demons. An unclean spirit obeys Jesus' mere order to be gone (Mark 1:23-27), as does an entire legion of demons, after being offered alternative quarters (Mark 5:1-20); or a demon of the most stubborn sort that causes epilepsy withdraws from a boy at Jesus' simple bidding (Mark 9:14-27). In these cases we usually hear of Jesus' exorcisms, and Jesus is regarded as one of the exorcists of the time. But the latter worked in a completely different way.

Flavius Josephus very vividly portrays an example from his own experience. He was personally present when, in A.D. 67 or 68 in Palestine, the Jewish exorcist Eleazar demonstrated for the future Emperor Vespasian and his entourage the expulsion of a demon according to customary method:

> He put to the nose of the possessed person a ring that had under its seal one of the roots prescribed by [King] Solomon [as effective, in his instructions on exorcism] and then, as the person smelled it, drew out the demon [who had greedily bit into the magic ring] through the person's nostrils. The person at once fell down. Whereupon Eleazar, speaking Solomon's name and reciting the incantations that he had composed, adjured the demon never to come back into the person. (*Antiquities* 8.46-47)

Subsequently Eleazar demonstrated to those present that the demon had actually left the possessed person by causing the demon to upset a nearby container of water (*Antiquities* 8.48).

This kind of exorcism always belonged to the Essenes' practice of healing. From the Qumran finds there is a scroll with four psalms that King David supposedly composed as an effective tool in the expulsion of evil spirits (11QApocryphal Psalms[a]), as well as an extensive collection of hymns of conjuration to be used for the same purpose (4Q510 and 511). Also in general use in the Judaism of the time were magic bowls, whose healing inscriptions and symbols transformed water that had been poured into them into a demon-expelling medicine, as well as formulas of conjuration filled with the names of gods and angels, along with mythological references, whose magic power, if used correctly, the demons could not withstand.

Jesus, by contrast, never performed like the exorcists. He used neither the names of God nor those of angels, neither magical prayers nor magical rites, neither Davidic nor Solomonic texts of conjuration, and he needed no equipment such as magic bowls or rings. The miracle accounts of the Gospels show that perfectly clearly.

Nor is it a coincidence that many of Jesus' miracles — the multiplication of the loaves, the expulsion of an entire legion of demons, the healing of the epileptic, or even the resuscitation of a person who, beyond any doubt, had died (esp. John 11:1-44) — were entirely absent from the customary repertoire of the miraculous healers or exorcists of that time. They far outstripped the professional capability of the latter. They are rather miracles *of God,* which have been presented in these accounts as having been performed through Jesus. For miracles of this kind there was no technique that Jesus could have learned from the Essenes or other contemporaries.

Faced with these wondrous events that went so far beyond the usual, Jewish contemporaries of Jesus reproached him to the effect that it must be the great power of Satan himself that effected the withdrawal of even the worst of demons without any discernible tools. Jesus retorted that their assumption was self-contradictory: Satan would be destroying his own power. Besides, there were people among them who drove out demons with an appeal to higher powers, which certainly were not powers subordinated to Satan. Granted, these effected little by comparison with the present events. "If it is by the finger of God that *I* cast out devils, then the *Reign of God* is upon you" (Luke 11:15-20; cf. Matt. 12:24-28; Mark 3:22-26).

Matthew 12:28 has, instead of the "finger of God," "Spirit of God." In context, that is not a significant difference. The Spirit of God is understood here as the active power of God himself already working on earth, exactly as the "finger of God" with Moses' wonders in Egypt (Exod. 8:15). The "finger of God" is the most understated way possible to formulate in human imagery God's own intervention in earthly affairs. This was once expressed more forcefully with the image of God having led the people of Israel out of Egypt "with his strong hand and outstretched arm" (e.g., Deut. 4:34; 5:15; 7:19).

For Jesus, those events in which demons withdrew without any sort of exorcism were an unambiguous sign that God himself was once more at work on earth. The victory of God's rule in the world, awaited in the future, was commencing. The event announced by the Baptist had actually begun. The proclamations of the prophet John could scarcely be fulfilled any better or quicker than this. The Reign of God was being inaugurated visibly, for all to see.

The miracle traditions of the Gospels thereby show, in manifold ways and with abundant clarity, that (3) it was *events of his own area of experience* that gave rise to Jesus' discourse on the Reign of God, which he owed neither to (1) the experience of a calling nor to (2) the linguistic and conceptual influence of his environment. The Essenes were of no recognizable importance here. Only Jesus' link with John the Baptist continued to have its effect, and indeed both fundamentally and fruitfully.

John baptized across the Jordan, within sight of the Holy Land as the coming realm of salvation. All of Jesus' "expulsion of demons" with which place names are connected in the Gospels occurred *within* the boundaries of the Holy Land as described in the Old Testament — the land that God was now publicly making his incontestable property once more. Granted, as his words concerning the "finger of God," and the miracle reports of the Gospels, show, Jesus was operating on the principle that he was personally involved in this activity of God's. But he did not regard it as being effected by himself or fundamentally bound to his person. Rather, he was sure that the same thing was occurring everywhere in the Holy Land: demons were withdrawing without the application of exorcising practices.

Out of this conviction, he sent people into localities at random to observe such occurrences in other places. When these people were asked how such wondrous happenings were to be explained, they were to inform the inhabitants there that the Reign of God was present. In the Gospels' presentation, this has become a regular mission of Jesus' disciples, whom he now assigned the task of driving out demons (Mark 6:6b-13; Matt. 9:36–11:1; Luke 9:1-6; 10:1-12; cf. esp. Mark 3:15; Matt. 10:7-8; Luke 9:2; 10:11). This mission is stamped, in a variety of ways, with the missionary concepts and experiences of early Christianity. Contrary to the interests of later presentation, the disciples' mission here indicates above all that for Jesus the event of the Reign of God at this point in time reached far beyond his personal realm of experience. He himself was a witness of that event, evidently the first. The imminence of God's active dealings on earth, of which Jesus had become aware since his baptism by John, probably decisively sharpened his perception of its very first signs. But at the same time, Jesus was from the outset the decisive interpreter of such events as *deeds of God* in which the Reign of God was beginning to prevail on earth.

Jesus' interpretation of generally observable events was held by his contemporaries to be extremely questionable. After all, one cannot draw the conclusion from the expulsion of a few demons that the Reign of God is already present. That Reign, everyone knew, was far more powerful, and at its coming it would have to shake the whole world to its foundations. In response, Jesus explained that evidently it was no different with the Reign of God than with a grain of mustard, in which, tiny though it be, a mighty mustard bush is nevertheless concealed, or with a bit of leaven, which, however small, nevertheless has the power within it to leaven a huge mass of dough (Mark 4:30-32; Matt. 13:31-33; Luke 13:18-21).

In the Gospels, these parables now illustrate allegorically the growth of the Church, from its smallest beginnings to its inclusion of the great pagan world. For Jesus, however, the point was the contrast between the invisible, but mighty power of God's Reign and the comparatively tiny, although already visible and characteristic signs of its effective growth on earth. Today one might perhaps select other images for such a contrast — for example, an AIDS virus that is visible only under a microscope, which makes the one infected by it a dead person; or a number on a bank account, invisible optically, which identifies its possessor as a millionaire. The contrast illustrates that it is a matter of the quality of the observable signs, not their quantity. The defeat of even one demon shows that God is establishing his rule, when obviously no one else — for instance, an exorcist — has effected it.

For Jesus, it was important in itself that human activities have no significance in bringing about the Reign of God. The Reign of God is like a field that has already been sown, which ultimately becomes, all by itself, a ripe field of grain, without anyone having bothered about it in the meantime (Mark 4:26-28). How God was establishing his rule — what he began with and what he did next — had to remain his own concern and was removed from any influence on the human side. Once underway, the process was irresistible and irreversible. No person or thing could be mightier than God, who was now beginning to establish his ruling power on earth. Jesus never sought to *bring* the Reign of God. It only began *to occur especially through him.*

The Last Judgment

Many Jesus researchers begin with the assumption that Jesus' discourse on the Reign of God bore fundamentally on the future (even if the near future). After all, before the dawn of the Reign of God, the Last Judgment would have to occur. Other scholars are of the opinion that, for Jesus, the Last Judgment announced by the Baptist no longer had a great deal of importance, if any at all. Instead, Jesus proclaimed the Reign of God or made it the new core of his own teaching. Common to both viewpoints is the Reign of God as a basically positive thing that must be sharply separated from the Last Judgment as the negative side of God's coming activity.

The Qumran texts finally bring decisive help to efforts to clarify these problems of the Jesus tradition. First, they have multiplied, in welcome measure, the material on which we base the already familiar idea that all human beings will be included in the Last Judgment, and that only there will the ultimate separation between good and evil take place. Still more important is a matter that one could have known from *Jubilees* or the Enoch writings, or indeed from the biblical Prophets, but to which only the Qumran finds call adequate attention: the duration of the Last Judgment and its relationship to the time of salvation.

In the *Melchizedek Midrash* from Qumran, the Last Judgment lasts seven years. The *War Rule* presents the coming settlement of accounts between light and darkness as an event that will last forty years in all, in the course of which all of the evil in the world will gradually be annihilated and good will correspondingly gain ground. At the same time, this event is reckoned as

God's execution of the Last Judgment. Likewise in those Qumran texts that see the Last Judgment one-sidedly as a punishment of the wicked, from which the good are removed or at which they cooperate at God's side, the event in question is one of lengthy duration, and over its course good becomes established more and more solidly.

That the Last Judgment can also be dubbed the "Day of God," invoking biblical usage, has led to its being regarded as an abrupt discontinuation of conditions in the world as they have prevailed until now, with the dawn of the time of salvation coming on the morrow. Actually, however, in these concepts — characteristic of Palestinian Judaism at the time of Jesus — the time of salvation and the Last Judgment begin simultaneously. A long-lasting process of gradual establishment of the Reign of God is necessary before that Reign will have definitively conquered. But it continues to spread ever further, displacing and annihilating evil in the world step by step, and continuously embracing more human beings in the constantly growing realm of salvation, until the latter will finally be complete and there will be no more evil.

Jesus, too, oriented himself to this way of conceiving things. For him, the Reign of God was not a static force that is either already present in its fullness or is still to come as a whole. It was a dynamic force, whose operation begins at a given point and reaches its completion only at a later time. Thus, Jesus promised those who had experienced with him the *beginnings* of the Reign of God: "I assure you, among those standing here there are some who will not taste death until they see the reign of God established in power" (Mark 9:1).

These words reflect the perspective of the half-century within which, around A.D. 70, Mark completed his Gospel, so it was no problem for him to accept these words of Jesus. The evangelists Matthew and Luke, who wrote later, have retained them with slight modifications (Matt. 16:28; Luke 9:27), reinterpreting them, of course, in the wider context. The decisive thing is that Jesus has clearly distinguished here between an already observable *beginning* of the Reign of God on earth, and its *completion,* to be achieved only in the future; and that Jesus' starting point is that only *some* of his contemporaries might live long enough to experience it in its perfection. The full establishment of God's power in the world must therefore still take considerable time.

Simultaneously with the time of salvation, whose beginning was becoming palpable in the demons' flight before the power of God, for Jesus the Last Judgment had already begun. For him, the Last Judgment was an integral component of the Reign of God, which, as the establishment of God's sole claim to rule in the world, naturally included the annihilation of all that was ungodly and the bestowal of salvation upon those who were pleasing to God.

This negative side of the Reign of God in the Jesus tradition often goes unrecognized. Usually only the salvific aspect is perceived, as if the Reign of

God were from beginning to end a matter of God's merciful, gracious, and loving approach to a humanity otherwise threatened with ruin. God is thought to have been, for Jesus, exclusively the good and generous Father, toward whom he had an especially deep relationship of trust. But Jesus' calling God 'abba, "Dear Father," which is supposed to prove this, was not limited to his person, but comes from the prayer that he gave his disciples, who were to call on God in this manner — the Our Father (Matt. 6:9-13; Luke 11:2-4; cf. Rom. 8:15; Gal. 4:6). But the disciples — like Jesus — were already included in the salvific area of God's activity and therefore represented only a part of what the Reign of God as a whole meant. The positive side must not be absolutized.

For Jesus, the Reign being established was that of the same God revealed in the Torah and the Prophets — the God who gave life as well as death, sickness and its healing, hope and corruption, blessing and curse. Wherever the Reign of God took form on earth, for some this was the salvation they yearned for, but for others it meant an agonizing end and everlasting annihilation.

Contemporaries objected to Jesus' view. For Israel as the chosen people of God, they held, the materialization of his Reign would surely be exclusively positive, and the simultaneous terror of the Last Judgment strike only others. Jesus referred them to the biblical picture of God's dealings. Wherever the Reign of God embraces human beings, it is like a dragnet used in fishing, whose content, as experience shows, is never more than partially fit for consumption; the rest is offal (Matt. 13:47-48). Or it is like a farmer's field, where not only grain, but weeds flourish (Matt. 13:24-30). Or it is like seed broadcast over farmland, which usually is partly eaten up by birds, partly left without adequate root soil, and partly smothered by weeds, so that never do all of the seeds yield the wished-for harvest of thirtyfold, sixtyfold, or especially, a hundredfold (Mark 4:3-8; Matt. 13:3-8; Luke 8:5-8; cf. Gen. 26:12).

In the Gospels, these parables are also accompanied and stamped by allegorical interpretations that now refer them to Jesus' own activity and the Christian mission. But what Jesus himself meant by these parables is that even with Israel God was not proceeding otherwise than he had always done: the Reign of God, even for Israel, was bringing in part salvation, and in part annihilation.

The Essenes' point of departure was that only the members of their union and other pious persons who had been led astray — especially by the Pharisees — without fault of their own (4QpNah 3:4-8; cf. CD 20:22-25) would survive God's Last Judgment. All other Jews, just as pagans who were unwilling to convert, would perish. Jesus shared this view in principle for the remnant of Israel, but he did not draw the same boundaries as did the Essenes. For Jesus, God himself made the selection in his own omnipotence, and obviously in a way that was frequently downright irreconcilable with conventional norms of piety.

Jesus had his most impressive experiences in connection with women. Owing to Eve's original guilt in the primeval Fall (Genesis 3), women were accounted as particularly guilt-laden beings and were generally excluded where religion was concerned. According to a widespread view, neither did they have souls, or any part in eternal life. Accordingly, it later became customary for pious Jewish males to thank God for not having put them in the world as women.

Now it happened, however, that the demons withdrew even from women, and a large number of them, among them one Johanna, wife of the Herodian courtier Chuza, and a woman named Susanna. Seven demons at once had departed from a certain Mary, from Magdala on the west bank of Lake Gennesaret, apparently a particularly hopeless sinner, who in the general estimation really need expect no grace from God whatever. Since these women supported Jesus and his group of followers financially from then on, it is to be supposed that the demons had withdrawn from them in their presence, though this is not expressly stated (Luke 8:2-3).

The full implications, however, of what happened for Jesus in the flight of demons only becomes clear if we keep in mind that, in the popular belief of Palestinian Judaism at the time, all diseases were attributed to the activity of demons. Malaria, for instance, from which Jesus delivered Peter's mother-in-law simply by grasping her hand and raising her from her sickbed, was reckoned an attack of the fever demon, which spontaneously left her as Jesus grasped her hand (Mark 1:29-31; Matt. 8:14-15; cf. Luke 4:38-39).

One became prone to diseases especially by sinning. Anyone who had transgressed God's commandments consciously or unconsciously would have God's protecting hand — or guardian angel — withdrawn, and the demons could take up residence in that person. The more serious the sin, the stronger or more numerous were the demons. Thus, illnesses were accounted God's punishments for unforgiven sins. The healing of the sick was basically regarded as impermissible interference with God's punishment.

But now it was God himself who caused the sick to recover on the spot, who made even the worst demons leave the possessed, without the latter having previously repented of their sins or even having received forgiveness. The fundamental connection between sickness and sin becomes clear, however, when Jesus forgives a crippled person his sins, and the latter, healed, is able to walk (Mark 2:1-12; Matt. 9:1-8; Luke 5:17-26).

The forgiveness of sins that John the Baptist had guaranteed for the coming Last Judgment, only after a conversion, was now visibly arriving in the execution of the Last Judgment, and even to the benefit of those who had not been baptized by John. At any rate, in the Gospels the expulsion of demons and other cures are never connected with John's baptism. If Jesus himself baptized in the course of his activity (John 3:22, 26; 4:1), his baptism nowhere appears as behavior accompanying the healing of the sick or the expulsion of demons.

What occurred here was God's activity on his own initiative, on behalf of persons who in no way deserved it. God was showing his unlimited power precisely where he had long since, by all acknowledged norms of piety, lost all to Satan. At stake in these events was not primarily help for those who otherwise could not be rescued, but the demonstration of God's power at central points of what until now had been the power of Satan — the victory of the Reign of God over the rule of evil in the world, where it held people in its power.

Against this background, it also becomes understandable why so many people were gathering in the now prevailing realm of God's rule. No one had expected so many. Jesus explained this striking state of affairs in his parables of the lost sheep, the lost coin, and the lost son (Matt. 18:12-14; Luke 15:3-32), and he observed that tax collectors and prostitutes were entering the Reign of God before the high priests and the elders (Matt. 21:31; cf. 21:23). Indeed, even pagans managed entry, while many Jews were excluded (Matt. 8:11-12; Luke 13:28-29). If only one proof were needed that Jesus was no Essene, then any of these parables or utterances could be adduced, for they contradict all that was holy to the Essenes.

Just as John baptized everyone who had undergone a conversion, so also Jesus regarded no one as excluded in principle from salvation. God himself had already included in the realm of his rule both women and others possessed by demons to the point of dereliction. For all others, the challenge was to recognize the signs of the times ("This is the time of fulfillment," Mark 1:15) and to surrender without reservation to the sole claim of God's rule.

For this, no one needed any prerequisites. To be like children, who were completely unqualified for anything in the area of religion, counted for Jesus as the best of all imaginable prerequisites for access to the Reign (Mark 10:14; Matt. 19:14; Luke 18:16; cf. John 3:3, 5). Those who were attached to their wealth (Mark 10:25; Matt. 19:24; Luke 18:25; cf. Mark 10:21-22; Matt. 19:21-22; Luke 18:22-23) or who regarded concern for their own support, and so for their future material security, as the most important thing (Matt. 6:25-34; Luke 12:13-34) had no chance.

But those who recognized the plenitude of blessing that was beginning to spill forth in the realm of God's rule, those who offered themselves without reserve to the claim of his rule, would bet everything on a single card in order to have a share in this Reign. Jesus likened their present situation to that of a wage earner on a farm who obviously would give everything he has to buy someone's field if he has discovered a treasure in it (Matt. 13:44), just as a wise merchant would give all for the acquisition of an especially valuable pearl, whose possession would eliminate all competition and promise unsurpassable gain (Matt. 13:45-46). Jesus likened their present situation to that of a business manager discharged from his position without notice who, immediately afterward, writes off considerable parts of what his employer is owed by debtors, so that the latter will have much less to pay, and the manager may subsequently live well at their appreciative hands (Luke 16:17).

Such ways of conducting business, though immoral, were not punishable and were very common in everyday life. Jesus did not recommend them for imitation but used them as universally comprehensible examples of total engagement in critical decision-making situations. Just such a situation was now at hand for all. In the definitive Reign of God, which would empty all previous arrangements of their value, everyone would have to face the simultaneity of definitive annihilation and salvation.

This change in all previous conditions for access to salvation was also the occasion for that symbolic action of Jesus in which he drove some businessmen from the outer court of the Temple and overturned the tables of money changers and dove merchants (Mark 11:15-17; Matt. 21:12-13; Luke 19:45-46; John 2:13-16). It is no longer ascertainable, nor is it of any particular importance, whether this symbolic action occurred shortly after the beginning of Jesus' public activity (as in John), toward the end (as in Mark, Matthew, and Luke), or somewhere in between. In any case it was neither a clarion call to revolt against the Romans nor a threat against the Temple hierarchy. Rather, it announced that the sacrificial worship, so important until then, had now lost every purpose and function, since God had now begun to impose his rule fully independently of it. The Essenes likewise boycotted the sacrificial worship in Jerusalem, but they held fast to the conviction that, even in the coming time of salvation, Temple and sacrifice would be indispensable. Jesus and the Essenes were worlds apart in their evaluation of the sacrificial worship as well.

Jesus saw in the further course of the Last Judgment, which was already beginning, not only the fate of the Jerusalem Temple as already sealed (Mark 13:1-2; Matt. 24:1-2; Luke 21:5-6), but likewise the fate of places like Chorazin, Bethsaida, and Capernaum, a majority of whose inhabitants failed to accept the wonders that had occurred among them as signs of the dawn of the Reign of God (Matt. 11:21-24; Luke 10:13-15; cf. Matt. 10:11-15). But Jesus refused to evaluate as God's present judgment the death of human beings caught in political conflicts or in the collapse of a tower rotted with age at the pool of Siloam in Jerusalem (Luke 13:1-5). For him, God passed judgment by letting people continue to be in the power of Satan and his demons, who only in the fullness of the time of salvation would finally finish their work as tools of God's punishment. On this point, coincidentally, the Essenes were of the same opinion as Jesus. Not that he needed to ask them for it; in this respect, almost all Jews had the same viewpoint.

A number of contemporaries were disinclined to believe Jesus that the departure of demons from a person without exorcism, the healing of the sick without the customary means of expert healing knowledge, or the conversion of tax collectors, prostitutes, and other worthless persons to a way of life pleasing to God without the bestowal of special enticements, were all obvious signs of the current victory of God's might. As proof of the correctness of his view, these skeptics frequently urged Jesus to work a wonder himself. Jesus always refused to comply with such demands for signs (Mark 8:11-13; Matt. 12:38-39; 16:1-4; Luke 11:16, 29; John 6:30; cf. 2:18), just as the report of his temptation by Satan presents him as averse to any wonder-working (Matt. 4:1-11; Luke 4:1-12).

Had Jesus accommodated these demands for signs, he would thereby have been presenting himself as a prophet. However, the last possible prophet, in Jesus' opinion, was John the Baptist, whose predictions were already being fulfilled (Matt. 11:13-14; cf. Luke 16:16). Further wondrous signs than those occurring in fulfillment of John's prophecy were really no longer needed. Jesus himself never regarded himself as called to be a prophet.

The implications of Jesus' rejection of any demand for a sign are usually missed. In actuality, it means nothing else than that Jesus always refused to work a single miracle. Yet the Gospels are full of reports of Jesus' independently wrought miracles.

It is the Gospel of John, especially, that has sought to find a compromise between these contrary statements of the facts. For example, it has Jesus sharply refuse the request of his mother to procure more wine by way of a miracle, but then has him accomplish the wonder nonetheless, even on his own competence (John 2:3-9).

Actually, Jesus never worked a miracle personally; rather, he was surrounded by miraculous heavenly occurrences in all their fullness. For Jesus, such miraculous occurrences were always mighty acts of God that happened in his presence, actions in which he saw himself involved, which he witnessed, and which he interpreted as occurrences of the Reign of God — happening, indeed, precisely through him. Owing to this strong connection of his person with the miraculous occurrences that happened during his time on earth, Jesus was increasingly depicted as an independent wonder-worker, indeed, as a wonder-worker filled with divine power who wrought deeds like a veritable new God on earth.

Jesus' own self-image, of course, in no way corresponded to this depiction. Even the miracle reports of the Gospels contain manifold elements referring to God as the actual wonder-worker in the case. Jesus' rejection of all demands for signs shows the underlying reality. At the same time, however, the fundamental connection of the mighty, wondrous deeds of the dawn of the Reign of God precisely with Jesus' appearance on the public scene makes it understandable that these deeds would have become more and more understood and described as the acts of his own person.

In this context, it is entirely correct to incorporate Jesus into the effective power of God, to designate him consequently as Son of God, and to say that God himself, acting in the person of Jesus, has appeared on earth. Whoever now maintains that Jesus was only a human being like any other, and in no way the Son of God, thereby denies the very activity of God to which Jesus committed himself with his whole person, and with which Christianity began. Anyone attempting to deny Jesus' status as Son of God in this fashion, far from being a champion of "historical accuracy," would be as far from Jesus' own concept as could ever be. The person of Jesus is firmly rooted in what occurred in those times as God's intervention in a world enslaved by the power of evil, and as indissolubly bound up with the particular persons and places among whom and in which a given event occurred — an event in which God himself, as judge and redeemer, has begun to cause the divine rule to prevail on earth.

Jesus once asked his disciples who they thought he was. Simon Peter, their spokesperson, replied: "You are the Messiah!" (Mark 8:29; cf. Matt. 16:16; Luke 9:20; John 6:68-69). Jesus forbade his disciples to propagate this view, since it was only half of the truth. The other half was his coming passion, death, and resurrection, whose meaning would become clear to the disciples only afterward (Mark 8:30-33; 9:9-10; cf. Matt. 16:20-23; 17:9; Luke 9:21-22).

This other half of Jesus' earthly existence is just as indispensable for his overall understanding of his person as his mighty activity as Son of God. The Church later gave this state of affairs, which was fundamental from the outset, adequate credal expression in the two-natures doctrine, which formulates Christ at once as true God and true human being.

Any talk of a "Dying Messiah," at least as far as the Gospels are concerned, is actually inappropriate, since in their framework Jesus as suffering, dying, and rising is characterized not as the Messiah, but as the Son of Man (Mark 8:31; 9:31; 10:33-34; Matt. 17:22-23; 20:18-19; Luke 9:22, 44; 18:31-32; cf. John 3:13-14; 6:53, 62; 8:28; 12:23-34; 13:31).

For a better understanding of these christological assertions, the Qumran finds unfortunately contribute nothing. The designation Son of Man is altogether absent. Nor is there any mention of a suffering, dying, or rising Messiah. Some decades ago it was regarded as a sensation that would shake Christianity to its foundations that some of the lines in the *Commentary on Habakkuk* had been interpreted by the Teacher of Righteousness as an anticipation of Jesus' suffering and crucifixion. The text actually refers to the disgraceful death of the Maccabee Jonathan at the hands of his enemies (1QpHab 8:13–9:2; cf.

Josephus, *Jewish War* 1.49). The messianic version of the *War Rule* from Qumran (4Q285) cites the coming execution of a death sentence *by* the Messiah — not, as so fondly supposed, *of* the Messiah. The Hebrew term occasionally used for the appearance on the scene of future savior figures such as the Messiah, *ʿāmad,* denotes, so to speak, their rising to office, not a rising from the dead. The figure of a suffering, dying, or rising Messiah was as foreign to the Essenes as to all of the rest of Judaism in pre-Christian times.

When Peter, as spokesperson of the disciples, characterized Jesus as the Messiah (Mark 8:29), he was referring to the wondrous works of Jesus previously portrayed in the Gospel of Mark, which had presented and named him as Son of God (cf. Mark 3:11; 5:7). That is new *Christian* coinage for the previous portrayal of the royal Messiah in Mark. It subsequently gained its strongest expression in the Gospel of Matthew, through the characterization of Jesus the wonder-worker as the Son of David (Matt. 9:27; 15:22; 20:30-31; cf. Mark 10:47-48; Luke 18:38-39).

In pre-Christian Judaism — including the Qumran texts — the Messiah never figured as a wonder-worker. Nor does 4Q521 (see above, pp. 31-32), erroneously appealed to by Eisenman and Wise as "messianic," report any wondrous deeds of the Messiah, but rather praises *God* as future wonder-worker even to the resurrection of the dead (4Q521 2 ii 4-15; 7 6).

Nor was the Messiah ever designated in pre-Christian Judaism as Son of God. The "Son of God" text, 4Q246, recently and frequently adduced as proof of the contrary, only criticizes the Seleucid King Antiochus IV Epiphanes for his presumptuous wish to be regarded as "Son of God" and "Son of the Most High" (4Q246 1:9–2:1). Granted, this is the first evidence from pre-Christian times of the linguistic occurrence of the designation "Son of the Most High," as we have it in the announcement of Jesus' birth (Luke 1:32). But it was entirely foreign to the Jewish messianism of the time. The understanding of the Messiah as Son of God, on the one hand, and as wonder-worker, on the other, is authentically *Christian,* and it only appeared in connection with the perception and presentation of Jesus as a wonder-worker.

The messianic depictions and expectations in the Qumran texts have no connection whatsoever with Jesus. Only in late stages of the formation of the Gospels did the manner of presenting Jesus assume traits that correspond to the Qumran messianic texts — as well as other Jewish texts, such as *Psalms of Solomon* 17 — where the Messiah as God's governor on earth destroys the enemies of the people of God and thereby helps the Reign of God to conquer. The time of the activity of the Messiah is thereby identical with the phase, of many years' duration, from the commencement of the Last Judgment until the completion of the time of salvation, which thus becomes an intermediate messianic reign between Satan's unbroken rule and God's sole rule in the world.

There is something corresponding to this in the Gospels, when Jesus characterizes not the Reign of God but its coming into being as "my reign" (Matt. 16:18; 20:21; Luke 22:29-30; John 18:36; cf. Mark 11:10; Luke 23:42). Jesus' lordship is also implied in the references in Matthew to the Reign of Heaven as the common power of God and Christ (Matt. 3:2; 4:17; etc.), or when this common exercise of lordship is simply called the Reign (Matt. 4:23; 9:35; 13:19; 24:14). The whole world is in view as the special realm of the reign of Jesus — here referred to as Son of Man, but conceived as Messiah — in the allegorical interpretation of the parable of the weeds in Matthew 13:36-43 (cf. 16:28). The oldest passage of this kind is 1 Corinthians 15:23-28, where Jesus as exalted Christ and Son of God destroys every godless rule, authority, and power still in the world, and death as the last of all, until his messianic task is finally completed in the future and only God reigns.

The Qumran texts now show, with a clarity that we did not previously possess, that in the Judaism of the time the royal Messiah as a future savior figure was important only for the interim, from the beginning of the Last Judgment until the completion of salvation. In statements concerning the subsequent time of salvation, a time free of all evil, one never finds him, not even in the descriptions of the time of salvation in other Jewish writings of unquestionably pre-Christian times. The time of the Messiah was not yet regarded then as the actual time of salvation, but only as the temporally bounded phase lasting from the beginning of God's coming salvific activity until its complete victory.

The years-long duration of the messianic age was always thought of in terms of the natural life expectancy of a human being. After all, as a physical descendant of David, the royal Messiah would have to be a human being. Since God protected him, any thought of the Messiah's dying before the completion of his task was completely foreign. Only the lethal fate of Jesus *before* the completion of the Reign of God changed the previous understanding of the Messiah — among Christians — and first occasioned the thought of a "dying Messiah." Never before in Judaism was the Messiah thought actually to have come, let alone to have such a fate awaiting him. Therefore no further rummaging around in Qumran fragments can bring to light such conceptions of a "killed Messiah."

The Books of the Prophets

Of real importance for Jesus and the beginnings of Christianity was the understanding of the biblical prophets that the Teacher of Righteousness had first introduced, that had become determinative for the Essenes and that, through Essene influence, had widely prevailed in the broad population of Palestine. John the Baptist had already used it. Jesus and the early Christians adopted it and now referred the biblical prophets' predictions of the future to the circumstances of their own time as constituting the dawn of the Reign of God on earth, just as the Baptist had done.

Jesus' response to the Baptist's inquiry (Matt. 11:5; Luke 7:22) is nothing other than a reference to the notion that what the prophets had announced for the time of salvation was now occurring before everyone's eyes and in everyone's hearing. The point in this response was not to give as complete a list as possible of the kinds of miracles that had now occurred in connection with Jesus. The withdrawal of demons, so important to Jesus, is not even mentioned. Further, the catalogue reaches its climax in the good news that has reached the poor, which does not fit the type of the other miracles.

The common meaning of all of the items in this catalogue is contained in the book of Isaiah. Through this prophet, God had communicated that, in the coming time of salvation, the blind would regain the light of their eyes, the lame their ability to walk, and the deaf their hearing; the dead would rise, and the poor would receive the good news (Isa. 26:19; 29:18-19; 35:5-6; 42:18; 61:1). All of that was happening now, which proved that the time of salvation, still lying in the remote future for Isaiah but proclaimed by the Baptist as immediately imminent, had actually begun. Only the cleansing of leprosy is not explicitly listed in the text of Isaiah, but only God's more general proclamations of healing (Isa. 30:26; 57:18; cf. 2 Kings 5:1-27).

The core content of Jesus' beatitudes in the Sermon on the Mount and in the Sermon on the Plain likewise refers to the prophet Isaiah's proclamations of healing. The beatitude of the poor, to whom the Reign of God now belongs, and that of the sorrowing, who now will at last receive solace (Matt. 5:3-4; Luke 6:20b, 21b), refer to Isaiah 61:1-2. The beatitude of the hungering, who will now finally be filled (Matt. 5:6; Luke 6:21a), has its precedent in Isaiah 55:1-2 (cf. 49:10). Those who until now could only be pitied are now to be congratulated since, precisely as poor, sorrowing, and hungering, they are the persons to whom God through Isaiah had unfailingly foretold for the time of salvation not only an end of their suffering, but superabundant well-being.

The Gospels and the other parts of the New Testament are filled with references to Old Testament passages that serve to demonstrate that with Jesus' earthly life the saving activity of God in the world, which had been prophesied, just as the annihilation of evil, had already begun.

This understanding of the Prophets comes to expression in a particularly impressive way in the teaching of the Gospel of Matthew, where, alongside many other Christian statements concerning salvation, every important stage in the earthly life of Jesus is supplied with a corresponding scriptural prooftext.

According to Isaiah 7:14, a virgin conceived him (Matt. 1:22-23); according to Micah 5:1, he was born in Bethlehem (Matt. 2:5-6); according to Hosea 11:1, he had to return from Egypt (Matt. 2:15); after which, according to Jeremiah 31:15, a lamentation over Herod's murder of the children was raised in his birthplace, Bethlehem (Matt. 2:17-18). Subsequently, according to a prediction "through the prophets," he came to Nazareth (Matt. 2:23), until at last, according to Isaiah 8:23–9:1, he took up his permanent residence at Capernaum (Matt. 4:13-16; cf. 9:1; 17:24).

Nowhere in the New Testament does it become as clear as it does here that what we now find in early Christianity is not only the same way of understanding the Scriptures, but also the same expository methods as we find in the midrashim and commentaries on the Prophets from the Qumran finds. Only, the Christians have now referred to Jesus and the Reign of God, which had begun with Jesus, that which the Essenes had regarded one to two centuries before Jesus' earthly life as God's prophetic references to their own current circumstances.

The Torah

The predictions of the biblical prophets could now be fulfilled. Their writings had attained the goal of their composition, and now essentially served only for the endorsement of actually existing circumstances as having been long since announced by God.

It was otherwise with the principal part of the Old Testament canon, the Torah. The Essenes, like all Jews of their time, regarded it as an inalterable and eternally enduring entity. Rabbis later held the opinion that not even God up in heaven could find a better use for his time than in the constant study of this basic ordinance for the whole of creation.

For Jesus, the Reign of God, as he experienced it, changed the entire previous understanding of the Torah — not on speculative grounds, however, but on the basis of a specific circumstance.

Even on the Sabbath demons fled without exorcism and therefore through God's active dealings; or those suffering from chronic illness, whose healing could easily have been postponed to one of the following workdays, were spontaneously healed through the workings of God (Mark 1:21-27; 3:1-5; Matt. 12:9-13; Luke 6:6-10; 13:10-17; 14:1-6; John 5:1-9; 9:1-14).

In the forty years' war of annihilation waged by God, the angels, and human beings against evil in the world, as the Qumran *War Rule* portrays it, the battle ceases every seventh year (1QM 2:8-9), because the Torah's instructions concerning the Sabbath years (Lev. 25:1-7; Deuteronomy 15) required this in connection with the Decalogue's prohibition of any work on the Sabbath (Exod. 20:8-11; Deut. 5:12-15). Above all, however, God himself had already fundamentally hallowed the Sabbath as a general day of rest at the creation of the world (Gen. 2:1-3).

But suddenly God was active even *on the Sabbath,* in the war of annihilation against the evil in the world, and thus no longer abided by his own ancient command to pause for rest on the Sabbath. In the time of the Maccabees, pious Jews had preferred to renounce self-defense and simply be cut down by their enemies, rather than protect themselves with their defensive weaponry (1 Macc. 2:29-38; cf. above, pp. 145-47). Now God continued his battle against evil even on the Sabbath, and this indeed as a war of aggression, where there was surely no need to renounce rest periods.

This state of affairs was difficult to comprehend and led Jesus to regard the ordering of God, world, and human beings, as established in the biblical presentation of creation (Genesis 1–2), with new eyes. On the very first day of the world, God had created light, but he had created the heavenly bodies that would emit it — sun, moon, and stars — only on the fourth day (Gen. 1:3-5; 14-19). Doubtless the case was the same, then, with the Sabbath: it had been subsequently subjoined to the sixth day, on which the human being was created (Gen. 1:26–2:4).

In this manner of regarding things, the Sabbath commandment can no longer have determinative authority over human beings. Rather, as light dominates the heavenly bodies that serve it, so also human beings must dominate the Sabbath that serves them. "The Sabbath was made for humankind, not humankind for the Sabbath," runs this new understanding of Scripture on the lips of Jesus (Mark 2:27). This new understanding of the Torah had not come to Jesus through other people's study of the Bible or outside exegetical prowess. It was forced upon him by God's own activities on the Sabbath, which required a rethinking.

The Torah, however, did not contain only manifold instructions for human behavior. Rather, at the same time God had revealed himself in the Torah, and this in his own way. God could never act counter to the self-revelation of his own nature given in the Torah. The Torah, as far as God's ways of acting were concerned, was unchangeable, as was unmistakably postulated by his own observation, "I am who am" (Exod. 3:14): "I *always* show (prove) myself the same as I *always* show (prove) myself." Therefore God's manner of obvious activity, irreconcilable with the customary understanding of Scripture, compelled Jesus to read the Torah with different eyes. Not only the Prophets but the Torah itself must be grasped anew in terms of the current event of the Reign of God, and it must be seen as being in harmony with that event.

The next step in Jesus' understanding was occasioned by the withdrawal of demons from women. That showed that the curse of the Fall (Genesis 3) no longer weighed on women, but a state of affairs was returning that had prevailed *before* the Fall. As God looked back after the creation of the human being and regarded his work of creation so far, he observed: "It is very good!" or "It all came out very well!" This positive appraisal included women, unrestrictedly, as a work of creation. From this, Jesus inferred that, in the current event of the Reign of God, the restoration of the order of creation that had prevailed before the Fall was occurring — that it had already begun with the activity of John the Baptist (Mark 9:11-13; Matt. 17:10-13) and was now continuing in a special manner with the unreserved inclusion of women, too, in the realm of salvation that was coming into existence through God's own activity.

The third and most effective step along the way to a new understanding of the Torah was that Jesus now proceeded to regard conditions prevailing in the realm of God's active rule as fundamentally identical with the circumstances that prevailed before the Fall. Where the power of sin was broken and all evil had fled, God alone prevailed, as God once had at the beginning of the history of the world. Here there was nothing ungodly any longer.

The curse pronounced upon the man as he was driven from Paradise, that in the future only through hard labor would he find adequate sustenance (Gen. 3:17-19), had lost its effectiveness in the newly appearing realm of God's rule. Just as God had once placed everything necessary to sustain human beings abundantly at their disposal in Paradise (Gen. 2:8-9), so this was now happening anew. God liberally gave their daily bread to those who asked him for it (Matt. 6:11; Luke 11:3), cared for them even without the work of their hands more generously than the birds under heaven and the flowers in the fields (Matt. 6:25-34; Luke 12:22-31), and made Jesus appear in the eyes of the people exactly like a glutton and a drunkard in well-to-do circles (Matt. 11:19; Luke 7:34) who did not have to bother about his daily sustenance. Jesus compared current life in God's new realm of lordship with the lavishness of a wedding banquet in the oriental style, which would last for many days and to which everyone would be invited, and at which everyone would be enormously entertained and no one would fast (Mark 2:19; Matt. 9:15; Luke 5:34). This is the way things are where evil has retreated and God has already established his rule (cf. also Luke 23:42-43; John 6:22-59). The fasting commandments of the Torah had become superfluous in the realm of salvation.

In Paradise, there had as yet been nothing unclean. The purity commandments of the Torah, the prohibitions against partaking of unclean animals, the ritual immersions of the Essenes and their numerous rules for conduct in daily life, served the purpose of avoiding uncleanness or restoring lost purity. God had given Israel the Torah particularly in order to facilitate the pure and holy life of the people of God amidst a world stamped by the power of sin and threatened with impurity. But in God's realm of lordship on earth, which was presently coming into being, there was no longer any such thing as physical uncleanness (Mark 7:1-23; Matt. 15:1-20).

Thus all purity prescriptions and food taboos were rendered null, just as sacrifices for the cancellation of sins were no longer necessary (Mark 11:15-17; Matt. 21:12-13; Luke 19:45-46; John 2:13-16). The first sacrificial offerings in human history were those of Cain and Abel, after the expulsion from Paradise. Their gifts came from their toil in the fields and in animal husbandry (Gen. 4:3-5). Now that conditions of former times prevailed once more, when God himself bestowed all foodstuffs, there was no longer any reason or occasion for these sacrificial offerings.

Jesus never criticized the Torah. Still, large parts of what had once been indispensable had now become superfluous. This was the case with rules like the one to the effect that, in case of divorce, the wife was to be provided with a document of proprietorship, which guaranteed her financial independence or facilitated remarriage (Deut. 24:1). The Essenes had deduced the principle of their lifelong single marriage principally from Genesis 1:27 (see above, p. 194), but had by no means ruled out the possibility of divorce, which was expressly provided for in the Torah. Jesus, on the other hand, concluded from conditions before the Fall that the existence of human beings in pairs must inviolably prevail as part of the primordial order of creation, so that divorce, or especially remarriage, even for women, was no longer licit in the realm of God's Rule (Mark 10:2-12; Matt. 5:31-32; 19:3-12; 1 Cor. 7:10-11). Thus there could no longer be any occasion for the drawing up of documents of divorce.

As these examples show, Jesus by no means abrogated the Torah. It is only that, for him, God's prophecy through Moses was being fulfilled in conformity with what had been announced through the other biblical prophets. Furthermore, the Torah had how reached the goal intended for it by God as its author. Jesus' Sermon on the Mount conveys this new understanding of Scripture with the words, "Do not think that I have come to abolish the Law [the Torah] and the Prophets. I have come not to abolish them but to fulfill them" (Matt. 5:17). Not a single, minuscule letter in the Torah may be changed in the course of this fulfillment. The Torah is still God's word in all of its component parts and will be God's word forever (Matt. 5:18-19; Luke 16–17). It was only that, for Jesus, the creation-Torah (Genesis 1–2) in its fulfillment now became the only authoritative criterion for the rest of the Torah, the Sinai-Torah (Genesis 3–Deuteronomy 34), whose character was thereby totally changed.

All of the now superfluous individual regulations of the Torah for Temple, priesthood, sacrifice, purity, food taboos, and so on, show from now on, in the course of this fulfillment, God's everlasting mercy, through which he had preserved his people Israel from all harm during the time of Satan's might in the world. The care God showed in the Torah, the power of blessing that came into effect in it, and the fidelity to the covenant he made with Israel on Sinai, which he kept not least by fulfilling his promises of salvation, continue to be effective in the Reign of God that is now dawning and moving toward completion. Jesus' witness is the guarantee for this. Nothing essential is changing — only, everything that until now had served the resistance that had to be mounted against the might of Satan has accomplished its task, wherever the might of Satan is already broken and God alone rules. The weapons have served their purpose, where the battle is over and God has conquered. But they continue to show everyone the incomparable might of God, with which he had once delivered Israel from Egypt and brought them into the Holy Land, where the definitive victory of God's rule on earth was now beginning.

For Jesus, the Torah was being fulfilled in another respect: the order of creation was now taking effect without restriction. This state of affairs introduced requirements that were far stricter than God's regulations for the time of Satan's rule after the Fall.

In the Reign of God, the creator of the world reigns absolutely. Here God's own righteousness is the greatest of all the gifts of salvation (cf. Rom. 3:21), but it also demands of the human beings to whom it has come more than merely following individual prescriptions. In the Sermon on the Mount, Jesus' standard is stated in these terms: "Unless your righteousness exceeds that of the scribes and Pharisees, you will never enter the kingdom of God" (Matt. 5:20). The Essenes were definitely included here (cf. below, pp. 267-68). But how do those who have been accepted into God's rule manifest this greater righteousness?

The new order of the Reign of God is seen most clearly in Jesus' manner of dealing with the Decalogue (Exod. 20:2-17; Deut. 5:6-21). Where God had definitively established his rule and was constantly present, no one had to be prevented anymore from revering foreign gods, from misusing God's name for magical purposes such as exorcisms, or from making idols. None of that needed to be dealt with any longer. Indeed, the human beings who had been spared God's just anger had now recovered their likeness of God (Gen. 1:27). Therefore not only must any thought of murder be foreign to them (Exod. 20:13; Deut. 5:17), but even anger toward others was irreconcilable with their new relationship with God (Matt. 5:21-26; cf. Matt. 18:23-35; 1 John 3:15). Anger had once driven Cain to murder his brother Abel (Gen. 4:5-6), but now it must be out of the question. As for divorce (Exod. 20:14; Deut. 5:18), it could no longer be, since the lifelong existence of human beings in pairs (Gen. 1:27) had been inviolably established, and it went altogether without saying that any lusting after the wife of another was to be excluded (Matt. 5:27-30). The relationship of mutual trust in the Reign of God, as it had prevailed in

Paradise between Adam and Eve before the Fall (Gen. 2:23-25), no longer tolerated any false statements whatsoever against others (Exod. 20:16; Deut. 5:20), and thereby also rendered any kind of oath superfluous (Matt. 5:33-37).

Thus, for Jesus even the Decalogue had been fulfilled in the realm of God's rule and was therefore rendered superfluous. Still, this example is the clearest demonstration that Jesus in no way wished to regard God's commandments as abrogated. In fact, his grasp of the will of God, as formulated for Israel's experiences on the front lines of the old battle against evil, was of the same kind, only far more demanding. His understanding of the Torah left everything behind that had been overtaken by the present event of the Reign of God, but that understanding filled the Torah with a new force that reached much further than what had previously been formulated by others in the simple interpretation of the Torah.

The Gospel of Mark has reduced this particularity of Jesus to a formula valid for all of Jesus' effectiveness. In the context of the evangelist's first report of Jesus' public activity — on the occasion of the expulsion of a demon on the Sabbath in the synagogue of Capernaum (Mark 1:21-27) — we read: "They were astounded at his teaching, because he taught them as one having authority, and not as the scribes" (Mark 1:22; cf. 1:27; 11:27-33).

Conclusion

The Gospel tradition makes all of the essential traits of Jesus and his activity very clear. The result is a comprehensive, self-consistent picture. This picture shows that Jesus was anything but a partisan of the Zealots or any other Jewish freedom fighters who were struggling against Roman power, as *The Dead Sea Scrolls Deception* and other books of the kind seek to suggest. When Jesus said, "Do not think that I have come to bring peace to the earth; I have not come to bring peace, but a sword" (Matt 10:34; cf. Luke 12:51), he was speaking not of any political conflict, but of the dawn of the Reign of God. He did not even mean merely the rescue of human beings from the power of Satan. He meant, at the same time, hostilities between God and the power of Satan, whose annihilation, accomplished in the form of the Last Judgment, brought suffering and death with it, as did every war. But in Jesus' overall view, this annihilation was in store especially for sinful members of the people of God, not the pagan Romans. Toward them, Jesus could have a completely different attitude (Matt. 8:5-13; Luke 7:1-10).

With the Essenes Jesus shared a high estimation of the Torah and the Prophets. But he took a totally different stance toward these writings than the Essenes did at the time. Especially in the interpretation of the Torah, he followed paths that neither the Essenes nor any other Jews before him had ever done. For Jesus, what was decisively new — and from this, Christianity took its rise — was the Reign of God entering simultaneously as Last Judgment and as commencement of the time of salvation, a Reign that presented itself concretely as God's active dealings on earth, and a Reign in which Jesus had been included from the very beginning. John the Baptist had foretold it powerfully a short time before. Now the prediction was coming true, the Torah and the Prophets were being fulfilled, and people were being led along a path that none had ever traversed.

At work here were neither human beings nor Satan but, for the first time since the biblical prophets, God with his own hand. God alone was beginning, on his own initiative, out of his omnipotence, to destroy everything in the world that was opposed to God. God made Jesus the authoritative instrument of his renewed saving activity and carried his work beyond Jesus' death on the cross by raising Jesus from the dead and installing him as the exalted Son of Man, in order to complete what had been begun during Jesus' time on earth, through Jesus as Christ and Son of God for all human beings and for all time. This is the basic orientation of the entire Christian faith: the renewed acts of God, on his own almighty initiative, through Jesus, for the salvation of all humanity.

CHAPTER TEN

Early Christianity

As far as can be ascertained, Jesus had no personal contact with the Essenes. At least he was never subjected to their three-year admittance procedure, which could have conveyed to him a more intimate knowledge of their ideas. But neither did the places he visited offer him any contact with the Essenes. In Bethlehem there were surely Essenes, but except for his birth, the Gospel tradition has him stopping there only a few days. At his baptism by John in the Jordan, it was John's proclamation that was front and center; there Jesus took no interest in matters Essene, nor, surely, did he make any visits to Qumran.

Furthermore, Jesus worked in Galilee, where in his time there were no Essenes at all. If Jesus did not first go to Jerusalem only a few days before his crucifixion, as John's Gospel presents it, but had already made the journey a number of times before for the pilgrimage festivals, then these were only very short visits, during which he could scarcely have become closely acquainted with Essenes. At all events, not even the Gospel of John suggests anything of the kind. Finally, as emerges from the Gospels, none of Jesus' activity shows any direct Essene influence, but instead a great deal that contradicted their basic orientation.

The case was different with Christianity, as it took form after Jesus' time on earth. The original community at Jerusalem arose in the same city in which there was also an important Essene quarter. This early community was the center of Christianity until the members who still belonged to it left Jerusalem at the outbreak of the revolt against the Romans in A.D. 66 and moved to the city of Pella east of the Jordan. Incidentally, this shows that the early Christian community adamantly eschewed any participation in the revolt against the Romans and preferred to set out for elsewhere, as it was becoming difficult to avoid camaraderie with the rebels preparing their uprising. The celebrated speculations of Robert Eisenman, that the early community was under the leadership of James the brother of the Lord and was a headquarters of the conspiracy against the Romans and in close collaboration with the Zealots, are automatically negated by these historical facts.

As the fundamental understanding of the writings of the biblical prophets on the part of John the Baptist and Jesus has shown, not every influence of the Essenes presupposes immediate contacts with them. The Essenes, during their long history, had had a lasting influence on the Judaism of Palestine, and this surely beyond Judea. Further, most of what we have at last come to know now through the Qumran texts was, in its time, in no way specifically Essene but the common property of Palestinian Judaism. This is true not only for linguistic usages, but also for the general worldview, concepts about the future, and ethics. Much in the New Testament that may appear to us at first glance to be a product of Essene influence turns out on closer examination to be simply characteristic of the Judaism of that time.

It would be an endless task to undertake an examination of all of the findings through which New Testament matters become more understandable in the light of the Qumran texts. We shall therefore confine ourselves to a few especially important questions in which, rightly or wrongly, it is supposed that Qumran or the Essenes had influenced early Christianity.

Christian baptism has nothing to do with Qumran. It is an adoption and continuation of John's baptism alone. Like the latter, from the beginning it was an act performed once and for all, was performed by someone other than the person being baptized, and had a sacramental character. The connection of baptism to the person of John had fallen into disuse; in principle, any baptized person could confer it (see above, p. 218). Instead, baptism became a fixed component of admittance into the Christian Church. Forgiveness of sins and bestowal of the Holy Spirit, both reserved by John to the future, but now occurring in the act of baptism itself (cf. above, pp. 219, 221), were therefore part and parcel of every baptized person's entire Christian being. Forgiveness of sins thereby occurred "in the name of the Lord Jesus Christ" (1 Cor. 6:11), as sacramental dedication to the saving import of Christ's expiatory death. All of this arose without any influence on the part of the Essenes and was entirely foreign to the ritual baths of purification practiced at Qumran.

The Eucharist, or Lord's Supper, had but scant connection with the Essenes' daily community meals. True, it was probably just as much a daily affair in the Christian communities of earliest times — although it was only held in the evening — and was indeed an actual meal, where those present ate their fill (cf. Acts 2:42, 46; 1 Cor. 11:25), but in which, in contrast with the Essenes' meals, women participated on an equal footing with men. The Essenes' community meals were ritual, it is true, but they were not sacramental like the Eucharist. Jesus' words of institution, which framed the (genuine) meal as a blessing over the bread and the chalice (1 Cor. 11:25) — as in later Christianity the prayers before and after the family meal — have no parallel whatever in the Qumran texts. Besides, the Essenes, like all Jews up to our very day, always pronounced the blessing over the bread and wine at the beginning of their meals, not as a framework to them.

These differences show quite clearly that there can be no question of the Eucharist having been celebrated at Qumran, or of the Christians having taken it over from the Essenes. The only connection consists in the fact that, apart from the Essenes and the Christians, neither in the Judaism of the time nor in the world around were daily meals held not in the family circle, but in common with all members of a local group, in a special meeting room, with all nonmembers excluded. The Essenes admitted only males who were full members, the Christians only the baptized. Here perhaps the Essene community meals influenced Christian procedures, at most only organizationally, and even this only partially.

It may be too that the Christian offices of bishop and deacon grew out of these contexts. But this is not certain, especially since we first meet them in remote Greece, and not in Palestine. Paul wrote his letter to the Philippians to the community there "with their bishops and deacons" (Phil. 1:1). From this we can conclude that there were a number of domestic communities in Philippi, each with a "bishop," who was responsible for financial administration and organizational matters, and with several "deacons," who assisted him in this, especially by seeing to purchases and serving table in the evenings. The Essenes' community meals were similarly organized. The meaning of the Essenes' designation *mebaqqer,* "overseer," even corresponds to that of *episkopos,* "bishop." But there were corresponding designations and organizational responsibilities even in Greek societies, so the Christian data can also be explained independently of the Essenes.

According to the presentation in the Gospel of John, Jesus took his last meal with his disciples on the evening of the Day of Preparation for the festival of Passover (John 13:1). The other Gospels have it one day later, on Passover Eve itself (Mark 14:12-17; Matt. 26:17-20; Luke 22:7). A good many calculations have been performed on this point. Theoretically it would be perfectly plausible that one and the same day would be the Day of Preparation according to the Essenes' old priestly calendar, and Passover itself according to the Temple's lunar calendar. From this it could be concluded that the Gospel of John followed the Essene calendar, and therefore that his Christian community stood on Essene foundations. But even apart from the fact that the two calendrical systems usually diverged substantially further from each other than by only one day, neither are there any traces whatever of the Essene calendar in the Gospel tradition. Therefore the supposition suggests itself that the author of the Gospel of John sought to have Jesus' death correspond symbolically to the slaughter of the Paschal lambs on the Day of Preparation (cf. also Jesus as "the lamb that was slain," Rev. 5:6, 12; 13:8), and accordingly predated the day of his death over against the tradition. Historical considerations or judicial-historical doubts over the presentation of the circumstances of Jesus' death in the other Gospels have certainly not been the occasion of John's earlier dating of the event.

The so-called community of goods of the early Christian community (Acts 2:42-47; 4:32-37; cf. 5:1-11) had no connection whatever with the Essenes' community ownership. The latter was the basis of contributions prescribed as obligatory for all Essenes for the support of priests and Levites, for the community meals, and for necessary social services. In the early Christian community, on the other hand, well-to-do members simply made rooms in their houses available for the evening gatherings. As for the community coffers stocked with voluntary contributions, these were devoted to the support of the socially needy and, in part, to the common meals. When available means became scanty, the community could be grateful to wealthy members like Barnabas, who disposed of a part of his land holdings on Cyprus and restocked community coffers with the proceeds (Acts 4:36-37).

The transgression of the married couple Ananias and Sapphira, which brought on their death, consisted merely in the fact that they returned to the community treasury only a part of the proceeds of a sale, while defrauding the Holy Spirit with the claim that this was all of the proceeds (Acts 5:1-11). Had they told the truth, no one would have taken it amiss that they had withheld some part of the proceeds for their private use. The Essenes, however, were strictly forbidden to sell property to outsiders.

Nor did concrete relations in the primitive community at Jerusalem have anything at all to do with the Essenes, but corresponded in every respect with what was customary worldwide in all Jewish synagogue communities. Only, because of the relatively small representation of well-to-do members in the Christian community, such members made extraordinarily large contributions.

Actual influences by the Essenes on early Christianity, if they are to be found at all, are to be found in the Gospel of Matthew. The manual of discipline in Matthew 18:15-17 corresponds in principle to Essene procedures. This is also the only Gospel to have used the concept *ekklēsia*, "church" (Matt. 16:18; 18:17), a concept that adopts the traditional biblical designations for the organization of the people of God, designations familiar to the Essenes, and develops them further.

Jesus' disciple Simon Peter is dubbed in the Gospels "fisher of men" (Mark 1:17; Matt. 4:19; Luke 5:10), as well as shepherd of the people of the Church (John 21:15-19). In the Gospel of Matthew, furthermore, he is called "the rock" upon which the Church is established (Matt. 16:18). Earlier, in the Qumran texts, there is a picture of the community as an edifice founded on a rock and therefore unshakably secure (1QH 6:25-29; cf. Isa. 28:16-17; further, Matt. 7:24-27; Luke 6:47-49). But here the rock foundation is not identified with a person.

Only in the Gospel of Matthew are the twelve disciples presented as composing a body at the court presided over by the Son of Man to judge the twelve tribes of Israel (Matt. 19:28; cf. Luke 22:28-30). The Essenes had a judicial body to which twelve men likewise belonged, and, of course, three priests (1QS 7:27–8:4; cf. above, pp. 111, 199). It is disputed, therefore, whether the Essene judicial group may be the prototype of the Matthean presentation (but cf. 4QpIsa^d 1 1-8).

Finally, more strongly than any of the other Gospels, Matthew has emphasized Jesus' descent from King David (Matt. 1:1), and presented him as messianic ruler, as would correspond to the Essene expectation of the royal Messiah. But this messianism was shared by all Judaism at that time, so that it is unnecessary to postulate a special Essene background here.

In the Gospel of John, the entire world is regarded dualistically as determined by the antithesis between light and darkness, between truth and lie, between life and death, This metaphysical dualism is also developed in the form of an ethical dualism, especially in the life of human beings. Here the dualistic texts from the Qumran finds — the *War Rule* and the *Teaching on the Two Spirits* (1QS 3:13–4:26) — present us with manifold parallels. At the same time, however, an analysis of the passages on both sides makes it clear that the Gospel of John has not gone back to these Qumran texts, but rather that both sides, independently of each other, were influenced by Mesopotamian Judaism, which in turn had taken over certain elements of ancient Persian dualism. These connections first became clear through the Qumran finds, and this corrected the once-favored derivation of Johannine dualism from pagan gnosis. This is the terminological background for the designation of the Christians as "children of light" (Luke 16:8), or for Paul's stern division between light and darkness (2 Cor. 6:14–7:1).

Thanks to the Qumran finds, we have at our disposal a plethora of aids to understanding the sense of difficult turns of expression in the New Testament. At least a few examples should be cited. It is now definitively clear, for instance, that "the many," or "the majority" (Mark 10:45; 14:24; 2 Cor. 2:6; etc.), always has in view the totality of humankind or of the members of the community. "Those on whom his favor rests" in the angelic proclamation of the Christmas story (Luke 2:14) are those who live their lives in a way that is pleasing to God, because they are marked through and through by an obedient following of God's directives. The "poor in spirit" of the first beatitude in the Sermon on the Mount (Matt. 5:3) are persons whom God's Holy Spirit has permeated and made capable of true humility. Likewise the Qumran texts now offer terminological parallels to the designation of a community as "church of God" (1 Cor. 1:2), to the identification of following the Torah as "works of the law" (Rom. 3:20; cf. above, p. 105), or of the divine work of salvation as the revelation of the "righteousness of God" (Rom. 3:21). The Qumran texts also shed new light on the meaning of the covenant bestowed by God as the conceptual context of these ideas.

Finally, a great deal of excitement has been generated by the claim that Cave 7 yielded an exceedingly old copy of the Gospel of Mark dating to as early as A.D. 50. The fragment referred to, 7Q5, is around the size of a silver dollar and offers the remnants of five lines of writing. Only ten letters have been preserved in their entirety, while ten others are mostly so fragmentary that the traces of writing can be fitted to no more than one letter of the Greek alphabet. The proponents of the Mark hypothesis identify the content of the text with that of words from Mark 6:52-53. They themselves admit that, in this case, instead of one indisputably preserved letter of the alphabet, another would be expected, and three other words witnessed in all of the manuscripts of Mark must have been omitted. Actually, however, the second line of 7Q5 is present in at least three other finds, which are all simply irreconcilable with the text of Mark. These three findings are either ignored or else distorted by advocates of the Mark hypothesis. But these findings definitively exclude their viewpoint. Unfortunately, no one has succeeded in an indisputable positive identification of the preserved text. In any case it is not biblical, coming from neither the Old nor the New Testament. Presumably we are dealing with a genealogical passage from a Jewish work of pre-Christian times, but even that is not perfectly clear as yet.

Beyond John the Baptist and Jesus, the Qumran finds are at any rate an unexpectedly rich aid to understanding the New Testament and early Christianity. They contain nothing that would even touch the foundations of Christian faith, let alone bring it down in ruins, as seems to have been hoped in some quarters. Instead, they enrich in highly gratifying measure our background knowledge of New Testament issues, of terminology unattested in Greek usage, and of the basic peculiarities of Christian origins in relation to contemporary Judaism.

How massive Christianity's peculiarities were perceived to be from the beginning is shown most clearly by Paul. Before his calling as Apostle of the Gentiles, he had sought in the radical ardor of his faith to exterminate Christian communities (Gal. 1:13). He was a Christian very early — three years after Jesus' crucifixion at the latest. The antagonism between Christianity and any sort of Judaism, which is still operative today, was already abysmal before that point in time. The principal reason was the belief of Christians that the humiliating crucifixion of Jesus was to be reckoned a saving deed of God on earth (cf. Gal. 3:6-14; Rom. 3:21-26; 4:25; 8:32; Mark 8:31; 9:31; 10:33-34). But for any believing Jew, a positive appraisal of a crucifixion as a saving deed of God is an intolerable scandal (cf. 1 Cor. 1:18-25). According to the Torah (Deut. 21:22-23), the crucified are to be regarded as cursed by God himself. For Torah-abiding Jews, such a contradiction in conceiving God was unacceptable.

CHAPTER ELEVEN

Rabbinic Judaism

The Qumran finds are revolutionary, not for the New Testament, but for the picture we have had until now of ancient Judaism. This picture has been shaped fundamentally by the works of the Rabbinic tradition, which arose around A.D. 200: the Mishnah, the Tosepta, both the Palestinian and Babylonian Talmuds, and much more. This body of tradition is the actual foundation of all Orthodox Judaism down to our own times. Its teachings rank as "oral Torah" and are in every respect of equal authority with the written Torah, or five books of Moses. It is regarded as having been revealed by God to Moses on Sinai at the same time as the written Torah.

This means that, according to today's Orthodox Judaism, the Rabbinic teachings already existed in the time between the Old Testament and the Mishnah, that they already had decisive authority then, and that they were strictly followed by mainstream Judaism. The Mishnah treatise 'Abot ("Fathers") lends support to this view by beginning with the statement: "Moses received the [oral] Torah on Sinai, and transmitted it to Joshua, and Joshua to the Elders, and the Elders to the [biblical] Prophets, and the Prophets have transmitted it to the men of the Great Assembly" ('Abot 1:1). There follows a chain of transmission from the Great Assembly (sixth/fifth centuries B.C.) down to the time of the author (about A.D. 200), the names and teachings in the chain being intended to authenticate the age and continuity of the Rabbinic interpretations.

Finally, in the Babylonian Talmud (third to fifth centuries A.D.) the Pharisees were increasingly regarded as the authentic vehicles and guardians of the oral Torah in pre-Rabbinic times, especially since the sages named in 'Abot were later thought of as Pharisees. On the basis of these considerations, not only the Sadducees, but also and above all the Essenes came to be regarded as dissident, marginal groups from bygone ages, sects long since disappeared, with whom a person standing on the solid base of the Rabbinic teachings would best have nothing to do.

We cannot go into detail here regarding the genesis of this extremely influential and often still uncritically adopted picture of ancient Judaism, or show how historically dubious it is. To do so is not really necessary here, since the Viennese Judaica and Rabbinics specialist Günther Stemberger has recently undertaken precisely this in his excellent book *Pharisäer, Sadduzäer, Essener* (1991). An intensive reading of this short work is heartily recommended to anyone interested in these matters.

Those who read Stemberger will be surprised to learn on what feet of clay the customary picture of ancient Judaism has stood throughout all of these centuries. Here we find, for example, that traditions in the Mishnah are interested in the Temple and the priesthood in the time after the destruction of the Jerusalem Temple, which would be very strange on the part of the Pharisees (pp. 131-33). Of course, this striking discovery raises the question of who nurtured these interests so late and so energetically, representing them in Rabbinic circles so that they made their way into the Mishnah. It was scarcely Sadducees, who at that time were encountering widespread rejection, as Josephus also attests (*Jewish War* 2.164-66), and who were not very numerous.

So the only ones actually left are the Essenes, as the "Fathers" of many component parts of even the Mishnah. The traditions of the Rabbis, which are authoritative for contemporary Judaism, were certainly influenced more extensively by the Essenes than is usually acknowledged today (see also above, p. 201). The main basis of their powerful influence was the enormous biblical knowledge possessed by all Essenes, which existed at that time neither among the Sadducees nor among the Pharisees, to say nothing of the wider population. The Essenes owed this knowledge to their entry procedures, which lasted at least three years and involved intensive study, as well as to the obligation incumbent on all members to read the Old Testament writings for several hours every day. Thanks to these religious obligations, the Essenes were the scholarly elite of Palestinian Judaism, barring none. This mighty potential in terms of scripture scholarship, now at last concretely demonstrable through the Qumran finds, cannot have remained without effect in the aftermath of the destruction of the Temple.

The misleading notion that the Essenes were substantially only in Qumran has led almost everyone today to regard the destruction of the Qumran settlement in A.D. 68 as the end of the Essenes as well. This view, of course, can no longer be sustained, once one realizes that at the time of Josephus' writings there were still more than 4,000 Essenes in the Holy Land. Certainly many of them lost their lives in the confusion of the revolt against the Romans. But the vast majority of the Essenes, just as the greater part of the rest of the population, survived this terrible period and influenced the aftermath in their own way.

It does not take a prophet to predict that, as investigation of the Qumran texts continues, free of the narrow view of the Essenes as "dissident" and "sectarian," it will demonstrate Rabbinic traditions to be, in a high degree, in agreement with Essene tradition, and will show that much of the material of the Rabbinic sages, however little it may have seemed to be the case to anyone before now, came from the Essenes.

Once we realize the significance of this state of affairs, the Essenes can at last be recognized as the center of Judaism in the time of Jesus, as they were then and as they deserve to be — we need only think of their high reputation with Philo and with Josephus — even though in the New Testament they appear not as "the Essenes," but as "the scribes" and "the Herodians."

In Gospel material formulated relatively late, the scribes are independently named alongside the Pharisees (Mark 7:1, 5; Matt. 5:20; 12:38; 15:1; 23:2; Luke 5:21; 6:7; 11:53; 15:2; John 8:3) and are therefore reckoned as a group to be distinguished from the latter. On the other hand, there were occasionally "scribes who belonged to the Pharisee party" (Mark 2:16; cf. John 3:1-12; 7:50-52; 19:39) and perhaps also scribes who were members of none of the great religious parties. In any case, the group designation "scribes" strongly suggests the thought of the Essenes as the elite group in Judaism at that time, even after the destruction of the Temple.

The oldest of our Gospels independently names, alongside the Pharisees, also the Herodians (Mark 3:6; 12:13; cf. 8:15; Matt. 22:16). They are usually regarded as partisans of Herod Antipas, who had John the Baptist executed and who was at the same time the ruler of Jesus in Galilee (see above, p. 212). But the context of the passages cited suggests a religious party instead of a political following. Also, some of the Church Fathers cite "the Herodians" as a religious group of ancient Judaism, next to the Sadducees and the Pharisees — namely, Hippolytus of Rome in his *Refutation of All Heresies,* completed about A.D. 222 (Pseudo-Tertullian 1), Epiphanius of Salamis in his *Medicine Chest* (19.5; 20; A.D. 374-77), and Philastrius (Filaster) of Brescia in his *Book of the Various Kinds of Heresies* (28), composed A.D. 385-91.

Epiphanius expressly emphasizes that "the Herodians," like the Pharisees, Sadducees, and other Jewish groups, survived the destruction of Jerusalem in A.D. 70 (19.5). He writes that their name was based on the fact that they had acknowledged Herod the Great (37-4 B.C.) as "the Messiah" (20), which had been Hippolytus' opinion as well. In the background is surely Josephus' story of the Essene Menahem, who is supposed to have greeted the schoolboy Herod as "King of the Jews" and thereby laid the groundwork for Herod's patronage of the Essenes during his reign (see above, pp. 160-61).

On account of this preferred status, the Essenes came to be designated the Herodians in the sense of "King Herod's special favorites."

The Essenes have left strong traces, not least in the New Testament and with the Rabbis. The Qumran finds definitively repair the undeserved disregard in which they have been held. The overwhelming importance, at least for the early history of the Rabbinic tradition in the Mishnah and Tosepta, which until now was erroneously conferred upon the Pharisees, actually accrues to the Essenes. Not only at the time of Jesus, but well into the Rabbinic age, the Essenes were the principal representatives of Palestinian Judaism.

Suggestions for Further Reading

Betz, Otto, and Rainer Riesner. *Jesus, Qumran, and the Vatican: Clarifications*. New York: Crossroad, 1994.

Cohen, Shaye J. D. *From the Maccabees to the Mishnah*. Library of Early Christianity. Philadelphia: Westminster, 1987.

Collins, John J. *The Scepter and the Star: The Messiahs of the Dead Sea Scrolls and Other Ancient Literature*. Anchor Bible Reference Library. New York: Doubleday, 1995.

De Vaux, Roland. *Archaeology of the Dead Sea Scrolls*. Schweich Lectures 1959. Rev. ed. London: Oxford University Press, 1973.

García Martínez, Florentino. *The Dead Sea Scrolls Translated: The Qumran Texts in English*. 2d ed. Leiden: Brill; Grand Rapids: Eerdmans, 1996.

García Martínez, Florentino, and Eibert Tigchelaar, *The Dead Sea Scrolls Study Edition*. Leiden: Brill, 1998.

Maier, Johann. *The Temple Scroll: An Introduction, Translation & Commentary*. Sheffield: JSOT Press, 1985.

Naveh, Joseph, and Shaul Shaked. *Amulets and Magic Bowls: Aramaic Incantations of Late Antiquity*. Jerusalem: Magnes Press/Hebrew University; Leiden: Brill, 1985.

Schiffman, Lawrence H. *From Text to Tradition: A History of Second Temple and Rabbinic Judaism*. Hoboken, N.J.: Ktav, 1991.

Shanks, Hershel, ed. *Understanding the Dead Sea Scrolls: A Reader from the Biblical Archaeology Review*. New York: Random House, 1992.

Stemberger, Günter. *Jewish Contemporaries of Jesus: Pharisees, Sadducees, Essenes*. Translated by Allan W. Mahnke. Minneapolis: Fortress Press, 1995.

Stendahl, Krister, ed. *The Scrolls and the New Testament*. Rpt. New York: Crossroad, 1992.

Talmon, Shemaryahu. *The World of Qumran from Within: Collected Studies.* Jerusalem: Magnes Press, 1989.

Trever, John C. *The Untold Story of Qumran.* Westwood, N.J.: Fleming H. Revell Co., 1965.

Vermes, Geza, and Martin Goodman. *The Essenes According to the Classical Sources.* Oxford Centre Textbooks. Sheffield: JSOT Press, 1989.

Index of Names and Subjects

271

Index of Citations

Maps

Figure 1: Places of Ancient Palestine

Sketch: Alexander Maurer

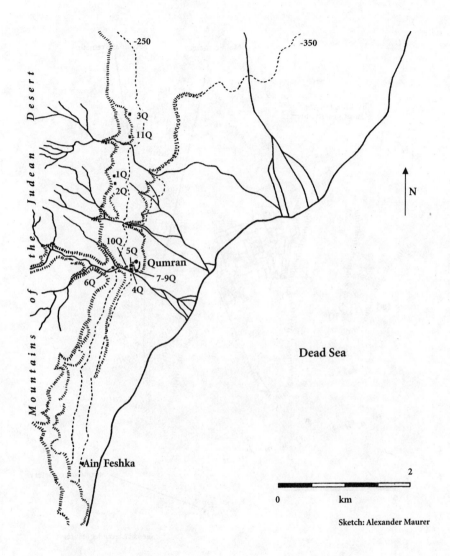

Figure 2: The Wider Area around Qumran

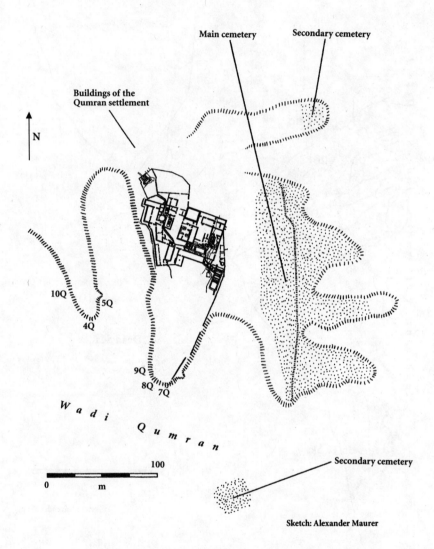

Figure 3: The Immediate Area around Qumran

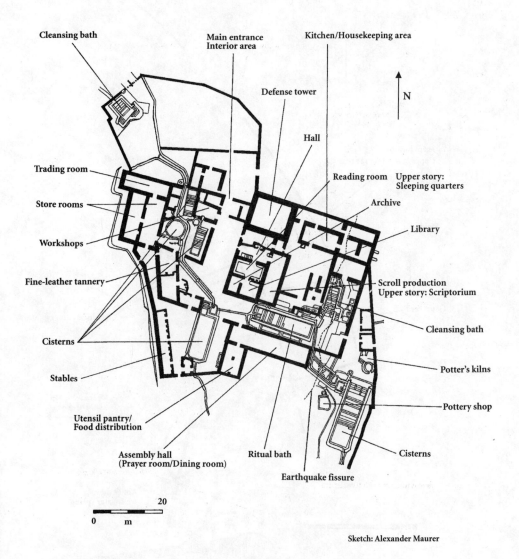

Cleansing bath

Main entrance
Interior area

Kitchen/Housekeeping area

Defense tower

N

Hall

Trading room

Reading room   Upper story:
Sleeping quarters

Store rooms

Archive

Library

Workshops

Fine-leather tannery

Scroll production
Upper story: Scriptorium

Cleansing bath

Cisterns

Potter's kilns

Stables

Pottery shop

Utensil pantry/
Food distribution

Cisterns

Assembly hall
(Prayer room/Dining room)

Ritual bath

Earthquake fissure

20

0   m

Sketch: Alexander Maurer

Figure 4: The Qumran Settlement

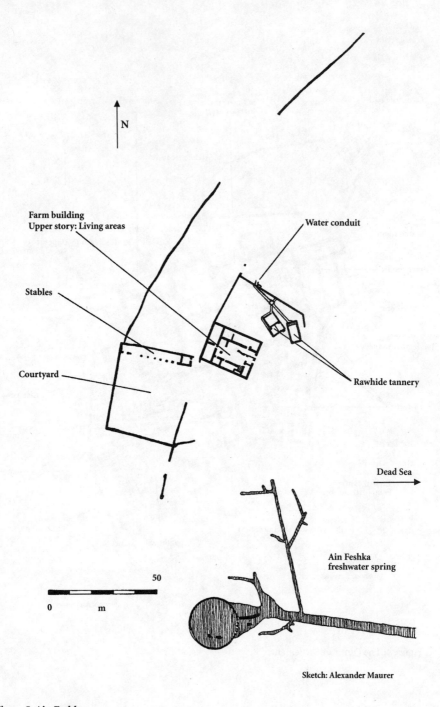

N

Farm building
Upper story: Living areas

Water conduit

Stables

Rawhide tannery

Courtyard

Dead Sea

Ain Feshka
freshwater spring

50

0   m

Sketch: Alexander Maurer

Figure 5: Ain Feshka